Constructing the
Little House

Laura Ingalls Wilder at eighty-five, signing books at Brown Bookstore in Springfield, Missouri, November 1952. The woman standing at the left is Wilder's friend Irene Lichty. Lichty later became the first curator of the Laura Ingalls Wilder Home and Museum in Mansfield, Missouri. Photo courtesy William Anderson.

Constructing the Little House

Gender, Culture, and Laura Ingalls Wilder

Ann Romines

University of Massachusetts Press   Amherst

Copyright © 1997 by
The University of Massachusetts Press
All rights reserved
Printed in the United States of America
LC 97–14675
ISBN 1–55849–121–X (cloth); 122–8 (pbk.)
Designed by Sally Nichols
Set in Weiss by Keystone Typesetting, Inc.
Printed and Bound by Braun-Brumfield, Inc.

Library of Congress Cataloging-in-Publication Data
Romines, Ann, date.
Constructing the Little house : gender, culture, and Laura Ingalls Wilder / Ann Romines.
p.   cm.
Includes bibliographical references and index.
ISBN 1-55849-121-X (alk. paper). — ISBN 1-55849-122-8 (pbk. : alk. paper)
1. Wilder, Laura Ingalls, 1867–1957—Criticism and interpretation.
2. Feminism and literature—United States—History—20th century.
3. Women and literature—United States—History—20th century.
4. Autobiographical fiction, American—History and criticism.
5. Children's stories, American—History and criticism. 6. Frontier and pioneer life in literature. 7. Mother and daughters in literature. 8. Women pioneers in literature. 9. Sex
role in literature. I. Title.
PS3545.I342Z83   1997
813'.52—dc21   97-14675
                                                                        CIP

British Library Cataloguing in Publication data are available.

Acknowledgments for permission to reprint previously published material,
archival material, and material under copyright appear
on the last printed page.

To my parents,
Ruth Rogers Romines and Elmer Romines,
and in memory of my grandmother,
Mayme Munson Rogers

Contents

Acknowledgments

The first friends of this book were my parents, Ruth Rogers Romines and Elmer Romines, who read to me, gave me books, and made me want—as powerfully as I have ever wanted anything—to read. My maternal grandmother, Mayme Munson Rogers, taught me to read and introduced me to writers—Alcott, Dickinson—who are still at the center of my life. She went to great pains to give me my first look at an actual woman writer, Laura Ingalls Wilder. This book began on that memorable day.

From the first, I have had friends and companions who shared and spurred my readings of the Little House books. Most faithful of these is my sister, Marilyn Romines, who is always game for yet another challenging discussion of Laura. I am also grateful to my fellow participants in the Third

International Willa Cather Seminar in 1987, who were patient with my inarticulate enthusiasm when I discovered that the Nebraska prairie made me want to write a book *not* about Willa Cather but about her Great Plains contemporary, Laura Ingalls Wilder. Later, friends, colleagues, and students helped me through the difficult process of finding a voice for this book, in which I could tap a lifetime of reading the Little House series. Susan Rosowski was responsive and supportive; Nancy Nelson encouraged me to write about Wilder in a personal voice and published some of my first efforts. My 1994 students in English/Women's Studies 251 debated issues of personal voice with me, while other students invited me to give a key-note address at a conference and thus gave me my first opportunity to talk publicly about the issues of writing this book. The friends and fellow scholars of my writing group, Phyllis Palmer and Susan Strasser, read and commented fruitfully on every page of this manuscript, and it owes a great deal to their expertise, care, and friendship.

At George Washington University, my colleagues and students have given me a stimulating and collegial climate in which to work on this project. I am particularly grateful to two supportive and attentive department chairs, Judith Plotz and Christopher Sten, and to my friends and colleagues in the English department office, Constance Kibler and Lucinda Kilby. The George Washington University Committee on Research has facilitated my project with summer research and travel funds. The university's Columbian School of Arts and Sciences and the department of English generously supplied funds for permissions and illustrations. This is the first book I have written on a computer, and I also thank the colleagues and friends who have guided me through a long (and continuing) electronic initiation, especially my student Patty Keefe Durso, who wrote me a computer handbook that I could actually understand.

Libraries and librarians have provided indispensable assistance to my writing of this book. George Washington University's Gelman Library delivered research materials promptly and provided work space and research advice. The Herbert Hoover Presidential Library opened the rich and extensive resources of the Lane-Wilder papers and supported my research there with two Hoover Scholar awards. Dwight Miller, senior archivist at the Hoover Library, gave me useful advice and assistance. The Pomona Public Library of Pomona, California, permitted me to quote from its collection of Wilder letters. The Western Historical Collection at the University of Missouri gave me access to important Wilder papers and manuscripts.

My cousin Julia Howard Helvey and my friend Edna Johnson Duff extended unfailingly generous hospitality when I returned to Missouri, again and again, for Little House research. At the Laura Ingalls Wilder Memorial Societies in Mansfield, Missouri, and De Smet, South Dakota, curators and staff members patiently answered my questions. William T. Anderson, author of many books about the Ingalls and Wilder families, was generous with his expertise and kindly shared a photograph from his personal archive. I am especially grateful to the late Irene Lichty LeCount, who introduced me to the Wilder collections in Mansfield when I was still a teenager (and, incidently, gave my sister and me a Wilder barn kitten). Mrs. LeCount's foresight and enthusiasm helped make the Mansfield museum possible.

Thanks, too, to the University of Massachusetts Press. Pam Wilkinson, managing editor, supervised the book's production meticulously, and Elizabeth Johns was an attentive copy editor. Bruce Wilcox, director of the press, nurtured my project through several years with his informed enthusiasm. It was wonderful to work with someone who was reading *Little House on the Prairie* to his daughter!

When I was a little girl, voraciously reading, I never thought in my most audacious moments that I might grow up to write a book myself. In the past few years, I have experienced a girlhood dream come true: I have been given space in which to read, think, and write about the presence of the Little House books in my life and U.S. cultures. For that gift, I thank everyone I have named here and many others I have not. I thank the stimulating climate of contemporary feminist scholarship. And I thank the fictional and actual figure of Laura Ingalls, who first showed me that a girl like me could become a strong woman and a writer.

Abbreviations

In notes and parenthetical references to often-cited works by Laura Ingalls Wilder, I have used these abbreviations:

BPC	*On the Banks of Plum Creek* (1953 ed.)
FB	*Farmer Boy* (1953 ed.)
FFY	*The First Four Years* (1971 ed.)
LHBW	*Little House in the Big Woods* (1953 ed.)
LHP	*Little House on the Prairie* (1953 ed.)
LTP	*Little Town on the Prairie* (1953 ed.)
LW	*The Long Winter* (1953 ed.)
SSL	*By the Shores of Silver Lake* (1953 ed.)
THGY	*These Happy Golden Years* (1953 ed.)

A Little House Sampler is abbreviated as *Sampler*.

Constructing the
Little House

By the mid-1950s, the Little House books were already considered "classics" of American children's literature, although the series had been complete for little more than ten years. This "Book Friends" program presented favorite book characters to children in a Licking, Missouri, elementary school, around 1953. Ann Romines (in Girl Scout uniform) is at extreme left, as narrator. Beside her are Georgia Ann Murfin (*standing*) and Jimmilee Brown (*seated*), portraying Mary and Laura Ingalls. Other girls portray characters from much earlier children's classics: *Little Women, Peter Pan, Heidi, Pinocchio, Alice in Wonderland, Tom Sawyer*, and others.

Introduction
The Voices from the Little House

I discovered them—the first thick, square volumes—on the low shelves of the children's library. They became a passion, potent as a drug. The Little House books by Laura Ingalls Wilder. A whole row of them, a series, to be traded back and forth with other girls, and then to be endlessly discussed, debated, enacted, and (more blissfully with each return) reread.

At the age of seven or eight, that was my introduction to a staple of twentieth-century U.S. children's literature. Wilder's seven novels of her Anglo-American girlhood on the nineteenth-century frontier, written in the 1930s and 1940s when she was in her sixties and seventies, were an immediate success with children (particularly girls) and their parents and teachers, even in a Depression market. By the time I found the Little House books, around 1950, they had been around for almost twenty years and had acquired the cachet of "classics"; in 1953 all the volumes were reissued in a uniform format with illustrations by Garth Williams, one of this century's best-known illustrators of U.S. children's books. In my small, underfunded Ozark public library, the new edition came none too soon. The original books, sturdy as they were, had been worn to tatters, their paper limp and frayed as old linen, by the grade-school girls who, year after year, discovered them on the shelves.

For me those fictional Little Houses that the Ingalls family built on the nineteenth-century prairie were inescapably compelling. They epitomized all the intensity, durability, and transience that I too knew, living at home in the 1950s. At the heart of them all was that entrancing protagonist—the brown-haired second daughter, Laura Ingalls. Her fresh, steady vision, printed out in a library book, seemed to legitimize my own vision, my sometimes-furtive life as a child. When my best friend Jimmilee won the part of Laura in the book pageant and I (too tall) was cast as the gawky narrator in my Girl Scout uniform, I was bereft. For that was the role *I* had dreamed of—as Laura, living in a Little House book.

Part of the allure of these books was the fact that they were multiple. When you had finished all seven (skipping *Farmer Boy*, the less satisfactory book about the boy Laura married), you could go back and begin again with the first House, *Little House in the Big Woods*—and on, again. That serial ritual of repetition was the deepest, most addictive satisfaction. The same houses, the same things, the same family, again and again. My adult life as an English professor began there, when I got hooked on rereading. And perhaps my interest in reading gendered cultures, an interest that fuels everything I write, began there too, inside the Little Houses that were books.

I did my childhood reading in rural Missouri, during the postwar 1950s. Fifty miles from my town, in a white farmhouse visible from the main highway, lived the famous author, Laura Ingalls Wilder. When we drove by with our parents, my best friend and I begged them to slow the car to a near-standstill, so we could look and look, scanning porch and lawn for Mrs. Wilder. But once, when Jimmilee's mother took pity on us and offered to drive us to the door so we could knock and say hello (as many children did, and were kindly welcomed), we were shocked. Unthinkable that we should knock at a Little House and speak to an Author!

Then came what promised to be the greatest day of my life. For my tenth birthday present, my grandmother drove me to Springfield, our nearest city, where Mrs. Wilder was scheduled to autograph books at Brown

Bookstore. (Such occasions were rare for her; this one, held when she was eighty-five, was to be her last.) In the stolid 1949 blue Chevrolet, the hundred miles to Springfield seemed to take forever. I sat on the edge of the front seat, chattering in high excitement to Grandmother, who always did me the honor of taking me seriously. When we arrived at the bookstore, with its towering dark shelves, Grandmother bought me the last book in the series, the only one I hadn't yet read: *These Happy Golden Years*. (On the last page was printed, "The End of the Little House Books.") We joined a line of girls I didn't know, city girls as intimidating to me as Laura's nemesis, Nellie Oleson.

Then I saw her, sitting at a table. Mrs. Wilder! She was tiny as I and my stout grandmother were not. Her hair was pure white and naturally curly (mine was not). Her dress was a rich dark red with a matching velvet hat (Grandmother and I wore navy blue). Grandmother nudged me forward and said, in her sociable voice, "Marjorie Ann loves your books, Mrs. Wilder." The Author smiled and opened my new book. On a blank page she wrote, in a squarish capable hand like Grandmother's. She wrote her name, "Laura Ingalls Wilder."

What did I say? Nothing. Like the young Laura Ingalls at moments charged with emotion and import, I "could not say a word" (LHBW 76), although I was ten and tall, above Grandmother's shoulder. Speechless, I took my book from its author's hand. Grandmother was probably embarrassed by her stony charge, mute among the charming, chattering little girls who filled the store. In the car on the long drive home, I stayed quiet. I was reading voraciously, lost in my last new Little House book.

In the forty years since that birthday, I have not stopped reading. My autographed copy of *These Happy Golden Years* is spineless, worn, and spotted with mold from a leak in my first apartment. Every few years I have returned to reread the Little House books—sometimes with a child as accomplice, most often alone.

But not alone. For the Little House books are longtime bestsellers. Since they began to appear in 1932, they have never been out of print. Although the final volume was published in 1943, the series has snowballed as a cultural phenomenon, spinning off more books as well as programs, pageants, restorations and reconstructions, and products ranging from dolls to bumper stickers. After Mrs. Wilder's death in 1957, her white farmhouse near Mansfield, Missouri, became a museum whose parking lot is regularly crowded with vans and station wagons from all over the United States. When I go there now (no longer too shy to approach the door), I find that the most avid of my fellow visitors are grown women like me. Intent, we crowd close to the glass cases, calling to our children and companions, "Look! Mary's nine-patch quilt! Pa's fiddle! Laura's bread plate!"

Such things, the ordinary keepsakes and accoutrements of a hard-pressed household, are mute in their cases. But for Wilder's readers, these familiar objects reiterate the Little House story. It is a story in which many American women have made deep, sometimes fatal investments. Now the books and the things seem inseparable. Relentlessly material, stubbornly domestic, they confirm each other and embody a complicated narrative of female survival. Wilder and her sisters and daughter are all dead now, leaving no descendants. Yet here these things still are, heavy with stories.

The survival of such objects is doubly important because the dwellings Wilder wrote about did not survive. The Little House, like the books, is serial. One by one, the houses are built, furnished, inhabited, abandoned, and left behind. These transient shelters derive enduring meaning from the repeated rituals of furnishing, maintenance, and housekeeping that are supervised by Laura's fictional mother and crowned with her signifier of domestic approval, a fragile, cherished china shepherdess that only Ma can touch and that she withholds from any dwelling that is below her standard. Such things as the shepherdess take on amazing weight and stability; they appear and reappear, recycled, refurbished, and reread, in consecutive chapters and volumes. When an occasional object must be left behind (such as the glass windows in the Kansas house of *Little House on the Prairie*), Ma preserves it in memories that her daughter, the future and actual Laura Ingalls Wilder, will eventually write. For me and many of my fellow readers, finding these very things physically present in the Mansfield museum seems to confirm the triumphant durability of the Little House myth. The serial house, the unchanging family, the undying things—all are preserved by women who, however transient their emigrant lives may have been, understood the powers of housekeeping. And the powers of writing.

Much of Laura Ingalls's story is about a girl's discovery of the voice in which she may speak and, eventually, write. Yet, as I have said, at moments of great stress the fictional Laura finds herself speechless. Why can't she speak?[1] And why did I, at ten, share her silence? In the world of these books, the Little House is the key term; it *must* signify. As Wilder's series makes abundantly clear, if a Little House is to signify, there must be a woman inside. (Until she marries, Laura Ingalls never enters a house kept by a man; as far as she knows, such houses do not exist.)

Throughout the series, in winter, months of fictional time pass without a single depiction of Ma's leaving the house, although Pa is out every day, by choice and necessity. Ma's confinement, shared by her daughters, is most severe in the fifth Little House book, *The Long Winter*, a narrative of blizzard-enforced indoor seclusion and near starvation. As Laura learns, the great peril of such seclusion, exacerbated by hunger, inactivity, and cold, is stupor and silence. If there are to be houses, the Little House series always implies, there must be housekeeping women. But if there are to be articulate women (such as Laura herself, in her triumphs of speaking and writing at school), those women must find a way outside the silencing, sheltering walls of the Little House.

Laura Ingalls, the fictional character, was a girl as ambivalent and headstrong as I was, as a reading child. That is what drew me to her. Had Laura and I met and recognized each other at Brown Bookstore, we could have spoken to each other. But Laura Ingalls Wilder, the author in the regal wine-colored dress, seemed to me a silencing figure. Calm, controlling, and assured, she handed me a commodity about which she appeared to have no doubts. A book, a name, a myth. She looked like a powerful woman— powerful because she had learned to speak, to write, and to sell her writing. What she sold was the Little House story, the series that held me quivering in its thrall. In the warm car with my sympathetic grandmother, hurtling toward the End of the Little House Books, I could find no words to tell her how this story seduced and frightened me. She was in the story. I was in it. What could we say?

Forty years later, as this book attests, I am still working to discover what I can say about Laura Ingalls Wilder and the Little House books. Much of my career as a teacher and scholar, which has focused on U.S. women's writing and gendered culture, has pushed me to question why this series has been such a freighted subject for me and for so many other Americans of my own and later generations. Several years ago, when I tentatively began to talk at conferences about Wilder's writing, I was amazed by the intensity with which people responded: women and men; senior professors and the bookseller's nine-year-old daughter, hunched over her Judy Blume at the back of the room. Given the immediacy and urgency of the conversations I found myself having about these books, I was surprised at the relative absence of sustained critical commentary on Wilder's writing (an absence that is just beginning to be rectified).

The history of U.S. literary studies in the years since the Little House series was published goes a long way toward explaining such absences and silences, of course. As an extremely popular children's series by an elderly rural woman, the Little House books were seldom considered as potential topics of scholarly discussion in decades when many taboos discouraged attention to "popular culture" and to texts produced by women, especially those who lived and worked outside "literary" culture, and when scholarship on "children's literature" was largely ghettoized. Recently, the flourishing of feminist scholarship, gender studies, and cultural studies has created tools and precedents for rereading the story of the Little House. Becoming a beneficiary of and participant in such ongoing scholarship has been one of the great strokes of good fortune in my adult life and a major impetus for the writing of this book.

However, all this does not entirely explain why thoughtful and theorized writing about the Little House series is still relatively scarce or why, despite my own nearly lifelong history as a passionate Little House reader, I was middle-aged before I ever mentioned these books in print or in my university classrooms. As I have begun to suggest, girls' problems with language and access to language are central to the Little House series. Both the published story of fictional Laura Ingalls's growing up and the publicly promoted account of Laura Ingalls Wilder's authorship of her own female childhood seem to celebrate girls' and women's voices. And yet—almost every Little House book ends with Laura's *silence*, as she listens compliantly to her father singing. His songs restate some of the most strongly patriarchal messages of nineteenth-century U.S. culture (one book, for example, ends with a verse from "Home, Sweet Home"); by featuring them in a twentieth-century series, Wilder and Rose Wilder Lane, her daughter and collaborator, renew their power, sometimes as obstacles to female voices. As a fan and a student of the Little House books, I learned some of those silencing lessons alarmingly well.

Rereading those books again and again as a quiet girl, I confirmed my Little House thralldom. Such rereading was also a way of retelling the story. I recast it in my mind, heightening the resemblances to my own close, midwestern nuclear family of middle class, Euro-American parents and daughters. And when I played with other girls at enacting Little House plots, I always vied (usually silently) for the part of Laura that I was too big to play convincingly. Jimmilee usually won the part because she looked like Laura: small, photogenic, and quick, with brown hair. She read the series as passionately as I did—and yet it must have resonated very differently for her, as an only daughter and caretaking sister to four younger brothers. My own younger sister Marilyn rejected my identification with Laura (perhaps because the protagonist was already "taken" by her preemptive older sister) and instead launched a semidurable alliance with Almanzo's story. Even now, when I discuss the Little House series with readers—such as African American friends, colleagues, and students—who did not "match" Laura Ingalls in race, class, region, gender, and ethnicity as closely as I did, I often discover that they choreographed their own internal retellings in order to stake a claim on the Little House story.

Like almost everyone else who has grown up in the United States since World War II, I came of age in a culture that was preoccupied with retelling, reframing, and reclaiming that story. Publishers sought "new" manuscripts by Wilder that might be added to the bestselling Little House list (even though Wilder had ended the series so definitively in *These Happy Golden Years*). Until her death in 1968, Rose Wilder Lane defended the myth of her mother's sole authorship against the strong evidence (overwhelmingly apparent in the Wilder-Lane papers) that Wilder and Lane collaborated on the series, thus suppressing an important part of her own career as an author. In the 1970s, the Little House story was retold for serial television; in the 1980s, President Ronald Reagan, with other nostalgic Americans, identified the reruns of *Little House on the Prairie* as his favorite television program. In the 1990s, biographers, critics, and readers are debating about how to reframe the story of Little House authorship in ways that will acknowledge the significant contributions of Lane. Meanwhile, Lane's heir Roger MacBride (until his death in 1995) proposed to extend the Little House series forward in time, by fictionalizing *Lane's* childhood in his "Little House in the Ozarks" books, which are available through the Book of the Month Club. Another author has begun a project that takes the series backward, fictionalizing Ma's childhood.[2] And Harper, Wilder's publisher—now corporately reconfigured as HarperCollins—is repackaging the series and adding a new line of Little House products, including paper dolls, calendars, diaries, and "retold" and newly illustrated episodes for very young children.

When I began to write this book, I realized slowly that I must add my voice to this cacophony of tellers and sellers. Even more slowly, I realized that the cacophony of voices was inside, as well as outside, my own head.

The feminist scholar with gynocritical and (new) historicist leanings told "her" Little House story in ways that competed, sometimes stridently, with the tales that the ardent fan desired to retell. The poststructuralist critic, weary of the close readings in which she had once been schooled, resisted writing a book that replicated the durable structure of Wilder and Lane's series, moving from little house to little house to little towns, while clocking the chronology of Laura Ingalls's life as child and adolescent. But the fan insisted.

All these voices have had their say in the shaping of this book. In the five chapters that follow, I discuss the Little House books in the order in which they were written and published, (re)telling their powerful and (for me) inescapable story. Using the rich resources of the Wilder-Lane papers, I also examine the unique story of daughter/mother authorship that is both written and suppressed in the series. And I discuss the "cultures of letters"[3] that facilitated the writing of the Little House and support readings of the series, even now.

At the same time, I have tried to foreground the issues that have kept these books in print and have, by the late 1990s, made them such widely read and powerfully contested texts for American readers, especially women. Each chapter is organized around one such issue, starting with one or two specific texts and then considering the issue's large cultural implications throughout the series. Chapter 1 discusses Wilder's and Lane's strong initial commitments to telling their fathers' stories, commitments that blocked and problematized the first two books, *Little House in the Big Woods* and *Farmer Boy*. I argue that Wilder and Lane finally overcame patriarchal constraints to succeed as women writers of stories about girls and women—but that they used their authorial successes to shore up the professional and personal failures of their actual fathers and to prop sagging patriarchal constructions.

Chapter 2 examines the problematic racial and ethnic discourse of the series. I propose that in their "Indian juvenile," *Little House on the Prairie,* Wilder and Lane broached some of the widest possibilities of multicultural experience in the historical United States. Then, in later books, we see those possibilities fading through contacts with immigrant neighbors and Laura Ingalls's infatuation with a "half-breed" man until, at the end of the series, the adolescent Laura's access to interracial, multicultural experience has dwindled to an amateur minstrel show at which, as a pubescent white girl, she can only take the role of acquiescent spectator.

In Chapter 3, taking off from *On the Banks of Plum Creek,* I look at the

Little House series as an account of frontier girls' education in material culture. In these books, more scenes of instruction occur in stores than in schools, and purchasing decisions are means of enlightenment and empowerment for girls and women, as well as indoctrination in a burgeoning consumer culture. Although the series—largely a product of the Great Depression—is often touted for its "antimaterialistic" values, I argue that one reason for its continuing appeal is that it acknowledges and scrutinizes the enormous importance for U.S. children of choosing and buying *things*.

Chapter 4 concentrates on the advent of Laura Ingalls's adolescence, when gender paradigms are impressed on her with increased force. Beginning with *By the Shores of Silver Lake*, the girl is pushed to choose between the influential and conventionalized gender models enacted by her parents as they conceptualize, build, and furnish a series of prairie Little Houses. The stringencies of such choices are dramatized by *The Long Winter*, in which the Ingalls women are confined for months to a single room and almost die of starvation.

Finally, Chapter 5 looks at the last two novels, *Little Town on the Prairie* and *These Happy Golden Years*, focusing on Wilder and Lane's efforts to devise a plot for their protagonist that both honors their patriarchal commitments and expands the possibilities of female storytelling and female lives. They manage this by interweaving multiple plots that indicate the historical range of possibilities for women in the late nineteenth-century West, as well as the complex allegiances of Laura's young womanhood. In the process, they suggest the ongoing multiplicity that has characterized the plots of most U.S. women's lives.

Finally, in a brief conclusion, I discuss the painful difficulties and implications—for authors and readers—of *ending* the Little House series and briefly consider some of the various cultural spin-offs that we have invented as ways to keep reading, and to keep revising, the sustaining and disturbing story of the Little House.

Writing these chapters, I have discovered some of the reasons why, for all the five decades of my life as a reader, Laura Ingalls Wilder's books have been a commanding textual presence. I have also become conscious that, more than any other text, the Little House story was a consuming passion I shared with everyone from scholarly colleagues to Ronald Reagan to my fourth-grade classmates to the upscale readers of *Martha Stewart Living* (which advertises a Little House video) to the little girls who, even now, are slitting the plastic wrappers on their new Little House paper dolls. For me a book about the cultural implications of the Little House series has been a way to participate in an ongoing conversation among U.S. readers and consumers about some of the largest and most personal issues of our lives: the questions about gender, mobility, housekeeping, materialism, and racial and cultural identity that have structured my chapters.

For Wilder and Lane, as for me and many other readers, these are gendered questions about girls' and women's agency and about how agency can be created and enacted by speaking and writing. Thus, as I wrote this book, voice was constantly on my mind. When I began, I imagined blissfully that, in my research, writing, and revision, I would be doing what I had dreamed of as a girl: living inside the world and the language of the Little House books. I also imagined that I would emerge from that dream with a manuscript in hand. That manuscript, I thought, would be written in my accustomed scholarly voice, wielding the feminist/historicist/post-structuralist argot that I have picked up in the last fifteen years and found, for the most part, useful and enabling. Actually, however, in creating a voice for this new book I discovered that I must go much further back, to access the continuity of my life as a North American female reader and writer, a dweller in and keeper of houses. Thus, I have tried to find places in this text to include (among others) the voice of the raptly reading girl I was in the 1950s. Today, reading the wider cultural history and dynamics of the writing and reading of the Little House story, I hear a clamor of voices—the voices from the Little House. In this book, I have tried to pay attention to these voices and to the intimate, difficult, and important questions they continue to ask about American lives.

Laura Ingalls Wilder's parents, Caroline Quiner and Charles Ingalls, were married on 1 February 1860, in Concord, Wisconsin. This tintype, their wedding picture, was inherited by their daughter Laura. Photo courtesy Laura Ingalls Wilder Memorial Society, Mansfield, Missouri.

Chapter 1

Preempting the Patriarchs
Daughters in the House

When Laura Ingalls Wilder's first book was published in 1932, the children's book market was beginning to be seriously affected by the Great Depression. Yet *Little House in the Big Woods* was reviewed respectfully and well, was designated as a selection of the Junior Literary Guild, and sold briskly. Seven additional novels would follow, and by 1943 the Little House series would be complete. And since 1932, a large body of Wilder's readers, adults and children, has invested heavily in the idea of a woman in her sixties and seventies, an untutored "natural" writer, independently recording the story of her frontier childhood and adolescence and simultaneously reinforcing values of individualism, cooperation, and survival that have come to seem seriously endangered. However, as critics and biographers of the past twenty years have begun to show, the authorship of the Little House series is more interesting and more culturally complex than this fans' version.[1]

As a successful twentieth-century writer at the age of sixty-five, Wilder was the beneficiary of a knot of Euro-American women's cultural traditions. For example, her New England–born mother (like Emily Dickinson and thousands of other women) had compiled her own handwritten and handsewn book of original and collected poems as a girl and had preserved it to pass on to her daughters.[2] Later, following her mother's example, young Laura Ingalls also wrote poems, which she carefully sewed into a homemade book and proudly signed:

> If you've read this book through,
> With all its jingles,
> I'll let you know that its been filled,
> By Laura E. Ingalls.
> (Handsewn, paperbound booklet, about 1881, Mansfield.)

She also remembered with particular pride her teacher's praise for her efforts at composition writing.[3] After her marriage, Laura Wilder became the family letter writer, as her mother had been. Historian Lillian Schlissel argues that in the United States, especially on frontiers, "'keeping the family together' has been the special charge of women" (1989, 244). In the Little House series, letters are the only means by which the Ingallses can maintain connections with distant relatives, and it is Ma who does the writing. One of the attributes repeatedly associated with Ma is her pen, its pearl handle carved in the shape of a feather. From early childhood, the books imply, young Laura connected her mother with that pen, which evokes a quill and thus a long history of writing women.

In addition, the one novel that the Little House series mentions the Ingalls family's owning is one written by a woman, *Millbank* (1871), by Mary Jane Holmes; Ma read aloud from this book so frequently that Laura memorized the first sentences before she learned to read. Holmes was one of the many U.S. women who had successful writing careers in the second half of the nineteenth century; much of the fiction in the magazines and papers that the Ingalls family read avidly on the nineteenth-century frontier was written by women.

It is not surprising, then, that writing for publication became a part of all four of the actual Ingalls daughters' lives. Mary Ingalls, after becoming blind, aspired to write a book, and as an adult, she published poetry and advised her sister Laura on literary markets. Carrie Ingalls Swanzey worked for the De Smet *News* for several years, and Grace Ingalls Dow was a local correspondent for the same paper. When Almanzo and Laura Ingalls Wilder immigrated to Missouri with their daughter Rose in 1894, Laura kept a lively, meticulous record of the trip,[4] following the example of the numerous nineteenth-century U.S. women who wrote narratives of their cross-continental migrations. Wilder's first publication was a brief, stilted account of this journey, printed in the De Smet *News*.[5] In all of these instances, which were closely woven into her life and her autobiographical fiction, Laura Ingalls Wilder was encouraged by the practice of other nineteenth-century women to write and to think of writing as an arena in which a woman might succeed.

Later, as the Wilders began to achieve some modest success in establishing Rocky Ridge Farm in the Missouri Ozarks, Laura Wilder entered the life of Mansfield's middle class. Like so many of her contemporaries, she became a clubwoman. Even Ma Ingalls as portrayed in the Little House series, who seldom left her house and lived in the most rudimentary communities, approved of women's organizing for church and temperance causes. Wilder's activities were more extensive; in an essay, she wrote of "the time I give to club work and lodge work and—yes, I'll admit it—politics. My mother and my mother-in-law had none of these" ("It Depends on How You Look at It," *Sampler* 112). Her correspondence often mentions the Aid society, the Athenians, embroidery club, bridge club, Eastern Star, and others. For such organizations, she might cook and entertain elaborately (for example, one letter to Rose Lane contains complicated instructions for Valentine tea sandwiches [LIW to RWL, 27 Jan. 1937, Hoover]); she also wrote and presented programs and papers. Like most of her contemporaries, Wilder took such tasks seriously; even when she was a well-known writer, in the mid-1930s, she still claimed intense nervousness when she read a carefully crafted paper to the nearby Mountain Grove Sorosis Club ("My Work," *Sampler* 176–80). Although, as Holtz observes, Rose Wilder Lane might chafe in her letters and her fiction (specifically *Old Home Town*, a portrait of Mansfield) against the limitations of small-town clubs and clubwomen, for Laura Ingalls Wilder and many of her contemporaries, clubs provided social and intellectual outlets that they associated with modernity and expanded opportunities for women.[6]

It was Wilder's club work that initiated the first phase of her professional writing career. Early in the twentieth century, as a member of the Missouri Home Development Association and the International Congress of Farm Women, she worked to organize clubs and to establish rest rooms, classes, and a circulating library for farm women in Mansfield and nearby rural towns. According to William T. Anderson, Wilder particularly "abhorred the image [common in small Ozark towns] of the lonely farm wife sitting uncomfortably in the farm wagon while her husband circulated and visited with the merchants and bankers." Thus she "worked" to "establish meeting rooms and restrooms" (*Sampler* 97) that provided space, comfort, privacy, and sociability in town. Such institutions were important to farm women like Wilder and her neighbors, offering "a place to rest from work . . . [and] a support. . . . Clubs were an essential part of the lives of rural women" (Jensen 77). In these projects, Wilder was very much a part of the Country Life movement popularized in the 1910s and 1920s United States as "the rural arm of American Progressivism" (Jellison 4). As Barbara Melosh has written, this movement "countered national stereotypes of rural isolation and decline through new images of modern farm families. Farm women actively participated in . . . [such] organizations devoted to the improvement of agricultural life. Rural reformers recognized women as a separate constituency in organizations such as the women's clubs of state agricultural extensions" (64).

According to Katherine Jellison, midwestern farm editors and journalists were "among the most visible proponents" of Country Life ideology, and they particularly wanted to reach women, like Laura Ingalls Wilder, "of the white, native-born middle class" (4, 9). Thus it is not entirely surprising that, when Wilder made an effective speech in 1910 about her work in a rural women's club, she was recruited by an editor of the *Missouri Ruralist* as a writer. Soon Wilder was a regular and popular contributor to this weekly; she became "household editor," and in 1919 the *Ruralist* created a special section for her columns, "The Farm Home."

Writing for the *Ruralist* gave Laura Ingalls Wilder several kinds of important writing experience. Many of her brief essays were frank and persuasive propaganda for the family farm; in one, Wilder argued that a farm family could live self-sufficiently on only five acres ("The March of Progress," *Ozarks* 30–33). Others honed her skills at description, narrative, and near-technical writing; one popular piece, for example, described how the Wilders rerouted a spring to provide running water for Rocky Ridge ("So We Moved the Spring," *Sampler* 108–11). Almanzo Wilder appears in these essays with the coy designation of "the Man of the Place," but Laura Wilder's primary attention is usually directed toward the work of farm women. She even tried an early stint at ghost writing, publishing "The

Story of Rocky Ridge Farm" under her husband's name to be eligible for a farm-home story contest (*Sampler* 104–6). Especially in the later essays, she experimented with autobiographical reminiscence; a few of these pieces provided the genesis of episodes in the Little House books. Writing for the *Ruralist* in her forties and fifties, Laura Ingalls Wilder served an effective apprenticeship, one that was facilitated by the culture of midwestern, middle-class farm women.

Wilder's mother, Caroline Quiner Ingalls, had given her daughter an example of a writing woman, but not of a woman who had made her writing a paying profession. When "Ma" Ingalls needed to earn money to support herself and her daughter Mary after her husband's death in 1902, she turned to her domestic skills, doing ironing and selling fruit to customers in De Smet (Glover). Laura Wilder worked with her husband to make Rocky Ridge a paying enterprise; she followed a common precedent for rural women by raising chickens and selling eggs to supplement the family income, becoming one of the leading egg producers in the state of Missouri. But to earn the large sums that would eventually bring her and Almanzo Wilder financial security, even in the Depression years, she had to turn to another woman, a professional writer, as a mentor and model: her daughter, Rose Wilder Lane.

By her early teens, Rose Wilder had completed all the public schooling offered in Mansfield, Missouri.[7] Living with a Wilder aunt in Louisiana, she completed high school and then returned to Mansfield, where she took up a career that had newly opened for women, telegraphy. At seventeen, she left home to work for Western Union in Kansas City and other western cities. By 1909 she had settled in San Francisco, where she married Gillette Lane and launched successful careers as a real estate saleswoman, a top reporter for the *San Francisco Call-Bulletin,* and a fiction writer. Encouraged by her own experience, Lane ebulliently urged Laura Ingalls Wilder to write for a wider audience and larger profits.

This lengthy postscript to a pre-1915 letter from California is typical of the barrage of pragmatic advice that the daughter sent to her mother at Rocky Ridge:

> . . . write the state agricultural high muckamucks . . . and ask them for the address of the largest certified milk dairy in Missouri and then write the dairy and tell them you are a professional writer and would like to write them up. . . . It will make a fairly good story for some farm paper—you can sell it to the Ruralist under some other name . . . I have

just written about two thousand words on one here for the special edition. By the time you get the writing . . . you can just clip my stuff, change a name or a sentence and resell it. (RWL to LIW, undated [pre-1915], Hoover)

Here Lane encourages her mother to think of writing as a commodity to be sold and, if possible, resold; details of individual authorship seem unimportant to her, as she advises that Wilder resell her daughter's words under her own name. She goes on to suggest that her mother think of recycling her letters, the private writing she has done all her adult life, into the autobiographical "thing" that is apparently already on Wilder's mind: "I bet the letter you wrote for grandma and Mary [Caroline and Mary Ingalls, in De Smet] could be put verbatim into that 'story of my life' thing. If I were you I'd have them save it and send it back."

Still in the same postscript, Lane urges that her mother make bolder use of the material around her, capitalizing on local events: "Why don't you write up Mansfield? Just write it as it happens, just a plain bald story of an Aid society oyster supper, for example . . . with conversation as nearly verbatim as you can get it. I think it would be great stuff—write it with real names, and describe real people." From the distance of San Francisco, the complications of "writing up" such local doings, saleably, while maintaining one's place as a respected participant in the Aid society and other institutions of Mansfield life, seemed negligible to Rose Lane. However, they must have been considerable to Wilder; she never followed this piece of long-distance advice.

However far Rose Lane lived from her parents—and later, she lived in places as distant as Albania—she always corresponded with her mother, often in the vocabulary of domestic work that they had shared since Lane's girlhood. For example, the same pre-1915 letter contains, among the rapid-fire writing advice, this typical note on fashion and sewing: "I have taken the tail from the new blue serge dress I got out here and with it entirely remodeled the blue serge dress I had with me there [Mansfield]—who says I am not my mother's daughter?"

Lane and Wilder's relationship, already complicated, gathered complexity as the daughter began to cast herself as aggressive, ambitious instructor and mentor for her less experienced mother. Many of Lane's copious instructive letters survive; most of Wilder's replies, until the mid-1930s and after, do not. So we know of Wilder's earlier responses largely through Lane's responses to them. For example, the daughter dismisses her mother's scruples about Lane's apparently extensive editorial changes in a *Country Gentleman* article that was published under Wilder's name: "All I did on your story was an ordinary rewrite job. Don't go saying that you're glad I liked your other one, that it gives you courage. The thing that should give you courage is that this one sold. You don't know how to write stuff for Country Gentleman. You never will know, until you stop and listen to what I tell you" (RWL to LIW, [1925?], Hoover).

Typically, Lane emphasizes her own professional savvy and financial competence. These are two women writers at very different stages of their careers, assuming very different stances. Wilder was secure in her "Farm Home" niche at the *Missouri Ruralist,* but when she attempted to write for a national *Country Gentleman* audience, she worried about maintaining an independent voice and summoning the "courage" to aim for a wider readership. Lane had early learned the benefits of projecting and—as far as possible—practicing a confident professional pragmatism (although her journals reveal her private doubts about her fiction). She had no patience with her mother's uncertainties, and she chided: "Dearest Mama Bess, in some ways you're like a frolicsome dog that won't stand still to listen." The parent is now the playful, undisciplined puppy, while the child has assumed the role of knowing, controlling trainer. In exasperation, Lane continues: "I go on yipping like this forever, like Andromache on the walls of Troy, and you won't listen. You'd rather do the washing. It isn't fair, now is it, really? Just because I was once three years old, you honestly oughtn't to think that I'm never going to know anything more than a three-year-old. Sometime you ought to let me grow up."

Finally, Lane concludes the letter by reminding her mother that, in devoting a morning to writing to her, "I've given you at least $100 worth of time" (RWL to LIW, 1925[?], Hoover). In the course of this entirely typical epistolary drama, she has run herself and her mother through a series of bewilderingly rapid changes. "Mama Bess" is cast as controlling matriarch, as an obliviously domestic parent who'd "rather do the washing" than take writing instruction from her now-mature child, and then recast as a lively puppy. Daughter Rose takes her turn as desolate wife, Andromache "yipping"—like a dog herself—at impervious maternal walls. Repeatedly, Lane reminds Wilder that her offspring's time and skills command high prices in the world outside the household, although she also continues to cram her letters with aggressively specific details of her own domestic prowess, which rivals her mother's.

After a 1918 divorce from Gillette Lane, Rose Wilder Lane left San

Francisco to work for the Red Cross and continue her successful writing career in postwar Europe. But by the late 1920s she had returned to Rocky Ridge from Albania, which she hoped eventually to make her permanent residence after establishing her own and her parents' financial security with a period of intensive, lucrative writing, in Missouri. According to William Holtz, Lane found it impossible to share the farmhouse with her parents; "problems" included Laura Wilder's requests for "trips, visits, and conversation" with the daughter who had been absent for several years, the "distracting conversations [that] rose from the rooms below" to Lane's second-story workroom, and the bickering of the Wilder and Lane dogs (Holtz 1993, 194–95). Lane's solution to these predictable incompatibilities was to build a fashionable "English cottage" on Rocky Ridge Farm as her parents' retirement home. The house was planned by an architect in the nearest city, Springfield; an architect-built house was very unusual in an Ozark town of the 1920s. Lane herself supervised every detail of construction and furnishing; she also dealt with the architect and paid him. Although she and the architect referred to the cottage as her "mother's house," the blueprints bore the traditional legend: "A residence for *Mr*. A. J. Wilder" (Hoover; emphasis mine). This contradictory language indicates the complicated dynamics of Wilder family relations in this period: matriarch, (putative) patriarch, and ambitious, affluent daughter were all in close, competing proximity.

For herself and her frequent guests, Lane remodeled the Rocky Ridge farmhouse, originally handbuilt by her parents. In the late twenties, she punctuated her residence there with long sojourns in New York, where she had many friends and literary connections. After the 1929 stock market crash, it soon became apparent that Lane's substantial investment account had been wiped out, and she found herself largely confined to Rocky Ridge.

It was in this intense climate of competition, building, and financial anxiety that the Little House books began to take shape. Clearly, Wilder was ready for a new stage in her life as a writer. At the age of sixty, in 1927, she had stopped writing for the *Ruralist*, which had been her primary market, and had ended her exacting work as secretary-treasurer of the local Farm Loan Association. Her few forays into national publications, such as the articles for *Country Gentleman* and *McCalls* that Lane had edited, were several years in the past. After her mother and her sister Mary's deaths in De Smet in 1924 and 1928, the last Ingalls home there had been closed, and Wilder's impulses to undertake life review seem to have intensified. The deaths of her mother and her older sister may have also removed a powerful female censoring presence. With daughter Rose nearby as mentor, editor, and rival, Wilder returned to the autobiographical project that she and Lane had been discussing for more than fifteen years. By 1930, she had completed a manuscript for adult or older juvenile readers, "Pioneer Girl," an account of her childhood and youth, up to her marriage. Lane revised this manuscript considerably and then enlisted her own New York agent, George Bye, to sell it for publication as a serial for older children. The manuscript got no offers, and Bye himself—who was effusive to Rose Lane about her fiction—could summon up no enthusiasm for Wilder's "Pioneer Girl." "It didn't seem to have enough high points or crescendo," he wrote to Lane; "no benefit of perspective or theatre" (George Bye to RWL, 6 April 1931, Hoover).[8]

Next, another version of the "Pioneer Girl" manuscript was reshaped by Lane and sent to her friend Berta Hader, a successful writer of children's books. This version "strung together" several stories Charles Ingalls had told his young daughters, within a sketchy narrative framework of the Ingalls family's domestic life in Wisconsin; Wilder and Lane first titled it "When Grandma Was a Little Girl."[9] Hader found an editor who was very interested in the project and asked Wilder to put "meat on the bones" (Farrow) of the minimal Ingalls family story. With Lane's assistance, Wilder provided the additional "meat," and the book was published under the title of *Little House in the Big Woods*, in 1932.

One wonders why Rose Wilder Lane, with her practiced eye for what was saleable in the popular fiction market of the 1920s and 1930s, settled on her grandfather's stories. They are not particularly unusual, and I recall skipping them as I read *Big Woods* as a little girl; they made this book my least favorite in the series. But they do have the "high points," "crescendo," and "theatre" that George Bye had missed in the "Pioneer Girl" manuscript. In fact, they are classic tales of male adventure, clearly and conventionally plotted. Such tales had been among Lane's most commercially successful publications; she had made her reputation with success-story biographies of Herbert Hoover, Jack London, Henry Ford, and the aviator Art Smith, and much of her fiction, such as *Free Land* and *Hill Billy*, foregrounded male protagonists. So it is not surprising that Lane turned first to these male narratives when she wanted to extract a saleable package from her mother's rather uninflected manuscript.

Wilder, too, although she seems originally to have written her autobiography as a story of her own, female life, soon came to think of Pa Ingalls's tales as her most important and promising material. In her 1937 Book Fair speech, written entirely without Lane's assistance, she spoke of those stories as being the part of her childhood that she and her sister Mary had remembered most vividly and "loved best." She concluded, "I have always felt they were too good to be altogether lost" ("Laura's Book Fair Speech," *Sampler* 216–24).

Is the first purpose of *Little House in the Big Woods*, then, to preserve a body of male narrative or to inscribe a girl's story? For the next few years, as the Little House *series* began to emerge, Wilder and Lane would find themselves struggling with the implications of this question. It is a crucial question about gendered priorities. As I've indicated, many features of nineteenth- and twentieth-century Euro-American women's culture had encouraged Wilder to think of writing as a woman's prerogative, and in the teens and twenties, Rose Wilder Lane had urged her mother toward the frank professionalism of the enfranchised New Woman. But in the Depression–New Deal years, when the Little House books were largely written, there was widespread hostility in the United States to such professionalism. In a 1917 *Ruralist* essay, Wilder had recalled from her adolescence a "Mrs. Brown" who had been chastised in De Smet for spending her time writing for pay while housework was left for her daughter to do.[10] Wilder justified such practice by explaining that Mrs. Brown had, unbeknownst to the town, been writing in order to pay for her daughter's "new winter outfit" ("If We Only Understood," *Ozarks* 309–10). In such a rationale, writing seems justifiable only if it serves the priorities of traditional domesticity and maternity. In the early 1930s, this reasoning had renewed force. According to Barbara Melosh, the New Deal was "the single example of a liberal American reform movement not accompanied by a resurgence of feminism. Instead, the strains of economic depression reinforced the containment of feminism that had begun after the winning of suffrage. As men lost their jobs, wage-earning women became the targets of public hostility and restrictive policy. One slogan exhorted, 'Don't take a job from a man!'" (1).

In many ways, *Little House in the Big Woods* reflects these conditions of the 1930s U.S. market. Although Ma, as Caroline Quiner, led a "very fashionable" and relatively affluent life as a teacher before her marriage to Charles Ingalls, those days are far behind her; she never speaks of them. In the Big Woods, she is unremittingly domestic; she would never venture into her husband's sphere to "take a job from a man." Much of the narrative is plotted to assure that the Ingalls daughters will follow their mother's example, never infringing on the prerogatives of patriarchy. Thus, although the book is presented as autobiographical fiction written by a woman, its centerpiece is men's tales told in Pa's voice.

In the thirties, Melosh observes, "socialworkers and public figures held women responsible for maintaining family morale" (1). *Little House in the Big Woods* justifies its female authorship by taking on that cultural task with a vengeance. In its very first sentence, this text zeroes in on the Little House: "Once upon a time, sixty years ago, a little girl lived in the Big Woods of Wisconsin, in a little gray house made of logs" (1). In Wilder's work, a house is a container for a heterosexual, patriarchal nuclear family. Years before, in a 1911 *Ruralist* piece, she had written that an "ideal home should be made by a man and a woman together" ("The March of Progress," *Ozarks* 30). When she wrote *Big Woods*, Wilder was living in a house commissioned and paid for by her single daughter; nearby, her daughter presided over the Rocky Ridge farmhouse, accompanied by a series of long-running guests, mostly women. However, although Wilder was well aware of such contemporary variations on the "ideal home," she never wrote about them. The first Little House, in particular, is a conventional family dwelling, and the book is a primer in the division of labor and culture that perpetuates such shelters.

Pa's stories provide some of the primer's most important lessons. Four of the tales are set apart by titles and spacing within the text. They are "inset stories" in the tradition of Willa Cather's *My Ántonia*. Cather's inset stories provide depth, distance, and a taproot to dream and myth. Wilder's tales also tap mythic resources, and three of the four are set in the past, featuring as protagonists Charles Ingalls's father, grandfather, and himself as a child. The effect of these tales is to bring the (male) past into the present, making it seem continuous with the world that young Laura and Mary inhabit. In the first story, for example, the girls' Grandpa Ingalls serves as protagonist. Grandpa breaks a taboo of the Big Woods: he ventures into the territory of the forest, which is reserved for men, without the protective attribute of his maleness, his phallic gun. There he is beset by an antagonist, a hungry panther, which is designated by the neutral pronoun "it" but has a terrifying scream "like a woman" (41). On horseback, Grandpa barely makes it to the safety of his house; as he slams the door, the panther leaps "on the horse's back, just where Grandpa had been" (42). Reunited with his house and gun, Grandpa executes a triumphant climax by shooting the panther off his horse's back. Then Pa delivers the cautionary denouement, his patriarchal legacy: "Grandpa said he would never again go into the Big Woods without his gun" (43).

However, the story also has a subtler agenda that would surely not be lost on the listening daughters. For the terrifying panther, which could kill a man and deprive a family of its patriarch, has a *female voice*. Roving wild in the Big Woods, such an uncontained predator is a deadly threat to Grandpa and his family; it must be killed. But when it dies, the female voice dies with it. Thus, even in this most traditional of male narratives, Wilder and Lane have inscribed the central problem of their text, the problem of female agency and the female storyteller's voice.

All the inset stories share themes of traditional male initiation, teaching boys and men the conditions of physical and psychic survival in the natural world. For example, Pa recalls a tale of his boyhood, when he ignored his father's orders and stayed in the woods after dark, only to be frightened by the voice of a screech owl and whipped by his father. Next, when Laura and Mary are squirming in resistance to the sedate behavior required of them on Sunday, Pa reaches back even further into the past for a tale of *his* father's childhood, recounting the boy's punishment by his father when he broke the parental rules and went sledding on Sunday. Then, in the last inset story, Pa tells of his own present uneasiness and danger when he travels through the woods without his gun; inventing perils, he fights with a dead tree stump that he envisions as a man-hungry bear. Loaded with furs that he will carry to town to trade for needed goods, Pa cannot hold the cumbersome gun; he is caught between his need for the commodities that can only be bought in town with his bulky currency—the furs—and the rules by which a solitary man may survive in the Big Woods. The same conflict between the need to trade with a profit-oriented community and the ritualistic rules by which a solitary man may hold his own in the natural world recurs throughout the Little House books, as Charles Ingalls wrestles with government regulations and natural forces to claim a homestead.

Pa's stories do not include a single female character. Instead, they construct an all-male world of significance and action. Laura and Mary listen raptly, memorizing every word. But the problem of female voice remains. One chapter, "Two Big Bears," dramatizes that problem by juxtaposing Pa's mock-heroic tale of his fight with an imaginary antagonist, the dead tree he mistook for a bear, with Ma and Laura's dark barnyard encounter with a real bear, which they at first mistake for their cow. Although Ma displays real valor toward an actual invader, rescuing Laura and herself from the hungry bear, her adventure does not become institutionalized as a part of the family fund of stories; it is not set off textually and ritually recounted as Pa's tales are, but is incorporated matter-of-factly into the ongoing narrative.

At another point, Wilder and Lane take an ingredient from Pa's storytelling, the predatory panther, and insert it in a tale with a female protagonist. Nothing in *Big Woods* rivets young Laura's attention more than this tale does, for it broaches some of the large problems of agency that are important to the book's child protagonist and to women authors. The story is told late at night at a family gathering, when the children are presumed asleep. Furtively, Laura attends to a forbidden adventure, one with a *woman* at its center. Visiting Uncle Peter, who was not present at the time of the recounted events, tells how his tame dog, Prince, refused to allow Aunt Eliza to leave the house to get water from the spring, but instead "kept pulling . . . till he tore a piece out of her skirt." Then Eliza interjects an aside to her sister, Ma:

> "It was my blue print.". . .
> "Dear me!" Ma said.
> "He tore a big piece right out of the back of it," Aunt Eliza said.
> "I was so mad I could have whipped him for it. But he growled at me."
> "Prince growled at you?" Pa said.
> "Yes," said Aunt Eliza.
> "So then she started on again toward the spring," Uncle
> Peter went on. . . . (69)

Uncle Peter has appropriated his wife's story and the prerogatives of telling. But the presence of a female listener encourages Aunt Eliza to reclaim some of those prerogatives. Although Peter controls the conventions of plot and delivers the denouement, Eliza brings the structure to life with specific and emotional detail that she knows will interest her sister. Clearly, Eliza and Peter are competing for control of this tale. Pa and Ma both continue to question and prompt and, among the four, the story gets told, compellingly. As it turns out, the dog threatened Eliza to protect her from a panther waiting at the spring.

By now Laura and Mary and their visiting cousins are wide awake.

This story articulates some of the most pressing dangers and rivalries of their lives. And Laura suggests, subversively, that storytelling is a game that even *children* may play.

> Laura put her head under the covers and whispered to Alice, "My! weren't you scared?"
>
> Alice whispered back that she was scared, but Ella was scareder. And Ella whispered that she wasn't. . . . They lay there whispering about till Ma said: "Charles, those children will never get to sleep unless you play for them."
>
> So Pa got his fiddle. (72–73)

The story of Aunt Eliza, Prince, and the panther has almost become a free-for-all, in which women, men, and children may all find voice. As Ma knows, such an occasion cannot continue unchecked. To restore control, she dutifully calls up the solo voice of the resident patriarch, her husband.

The details of dress, dimension, and feeling that Eliza adds to this tale are just the sort of detail that Wilder and Lane added to the "bare bones" of Charles Ingalls's adventure stories to ready them for publication in *Little House in the Big Woods*. In fact, this tale is like a model for the creative process of combining memory, invention, and adventure from male and female experience that produced many of the best qualities of the Little House series. But this riveting story, to which the children are so attentive, also emphasizes the enforced helplessness of Eliza. Unlike the men in the woods, who can fight or ride or run, she can do nothing but stay imprisoned in the house. To her sister, Eliza says, "I didn't know what to do. There I was, shut up in the house with the children, and not daring to go out. And we didn't have any water. I couldn't even get any snow to melt. Every time I opened the door so much as a crack, Prince acted like he would tear me to pieces. . . . Peter had taken the gun, or I would have shot him" (70).

Peter has gone away, carrying the emblem of male power that allows a man to move outside the house with impunity. In his absence, patriarchal priorities are enforced by Peter's surrogate, Prince. "Shut up in the house with the children," what can a woman do?

For Laura and Mary Ingalls, their mother's domestic indoctrination provides one classic response to that question. Caroline Ingalls teaches the girls the routines of daily and weekly tasks that comprised the usual work order for Euro-American housekeepers in the nineteenth century. Instructing her daughters,

Ma used to say:

"Wash on Monday,
Iron on Tuesday,
Mend on Wednesday,
Churn on Thursday,
Clean on Friday,
Bake on Saturday,
Rest on Sunday." (29)

When Lane advised Wilder about how to expand Pa's stories into the longer book manuscript her editors wanted, she suggested that the sketchy narrative frame be stretched to comprise the cycle of a year in the Big Woods, with "any and all details about the way of living" (RWL to LIW, 16 Feb. 1931, Hoover). Following this advice, Wilder elaborated on her mother's household work. The Thursday task of churning, for example, is detailed step by step, from the preparation of the milk to the molding of the butter. Consistency is emphasized; in the winter, when the cream is paler, Ma colors it with grated carrot to replicate the yellow of rich summer butter. Every day, then, Ma serves forth her yellow butter, and she and her daughters perform the same tasks; even at four, Laura knows that "Every morning there were the dishes to wipe" (28). Of course, Charles Ingalls's work as a farmer, hunter, and trapper is repetitive too. But this book is written from the point of view of a little girl who spends most of her time in the house with her mother and sisters, engaged in what Kathryn Allen Rabuzzi has called "the traditional mode of being" for housekeeping women: waiting indoors for a man's return from outside (141). To young Laura, her father's doings seem exciting and unpredictable; who knows when he will shoot a bear or encounter an undomesticated panther? In *Little House in the Big Woods*, the stuff of plots—action, adventure, and completion—belongs to men. Thus Pa's fund of male stories can be formatted, titled, and inserted as what Wilder viewed as "the best" feature of her text. But the uninflected, repetitive life inside the Little House has different precedents and priorities. Although the two little girls can be raptly fascinated by their mother's work as well as their father's tales, they agree that "the best time of all was at night, when Pa came home" (33).

Little House in the Big Woods is dominated by family and family relationships. The Ingallses exchange (rare) visits almost exclusively with family members, and—because Ma's sister Eliza Quiner has married Pa's brother Peter Ingalls—the closest relationships are doubly intense, and Laura's favorite cousins are *double* cousins. In the large, extended Ingalls family, Charles Ingalls and his brothers and their families live on adjacent farms and frequently trade work. The babies all look indistinguishably alike, and even Laura's name is not exclusively her own; there is another child named "Laura Ingalls" in the family. In the course of the book, Laura almost never exchanges a word with a person who is not her relative. Thus Wilder and Lane's first book portrays a profoundly endogamous world, with the Little House as its stable center.

As the loving daughter who privileges and preserves her father's patri-archal tales, Laura Ingalls the character and Laura Ingalls Wilder the woman writer are in the tradition of the sentimental, woman-authored daughter described by Linda Zwinger. According to Zwinger, father-daughter rela-tions in such novels reflect the tensions between the endogamous family, which is "the foundation of desire," and the exogamy that has facilitated most Western culture by a marital exchange of women. An implied subject of such fictions, Zwinger says, must be the "unspoken" and unspeakable story of father-daughter incest. She argues that in "Western, middle-class family stories," the father "always has a question he will neither articulate nor take responsibility for." Whatever her response to that paternal ques-tion, "the daughter is positioned as the one who provides the questions, who *makes* the unspoken story happen" (3).

Even at four, young Laura Ingalls clearly takes such a position with her father. For example, the girls' favorite game is one in which their father plays the role of a "mad dog," divesting himself of the controls of culture and rationality to chase his daughters about the house, "trying to get them cornered where they couldn't get away" (36). Within the frame of game playing, Pa enacts his vigorous, passionate, and potentially incestuous pur-suit. But it is the daughters who take the pursuit beyond the constraints of a game:

> Pa growled so terribly, his hair was so wild and his eyes so fierce that it all seemed real. Mary was so frightened that she could not move. But as Pa came nearer Laura screamed, and with a wild leap and a scramble she went over the woodbox, dragging Mary with her.
>
> And at once there was no mad dog at all. There was only Pa standing there with his blue eyes shining, looking at Laura.
>
> "Well!" he said to her. "You're only a little half-pint of cider half drunk up, but by Jinks! you're as strong as a little French horse!" (36)

It is the girls who have decided that *this* time the game of mad dog will "seem real." Unlike cowering Mary, Laura has chosen to become an equal player in the game, running and dodging with ferocious energy. Clearly she is the winner here, and her reward is the gaze of Pa's shining blue eyes. Although the male gaze traditionally enforces patriarchal proprietorship, here it also indicates Pa's recognition that his daughter Laura is *not* a passive pawn in this game. Laura's blue eyes *exchange* a look with her father, expressing a special bond between them that is intensely romantic and potentially incestuous in ways that will become increasingly problematic as the Little House series continues. Playing the game of "mad dog," young Laura assumes the tasks of interpretation and action that will make her an active storyteller and a fit match for her seductive father.

Laura's aptitude for active agency is an incipient problem, especially in relation to her father. In the family romances Zwinger discusses, "the sentimental daughter" is supposed to "remain provocatively passive, submissive, composed by the language and stories of the fathers" (66). Life in the Ingalls family constellation is life in a *man's* family, in which Pa calls the songs and tells the stories of his male ancestors. Just a few incidents, such as Laura's triumph in the game of "mad dog," suggest the possibility of a woman or girl's becoming an active, initiating player within this patriarchally dominated framework.

Another such incident occurs at the sugaring-off dance, when Laura's Grandma Ingalls, who has been much occupied in the kitchen with preparing food and boiling the sugar sirup, comes forth to challenge her son George in a jigging contest. Tossing away her spoon,

> She put her hands on her hips and faced Uncle George, and everybody shouted. Grandma was jigging. . . . Grandma's eyes were snapping and her cheeks were red, and underneath her skirts her heels were clicking as fast as the thumping of Uncle George's boots. . . . Uncle George began to breathe loudly, and he wiped sweat off his forehead. Grandma's eyes twinkled. "You can't beat her, George!" somebody shouted. All at once he threw up both arms and gasped, "I'm beat!" (149–50)

Just as she is enjoying her triumph, "Suddenly Grandma stopped laughing. She turned and ran as fast as she could into the kitchen. . . . Everybody was still for a moment, when Grandma looked like that" (150). This incident, which occurs near the end of *Big Woods*, indicates how much is at stake when a woman emerges to take center stage in the narrative, especially when she "beats" a man. Dancing, Grandma has almost overcooked the sirup. The high point of the sugaring-off party should occur when the guests feast on candy made from the thickening sirup. If Grandma abandons her spoon for too long, the evening and the large, valuable batch of maple sugar will be spoiled. Thus the suspenseful silence when she runs back into the kitchen. However, she has returned to the stove just in time, to everyone's great relief: "[Grandma] came to the door between the kitchen and the big room and said: 'The syrup is waxing. Come and help yourselves.' Then everybody began to talk and laugh again. They hurried to the kitchen for plates . . ." (150–51).

Grandma's story demonstrates what a lively and compelling protagonist an energetic woman can be, even when she is up against a male rival. But it also shows the tremendous danger to social order implicit in such a female performance, especially when a woman "beats" a man. Significantly, this is Grandma's first and last speaking appearance in the Little House series. She seems a dangerous, potentially disruptive presence.[11] By contrast, Ma, who is a staple presence in all the books, will never preempt the narrative stage with such a performance.

Another disruptive incident, very near the end of *Big Woods*, has at its center the most problematic person Laura has yet encountered in her young life: her cousin Charley. More than anyone else in *Big Woods*, Charley challenges the patriarchal authority of the large, endogamous Ingalls family. A recalcitrant eleven-year-old, he refuses to observe the family tradition of joining his father and uncles in field work; instead, he pesters them, diverting their attention from harvesting oats. When Charley steps on a nest and is attacked by the yellowjackets in it, the men assume that he is up to yet another trick and ignore his cries; meanwhile, he is severely stung. Ma and Aunt Polly plaster him with mud and wind him tightly in cloth: "only the end of his nose and his mouth showed. . . . Laura and Mary and the cousins stood around for some time, looking at him. . . . Laura and Mary were horrified. They were often naughty, themselves, but they had never imagined that anyone could be as naughty as Charley had been" (208–10).

Charley is the only Ingalls child who resists the patriarchal Ingalls plot, enacted by his father and grandfather and uncles, who "trade work" and harvest the grain. His punishment for this playful resistance is intense pain and near-ultimate confinement. Swaddled to the point of immobility by the women, he horrifyingly resembles a very young infant or a corpse. Acting on his own desires, Charley is a nest-spoiler and a threat to an endogamous plot; he enacts a resistance so monstrously "naughty" that Laura and Mary, good daughters, cannot even imagine committing it. In fact, no Ingalls, child or adult, laughs at Charley's plight. It is a solemn spectacle, the scapegoating of a pariah.

Interestingly, Wilder tried reintroducing Charley in a later novel, *By the Shores of Silver Lake*; she drafted a scene in which he teased and annoyed Laura until she angrily threatened him with a knife when he tried to kiss her. In a letter, Rose Lane criticized this scene:

> Here you have . . . a girl twelve years old, who's led rather an isolated
> life . . . and you cannot have her acting like a slum child who has
> protected her virginity from street gangs since she was seven or eight.
> Maybe you did it, but you cannot do it in fiction; you cannot make it
> credible in under ten or twelve thousand words and if you do make it
> credible it's not a child's book. (RWL to LIW, 21 Jan. 1938, Hoover)

Wilder protested her daughter's reading: "It was no question of sex or protecting her virtue. . . . It was just the idea of being manhandled." Although the scene was eventually excised from the book, this confrontation between Charley and Laura was obviously important to Wilder, and she argued vigorously for its retention: "Charley was given a character in Big Woods and in Silver Lake I have only shown that his character was still the same" (LIW to RWL, 25 Jan. 1938, Hoover). In both books, Wilder sees him as a troublemaker, and the later draft scene made explicit the sexual nature of Charley's threat. (Wilder's protest of this sexual issue actually reiterated it; Charley threatens to *manhandle* Laura, she says.) The boy suggests a knot of enigmas so difficult that he is eventually almost written out of the series, reappearing only as a shadowy, briefly mentioned young man in *Silver Lake*.

As Wilder originally conceived him, Charley articulates the unthinkable; he resists the benign stasis of Ingalls family relations. He makes explicit the incest that is always implicit in endogamy and challenges Pa's sexual dominion as the sole male in the Little House. Lane, with her acute awareness of what the fiction market would and would not tolerate, saw the danger in Charley's story; it was too long, not "normal," and unsuitable for children, she warned her mother. Charley was important to young Laura, and to the author Laura Ingalls Wilder, because he raised crucial questions about agency, limits, and sexuality within the Little House plot that is launched in *Big Woods*.

By the end of the first Little House book, Wilder and Lane had established the Ingallses' daily and weekly domestic routine, within the cycle of a year's work and rituals: Christmas, Laura's birthday, sugaring-off, butchering, harvest. In that cyclical framework, Pa's stories are embedded. Repeated again and again, they reinforce the Ingalls family's patriarchal values. The book's last chapter, "The Deer in the Wood," both continues and counters those values. In late fall, Pa goes out to shoot a deer at his deer lick. When he returns empty-handed, "Laura and Mary did not know what to think." "Pa had never before gone out to get a deer and come home without one" (231). To explain this lapse, Pa tells the girls a story. At the moonlit clearing, he says, he watched a buck, a bear, and a doe and fawn come out of the forest. Each time, remembering that his daughters and wife were "waiting for me to bring home" meat, Pa resolved to shoot; each time he became so "interested in watching" that he did not fire. The animals were "so beautiful . . . so strong and free and wild" and in such perfect harmony with their environment that Pa "forgot all about my gun" and returned to the Little House without game (232–35). Laura and Mary respond sympathetically to this tale, and Mary says consolingly, "We can eat bread and butter" (236).

In many ways, this is a story about the burdens of enacting a patriarchal role. For once, even though he has baited the trap of the deer lick, Charles Ingalls is reluctant to "bring home the bacon" as a competent provider should. Instead, he wants only to *watch*, an intent observer, and to live in the woods in a way that will not disturb or destroy the indigenous animals. (In later books, Pa will bemoan the disappearance of wild birds and animals on the prairie, as he and other "white settlers" claim the land.) This story, unlike the others Pa has told, is a story about *not acting*, and at its end there is no prize for the triumphant protagonist and no moralistic denouement that encapsulates patriarchal lore. Pa's storytelling style is also somewhat different, more descriptive and reflective, less relentlessly plot oriented. Recounting his experience for his beloved daughters, he also seems to be thinking about another way a man might live.

In "The Father's Breasts," Patricia Yaeger urges that feminists read stories of patriarchs in less binary and programmed ways; she warns against reductively phallogocentric reading of fathers' texts. Yaeger argues for readings of men's texts that do not see the father simply as an abstract, authoritative, and bodiless force but also acknowledge his bodily, personal, mortal specificity (6). My reading of the male stories in *Big Woods* has so far emphasized their phallogocentric qualities and the ways they lay down the fathers' law. But this last of Pa's tales invites a different kind of reading; Charles Ingalls enjoys a moment of stillness and receptivity that he honors even though he is guiltily aware of his patriarchal duty to hunt. And, importantly, he shares this lapse with his daughters, insuring its repetition by making a story of it. Such a father may be the "being" to whom Yaeger calls our attention, one "who can be anatomized, fragmented, shattered— or cherished—as someone who no longer operates [patriarchally] from an abstract and transcendental realm" (19).

The result of Pa's lapse in hunting is a change, at least temporarily, in the Ingalls family's ethos and diet, to vegetarian "bread and butter," both foods the book has portrayed Ma preparing as part of her domestic routine. Interestingly, this last chapter is preceded by one called "The Wonderful Machine," in which Charles Ingalls performs an agricultural coup in the spirit of the shared patriarchal values of his paternal family, organizing his male neighbors and relatives to take advantage of modern technology by hiring a threshing machine. In "The Deer in the Woods," it is almost as if he is taking a respite from this active, ambitious, success-oriented version of himself, allowing himself to tell another story about his manhood.

Big Woods is a compendium of such competing stories. But Wilder and Lane chose to end the book with a scene that mutes all the potential conflicts of this first book, focusing instead on the satisfying repetitions of cyclical time. From her trundle bed, Laura watches her parents, sitting by the fire. "The long winter evenings of firelight and music [with which the book began] had come again." Ma sits "swaying gently in her rocking chair and her knitting needles flashed in and out"; her motion and her domestic task suggest hypnotic, soporific repetition. And Pa sings a song that is new to Laura, one by which his culture yearly, ritually marks the passing of time, "Auld Lang Syne." He tells the child that "the days of auld lang syne" are "the days of a long time ago. . . . Go to sleep, now." Laura's drowsy reflections end the book: "She thought to herself, 'This is now.' She was glad that the cosy house, and Pa and Ma and the firelight and the music, were now. They could not be forgotten, she thought, because now is now. It can never be a long time ago"(236–38).

Laura rejects the adult concept of passing, irretrievable time that "Auld Lang Syne" proposes. Instead, in her mind, the little log house and its daily, weekly, yearly routines are permanent and static: a satisfyingly endogamous arrangement. But if *now* can never become "a long time ago," it is impossible to tell any new stories about the Ingalls family. As the tellers of a growing girl's story, Wilder and Lane found themselves in an impasse on the publication of *Little House in the Big Woods*. In a Depression market that was hungry for nostalgic certainties of "a long time ago," they had begun to create a demand for serial stories of Laura and the Ingalls family. But the format of *Big Woods* had left them nowhere to go.

Thus it is not surprising that Laura Ingalls Wilder's second book for children, published in 1933, turned to a *boy's* story. *Farmer Boy* (the only Wilder title that denotes a character's gender) is a fictionalized account of the tenth year of Almanzo Wilder, Laura Ingalls Wilder's husband and Rose Wilder Lane's father. Unlike his wife and daughter, both writers and loquacious storytellers, the actual Almanzo Wilder was reticent and seldom committed words to paper. Only a few letters to his daughter are included in the voluminous Wilder-Lane papers, and when he was in business, his wife wrote up much of the paperwork. As William T. Anderson has suggested, Almanzo Wilder seems to have "subscribed to the notion that correspondence and written communication were the realm of the female spouse" (1986, 126). Laura Wilder called her husband by a nickname that suggests prototypical masculinity—Manly—and she made him an ongoing character in her *Missouri Ruralist* essays, as "The *Man* of the Place."

Rose Wilder Lane also thought of her father Almanzo's story as a rich potential source of fictional material; fairly early in her career (perhaps sometime in the 1920s) she outlined a proposed novel based on her father's life, to be called "A Son of the Soil" and apparently to follow from her earlier biographies of Herbert Hoover and Henry Ford, both popular projections of male heroism. Lane's materials for "A Son of the Soil" (which was never written) include notes from interviews with her father about his vivid, specific memories of a rural boyhood—"Gosh! Sure was a happy childhood," she records his saying (Lane, Notes for "A Son of the Soil," Hoover). Eventually, Lane did make a fictionalized version of her father the central character of one of her best novels, *Free Land* (1938).[12]

In their correspondence throughout the composition of the Little House series, Wilder and Lane expressed their concern about whether the books would appeal to boys as well as to girls. *Farmer Boy* must have seemed the logical successor to *Big Woods*, which had been the cyclical, endogamic tale of a girl's life. Before the first book was even published, and its success assured through selection by the Junior Literary Guild, both mother and daughter were at work drafting and revising *Farmer Boy*. William T. Anderson has provided the most complete account of the composition of this book (1986), but even he admits that documentation of that composition process is less than complete, compared to other Little House novels for which we have multiple drafts, handwritten by Wilder, typed by Lane, revised by both. Anderson, while he depicts a process of profound "collaboration," emphasizes that Lane was "editing" and revising her mother's material. William Holtz, on the other hand, implies that Lane substantially wrote the book (1993, 228–32). Whatever the balance of the collaboration, its first round led to uncertainty and failure for both mother and daughter. Despite the success of *Big Woods* and a burgeoning market for Wilder fiction, Harper rejected the first submitted draft of *Farmer Boy* and sent it back for a complete rewrite. Eventually the publisher accepted a revised version (produced after Lane had traveled to Malone, New York, her father's childhood home, to gather additional impressions and materials), but with less enthusiasm than for the first book. Citing the pressures of a Depression market, Harper offered Wilder only half the royalty rate she had received on her first book. Since both Wilder and Lane saw the books as a hedge against the family's declining fortunes in economic hard times, the reduced royalty was alarming. This "boy's story," which may have seemed a sure thing after *Big Woods*, demonstrated that traditional male storytelling was *not* entirely an answer to the problems and promise of the emerging Little House series.

In *Farmer Boy*, nine-year-old Almanzo is the youngest in a family of two parents, a farmer and a housekeeper, and four children—two girls, two boys. Unlike the five-year-old girl Laura, Almanzo has a powerful, plotted sense of passing time; he longs to grow older so he can leave school, train and sell horses, and become a farmer himself. Although his "now" is full of immediate satisfactions, he is gladly aware that it *will* soon become "a long time ago," and the narrative presents him as an active protagonist. With his father, he learns to work in the fields: "There was no time to lose, no time to waste in rest or play. . . . All the wild seeds . . . are trying to take the fields. Farmers must fight them with harrow and plow and hoe; they must plant the good seeds quickly. Almanzo was a little soldier in this great battle. From dawn to dark he worked, from dark to dawn he slept, then he was up again and working" (124).

Almanzo's agricultural work as a "farmer boy" is just as cyclical as the life young Laura led in the Big Woods, but his presentation is strikingly different—as a prototypical male protagonist, a "soldier"—and his story repeatedly emphasizes goals, achievements, and rewards (often monetary). He raises an enormous pumpkin to take to the fair and win a prize; he saves money to buy a pig and dreams of buying horses.

This book, like *Big Woods*, depicts the repeated processes of rural life, inside and outside the house: cutting ice, weaving cloth, making shoes, harvesting and harrowing grain, shearing sheep, selling horses (by Father) and butter (by Mother). However, Almanzo seldom listens to stories of male adventures, like those Pa Ingalls told his daughters. Instead, he enacts his own end-stopped plot. In the book's last chapter, the ten-year-old is offered an apprenticeship in a thriving carriage business, and his father tells him he must choose between that opportunity and a future as a farmer. Almanzo is surprised; "He hadn't supposed he could say anything. He would have to do whatever Father said." For this boy, the choice is easy: "He wanted to be just like Father," a farmer (370–71). Delighted with his son's choice, Father gives the boy his heart's desire, a colt to train and to own. By meeting goals, making plans, and speaking for himself, Almanzo achieves property, pleasure, and self-possession (and, incidentally, the horses provide the mobility that will eventually take the young Almanzo west, where he will meet Laura Ingalls). In the original ending that Wilder drafted for *Farmer Boy*, the Wilder family sells the New York State farm and moves to Minnesota, as Almanzo Wilder's parents actually did. In that ending, Almanzo is the pawn of his father's wanderlust, much as young Laura was.[13] But the revised, published ending emphasizes Almanzo's volition, his education in self-knowledge and self-determination.

Although Almanzo admires and loves his mother, his feelings for his father are far more powerful, nearly worshipful: "Almanzo was sure that Father was the smartest man in the world, as well as the biggest and strongest" (48). Father's authority comes from his respect for the value of traditional labor and for the money into which that labor is translated. For example, he discounts the time- and labor-saving values of the newly available threshing machine (unlike Charles Ingalls, who adopted it eagerly in *Big Woods*). James Wilder threshes his grain by hand and teaches Almanzo to do the same. The older Wilder son, Royal, has chosen to be a storekeeper rather than a farmer. Both parents are saddened by this decision. Mother sees it as a sign of masculine decline and says to her husband: "It's bad enough to see Royal come down to being nothing but a storekeeper! . . . he'll never be the man you are" (367). Almanzo, here presented as the youngest Wilder son,[14] is his father's last chance to pass on patriarchal values and nonmechanized agricultural practices to the next male generation.[15] The boy's decision to be a farmer confirms all-important values of stability, tradition, and paternal authority. Technology, towns, and higher education seem to be enemies of those values. For example, Almanzo is the only Wilder child who does not attend a winter term at the Malone Academy. When his older sister Eliza Jane comes home from the Academy, she is "mortified" that her father drinks tea from his saucer, upholding an outdated tradition. Her mother reprimands her severely, saying "I guess a thing that folks have done for two hundred years we can keep on doing. We're not likely to change, for a new-fangled notion that you've got in Malone Academy" (296–97). Eliza Jane Wilder, who reappears in the last two Little House books, is one of the least attractively presented characters in Laura Ingalls Wilder's fiction. Yet the readers of *Farmer Boy* must recognize that her "new-fangled notion" of drinking tea from the cup has indeed prevailed over the two-hundred-year-old custom defended by her mother. However unfilial, her critique of paternal manners suggests that the reign of her father, the Farmer *Man* venerated by this novel, is soon to end.

As Wilder and Lane worked on drafting and revising *Farmer Boy*, they were becoming aware of how drastically the national Depression would affect their financial security. In December 1931, the investment company that provided substantial income to both Lane and the Wilders went bankrupt. In early 1933, President Roosevelt began proposing the New Deal recovery policies that Wilder and (especially) Lane would vehemently oppose.[16] *Farmer Boy* bears many marks of the financial and political climate in which it was written. According to Almanzo's father, the farmer is an exemplar of self-determination and self-sufficiency: "A farmer depends on himself, and the land and the weather. If you're a farmer, you raise what you eat, you raise what you wear. . . . You work hard, but you work as you please, and no man can tell you to go or come. You'll be free and independent, son, on a farm" (371).

All through her career with the *Missouri Ruralist*, Laura Ingalls Wilder had been an enthusiastic propagandist for the small family farm, an institution she and Lane saw as threatened by the New Deal. In many ways, the fictionalized James Wilder of *Farmer Boy*, based on the father-in-law and paternal grandfather of the two authors, was their most effective advocate for traditional, stable agrarian values. Interestingly, to find such a spokesperson they had to go further back in time than the Little House books, into the childhood of Almanzo Wilder, who was ten years older than his wife. They also returned, for this one book, to the longer-settled territory of New York State, one of the original colonies. With the Wilder family, prosperously established near Malone, they could make their strongest argument for the rewards of the farmer's life. In *Farmer Boy*, young Almanzo sees his farmer father as "an important man" with "a good farm" and "the best horses. . . . His word was as good as his bond, and every year he put money in the bank. When Father drove into Malone, all the townspeople spoke to him respectfully" (22–23). Aside from the emphasis on Father's integrity, every other clause in this description underlines what James Wilder *owns:* farm, livestock, money, respect. Although *Big Woods* portrays the Ingalls family in more prosperous circumstances than in any of the other Little House books, the modest comfort of their small cabin and plot of cleared land is on a very small scale compared to the spacious house, wide fields, and numerous barns owned by James Wilder.

Again and again, Laura Ingalls Wilder's second book emphasizes plenty, abundance, wealth, even excess. For example, Father sells two colts for four hundred dollars, and by canny marketing, he sells five hundred bushels of potatoes for a dollar a bushel, while Mother earns two hundred and fifty dollars for her five hundred pounds of butter. This book is full of food and full of money.[17] The abundance of the Wilder table is too much for even Almanzo, an epic eater. Here is a description of an ordinary family supper:

> Almanzo ate the sweet, mellow baked beans. He ate the bit of salt pork that melted like cream in his mouth. He ate mealy boiled potatoes, with brown ham-gravy. He ate the ham. He bit deep into velvety bread spread with sleek butter, and he ate the crisp golden crust. He demolished a tall heap of pale mashed turnips, and a hill of stewed yellow pumpkin. Then he sighed, and tucked his napkin deeper into the neckband of his red waist. And he ate plum preserves, and strawberry jam, and grape jelly, and spiced watermelon-rind pickles. He felt very comfortable inside. Slowly he ate a large piece of pumpkin pie. (28–29)

No matter how prodigiously Almanzo eats, he never makes a dent in this inexhaustible abundance. Financial insecurity, the Ingalls family's constant state, is never experienced by the fictional Almanzo. For this child, being a Farmer Boy means self-determination and *ownership;* he wants to "have horses and cows and fields. . . . just like Father" (371). Thus the book is full of lessons in investment and in caring for property. Given a fifty-cent piece, Almanzo must decide what to buy: pink lemonade or a suckling pig? Schooled by Father, he chooses the pig, giving it attentive care and preparing it for the market. Fifty cents is a significant sum, Father reminds him; "That's what's in this half-dollar, Almanzo. The work that raised half a bushel of potatoes" (and Almanzo well knows how *much* work that is). In such lessons, farm labor becomes the basis for a monetary system and for the nation's success. According to Father Wilder, "it was axes and plows," wielded by farmers, "that made this country" (184, 188).

As I've said, Almanzo admires his mother, particularly when she performs her own feats of bargaining and selling. Having sold her butter for a record price, Mother drives into town alone to put her money in the bank, and "Almanzo was proud. His Mother was probably the best butter-maker in the whole of New York. People in New York City would eat it, and say to one another how good it was, and wonder who made it" (239). Mother's success with her butter depends on her proximity to the largest U.S. city, fast-growing New York; this links her to modernity and to the rapid urbanization of the years just after the Civil War. At the same time, her domestic work is almost archaically traditional. Although she makes the clothing for her entire family, there is no mention of a sewing machine or of any assistance. For much of this clothing, including every stitch Almanzo wears, she spins and dyes the thread and weaves the cloth that she cuts and sews. The Wilder family keep sheep and produce their own wool. Thus Mother Wilder draws on much older traditions than the Ingalls family in the West, which never owns sheep nor produces cloth. Although Mother Wilder is living after the Civil War and benefiting from the rewards of an urban market, most of her work proceeds as if the Industrial Revolution had never happened. Such traditional self-sufficiency must have appeared especially attractive to Wilder and Lane in the early 1930s, when the benefits of "modern times" seemed suddenly to have turned against them. Thus it is not surprising that, in a revision, Lane eliminated the ending her mother had proposed for *Farmer Boy*, which abruptly sold off the Wilder farm and propelled them toward an unknown destination in the "West." Instead, in the finally published version, the security and stability of the Wilder farm ethos and economy are guaranteed and perpetuated by Almanzo's last-chapter decision to become a Farmer Man, like his father.

Must *farmers* be boys and men? Almanzo's sisters help in some of the field work and regularly assist their mother with cooking and housework. And Mother is a multiskilled worker, as we have seen. Yet, however high the price her butter brings, it is only half the sum Father gets for his potatoes, and all the farm profits presumably go into *his* bank account.[18] Laura Ingalls Wilder's *Missouri Ruralist* essays had advocated partnership for men and women on family farms. In this book, written and marketed by a mother and daughter about a husband and father who does not write, patriarchy, paternity, and farming are clearly linked. Such an agenda is potentially problematic for women—although, as we have seen, the conservative Depression climate pressured women to promote jobs for men. Writing *Farmer Boy*, Wilder and Lane pursued income and professional success for themselves (especially Wilder), by glorifying *the* most traditional of male professions.

Yet the portrayal of both Almanzo's sisters raises questions about these values. The oldest child in the fictionalized Wilder family, "bossy" Eliza Jane, is Almanzo's least favorite sibling and the only one to challenge Father Wilder even on such a small matter as drinking tea from his saucer. Nevertheless, on one occasion Eliza Jane is portrayed as Almanzo's most effective ally; when he angrily throws the stove-blacking brush at her and mars their mother's cherished parlor wallpaper, Eliza Jane skillfully and laboriously patches the paper so that Mother never sees the damage Almanzo has done. Here Eliza Jane's initiative and assertiveness are positive values, but Almanzo's more usual irritation with his older sister shows that a female like her is potentially a problem for a Farmer Boy. In the next-to-last Little House book, *Little Town on the Prairie*, Eliza Jane reappears as a woman homesteader and Laura's beleaguered, ineffectual schoolteacher; this problematic future sister-in-law becomes a model for an unsuccessful professional woman, as young Laura contemplates launching her own teaching career. Among the Wilder and Ingalls women, Eliza Jane is portrayed as most at odds with the traditional role of a nineteenth-century farm woman.

The actual Eliza Jane Wilder was an interesting and original person who did attempt for several years, in difficult circumstances, to prove up a homestead in South Dakota. As a single woman, she worked in several states and as a clerk for the Department of the Interior in Washington, D.C. At forty-three she married a well-to-do Louisiana rice farmer, moved to Louisiana, and bore a child. After her husband's death, Eliza Jane Thayer was left without financial resources.[19] Nevertheless, her descendants remembered her as resourceful and indomitable. A granddaughter recalled, "my grandmother was a strong one. . . . She did anything to make a nickel. I think she sold Watkins products [flavoring extracts] door to door. She was never at a loss; she always had something to do" (Francis Gervaise Thayer, interview in Hines 1994, 230).

Eliza Jane's relationship with her younger sister-in-law, Laura Ingalls Wilder, was always somewhat strained, as the largely unflattering portrayal of her in Wilder's fiction suggests. In 1945 Wilder answered schoolchildren's inquiries: "I never learned to care very much for Miss Wilder. She died long ago" (LIW to Las Virgenes School, Calabasas, Calif., 7 May 1945, Mansfield). Nevertheless, Eliza Jane provided important assistance to her brother's family in Missouri. When, at sixteen, the precocious Rose Wilder had completed the minimal high school curriculum in Mansfield, her parents considered her dangerously at loose ends. Wilder-Ingalls family stories, cited by William Holtz, suggest "that Rose was slipping out of parental control" and perhaps conducting "a worrisome dalliance with a Latin tutor" (1993, 42). At this point, in 1903 Rose was sent to live for a year with her Aunt Eliza Jane in Crowley, to undertake a more ambitious and challenging high school curriculum. A year later, at seventeen, Rose graduated with honors, completing her formal education. Obviously, the support of her rather unconventional aunt "E.J.," as the family (but not the books) called her, was extremely important to Rose as she began to launch herself as an independent woman.[20]

Eliza Jane's support had increased in importance to the Wilder family after James Wilder sold all his property in Minnesota,[21] where the family had emigrated from New York, and sunk the proceeds in rice plantation investments, which failed within a year.[22] When James Wilder died soon thereafter in 1899, he was "a broken man" with a much-diminished estate; his legacy to Almanzo Wilder was five hundred dollars, the amount of a single year's potato profit in *Farmer Boy* (Holtz 1993, 41).[23] Thus the actual history of the Wilder family records the ascendancy of the independent woman, Eliza Jane, and the decline of the Farmer Man. *Farmer Boy* is obviously an effort to restore and perpetuate the myth of the Farmer Man in the persons of James Wilder and his son Almanzo. But for two women with financial and literary ambitions and anxieties, who had seen Eliza Jane Wilder Thayer both as a rival and an ally, both as a financial supporter and as someone who had *not* lived out the traditional role of the farm wife, the character of Eliza Jane was a problem and a challenge. This is apparent in her rather contradictory portrait in *Farmer Boy*.

The fictional portrait of Almanzo's sister Alice, his closest sibling in age and temperament, is far more consistent. These two are always friends and allies, although Alice never appears in the later books. In *Farmer Boy*, their relationship raises important questions about gender constructions. For example, because they are about the same size and age, the two siblings sometimes work together in the fields. One spring day they are both kept home from school to plant carrot seeds.

> Their bare feet felt good in the air and the soft dirt. . . . Almanzo could see his feet, but of course Alice's were hidden under her skirts. Her hoops rounded out, and she had to pull them back and stoop to drop the seeds neatly into the furrow.
>
> Almanzo asked her if she didn't want to be a boy. She said yes, she did. Then she said no, she didn't.
>
> "Boys aren't pretty like girls, and they can't wear ribbons."
>
> "I don't care how pretty I be," Almanzo said. "And I wouldn't wear ribbons anyhow."
>
> "Well, I like to make butter and I like to patch quilts. And cook, and sew, and spin. Boys can't do that. But even if I be a girl, I can drop potatoes and sow carrots and drive horses as well as you can."
>
> "You can't whistle on a grass stem," Almanzo said. (129–30)

Clearly these children have already received rigid educations in gendered behavior. Neither of them questions that Alice must wear her cumbersome hoop skirts, even though they impede her while she is doing field work. Almanzo, the Farmer Boy, disdains taking on any "feminine" attributes, wearing ribbons or patching quilts. The questions and quandaries in this passage are all for Alice, who wants to be pretty, to dress in conventional feminine style, to do the traditional domestic work at which her mother excels, *and* to be her brother's equal at field work and handling horses. These culturally contradictory desires will surface again in the Little House character of Laura Ingalls. Alice is an interesting and attractive character, and she suggests a relatively wide range of behavior and work available to a female child in the nineteenth century. Almanzo, although he is customarily confident and assertive with this slightly older sister, can't come up with an effective rejoinder when she claims to be his equal at the work he values most, driving horses. He only cites his superiority at whistling, a practice forbidden to decorous Victorian girls: "Whistling girls and crowing hens / Always come to some bad end." Alice and her older sister Eliza Jane, although they are clearly secondary characters, provide much of the cultural complexity of *Farmer Boy;* they suggest that an unbroken inheritance of an agricultural vocation from a patriarchal parent is as difficult—if not impossible—for a girl as it is effortless for their brother Almanzo.

Laura Ingalls Wilder called her first book a "memorial" to her father, Charles Ingalls. Although Almanzo Wilder was still alive when Rose Wilder Lane worked on *Farmer Boy*, this book is also obviously a tribute to a father's choice of vocation, farming, and to his lifelong involvement with horses. Lane's relationship with her father appears to have been far less conflicted and intense than her relationship with her mother; her journal, which complains frequently about her mother's demands and "insensitivities," seldom complains about her father. When Lane traveled to Malone, New York, to do research for the revision of *Farmer Boy*, she sent her father packets of annotated postcards of local views, trying to link present scenes to the memories her father had recounted. For example, on one card she wrote, "We went to Burke and the starch factory [owned by Almanzo Wilder's uncle and subject of a deleted manuscript chapter in *Farmer Boy*] is gone. We met Ralph Bissett there and he remembered hearing about your father and his good horses." On the next card she added, "I am sending you by express some wintergreen plants [not native to the Ozarks]. . . . I believe they will grow there [Mansfield]" (RWL to Almanzo Wilder, Malone post-cards, undated, 6–7, Hoover). Wintergreen berries had been a favorite childhood treat that Almanzo Wilder had recalled to his daughter and are the subject of a memorable episode in *Farmer Boy*.

With her research and writing on the second Laura Ingalls Wilder novel, Rose Lane was involved in a complex project of preserving and transplanting *her* father's childhood memories. But the character of Almanzo is handled very differently from that of Charles Ingalls, who is seen both from his daughter Laura's perspective, as she reimagines her own childhood vision, and through his own inset narratives (as remembered by Laura Ingalls Wilder) in *Big Woods*. *Farmer Boy*, by contrast, is entirely written from the boy's third-person point of view; the female authors have assumed a "male" perspective. This was a practice to which Lane had returned again and again in her writing career; she had even ghostwritten for men, such as Lowell Thomas.[24] But almost all of Laura Ingalls Wilder's published writing, beginning with her early work as women's editor of the *Missouri Ruralist*, had been from a specifically female perspective.

Thus the first two Wilder books raise important questions about how *daughters* might write the stories of beloved fathers. *Farmer Boy* is the story of a son's inheritance of his father's vocation. But Lane and Wilder were ambitious daughters of fathers who had no surviving sons. (Each woman lost a male infant child and had a brother who died in infancy.) May a daughter become her father's heir? This question is further complicated by the facts that neither Charles Ingalls nor James Wilder nor Almanzo Wilder ended his life as a fully successful farmer. Laura Ingalls Wilder wrote to

Rose Lane in 1937 that "Pa was no businessman" but a "hunter and a trapper, a musician and a poet" (LIW to RWL, 23 March 1937, Hoover). When he died at sixty in 1902, Charles Ingalls had abandoned his homestead farm to live in town, doing odd jobs and carpenter work. James Wilder lost the profits of his farming through unwise investments late in his life, and even the thrifty Almanzo and Laura Wilder had needed financial help from their daughter, from the 1920s onward, to keep Rocky Ridge Farm going. Recalling his farming career to Rose Lane in 1937, Almanzo Wilder wrote, "My life has been mostly disappointments" (*Sampler* 213). The failures, stringencies, and disappointments of farming, for these men, were among the reasons why Laura Ingalls Wilder and Rose Wilder Lane were writers. Their publications, especially the Little House books, are still earning royalties for their heirs, and were a far more reliable source of family income than the farms ever were.

A pertinent subtext to this debate about inheritance is "Grandpa's Fiddle," written by Lane, unpublished during her lifetime and found in her papers after her death. This story is an account, from seven-year-old Rose's point of view, of Laura, Almanzo, and Rose Wilder's departure from South Dakota (where their farm had failed) to make a new start in the Missouri Ozarks. The central event of this tale is Charles Ingalls's announcement of his legacy to his daughter Laura, whom he will never see again. Having played his repertoire of old songs for her one last time, he says,

> "Laura, you've always stood by us, from the time you was a little girl knee-high to a grasshopper. Your Ma and I have never been able to do as much for you girls as we'd like to. But there'll be a little something left when we're gone, and I hope, I want to say now, I want you all [the assembled Ingalls/Wilder family] to witness, when the time comes, Laura, I want you to have the fiddle."

Laura is overcome by the implications of this gift, and later she says to her husband,

> "To think, Manly, he gave me the fiddle. . . . It's the first thing I remember, Pa's playing us to sleep. . . . by the campfires . . . all the way out here. . . . I see it now, though I didn't then—we never could have gotten through it all without Pa's fiddle." (68)

In both the Ingalls and Wilder families, there were few tangible assets to pass on to the next generation. The fiddle represents music, spirit, endurance, and a vast repertoire of cultural inheritance; on the last night

Pa plays for Laura, for example, he begins with Mary's request, the Scottish "Bonny Doon"[25] (the Ingalls/Quiner family is of Scottish descent), and ends with a Civil War campground song, "Tenting Tonight." In this story, Rose Wilder Lane is obviously rethinking family issues of father-to-daughter inheritance, suggesting that the continuity of song that Charles Ingalls created with his fiddle was passed to his daughter Laura and perhaps became the central motif and resource of the Little House books. *If* we see the Little House books as starting from Pa's stories and music, he is not the half-failed patriarch who has not been able to do as much as he and his wife wished to do for their daughters. Instead, he becomes the founder of the family fortune, the Little House books. Rose Wilder Lane's ambivalence about the patriarchal implications of her story, "Grandpa's Fiddle," may explain why she never published this tale.

Charles Ingalls's fiddle was indeed willed to his daughter Laura after his death in 1902. Her correspondence records her elaborate efforts to assure that it would be given careful conservation; at first she made it a bequest to the South Dakota Historical Society, with the proviso that it be played for an audience at regular intervals.[26] When Rocky Ridge Farm became a museum, after the Wilders' deaths, the fiddle returned there, and it is still the most popular exhibit in the museum. Every year a fiddler plays it at Mansfield's Laura Ingalls Wilder Days. In this complex interaction of texts, artifact, music, and ongoing ritual, the issues of father-daughter inheritance that were such an important part of the Little House project are perpetuated to this day.

In a pertinent 1989 essay, "Reading the Father Metaphorically," Beth Kowaleski-Wallace writes that metaphoric readings of paternal figures, in which father equals patriarch, have been important to many feminist readers of the past two decades. Such readings, "working by means of resemblance . . . give us a sense that we are finally able to comprehend, to take hold of, the elusive force [patriarchy] that enthralls us" (298–99). But Kowaleski-Wallace goes on to argue that metaphoric readings often cannot plumb the full complexity of daughters' reading and writing of patriarchal fathers. She asks, "how . . . does reading the father metaphorically account for the daughter's tendency to identify so strongly with the father, even when his masculine inclinations involve her in behavior so antithetical to her own feminine interests?" (303).

From the beginning, and most explicitly in the first two volumes, the Little House series offers a complex treatment of the issues Kowaleski-Wallace defines. Shoring up the aging, newly fragile farmer patriarchs is a major project of these books—but to write and publish the books, Wilder and Lane had to expand and partially to repudiate the traditional roles of farm wife and farm daughter.[27] Through their writing careers, they concurrently defend and dismantle patriarchy. According to Kowaleski-Wallace, "all daughters are . . . simultaneously attracted to and horrified by the possibility that the father's power might *not* be inviolable" (309). The account of Pa Ingalls as "mad dog," for example, does not lend itself fully to metaphoric reading; clearly this father is not entirely the out-of-control "beastly" seducer and pursuer *or* the playful, protective parent. Four-year-old Laura, when she chooses to respond actively and aggressively to her father's pursuit, is becoming aware of how complexly he must be read. Kowaleski-Wallace argues that metaphoric readings of patriarchs are built on the assumption of an autonomous self, "a dualistic model of the male oppressor and his female victim" (296). Theorists who advocate metaphoric reading "posit the result of a woman writer's identification with her father as a profound *self-division*" (304), and if the ideal self is *autonomous*, such division must be destructive. But if, like Juliet Mitchell and others, one views a "sense of being 'split'" as "an inevitable part of what it means to be *human*" (305), we need ways of reading and writing that begin to free both daughters and fathers from rigid, restrictive formulations of patriarchy. In *Farmer Boy*, for example, Alice Wilder speculates about such a reading of gender prerogatives when she claims a traditional feminine role for herself *and* also claims the most desirable skills of a farmer-patriarch, such as horsemanship. In *Big Woods*, Charles Ingalls has a similar experience when he lays down his phallic gun and his aggressive hunter's role to become a passive, receptive, conventionally *feminine* observer of the forest animals. The Little House books, espousing traditional gender roles and agricultural values in a shell-shocked Depression culture, are the work of dutiful daughters honoring their farmer fathers; but they are also subtly iconoclastic works, dismantling patriarchal prerogatives to facilitate the emergence of wide-ranging female sensibilities.

Debate about the authorship of the Little House series has dominated much discussion of Laura Ingalls Wilder's career in recent years, especially since the 1993 publication of William Holtz's biography of Rose Wilder Lane. Holtz is Lane's advocate; he aims (quite justifiably, in my view) to direct more attention and respect to her long and various writing career. He points out what must be apparent to anyone who examines the Wilder/ Lane papers with care: that Lane did a substantial and important amount of writing and rewriting of the Little House series. But Holtz also goes further; he attempts to anatomize and evaluate the contributions of each woman to the series and concludes, "Almost everything we admire about the Little House books—the pace and rhythm of the narrative line, the carefully nuanced flow of feeling, the muted drama of daily life—are created by what Mama Bess called Rose's 'fine touch,' as shining fiction is made from her mother's tangle of fact. Laura Ingalls Wilder remained a determined but amateurish writer to the end" (1993, 380).

Having looked at the same manuscript materials, which constitute an incomplete and various record of the two women's collaboration, I cannot draw the same conclusions.[28] The relatively uninflected narrative that Wilder initially lays out is sometimes enhanced and enriched by Lane's additions and suggestions (she also made some significant cuts). And sometimes I prefer the Wilder draft to the Lane revision; for example, the Fourth of July chapter in *Little Town on the Prairie*, which Holtz cites as one of Lane's most successful revisions, has always seemed to me a leaden chunk of propaganda and one of the least successful passages in the series. However, as far as I am concerned, such designations are ultimately an unproductive line of argument. While writing this book, I have come to see the Little House books as the work of a composite author, with strengths and qualities that do not exactly match the independently produced publications of either collaborator.[29]

I also see these issues of authorship as related to a patriarchal publishing tradition that is uncomfortable with acknowledging collaborative work, especially if that work has the marks of "literary" merit that Holtz and many other readers have found in the Little House series. The publishing prerogatives of single ownership and authorship, like those of legal sanctions and names on paper, have been primarily male-administered. (Although successful U.S. women authors were numerous in the second half of the nineteenth century, most of them got published through negotiations with powerful male editors and publishers, as Susan Coultrap-McQuin has shown in *Doing Literary Business*.) Such patriarchal precedents are apparent in the Little House books. It is Pa who owns the Ingalls land and property; his name alone appears on the homestead papers, even though his wife and daughters all help him to claim the land. And, as we have seen in *Big Woods*, it is Pa's storytelling that specifically invokes male ancestors, his father and grandfather. Ma tells her daughters no corresponding stories about specific female ancestors.

Rose Lane, despite her feminist leanings, conducted her writing career in a publishing industry where ultimate decisions were still made largely by men. She placed high value on her name and writing reputation as a commodity and she often urged her mother to make "Laura Ingalls Wilder" similarly marketable. Lane saw unacknowledged collaboration, the occasional ghostwriting that had been a substantial source of her income since around 1918,[30] as a detriment to her valuable reputation. She explained to one of her informally adopted sons, "This kind of work is called 'ghosting,' and no writer of my reputation ever does it" (RWL to Rexh Meta, 23 March 1931, Hoover). Thus Lane took pains to separate herself from her mother's writing in the eyes of the public. For example, when negotiations for publishing *Big Woods* seemed to be complete, Lane wrote to the children's editor at Knopf that she had sent her mother's contract to agent George Bye, "and now I fade, gracefully I hope, from the scene" (RWL to Marian Fiery, 6 Oct. 1931, Hoover)—even though she was very much *on* the scene for the ongoing marketing and editing of Wilder's work. Later, after her mother's death, as William Anderson and others have noted, she fiercely argued for the separateness of their two careers. In a typical letter to Louise Hovde Mortensen, she asserted: "A fiction writer myself, I agree that my mother could have added to artistic effects by altering facts, but she did not write fiction. She did not want to" (Mortensen 428–29)—despite the fact that the voluminous surviving correspondence between Lane and Wilder about the later Little House books clearly shows Wilder making a fiction writer's decisions about how to shape, use, and alter her autobiographical materials. Furthermore, Lane always presented her mother as a writer for children, which she herself was not. Preserving this distinction between them was obviously very important to Lane. When the Little House books were clearly established as a literary and monetary success, she advised her mother that children's fiction was a surer investment than adult fiction: "there is much more money in juveniles. I'd do one myself if I could get the time" (RWL to LIW, n.d., on the reverse of Ida Louise Raymond to RWL, 18 Dec. 1937, Hoover). Although she was sometimes desperate for money, Lane never "got the time" to write for children under her own name, even though she had been involved in the success of two very lucrative juvenile serials of the 1930s—the Little House books and the Sue Barton nurse series, which her longtime companion, Helen Boylston, began at Lane's suggestion. To George Bye, Lane made it clear that her mother's "little" project was very small potatoes compared to the larger business of Rose Wilder Lane's career. When the final contract for *Big Woods* was completed, she wrote Bye apologetically, "From now on I think there'll be nothing to it but royalties coming through. My mother will continue to write juveniles and I'll go on placing them, and I hope the dribbling commissions will be worth while to you." She ended the letter with more important news of her own career: "Another short story is coming shortly" (RWL to George Bye, 27 Nov. 1931, Hoover).

It seems apparent, then, that Lane intended to dissociate her own publishing reputation, initially much more illustrious than her mother's, from the Little House project. Additionally, Lane's private diaries establish that she was particularly anxious about her own career at the time the Little House books began to be written and published; she felt that her reputation had slipped and her literary ambitions were as yet unfulfilled. In the diaries she alternated between large-scale plans and personal, professional, and financial despair. In early 1933, for example, she ambitiously projected an "American novel in many volumes, an enormous canvas, covering horizontally a continent, vertically all classes" (RWL diary, 11 Jan. 1933, Hoover). But a few days later, working on *Farmer Boy* rewrites, Lane lamented: "I am getting nothing whatever done. . . . my own work stagnates: I do not even think of it" (RWL diary, late January, 1933, Hoover). She continued to take notes on her voracious reading; for example, Virginia Woolf's *Orlando* evoked this discriminating praise: "The impression is that made by a waterfall. I do not know how otherwise to express the rushing force and delicacy of the book . . . quite real, profound, and yet resulting in nothing definite, concrete, graspable." But Lane then turned on herself: "I haven't an intelligence competent to meet her [Woolf], or to enter her field" (RWL diary, 7 Dec. 1928, Hoover).

Lane's self-appraisal is acute. In the 1930s, as the Little House books appeared under her mother's name, she wrote most of the fiction readers now generally consider her best: *Let the Hurricane Roar* (1933), *Old Home Town* (1935) and *Free Land* (1938). But no one has yet argued—and I certainly can't—that these volumes stand among the very best U.S. fiction of their time. Instead, these books, all of which were profitably first published serially in such magazines as the *Saturday Evening Post,* often seem stale and formulaic. It is as if Lane's market savvy, her near-infallible knowledge of what would sell to magazines, had incapacitated her for writing any other kind of fiction. The extraordinary innovations of a book like *Orlando* no longer seemed a possibility for Rose Wilder Lane in her anxious middle age. And Lane's fixed ideas of what a "writer of my reputation" could and could not publicly do cut her off from strategies that might have allowed her to recharge her career and to make fuller use of her own remarkable gifts (which had been well demonstrated by a fine story, "Innocence," that won the O. Henry Award for 1922). Lane was "being an author" as the male-dominated publishing industry had taught her to be.

But her mother was less constrained. Her journalistic career had been largely as a woman writing specifically as a woman and for women; at the *Missouri Ruralist* she was probably considered the spokeswoman for a large body of farm women. Wilder's traditional Anglo-American midwestern upbringing had given her broad experience with women's collaborative work. She worked with her mother and sisters on domestic tasks every day: sewing, housekeeping, gardening, cooking. Although Ma Ingalls, as portrayed in the Little House books, told her daughters no didactic tales of their female ancestors that parallel Pa's patriarchal lore, she thoroughly instructed them in a powerful and largely anonymous tradition of women's domestic work. Thus, in the 1920s, when both Wilder and Lane were thinking of writing about "pioneer days" for publication, Wilder had no qualms about writing her mother's one surviving sister, "Aunt Martha" Carpenter, and asking for her reminiscences of early frontier experiences. She told her aunt that Rose might use these memories in her writing or that she, Laura, might produce an article on frontier cooking for the *Ladies' Home Journal*. Her assumption was that family stories and family history were family property, and that the practice of women's collaboration that she had learned in her mother's house was still a part of the family tradition that her aunt would be glad to honor.[31] This tradition is portrayed throughout the Little House series; in fact, the very last culinary achievement mentioned in the series is a collaborative one: Laura beats the eggs for her own wedding cake, baked by Ma. Unlike her daughter, who was an isolated only child, Laura Ingalls Wilder had received her education in a household of five girls and women, and as she began to work on the Little House series she spent many of her waking hours in her memories of that world. These conditions almost certainly made it easier for her to accept (and perhaps to take for granted) her daughter's substantial contributions to the series that appeared solely under the mother's name.

In the first two books of their collaboration, *Big Woods* and *Farmer Boy,* Wilder and Lane had essayed a girl's story and a boy's story—Laura's and Almanzo's—and they had experimented in combining traditions of male storytelling with narratives of female experience, whether through young

Laura's point of view or the near-submerged stories of Almanzo's sisters. When these two books were complete, it was obvious that a substantial market for Laura Ingalls Wilder fiction had been created. As we've seen, Wilder and Lane had also drawn from their complex heritage of gendered culture: patriarchal stories and priorities, matriarchal domestic education, the male-oriented doctrine of individual success that had governed much of Lane's career and toward which she urged her mother, and the traditions of domestic collaboration in which Wilder had come of age. Additionally, both women were daughters of beloved (and partially failed) fathers who had no male heirs. Writing was their way of preserving their fathers' myths and priorities, but to do their best writing, they had to find ways around the traditions of male dominance that suppressed female voices and ignored female stories.

One of the ways they had begun to work at these problematic issues was through the plotting of the books. In this respect, as we've seen, *Big Woods* and *Farmer Boy* are very different. *Farmer Boy* has an Aristotelian plot of conflict, growth, conscious effort, and achievement, the sort of plot that is usually considered to be a traditional resource of male-dominated Western culture. *Big Woods* confines such plotting to Pa's tales; the rest of the book, dominated by young Laura's perception, is reflective, sensory, and cyclical. In a pertinent essay, Susan Stanford Friedman emphasizes the differences between two fictional modes: narrative and lyric. "Narrative is understood to be a mode that foregrounds a *sequence* of events that move dynamically in space and time. Lyric is understood to be a mode that foregrounds a *simultaneity*, a cluster of feelings or ideas that project a gestalt in stasis. Where narrative centers on *story*, lyric focuses on *state of mind*" (164). Friedman argues from Virginia Woolf's assertion that, to tell as yet untold stories, women writers must "'tamper with,' 'break' and subvert narrative" (162). Since Woolf views traditional narrative plot as an instrument of male control, a woman writer's subversion of plot may be read as "a critique of the traditional family," which suppressed the daughter's voice. "Overthrowing the tyranny of plot is for the woman writer tantamount to overthrowing the power of the father" (163). In this context, we can see more clearly why plotting is such a freighted issue for Wilder and Lane. Furthermore, narrative plot is often considered to be an Oedipal strategy (thus Roland Barthes' assertion that the story of Oedipus is "paradigmatic of all narratives" [Friedman 163]). Lyric, by contrast, may evoke the rich sensory simultaneity and proximity of "pre-Oedipal" time, dominated by the child's closeness with her mother. *Big Woods* is located in the sensibility of a fictional four-to-five-year-old; because Wilder made the fictional Laura two years older than she herself was at the same period, she was drawing from even earlier childhood memories (or family stories) when she wrote the book. Friedman sensibly warns against oversimplifying the narrative theory she articulates,[32] but she does conclude that, used carefully, this body of theory can "provide illuminating metaphors for the inscription of adult desires and fantasies about childhood in an historically constituted literary discourse" (166).

With similar caution, I propose that this body of theory can illuminate the Little House fictions of childhood, and particularly *Big Woods*. Much of the richness of the first Little House book comes from its lyric qualities, and those qualities are usually associated with Laura's solitude or the experience she shares with her mother and sisters: Laura's long, rapt scrutiny of her Christmas rag doll (made by Ma), for example, or the girls' worshipful look at their mother's best delaine dress, in a freighted, often-silent state of sensory/emotional intensity. In recurrent passages like these, cues to time and sequence are largely external, as when Pa wakens Laura with the announcement that today is her fifth birthday. Such passages were added late in the long process of revising *Big Woods*; Wilder told a friend that her editor had asked her to put "meat" on the "bones" of Pa's stories (Irene Lichty, quoted in Farrow). The intense evocation of *things* that has made the Little House books so powerful for so many readers comes largely from these additions, such as the repeated evocations of Ma's talismanic china shepherdess that begin in *Big Woods*. These lyric passages link the Little House series to resources of nineteenth and early twentieth century U.S. women's culture, which was often encoded in things, especially domestic objects and textiles.

Friedman also reminds her readers that Virginia Woolf, like most other twentieth-century women who wrote fiction, did not write exclusively in the lyric mode. "Ultimately, Woolf does not dismiss the need for narrative any more than she ever abandoned the novel for lyric poetry, any more than she denied father for mother. . . . Woolf drew from her mother and her father, just as *To the Lighthouse* is ultimately a lyric novel, an interplay of both discourses" (174). The Little House books too are built on "an interplay of both discourses." It may seem that Lane, with her practiced professional skills, brought the "masculine" resources of sequential narrative to the process, while the "feminine" lyric qualities came from Wilder. Ultimately, however, such a simplistic formulation does injustice to both authors of the Little House series. What's particularly timely and durably compelling about these books is their efforts to claim the widest resources of language and experience—lyric, narrative, female, male—to tell stories about daughters who wanted to expand and grow without entirely repudiating the structure of patriarchy.

For this project, *Farmer Boy* was a dangerous and necessary experiment. The kind of Oedipal narrative expressed in Almanzo's story *did* significantly frame Laura Ingalls's experience. She was a (male) farmer's daughter who would marry a farmer, Almanzo Wilder. But the foregrounding of these men's stories threatened to suppress Laura's own, just as Alice and Eliza Jane Wilder became bit players in *Farmer Boy*. As a child, I sensed this, uneasily. *Big Woods* and *Farmer Boy* were my least favorite books by my favorite author because they emphasized Pa and Almanzo in ways that obscured the centrality of Laura, the girl protagonist who had become so important to me.

To create a Little House *series* that would become one of the most memorable and problematic U.S. narratives of a girl's experience, Wilder and Lane had to find new narrative strategies and to preempt the patriarchal voice that is such a strong presence in the first two books. They began to discover their strategy in the third book, *Little House on the Prairie*, in which Laura Ingalls Wilder's juvenile fiction becomes a series. In it, the stable, static Little House in the Big Woods becomes a covered wagon traveling west, at the center of a mobile, exploratory lyric narrative, with a female sensibility at its center.

This photograph of Laura Ingalls Wilder appeared in the *Missouri Ruralist* in 1918. By this time Wilder was well established as a successful editor and columnist at the *Ruralist* and was considering ways to expand her writing career. Courtesy Herbert Hoover Presidential Library-Museum.

Chapter 2

"Indians in the House"
A Narrative of Acculturation

Little House on the Prairie is probably Laura Ingalls Wilder's best-known book, and certainly her best-known title. It takes the Little House, container for an intensely defined and defended domestic culture, and surrounds it with vast, fluctuating, contested space. When I was seven or eight, it was this book that first caught me, invaded my imagination, made me a fan. Already I was spending every Saturday afternoon at a Western double feature and playing "Indians" with my cousins (I vied for the only girls' parts I knew, Sacajawea and Pocahontas). This book returned to Laura; it freed her—and me—from the suffocating smallness of the Little House in the Big Woods and gave her space to run and imagine on the Kansas prairie. And it held out the tantalizing possibility that Westerns and Indians were games, and genres, in which (white) girls too could play.

In this third book, published in 1935, Wilder and Lane resumed the story of the Ingalls family, with Laura as protagonist. To do so, it was necessary to disrupt the secure, static *now* of *Big Woods*. The new book begins with a powerful stroke of radical change: "Pa said to Ma, 'seeing you don't object, I've decided to go see the West. . . . We can sell [the Big Woods farm] now for as much as we're ever likely to get, enough to give us a start in a new country'" (2–3). Although historically predictable, this is an astounding decision for the Charles Ingalls of *Big Woods*, who was a devoted son, brother, and uncle, as well as a husband and father. After leaving the extended, exogamous Ingalls family behind, he will never again share work with brothers on adjacent farms or join in communal sugaring-off with his parents; in fact, he will apparently never see his parents again.[1] His wife Caroline *does* object, at least to the timing; "Oh, Charles, must we go now?" she says (3). Nevertheless, with remarkable dispatch, the young family load a wagon with their few portable possessions, say farewell to the assembled relatives, and ride away "from the little log house. . . . It stayed there. . . . And that was the *last* of the little house" (6, emphasis mine).

However, this is the true beginning of the Little House *series*. The move dislodges the hegemonies of both Laura's parents: Pa's heritage of patriarchal prerogative and Ma's legacy of domestic order and prowess. It initiates a pattern, which will persist throughout the Little House books, of moving, establishing, building, settling, and then uprooting to move again and then to resume the settling process. Neither parent entirely controls this pattern; as Laura grows older, she sees that sometimes the family travels because of Pa's love for moving, exploration, and new beginnings; sometimes they stay put because of Ma's insistence on an established community where she and her daughters can have the benefits of schools, church, and a stable middle-class culture. And on many occasions, neither Pa nor Ma decides the family's fate; they are compelled to move or stay by such powerful circumstances as weather, illness, or U.S. government policy. The initial move out of the Big Woods jolts young Laura Ingalls out of endogamy; as her family sets out for the West, she is released into growth, sequence, and seriality.

This seriality is the solution to the stultifying plots that endangered the two previous novels and hampered Wilder and Lane's efforts to continue a girl's story. On the prairie, Laura Ingalls is dislodged from *now* into time, and into a new awareness of cultural multiplicity. No longer will she live surrounded only by Ingalls relatives.

On the first page of *Little House on the Prairie*, Laura thinks of her family's westward move, as she has been schooled to do, as "going to the Indian country" (1) where, Pa promises, she will "see a papoose" (6). Up until now, the only other children Laura and Mary have met have been cousins; all these children share the same names and the same genes. The new word, "papoose," suggests that there is another way to be an American child, in a country that is not owned by Ingalls men but is marked and named by other cultures: "Indian country."

Laura looks forward to encounters with Indians; she asks eagerly, "What is a papoose?" and Pa replies, "A papoose is a little, brown Indian baby" (6). Part of this is familiar language to Laura; "little babies," sister and cousins, are part of her own family. But the other two words expand her vocabulary. "Brown" and "Indian" signify racial and cultural difference from herself. Laura's interest is piqued and, as the family travels toward Kansas Territory, she repeats her question again and again: "What is a papoose?"

Laura's question signifies that her conscious frontier experience has begun. As she grows into girlhood and womanhood in Kansas Indian Territory, western Minnesota, and the Dakota Territory, she becomes part of a process of cultural interaction, defense, resistance, and exploration that had especially high stakes for young females, who might eventually intermarry and bear racially and culturally mixed children. As a mobile *serial*, the Little House narrative could expansively explore that process, showing how possibilities and prohibitions of acculturation were built into the maturation process for a borderland U.S. child in the late nineteenth century. Beginning with *Little House on the Prairie*, Laura Ingalls Wilder and Rose Wilder Lane began to propose some of the hardest and most persistent questions for an emigrant nation: questions of possible cultural interaction, cultural collision, and a potentially multicultural life. What happens when housekeeping hits the road, encounters other cultures, and the Little House becomes a serial project? The complexity with which the Little House series responds to these questions (always from the point of view of its Euro-American protagonist and her family) is one of the major reasons why these books have been so compelling and so perennially troubling for U.S. readers.[2]

As five-year-old Laura Ingalls continues to ask her question—"What is a papoose?"—she discovers that her mother will not answer her. Instead,

Ma deflects the child with evasions and instructions in manners. Laura draws obvious conclusions and asks,

> "Why don't you like Indians, Ma?"
> "I just don't like them; and don't lick your fingers, Laura," said Ma.
> "This is Indian country, isn't it?" Laura said. "What did we come to their country for, if you don't like them?"
> Ma said she didn't know whether this was Indian country or not. She didn't know where the Kansas line was. But whether or no, the Indians would not be here long. Pa had word from a man in Washington that the Indian territory would be open to settlement soon. It might already be open to settlement. They could not know, because Washington was so far away. (46–47)

In Kansas, Caroline Ingalls finds herself in a fluctuating, unreadable territory; she cannot be sure about where the lines are or how they signify. In the immense, uncultivated prairie, the very idea of lines at first seems a fiction imposed on the wide, uninscribed land. Ma has reluctantly left the bounded world of the Big Woods for a classic borderland much like that described by Gloria Anzaldúa: "a borderland is a vague and undetermined place created by the emotional residue of an unnatural boundary. It is in a constant state of transition" (3). In the border culture Anzaldúa describes, "Males make the rules and laws; women transmit them. . . . The culture expects women to show greater acceptance of, and commitment to, the value system than men" (16–17).[3] Now that the Ingalls family owns no land and has no fixed address or surrounding relatives (throughout this book, they are squatters on property to which they have no title), such matters take on redoubled importance. Against the unseen Indians who have already made their claims to this new, unknown place, Caroline Ingalls marshals all the sources of authority she knows: the patriarchal "word" of a male government, as passed on to her husband, and the codes of manners and ongoing domestic rituals of her Little House. As we have seen, *Big Woods* described the traditional female work order Ma observed. As soon as the wagon stops in "Kansas," even temporarily, she resumes that order. Alone with her daughters (Pa is hunting) in an absolutely unknown place, Ma heats her sadiron and irons clothing for them. In their meticulously ironed dresses, Caroline Ingalls and her daughters will be a colonial outpost of Anglo-American propriety on the Great Plains.

In the nineteenth-century United States, a woman's pale complexion often signified privilege, shelter, protection, and confinement; it was also an external indicator that she did not belong to one of the darker-skinned races against which U.S. law and custom discriminated. Thus, in Indian territory, Ma Ingalls becomes even more preoccupied with protecting her daughters from the strong sunlight that will tan their skin. Laura, who loves to feel sun and air on her bare skin, is constantly ordered to wear her sunbonnet, lest she become "brown as an Indian." As Glenda Riley notes, "the sunbonnet was often the focus of the contest" between mothers and daughters on the Great Plains; the freckled or tanned skin of a bonnetless daughter seemed a dangerous rejection of "conservative" Euro-American standards of womanhood and of "ideals of [female] beauty that emphasized clear and pale skin" (1988, 85). Importantly, such advice also implies another fact that Ma must have found particularly threatening: that race is not a fixed, absolute condition but is as fluctuating as the Kansas border seems to be. In this new country, young Laura might *become* the fascinating Other: "brown as an Indian."

The child's curiosity does not abate; nearly halfway into the novel she is still asking, impatiently, "Pa, when are we going to see a papoose?" Her mother intervenes, "'Goodness!' Ma exclaimed. 'What do you want to see an Indian baby for? Put on your sunbonnet, now, and forget such nonsense'" (123). In *Big Woods*, Laura and Mary begged their father for stories of the male Ingalls past. Here Laura asks, instead, to "see" unknown cultures. To Ma, such desires are dangerous "nonsense," and they threaten her daughter's place in white, female culture.[4]

With her parents and sister, the actual Laura Ingalls moved to postbellum Kansas about 1869. There, the Ingalls family settled into a turbulent political and cultural situation, many conditions of which are mirrored in the fictional Laura's experience in *Little House on the Prairie*. "Bleeding Kansas" had been torn by strife about issues of race and abolition in the years before the Civil War and scars of that conflict were still fresh when the Ingalls family arrived. The region was marked even more definitively by the efforts of the U.S. government to control and contain the presence and property of Native Americans. While many surviving members of the traditional tribes of the Great Plains remained in Kansas, thousands of members of other tribes were also there, having been relocated by the government. The "Indian country" where the Ingalls settled was, unbeknownst to them, a part of the Osage Diminished Reserve.[5] Grant Foreman, a local official writing from Muskogee, Oklahoma, in 1933, in response to inquiries from Rose Wilder Lane, described the fluctuating borderland conditions of Kansas in the late 1860s: "there were doubtless many wandering tribes passing through and camping there; and in all probability your mother as a child may have seen wild [sic] Indians from various of these tribes, whose identity it would be difficult to determine. There were doubtless Cherokee and Osage Indians there of course" (Grant Foreman to RWL, 27 March 1933, Hoover).

From midcentury on, Kansas was ravaged by the conflict generated by farmers' and railroads' greed for these Indian lands, from which most Native Americans were eventually forcibly removed. Thus when young Laura asks, "This *is* Indian country, isn't it?" she is voicing one of the most telling moral questions of the nineteenth-century United States and is raising a great issue that was still problematic in the 1930s, when *Little House on the Prairie* was written, and remains so today: the Euro-American preemption of lands occupied by Native Americans. As H. Craig Miner and William E. Unrau have established, from midcentury Kansas had been "a moral testing ground . . . there is no better example of America experiencing a failure of institutional nerve" (2).

Clearly these issues were very important to Wilder and Lane as they worked on *Little House on the Prairie*. This is indicated by Lane's entry in her diary for 1 February 1934: today "Mother finishes her *Indian* juvenile" (RWL five-year diary, 1 February 1934, Hoover; emphasis mine). The working title for the novel was "Indian Country."[6] However, since Wilder was very young, even younger than her fictional Laura, when her family resided in Kansas Indian Territory, she had few memories of the period. No longer relying on her fund of paternal stories as material, she did unprecedented research for this third book; she and Lane both traveled in Kansas and corresponded with historians of U.S.-Indian relations. This research continued a longstanding interest for both women. For example, when Wilder wrote a 1923 historical essay about Wright County, Missouri, where Mansfield is located, she included a brief but respectful account of the local Indian history ("Our Little Place in the Ozarks" *Ozarks* 25). And in the 1930s Lane became immersed in research for a (never published) history of Missouri in which Indian issues would have figured significantly. These concerns came to bear in *Little House on the Prairie*'s minutely observed portrayal of "Indian country" through the eyes of a white child, Laura Ingalls.

At first this complexly inhabited territory appeared a blank page, marked only by animal life. When the Ingallses first arrived, it seemed to Laura that "on the whole enormous prairie there was no sign that any other human being had ever been there" (40).[7] Significantly, in this book Laura has not yet learned to read words (although she is about six, the traditional age for first reading lessons). So she must constantly question her parents, particularly Pa, who can read newspapers and maps and tell time. To Pa, the conventional boundaries of patriarchal culture are charged with importance; when the Ingalls family has dangerously crossed the frozen river and made the traditional entry into the West, he is elated:

> "We're across the Mississippi!" he said, hugging her [Laura] joyously. . . . "do you like going out west where Indians live?"
>
> Laura said she liked it, and she asked if they were in the Indian country now. But they were not; they were in Minnesota. (9)

As they approach the Kansas borderland, such traditional markers and received texts seem to matter less and less; the sensory experience of the prairie is overwhelming and imposes its own geography and geometry. "Day after day they traveled in Kansas, and saw nothing but the rippling grass and the enormous sky," a "perfect circle" with the wagon in its "exact middle." At night, the stars seem newly close; "Laura felt she could almost touch them" (13). The land is no longer a distanced page that must be read to a passive Laura by a male interpreter. Instead, she is enveloped in this immense, intimate text. "Laura had never seen a place she liked so much as this place" (49).

When the wagon finally stops, the first signifying mark the child recognizes in the prairie grass is an old trail near the site where the Ingallses begin to build a house. The trail motivates Laura to ask yet again when she will see a papoose. "Pa didn't know. He said you never saw Indians unless they wanted you to see them" (55). This is a new idea for Laura: that what she sees and experiences could be controlled by someone other than Pa or Ma, someone outside her family and her culture. Her curiosity about Indians continues to grow.

Later, when Indian men begin to make occasional appearances near the Ingalls home, Pa takes Laura and Mary to see an abandoned Indian camp nearby. In this important lyric sequence, the Ingalls daughters are instructed in the rudiments of sympathetic ethnology. Until now the Ingalls family may have seemed endogamic and self-absorbed; their solitary wagon is always the center of the world, and other cultures are dismissed by Ma as "nonsense." But this overt self-absorption dissipates as Pa, the dog Jack, and the two girls walk away from the Little House, leaving Ma behind: "Laura felt smaller and smaller. Even Pa did not seem as big as he really was. At last they went down into the ["secret"] little hollow where the Indians had camped. . . . from this hollow she [Laura] could not see the house. The prairie seemed to be level, but it was not level" (174–75). Instead of a blank, flat page, the prairie is folded, full of small, complete cultural domains that cannot fully see each other. Here the familiar signs of the Little House appear changed; in a realm of cultural relativism, Laura and even her patriarchal Pa seem "smaller and smaller."

Carefully, Charles Ingalls begins to teach his daughters to "read" the marks of their domestic practices that the Indians have left behind; he questions and instructs the girls like a skilled teacher. Although they have seen no Indian women so far, Pa shows Laura and Mary how to decipher the cultural evidence of such women's lives:

> Pa read the tracks for Mary and Laura. He showed them tracks of two middle-sized moccasins by the edge of a camp fire's ashes. An Indian woman had squatted there. She wore a leather skirt with fringes; the tiny marks of the fringe were in the dust. The tracks of her toes inside the moccasins was deeper than the track of her heels, because she had leaned forward to stir something cooking in a pot on the fire.
>
> Then Pa picked up a smoke-blackened stick. And he said that the pot had hung from a stick laid across the top of two upright, forked sticks. He showed Mary and Laura the holes where the forked sticks had been driven into the ground. Then he told them to look at the bones around that camp fire and tell him what had cooked in that pot.
>
> They looked, and they said, "Rabbit." That was right; the bones were rabbits' bones. (176–77)

Here Pa follows the model of the nineteenth-century ethnologists (also mostly white men) who were beginning to study Native American lives, and like them, he may be imposing his models of Euro-American gender roles on the cultures he observes. Nevertheless, this is an enormously important passage for Laura's expanding awareness and for the whole Little House series. With all the force of his male and parental authority, Pa presents Native American life as worthy of respect and attentive reading, and he includes women and their traditional domestic work (as defined by Euro-Americans) in his instructive text. Ma also cooks over an outdoor fire, and the Ingalls family often eats prairie rabbit stew, as the departed Indians did. Just as Pa and the Indian men use the same ancient trail, as cohabitants of the prairie, the Indians and the Ingalls family share some features of a prairie life. When Pa and the girls set out on their walk to the Indian camp, Ma objects: "It is so far" to go, she says, "in this heat." But her husband replies merrily, "This heat doesn't hurt the Indians and it won't hurt us. . . .

Come on, girls" (173). Leading his daughters into the hollows of the complex, convoluted prairie text, he also leads them beyond the limits of
prescribed reading for nineteenth-century white American girls.

During their explorations of the Indian camp, the girls' attention is
deflected when Laura joyously spies plunder, "a beautiful bead" in the dust.
She and Mary begin to find more, and at once "they forgot everything but
beads" (177). When they rejoin Ma in the Little House, the whole family is
excited by their glittering find. The annoyingly "good" and "unselfish"
Mary gives her beads to Baby Carrie; Laura, who will not "let Mary be
better than she was" (179), gives up her beads too, angry that her sister has
manipulated her into surrendering something she wanted to keep.

The beads are probably evidence of cultural exchange; their bright
colors suggest that they were glass trade beads, made in Europe, which
were commonly circulated among Plains Indians in the nineteenth century
and were widely used for decoration and beadwork. That the actual Ingalls
family valued such beads is indicated by a picture taken about 1881 of the
three oldest sisters, dressed in their modest best for their first surviving
photograph. Carrie, age eleven, appears to be wearing the string of carefully preserved trade beads.[8]

Wilder's important "Indian Camp" chapter is almost a parable of Euro-
Americans' relations with Native American cultures on the Great Plains. It
posits the possibility of a partially shared culture, of mutual acculturation,
and it encourages the study of another culture, with all the potential benefits and abusive misreading that such study can entail. It also suggests the
greed and quarreling that desirable Indian property (such as the beads and,
historically, Indian lands) engendered among competing non-Indians.

According to Joseph B. Herring, who has studied the Native American tribal members who refused to be removed from Kansas and whose
descendants have remained there, the history of Kansas "Indian territory"
provides a telling study in acculturation, which Herring defines as "the
intercultural borrowing that takes place when two or more diverse peoples
come into close contact. Each adopts certain cultural traits of the other,
resulting in new and blended forms; yet each retains a certain degree of
cultural autonomy" (1–2). Particularly in her Kansas novel, *Little House on the
Prairie*, Laura Ingalls Wilder addressed what acculturation might mean for
Euro-Americans newly settling on the Great Plains, and especially for
young Laura, newly eager to expand the confines of the Little House.

Taking up this theme in the 1930s, Wilder joined a tradition that
had persisted for at least several generations in the United States, that of

children's literature responding to non-Indian children's interest in Native American cultures. Many of these books reflected a "romantic" view of Indian life, as indicated in Charles Eastman's *Indian Boyhood,* published in 1902: "What boy would not be an Indian for a while when he thinks of the freest life in the world?" Eastman's work was enormously popular, especially with the burgeoning Boy Scout and Camp Fire Girl organizations (Penney 338–39). According to Holling C. Holling, who produced several popular books "on Indian subjects" in the 1930s, there was a considerable potential market for such material, and children's magazines such as the *American Boy* and the *Youth's Companion* ran stories and articles about Native Americans, as well as "ads from dealers who sold Indian material." Holling summarized the childhood interest in Native American cultures that he shared with many other Americans: "As a boy, I wanted to know all about Indians. How did they really live? . . . How did they make those arrow points that Grandfather found in the fields? There were a thousand questions in my mind, and very few answers in the books I had" (Penney 299, 340–41).

Thus, in 1935 when *Little House on the Prairie* was published, an "Indian juvenile" may have seemed a promising commodity even in a Depression book market. But Wilder's book, as we have seen, attempted a more complex cultural study than much of the other available children's literature. Laura Ingalls *is* attracted to the apparent lack of constraints she witnesses in Kansas Indian cultures. She notes approvingly that the Indians' horses are unimpeded by any harness or bridle and envies the Indian children because they are not required to wear clothes. But she sees more than the hypothetical attractions of "the freest life in the world." In the Indian camp, the Ingalls daughters read a story of work, ritual, and domestic care that appears to be much like their own.

The problem of the Indian camp episode, of course, is that there are no Indian *people* in it. Instead, Pa and Mary and Laura become voyeurs, if not trespassers and looters, in a secluded, occluded cultural domain. In a slightly earlier chapter, "Indians in the House," the girls meet their first Native Americans. Played against each other, these two chapters suggest the two kinds of language Laura encounters in her efforts to learn about Indians. One is a language of attention, respect, and potential mutual acculturation. The other is a language of abuse, conflict, and violent opposition. For example, Ma customarily compares any unseemly yelling and "wildness" from Laura with Indian behavior. When a neighbor, Mrs. Scott, begins to speak of her fear and hatred of Indians and of the "Minnesota massacre" of white settlers, Ma silences her and refuses to tell the listening

Laura what a massacre is (211–12). Thus Indians are associated with violent intensities that Ma (inadvertently) further intensifies by excluding them from the spoken discourse of her house. Even Pa, though he teaches his daughters the language of acculturation, sometimes lapses into the other way of talking about Indians; he tells Ma, "The main thing is to be on good terms with the Indians. We don't want to wake up some night with a band of the screeching dev—" At this point Ma silences him, although "Laura dreadfully wanted to know what he had been going to say" (144).

The language of violence is barely suppressed in "Indians in the House," the chapter in which two Indian men visit the Ingalls house while Pa is away, order Ma to cook cornbread for them, and take Pa's tobacco. By bringing actual Indian men into the world of Euro-American girls and women, Wilder and Lane evoke powerful fears of violated boundaries, fears that have been expressed in the nineteenth- and twentieth-century United States through hysteria about the possibility of interracial rape of white women. Laura and Mary are outdoors with the chained dog, Jack; they see the Indian men disappear into the house where Ma and Baby Carrie are. The girls are shaken with amorphous fear of what could happen in the house between Indian men and a white woman. "'Oh, what are they doing to Ma!' [Laura] screamed, in a whisper" (136). Jack strains against his chain, and Laura longs to set him free to "kill" the men, even though Pa has ordered her not to.

The tension of this scene is extraordinary. The two girls vibrate between the protective masculine presence of Jack, who is "panting" to attack, and a strong sense of obligation to join and "help" their mother in the house. When Laura tries to go inside, she involuntarily "turned and flew back to Jack. . . . and hung on to his strong, panting neck. Jack wouldn't let anything hurt her" (136). Leaving Jack behind and entering the house with Mary is the most difficult decision of Laura's short life. By this act, she turns her back on the male strength that promises to protect her by "killing" the racial Other and joins her mother in the Little House.

Inside, the girls witness what is potentially a classic scene of sexual abasement: the "wild men," dressed only in fresh skunk skins, stand by the fireplace while Ma kneels before them, cooking for them, with Carrie clinging at her skirts, in a posture that suggests sexual and domestic submission. At this sight Laura hides behind a plank that obstructs her view of the Indian men, so she feels "safer. But she couldn't help moving her head just a little," to see the intruders. Thinking herself unobserved, Laura takes in every detail of the men's clothing, bodies, demeanor, and smell. Despite their traditional Native American dress and hairstyle, which are new to Laura, she notes familiar similarities to Pa; each man carries "a knife like Pa's hunting knife, and a hatchet like Pa's hatchet" (138), and they command a woman's housekeeping as the girls have seen their white father do. Before Laura's gazing eyes, the scene's complexities multiply. Although she wants to read these men, they will not stand still to be cataloged and objectified, like the objects at the Indian camp. Instead the men speak syllables that Laura cannot interpret and *return* her gaze. In the intense eye contact is Laura's most difficult lesson: the "wild men" whom she longs and fears to see are subjects, not objects, and they share her space and her humanity.

Dennis McAuliffe, Jr., in a personal history of his Osage family, who lived near the Ingallses in Kansas Territory, views *Little House on the Prairie* as entirely abusive of Indians. McAuliffe writes, "I would not want my child to read *Little House on the Prairie*. I would shield him from the slights [it] slings upon his ancestors." McAuliffe finds the depiction of the Indian men in "Indians in the House" particularly offensive, noting that "Mrs. Wilder assigns them descriptive adjectives that connote barbarism, brutality, and bloodthirstiness" and "makes light of their obvious plight" (intense hunger resulting from the incursions of white settlers) (113). I read no evidence of a "light" or mocking attitude in this scene; instead, I see its tone as intensely serious; Ma, Laura, and Mary seem almost paralyzed by their fear of these unfamiliar men. Laura's view of them again and again emphasizes their *unreadability* to her: first their eyes are described as "black and still and glittering, like snake's eyes" (134), which indicates how frighteningly alien to her own humanity these men seem. To Laura, the men have remarkable self-possession; "their faces were bold and fierce and terrible" (139). They behave with control and decorum; they do not touch or harm any member of the Ingalls family, and they wait until Ma's cornbread is baked and served to them, then eat "every morsel of it, and even picked up the crumbs from the hearth" (140). Then one man attempts to speak to an uncomprehending, silent Ma before they depart. Repeatedly, the text returns to the image of the men's glittering eyes. "Shining" eyes and eye contact are a recurrent motif in the Little House books, and are especially used to express the strong bond between Laura and her father. The sharper light of the Indian men's eyes both frightens Laura and attracts her; the device of the plank, behind which she periodically retreats to cut off her vision of these men, expresses Laura's warring fear and desire to see and comprehend them. Unlike McAuliffe, I view this extremely complex scene as an attempt to convey, from a white girl's viewpoint to a readership of children, the extraordinary stresses and tensions that burdened even the simplest contact between Euro-American females and Indian men.[9]

The large issues of race and acculturation that pervade this scene and this book are inseparable from matters of gender. Pa is the parent with whom Laura persistently identifies; her eyes lock with his in commonality and passion. But both "Indian Camp" and "Indians in the House" force Laura to scrutinize a woman's position in the Little House equation (both chapters center on a woman cooking at a fire) and to assess her own position in relation to the hearthside woman. The complexities of Laura's relations with her mother (which I explore more fully in Chapter 4) are especially evident here. It is apparent to the Ingalls daughters that their mother "hates Indians," as Laura and Pa do not. And in this book, hating Indians is a denial of the widest possibilities of North American cultures. For Caroline Ingalls, Indians become a code for everything that seems to threaten the settled, white life she wants for her daughters: they signify tan skin, loud voices, transience, and interrupted housekeeping. Their scanty attire (which Laura envies) is a refusal of the layers of rigid clothing by which Ma is determined to mold her girls into Victorian ladies.

Ma's values are clearly at risk in Kansas territory. Despite her staunch strengths, she is presented in this book as the most vulnerable member of the Ingalls family. In "Indians in the House," as we have seen, Laura and Mary are frantic with worry about their mother. And earlier, when Ma was helping Pa build the log house, a log fell on her, knocking her unconscious and nearly crushing her foot. The Little House is Ma's shelter, her justification, and perhaps her greatest danger as well; as the girls can plainly see, their mother is the person most at risk in the house's construction, and she is most endangered by Indian men's incursions.

As was typical of many nineteenth-century westering women, Ma did not make the decision to emigrate to Kansas. Instead, she acquiesced to her husband's wish. Historian Lillian Schlissel has suggested that western immigration often "played a vital role in the life cycle of men, corresponding to 'breaking away,' improving, or bettering oneself, the stages that mark a man's life." Thus westward migration often became a male mythic experience, "an expression of testing and reaching for men." Clearly Charles Ingalls, leaving his close family of origin behind and setting out independently for the challenges of the frontier, is testing himself in these traditionally masculine ways and confirming his maturity. But Schlissel postulates that the dynamics of emigration were very different for most nineteenth-century women. For them, the move West was likely to be "an 'anti-mythic' journey. . . . It came when the physical demands of their lives drained their energies into other directions" (14).[10] A large percentage of the emigrant women Schlissel studied in *Women's Diaries of the Westward Journey* were pregnant and/or the mothers of babies or very young children. In the Little House books, Carrie, the third Ingalls daughter, is portrayed as a baby in Wisconsin and a toddler in Kansas. However, in the history of the actual Ingalls family, Carrie was born in 1870 in Kansas.[11] Thus it is probable that Caroline Ingalls was pregnant when the family traveled to Kansas and in the first months when they were settling there. The Kansas memories of Ma, Pa, and Mary, which were Wilder's material for this book, along with her own early childhood impressions, must have been touched by the impact of Ma's pregnancy and Carrie's birth, which would have displaced Laura as the smaller, younger child and deflected her mother's attention.

The six-year-old Laura of the *Little House on the Prairie* is newly eager to explore possibilities beyond the confines of the Little House, moving beyond the rituals, prescriptions, and intimate nurturance she associates with her mother. She turns, as Lacanians would predict, to her wider-ranging father for language (songs, stories) and space. But at the same time, she becomes more conscious that she is a *girl* who will be a woman, and thus her place and her territory are with her mother. Some of the anger that attended this realization seems to have become a part of the sometimes-troubling portrait of Ma in this book. As children reading the earlier Little House books, my girlfriends and I found Ma far less attractive than romantic Pa; her combination of authority, vulnerability, and narrow-mindedness was painful to acknowledge. Michael Dorris calls Ma a "know-nothing racist." Remembering his negative reaction to her when he was enthusiastically reading the Little House books as a child, he concludes, "I had Ma to thank, possibly more than anyone else in real life or literature, for my first startling awareness that an adult authority figure could actually be wrong and narrow-minded" (1821–22). It is largely because of this portrait of Ma that Dorris decided not to read Wilder's books, which he had loved as a child, to his own young daughters.

Why is "gentle" Ma portrayed as an Indian hater? As Sarah Deutsch reminds us, women have traditionally been considered "the repository of racial purity," and on western frontiers there were stronger taboos against interracial sexual relations for white women than for white men (117). For Laura and her other daughters, Caroline Ingalls consistently desires the security and propriety of white, settled girlhood and womanhood. But even at six, Laura is beginning to chafe against the restrictions of the life that her

mother desires for her, restrictions that would curb her exploration, prevent her acculturation, and block her access to Indian cultures. Her perceptions of her mother reflect these budding frustrations as well as her ongoing
love and admiration. Also, I would suggest, Indian-hating (an attitude Ma
shares with the only other white woman character in Kansas, Mrs. Scott)
allows Ma to express her anger at the demands and dislocations of her
emigrant western life. Her husband Charles, of course, is largely responsible for her emigration, and behind him is the whole institutional structure
of white nineteenth-century patriarchy, which promoted manifest destiny.
But Ma does not permit herself to express opposition to her husband.

Thus, when Indian men (for Ma's hostility seems entirely directed
toward male Native Americans) enter Ma's kitchen, conscripting her labor,
interrupting her cherished routine, and filling her space with their alien
smell, her response, once they are gone, is fear and anger that become her
hatred of Indians. As the girls have been told, their mother was a self-
supporting, self-possessed young woman who could afford dressmaker-
made clothes "back East," when she married Charles Ingalls. A young
woman still in Kansas Indian Territory, Caroline Ingalls, who had previously lived in a closely knit Big Woods community that included sisters
and many other women, finds herself almost entirely isolated and entirely
dependent on her volatile husband's decisions. She is largely portrayed as
calmly acquiescent, but her one major outlet for anger, resistance, and
defense of the values of feminine domestic culture on the unsettled prairie
is her intense, vocal rejection of Indians and Indian cultures.[12]

Consequently, the chapters of *Little House on the Prairie* in which the
Ingalls family encounters Indians, and particularly "Indians in the House,"
are charged with extraordinary import for Ma and her daughters. When Pa
comes home after the Indian men's intrusion, he does not share the females'
intense emotions. Instead he jokes with them about seeing Indians "at last,"
despite Ma's unprecedented admission, "Oh Charles! I was afraid!" (143).
While Ma prepares supper, he takes the girls with him to dress the game he
has shot, using his knife, which is like the Indian men's, and saving the
rabbit skin to make a child's hat, just as the Indians used animal skins for
clothing. He becomes alarmed only when the girls admit that they considered releasing Jack and warns them solemnly that to unleash the angry dog
would have caused unspecified "bad trouble" (146). These events emphasize that Pa is a Kansas *man* with a primary interest in male relations among
himself, his male dog, and the Indian men, who are all subjects, while he
views his wife and daughters as objects who must accede to male demands.

He presents the situation to Laura as one in which *her will* is the true danger, for if she had exercised it, she would have released Jack. Here as elsewhere, Laura's encounters with Indians evoke her culture's sternest strictures about what a girl must not think. Pa voices those strictures: "'After this,' he said, in a terrible voice, 'you girls remember always to do as you're told. *Don't you even think* of disobeying me. Do you hear?'" (146, emphasis mine).

In other Kansas experiences, Laura and Mary are encouraged by their elders to be open to acculturating influences. At Christmas they accept an account of a Santa Claus without the reindeer and sleigh he used in the Big Woods; in Kansas, they believe that Santa is equipped with a pack mule, Southwest fashion. And their favorite neighbor is Mr. Edwards, a spirited bachelor (who resurfaces in *By the Shores of Silver Lake* as a speculator, gambler, and drinking man) who wears a coonskin cap, describes himself to a fascinated Laura as "a wildcat from Tennessee" (63), and specializes in a piercing rebel yell. Despite their regional differences, Ma clearly likes "wild" Mr. Edwards; he is always welcome in the Little House and is the honored guest for Christmas dinner.

Another interracial encounter occurs when the family contracts malaria. Then Laura meets her first African American, Dr. Tan, a "doctor with the Indians" (192) who happens upon the Ingalls family when they are severely ill and cares for them, probably saving their lives. Laura is very conscious of the doctor's dark skin—"he was so very black" (191)—but no word of racial prejudice is spoken against him, not even by the rabidly anti-Indian Mrs. Scott, who nurses the Ingalls family and carries out Dr. Tan's orders. They all like the jovial doctor very much, enjoy his company, and value his competence—indeed, he is the first educated professional person that Laura has ever met. In Kansas it is possible for her to believe that an educated, compassionate man can move safely among white settlers, African Americans, and Native Americans. In fact, Dr. Tan was a documented historical personage who lived with his parents near Independence and practiced in postbellum Kansas.[13]

Nevertheless, as the Indian trail that runs close by the Ingalls house begins to be used by more and more Indian men, it becomes clear that this shared trail will not be an avenue of mutual acculturation. Even Pa regrets building so close to the trail, and Ma vetoes any possibility of a shared life: "'Let Indians keep to themselves,' said Ma, 'and we will do the same'" (229). Obviously the possible similarities between her housekeeping and that of the unseen Indian women who are camped nearby are alarming to Caroline Ingalls; when her husband hauls her laundry water, he half-teases, "you could wash clothes in the creek. . . . Indian women do." Ma retorts, "If we wanted to live like Indians, you could make a hole in the roof to let the smoke out, and we'd have the fire on the floor inside the house. . . . Indians do" (76). In fact, their log house *does* have a rudimentary fireplace, with a cooking fire at floor level and a chimney hole for smoke. In this way and many others, the Ingallses are very close to "living like Indians," and this unadmitted fact intensifies Ma's efforts to draw clear cultural lines between her Euro-American family and a Native American lifestyle.

Conversation with Native Americans is impossible for the Ingallses, who know no language but English. On the one occasion when Pa converses with an Indian, it is because the Indian has learned English. According to Herring, for Kansas tribes "acculturation has been a largely one-sided process; they have adopted far more Euro-American traits than vice versa." Such "acculturative concessions," especially if assumed by the Indians "on their own terms," were "a defense mechanism that proved crucial to their survival" (2). In *Little House on the Prairie*, acculturation is clearly a one-way path; Indian men use guns and occasionally speak English, but the Ingallses stay within the walls of their Little House.

The most compelling Indian who appears in *Little House on the Prairie* is "The Tall Indian" (another chapter title) whom Pa identifies as a "perfectly friendly" Osage, "no common trash."[14] After companionably eating and smoking by the hearth with Pa, served by Ma, this man tries to converse with Pa in French, a traditional diplomatic language. But Pa must reply, "No speak." When the Indian has left, Pa expresses singular regrets; he says, "I wish I had picked up some of that lingo" (229). The stubborn insularity of a monolingual life in a multilingual territory is subtly critiqued here—especially since the Indian man, who obviously speaks both French and Osage, probably speaks other Native American languages as well.[15]

The tall Indian becomes the Ingallses' hero; he persuades the prairie tribes, gathered for their annual spring "jamboree" near the Ingalls homestead, not to kill the encroaching white settlers. Pa learns that the Osages "called him a name that meant he was a great soldier": Soldat du Chêne. Wilder struggled to recall this name; obviously the character and the situation had special importance, both personal and historic, for her. She told an audience, "I could not remember the name of the Indian chief who saved the whites from massacre. It took weeks of research before I found it. In writing books that will be used in schools such things must be right" ("My Work," *Sampler* 179). The powerful figure of this much-admired warrior, who can bring nonviolent concord out of a multicultural cacophony of assembled tribes that are eager to wage war against whites, expresses a version of male heroism articulated nowhere else in the Little House series, where even Pa is susceptible to fatigue and error. Soldat du Chêne is certainly noble—and perhaps stereotypically a "noble savage" as well. He suggests a multilingual, acculturated life in the context of which Indians and Ingallses might coexist in Kansas Territory. But he may also suggest an assimilationist leadership that persuaded some Native Americans to surrender their embattled rights and property. The tall Indian is an eminently and perhaps even excessively civilized "wild man."

All the Ingalls family members, even Ma, recognize something awe-inspiring in Soldat du Chêne. The chapter titled "The Tall Indian" ends as Pa plays and Ma sings "The Blue Juniata." This is a song about a "wild and free" "Indian maid," Alfarata, a hunter with "strong . . . arrows" who sings about her warrior-lover as she navigates the rapids of a small Pennsylvania river. The song ends:

> Fleeting years have borne away
> The voice of Alfarata,
> Still flow the waters
> Of the blue Juniata. (235)

Although Pa's songs are frequently partially quoted in the Little House books, this one, written by Mrs. Marion Dix Sullivan in 1844 (Garson 92–93), is among the few for which a complete text is provided—a fact that signals its special importance.[16] To Pa's accompaniment, Ma recites a persistent Victorian American "solution" to "Indian problems." An Indian woman and artifacts of her culture are condensed into a few charged romantic images and firmly removed from present presence, leaving behind only the (ostensibly) unmarked Eastern territory where she once "roved," "wild." Alfarata is much like the "Indian princess" archetype described by Rayna Green as one of the most common distortions on Native American women; she is presented as James Fenimore Cooper's Eastern Indians are, near extinction. The pastiche of images associated with her is a far cry from the evidence of a functioning community of Great Plains Indians that Pa and his daughters read at the Indian camp. It is Alfarata Ma can comfortably acknowledge, for she is romanticized, Anglicized, and *gone*.

Laura, however, has not learned the tactics of distancing and forgetting by which many adult Euro-Americans "dealt" with Indians. Instead of luxuriating in the soporific strains of her parents' song, she pleads, "please tell me where the voice of Alfarata went?" Ma replies that she "went west," as Indians "have to," and when Laura asks why, Pa answers, because "the government makes them." But Laura is not satisfied and pleads:

> "Please Pa, can I ask just one more question?"
> "May I," said Ma.
> Laura began again. "Pa, please, may I—"
> "What is it?" Pa asked. It was not polite for little girls to interrupt, but of course Pa could do it.
> "Will the government make these Indians go west?"
> "Yes," Pa said. "When white settlers come into a country, the Indians have to move on. . . . That's why we're here, Laura. White people are going to settle all this country, and we get the best land because we get here first and take our pick. Now do you understand?"
> "Yes Pa," Laura said. "But, Pa, I thought this was Indian Territory. Won't it make the Indians mad to have to—"
> "No more questions, Laura," Pa said, firmly. "Go to sleep."
> (236–37)

Laura immediately apprehends the connection between Alfarata and the Indians who are her family's Kansas neighbors, connections her parents are struggling to suppress (thus, throughout this scene, they order Laura to sleep). In this troubling account, the story of the solitary, roving Indian woman who luxuriates in her freedom, her love, and her voice becomes a story of a woman compelled by a force she cannot control (the white, patriarchal "government") to "go west" and leave the territory with which she is intimately linked, the Juniata—or the Little House in the Big Woods. As a white settler herself, Ma is clearly committed to the removal of Alfarata. And yet, as she tells it to Laura, the story of the Indian woman's forced westward migration resembles Ma's own story. As an independent wandering woman and a subject of male removal, Alfarata suggests that an Indian woman might be both an ally and an alternative model for Caroline Ingalls and her emigrant daughters. Even the implication of such alliances is so troubling and so potentially revolutionary that, as Laura's parents insist, they must be pushed back into the unconscious, muffled by sleep. Alfarata is gone beyond acculturation, for removal prevents acculturation, at least for the white settlers who intend to take Indian territory for their own. "*We* get the best land," says Pa.

The best land, Laura's parents imply, is a blank page, smoothed flat for the settler's plow, from which all traces of Native American habitation have been erased. As Elizabeth Segel has written, Pa instructs Laura here in the most blatant fundamentals of manifest destiny (although he may be reluctant to admit them) (68), and he denies the importance of the very cultures that, at the Indian camp, he earlier taught his daughters to read and to respect. Significantly, this is one of the few passages in the early Little House books in which both Laura's parents appear obviously, negatively repressive. They exercise rigorous control over Laura, determining when she may speak and when she may and may not be awake to reflect and to question. Correcting and interrupting (even though their children are forbidden such practices), they make it very difficult for Laura to ask the questions that are most disturbing and pertinent to her; finally Pa "firmly" shuts off the process of voiced questioning entirely. Sixty-some years after her childhood experience in Kansas Indian Territory, and despite her commitment to the heroism of her parents (especially Pa), Laura Ingalls Wilder and her daughter used their hard-won authorship to give voice to those forbidden questions about the relation of the "Little House" story of Great Plains settlement and the story of the removals of Great Plains Indians. As Segel has convincingly argued, Wilder and Lane "believed that the complexity and the tragedy [generated by the competition of settlers and Indians] were not beyond the comprehension of young children" (70), although the articulation and inscription of such complexity and tragedy were forbidden by the most powerful agencies of young Laura's culture.

Such complexity qualifies *Little House on the Prairie* as a frontier text, according to an updated conception of "frontier" proposed in 1992 by Annette Kolodny, who urged that we "recognize 'frontier' as a locus of first cultural contact, circumscribed by a particular physical terrain in the process of change *because* of the forms that contact takes, all of it inscribed by the collisions and interpenetrations of language. . . . [This is experienced by] a currently indigenous population and at least one group of newcomer 'intruders'" (3, 5).

Such narratives may be composed "in that first moment of contact" or, like Wilder and Lane's novel, "after the fact, reworking for some alternate audience or future generation the scene and meaning of original contact" (5). One of the striking features of *Little House on the Prairie* is how fully it takes on the post-Turnerian frontier agenda Kolodny describes, filtering it through a white girl's sensibility as she experiences "first cultural contact" and the competition of indigenous Indians and intruding settlers over land use in Kansas territory, in a buzz of competing languages that Laura and her parents cannot comprehend. Because Wilder and Lane attempted so much in this children's book, the bright romance of expansion and acculturation that Laura initially reached toward is supplanted by an atmosphere of tragedy that still seemed immediate in 1935. And in the 1950s, I also found this book unforgettable because it admitted a girl like me to frontier territory, and then forced me to face some of the human losses that were implicit in settler-Indian relations, raising questions that were elided by my grade-B Saturday Western movies.

Thus, in the book's final chapters, the ideal of mutually beneficial acculturation seems less and less possible. Competition for this strip of Kansas accelerates. Pa obtains a newspaper that "proved that he [Pa] was right, the government would not do anything to the white settlers" (273), although there are rumors in Independence that settlers like the Ingalls family will soon be expelled and that this territory will remain reserved for Indians. Planning his crops and setting up a rudimentary farm, Pa struggles to impose the authority of his patriarchal culture on the disputed prairie, so that he may own and inhabit it as a "white settler." Meanwhile, the Indians, as is their yearly spring custom, burn off the prairie, sending a raging fire, which Ma and Pa are narrowly able to deflect, toward the Ingalls homestead. According to Pa, the Indians burn off because the practice encourages the growth of new grass and makes horseback travel easier; however, other settlers suspect that the burning is intended to expunge them. At any rate, the Indians assert their authority over the territory, altering it to meet the needs of their culture and acting out their dominion over this page of disputed prairie text.[17]

Throughout *Little House on the Prairie*, two stories have alternated. The episodes in which the Ingalls family approaches and recedes from Native American cultures, which I have been discussing, are interwoven with the construction of a house—a house that Charles and Caroline Ingalls hope will be their permanent dwelling on a settled Kansas farm. For example, the important chapter "Indians in the House" is framed by two such chapters, "A Roof and a Door" (in which Pa constructs same) and "Fresh Water to Drink" (in which Pa digs a well to provide water for the house). These two adjacent narratives are in constant competition. The house story is one of step-by-step construction, both physical and psychic. Intently, Laura and Mary watch and help their parents assemble a shelter, erecting logs, crafting doors, building a fireplace, arranging possessions, defending the house from fire, and triumphantly completing it by installing glass windows, hallmarks of affluence and permanence. Rituals, like Ma's household work order and the family's Christmas festivities, are also an important part of constructing this shelter. Building their Little House in Kansas, the In-gallses are laboring to construct the center of a centered universe.

But Indians endanger that center. They may interrupt Ma's house-keeping, burn the prairie, and threaten to steal the commodities (furs) by which the Ingallses will finance their homestead project. As their awareness of Indians' presence intensifies, the Ingallses cannot maintain the ethno-centrism that supports the reign of the Little House. Investigating the complex culture of the Native Americans with whom they share this prairie borderland, Pa and his daughters have also begun ethnological investiga-tions. As Jacques Derrida has observed, "ethnology could have been born as a science only . . . at the moment when European culture . . . had been *dislocated*, driven from its locus, and forced to stop considering itself as the culture of reference. . . . [T]he critique of ethnocentrism [is] the very condition of ethnology" (233). In postbellum Kansas, ethnology (widely attempted by nineteenth-century white investigators of Native American cultures) signals the fall of ethnocentricity—and thus the decentering of the Little House.

The intense stress generated by the accelerating conflict of these two stories in *Little House on the Prairie* mounts to a peak of intensity during the annual gathering of prairie tribes near the end of the book. As Segel has importantly observed, the "vivid description" of this terrifying period "is an essential component of the books; it provides an empathy with the settlers to match that which Laura experiences for the Indians, and it forestalls the one-sided view of the Western conflict that marks most children's books on the subject" (68). Laura is stimulated to heightened awareness by the sounds of a discourse she cannot decipher—the Indians' "fierce yells of jubi-lation. Faster, faster, faster they made her heart beat. 'Hi! Hi! Hi-yo! Hah! Hi! Hah!'" (275). One night she awakens screaming; "some terrible sound had made cold sweat come out all over her." Pa tells her, over Ma's protest, "It's the Indian war cry, Laura" (290–91). Laura, acceding to Pa's authority as the family interpreter, is placed in a position where she *must* read the surrounding Indian culture as a direct threat to her home, her family, and her life. The sleepless days and nights that follow are a period of almost hallucinatory horror; the Ingallses huddle in their house, listening and speculating about if and when the Indians will attack. The confinement, at the season when spring planting should be underway, is almost unbearable; "the plow was in the field where [Pa] had left it. . . . Mary and Laura could not go out of the house" (296–97). The snug Little House has become a terrible prison, and the process of its construction is stopped dead.

Inexplicably the Indians disband, and Pa hears that Soldat du Chêne has forestalled an attack on the whites. Although Pa, as he says, may long to join in such Indian rituals as a buffalo hunt, there is never any possibility that he or other settlers might join the intertribal council deliberations. Despite their proximity, whites and Native Americans remain separate. As the long lines of Indians depart (permanently, the book implies), they ride past the Ingalls house. When the last group, the Osages, pass, led by Soldat du Chêne, the Ingallses stand for hours in their doorway, watching. This rendingly elegiac chapter is titled "Indians Ride Away." Although Pa raises his hand "in salute" (305) to the heroic Osage leader, no word is spoken and no eye contact is exchanged between the Ingallses and the Osages; the Indians "went by as if the house and stable and Pa and Ma and Mary and Laura were not there at all" (305). Despite efforts at intercultural accommodation, there seems to be no available vision that can encompass both Indians and Euro-American settlers living together on the Kansas prairie.

Indian women and children, unseen until now, are part of the procession. As was the custom among the Osage, the younger children are naked.[18] When Laura sees her unfettered contemporaries, she initiates eye contact and begins to wish herself beyond the constraints of her familial Little House. "She had a naughty wish to be a little Indian girl. Of course she did not really mean it. She only wanted to be bare naked in the wind and the sunshine, and riding one of those gay little ponies" (307). Even at five, Laura Ingalls is sufficiently socialized to know that acculturation, adopting some of the behaviors of an Osage child, is very "naughty," something she must not "really mean"—despite the insistence of her desire.

Then, at last, Laura sees her long-awaited "papoose." Her eyes lock with those of an Osage baby, riding in a basket alongside its mother. As the two children exchange a "deep" mutual look, Laura addresses a forceful imperative to the most powerful person she knows, challenging both adulthood and patriarchy: "Pa," she said, "get me that little Indian baby!"

Shocked, Laura's parents remonstrate; Pa says, "The Indian woman wants to keep her baby" and Ma adds, objectifying the alien child,

> "Why on earth do you want an Indian baby, of all things!" . . .
>
> "Its eyes are so black," Laura sobbed. She could not say what she meant.
>
> "Why Laura," Ma said, "You don't want another baby. We have a baby, our own baby."
>
> "I want the other one, too!" Laura sobbed, loudly. (309–10)

In all the Little House series, Laura never makes a larger claim than her demand for the Indian child. Her passionate cry gives voice to the most piercing tensions of the settlement of the Great Plains *and* of the multicultural possibilities of American life. Laura's demand for the baby may express an imperious, hegemonic sense of cultural entitlement by which the Indian child becomes an object of desire, a possession like the trade beads. But the intense look that Laura exchanges with the baby also suggests possibilities of a shared lifestyle and a shared life between the Euro-American and Native American children. Laura is reaching toward an extended family that she might share with both her white sisters and an Indian baby. As Lucy Maddox has pointed out, familial language—often used by nineteenth-century white U.S. writers, as in "our red brothers"— is obviously problematic because it may elide "those differences in ethnicity, social organization, belief, and behavior that are . . . at the heart of Indian-white incompatibility" (170–71). I would argue, however, that young Laura's desire reaches—however futilely—beyond this model of incompatibility, suggesting a *delight* in difference that may even move toward the heightened multiplicities of *jouissance*. Laura resists her parents' and her culture's prescription that she cannot have both babies; she resists the prohibitions on plurality and on acculturation.[19]

Laura's assertive, imperative, desirous demand for the baby taps an impulse that her Euro-American upbringing has offered no way for a girl to express: "she could not say what she meant." Her outburst is a female child's explosive critique of the languages offered her by her culture; it *voices* her yearning for a life of expansion and inclusion. In the early chapters of *Little House on the Prairie*, the wide expanses of multicultural Kansas seemed to offer a model for such a life. But now, as the Osage baby is carried away in its mother's containing basket, Laura experiences the pain that Anzaldúa says is characteristic of a borderland life: "the emotional residue of an *unnatural boundary*" (3, emphasis mine).[20]

When the Indians have departed, the Ingallses all feel a pervasive sense of emptiness and depression. Surprisingly, even Ma is "so let down" that, unprecedently, she abandons her housework. Significantly, this response occurs when she has seen—presumably for the last time—her first Indian woman. If we read the absences in this book, we discover that the most striking absence is that of women of color, especially Indian women. Although Pa communicates haltingly with a few Indian men and a black male doctor cares for the Ingalls family members, they encounter only one other woman, Mrs. Scott, a white Indian hater. However, according to historian Glenda Riley (1984), there was actually considerable interaction between white and Native American women on frontiers, and the white women, more than their male counterparts, were likely to alter previous negative views of Indians and to admire (and sometimes adopt) some features of Native American cultures. The series' portrait of Caroline Ingalls certainly does not confirm Riley's findings. Yet, as we have noted, Ma's isolation and her special vulnerability are apparent in this book, where, more than anywhere else in the series, she is cut off from communities of women. On the prairie, Indian women are always unseen but present in the nearby camps. Ma, struggling to adapt her domestic routines to the new Great Plains and grappling with childbirth and child care, might have a great deal to gain from interchange with these Indian women.

Although the Indians' departure supposedly brings "a great peace" (312), that peace is brief (only four pages) and regressive. As the Ingallses' seeds begin to sprout in the newly plowed prairie sod, their routine more and more resembles life in the settled, agricultural Big Woods; the reign of the unimpeded "white settler" seems to have begun in Kansas. As she watches the flourishing garden, Laura thinks, as Pa has schooled her to, "Pretty soon they would all begin to live like kings" (315).

Then, one spring morning when "Mary and Laura were washing the dishes and Ma was making the beds" (316), the domestic rhythms of the new Little House are interrupted again by loud male discourse and the sound of Pa's angry voice: "I'll not stay here to be taken away by the soldiers like an outlaw! If some blasted politicians in Washington hadn't sent out word it would be all right to settle here, I'd never have been three miles over the line into Indian territory. But I'll not wait for the soldiers to take us out. We're going now!" (316).

Despite the assurances of Kansas newspapers, non-Indian settlers are to be forcibly expelled from this strip of Kansas "Indian territory." And the Ingallses find themselves at odds with the prevailing, patriarchal U.S. government—it considers them "outlaws," not "kings." Facing forced removal by government military forces, they are in the position of the departed Indians. They have no legal recourse for, like the Indians, they have no U.S. title to the land on which they have been living as squatters.

Because Pa's prerogatives of kingly self-determination have been violated, he is enraged as his daughters have seen him only in his performance as a "mad dog." Stripped of power by the government, which he thought was his ally, Pa becomes the absolute dictator of his female family; he decrees, "We're going now!" Laura, who has been her father's adoring ally, now cowers silently against her mother, frightened of Pa. As on the day of "Indians in the House," gender lines are clearly drawn and females are silenced. "Ma didn't say anything. She . . . looked around, at the dishes not washed and the bed only partly made, and she lifted up both hands and sat down" (319). By the next morning the Ingallses have given away their cattle, eaten their hoarded seed potatoes, abandoned their house, their furniture, and their precious plow and packed their portable belongings in the covered wagon. They do not know where they are going, only that they are leaving Kansas behind.

Pa says, as they look backward at their prairie home, "It's a great country, Caroline. . . . But there will be wild Indians and wolves here for many a long day" (325). Despite Pa's sporadic respect for Indian cultures and his desire to live in a country with plentiful wild animals, he renounces the beautiful, fertile Kansas prairie as an uninhabitable country. He is a white man who refuses to live as an "outlaw"; thus he cannot remain in an acculturated Kansas, sharing space with "wild Indians and wolves." This book began with the image of a Little House in the Big Woods, left behind; at its end there is a similar framing image of the abandoned Little House on the Prairie. The Big Woods of Wisconsin was not wild enough for Charles Ingalls; he wanted to "see the West." But Kansas is *too* wild, he now says. *Little House on the Prairie* is the only one of the Little House books that ends (or begins) with a journey to no destination. For the prerogatives that Pa enacts in his departure from Kansas there seems to be no viable destination.[21]

Though Laura's parents are largely calm and matter-of-fact during their hasty departure, Pa's language signals his submerged anger, bitterness, and sense of loss. On their first night of travel, which ends the book, he plays his fiddle and sings as usual, but his music tells the story of his conflicted feelings. He chooses two songs from the recent Civil War (which had early erupted on the Kansas border), the Confederate anthem "Dixie" and a Union song, "The Battle Cry of Freedom." Is he an "outlaw" Rebel or a soldier of the defending Union? Defying the soldiers who threaten to eject him or joining them? He also sings the western Gold Rush parody of Stephen Foster's "Oh, Susanna" (Garson 46–47), which mocks the riches of the "golden" West:

> I went to California
> With my wash-pan on my knee,
> And every time I thought of home,
> I wished it wasn't me. (333)

The sardonic song allows Pa to voice the disillusion and homesickness he will not speak, at least not where Laura can hear.[22] He interrupts his rendition of "Oh, Susanna" to tell his wife, "I've been thinking of what fun the rabbits will have, eating that garden we planted" (333), mourning the relinquishment of the Kansas farm to wildness. But Caroline Ingalls silences the expression of such mourning: "'Don't, Charles,' Ma said" (334).

As always, Ma speaks for silence. The tempestuous feelings aroused by the Ingallses' expulsion from Kansas are too dangerous for expression; they are a story that the young daughters must not hear but will always remember. The reader of the final chapter of *Little House on the Prairie* cannot directly perceive Pa's grief and agitation through Laura's point of view, which controls the book's narration. Content in the intact circle of her family, the little girl responds happily to the "lilt" and "swing" (334) of her father's songs, not to the bitter ironies implicit in the lyrics and their contexts. To construct Charles and Caroline Ingallses' frustration and sense of futility, one must read through the child's perspective on her parents' discourse, and the book provides subtle cues by which readers (especially older ones) may do so. For example, when Charles assures Caroline that they are "taking more out of Indian territory" than they took in, she responds, "I don't know what" and Pa replies, "Why, there's the mule!" (334). To Laura, who loves to pet the appealing mule colt, this is clearly an important gain. But to her parents, who know that a mule is a hybrid animal and almost always sterile, it is an ironic gain, emblematic of their abortive Kansas experiment in acculturation.

Even a dozen years later, in *These Happy Golden Years*, the last Little House book, the pain of leaving Kansas is still clearly on Ma's and Pa's minds. When Ma's brother tells a parallel story of being expelled from Black Hills Indian territory by government soldiers, Pa blazes with still-hot indignation: "I'll be durned if I could have taken it," he declares (109). And Ma mourns her brother's loss as she still mourns her own; when he tells of his regrets, she says, "I know. . . . To this day I think of the house we had to leave in Indian territory" (110). Never, until this late moment in the series, has Ma *voiced* this thought.

A large part of Wilder and Lane's task in writing the Little House books was to acknowledge the power of such suppressions. Nowhere was this task more complex than in the writing of *Little House on the Prairie*. In her later years, Wilder "told a friend . . . that she remembered everything in her books except the stories of her life on the prairies of Kansas, in Indian

territory. Those were Pa's stories and Ma's stories and Mary's stories, because they had been old enough to remember" (Zochert 50). This book,
freed from the strictures of conscious memory, dramatizes some of the
largest issues of Laura Ingalls's life as the daughter of white settlers in Indian
territory, issues that followed her to all the other Little Houses of her life.
Here, as epitomized in Laura's desire for the Indian baby, Wilder and Lane
tap their own impulses toward the acculturated life that has always been
one of the great potential resources of post-Columbian North America. But
these impulses are a threat to the project of *white settlement* to which Laura's
parents were committed. So the child's very consciousness becomes a danger to be suppressed.

For Laura the Kansas episode does not end in defeat or anger; her
father's agitation, when briefly visible, is alien and surprising to her. Instead, the expulsion returns her to her favorite state: nomadic covered-
wagon life. As she has learned, life in the West demands mobility, flexibility, and the ability to leave some things behind. These are the qualities
Laura observed in the departing Indians, many of them native to the West,
and she is delighted now to be leading such a life herself. "Laura felt all
excited inside. You never know what will happen next, nor where you'll be
tomorrow, when you are travelling in a covered wagon" (327). "Everything
was just as it used to be before they built the house" (332). Laura's joy at the
end of this book is subversive because it can potentially undermine the
whole *Little House* project; she delights in the freedom—rare for a girl—of
being unhoused.

In this state of dangerous arousal, Laura is not disposed to fall asleep.
Her parents' double-edged talk and her father's passionate, stimulating
music excite her further; although the other children are sleeping, "Laura
had never been wider awake" (334). Ma, observing her daughter's state,
instructs Pa to change his tune, as the book ends:

> [T]he voice of the fiddle changed. Softly and slurringly it began
> a long, swinging rhythm that seemed to rock Laura gently.
>   She felt her eyelids closing. She began to drift over endless
> waves of prairie grasses, and Pa's voice went with her, singing.
>
>   "Row away, row o'er the waters so blue,
>   Like a feather we sail in our gum-tree canoe.
>   Row the boat lightly, love, over the sea;
>   Daily and nightly I'll wander with thee." (335)

At last the problematically wakeful daughter is put to sleep by the power of her father's hypnotically effective song. But the prairie/sea equation, so common to Great Plains writing, returns her, beyond consciousness, to an oceanic, amniotic, unhoused intimacy with the unbordered prairie, with its "endless waves of . . . grasses." The song further cements Laura's bonds with her wandering father; "Pa's voice went with her." As the girl drifts into sleep, the lyric acknowledges the romantic bond of Charles and Laura Ingalls that, as she matures, the waking Laura must increasingly repress.

Additionally, Pa's song, "The Gum-Tree Canoe,"[23] recalls an earlier song from this novel that provoked some of Laura's most problematic questions: "The Blue Juniata," in which Alfarata in her *canoe* on the *blue* river longed for her absent *love*. In this second song, the vanished Alfarata might seem to be reunited with her beloved warrior, and her voice could be the rejoinder to Laura's urgent earlier question: "where did the voice of Alfarata go. . . ?" (236). *Little House on the Prairie* ends with a powerful vision of a prairie life without boundaries or taboos, where the voice of an female Indian, Alfarata, seems indistinguishable from the song of Laura's beloved father. But clearly and sadly, such a vision is only a dream, not a possibility of the Ingalls family's present, waking life.

As a series the Little House books became a far more complex cultural document than critics have yet acknowledged. When Wilder and Lane moved beyond the static situations of the first two books to launch the Little House *serial*, they found in the newly mobile Laura Ingalls a sensibility that could begin to express the accelerating desires and pressures of a borderland girlhood. And these volatile issues did not disappear from the Little House series at the end of *Little House on the Prairie*. Instead, as the fictional Ingalls family moves from Kansas Territory to western Minnesota to Dakota Territory, in five succeeding volumes, facts, dreams, and nightmares of American acculturation continue to surface in their waking lives.

In Minnesota, to Ma's delight, they move into a relatively established community of "white settlers" like themselves. Their nearest neighbors in the fourth novel, *On the Banks of Plum Creek*, are Norwegian. Here Pa and Ma encounter a new dilemma, one that many settlers on the Great Plains shared. They want to teach their daughters the importance of community and cooperation; for example, when Norwegian neighbor Mr. Nelson has helped to save the farm from a fire, Ma forcefully tells her girls that "there is nothing in the world so good as good neighbors" (274). But at the same time, Pa and Ma want to preserve their own Anglo-American ethnic identity and heritage. The novels often mention this heritage, particularly Ma's Scottish ancestry, and in her 1937 "Book Fair Speech," Wilder described it proudly. Both her parents were "raised on the frontier," she said. "Mother was descended from an old Scotch family and inherited the Scotch thriftiness. . . . Father's ancestors arrived in America on the Mayflower" (*Sampler* 216).

The fictional Ingallses never undertake to learn any language other than their hereditary English. Pa cannot understand why the Norwegian farmer from whom he bought his land, who spoke almost no English, planted so little wheat, nor does he comprehend when friendly Mr. Nelson says that the warm winter is "grasshopper weather." He and Ma dismiss this comment as "likely . . . some old Norwegian saying" (66). Thus they miss the omens of their biggest financial disaster, when their first-year bumper crop of wheat is destroyed by a predictable infestation of grasshoppers. Trouble and misunderstandings persistently arise from the language barrier.

The complexities of such issues emerge when the family acquires, through the kindness of Mr. Nelson, a new cow with a circle of rosy spots on her side. "Her name is Reet," Pa announces.

> "Reet?" Ma repeated. "What outlandish name is that?"
>
> "The Nelsons called her some Norwegian name," said Pa. "When I asked what it meant, Mrs. Nelson said it was a reet. . . . I guess I looked as foolish as I felt, for finally she said, 'a reet of roses.'"
>
> "A wreath!" Laura shouted. "A wreath of roses!"
>
> They all laughed till they could not laugh any more, and Pa said, "It does beat all. In Wisconsin we lived among Swedes and Germans. In Indian territory we lived among the Indians. Now here in Minnesota all the neighbours are Norwegians. They're good neighbours, too. But I guess our kind of folks is pretty scarce."
>
> "Well," said Ma, "we're not going to call this cow Reet, nor yet Wreath of Roses. Her name is Spot." (43–44)

With assurance and adamic entitlement, Ma rechristens the cow with a name that strikes familiar chords in her native tongue. Clearly, something is being lost from the Ingalls vocabulary; the specificity and poetry of the evocative Norwegian name are not retained in the blunt cliché, *Spot*. When she dictates the change, Ma claims a victory for her own ethnic heritage.

Here and elsewhere, the Ingallses' sense of "good neighbours" wars with their insular sense of themselves as a scarce and singular (and probably superior) "kind of folks." The Norwegians, unlike the Indians, are white like themselves (descriptions of them, filtered through Laura's perceptions, tend to emphasize their fair skin and light hair), yet they are culturally other in ways that Ma, at least, finds "outlandish." Laura begins to associate cultural differences with language differences; when she sees Mr. Nelson's house and stable, built very differently from Pa's, they look to her "as if they spoke Norwegian" (215). Significantly, when the Ingallses encounter the primary cultural institutions of the little town, the church and school, there is no indication that recent Norwegian immigrants like the Nelsons are included in either. Although Laura protested the cultural boundaries in Indian territory, she makes no such outcry in Minnesota. Even among white settlers and good neighbors, it seems, there are dividing lines that cannot be broached.

In the next book, *By the Shores of Silver Lake*, Laura enters adolescence and the Ingalls family migrates yet again, to Dakota. There Laura's early Kansas yearnings for cultural multiplicity are rekindled in the mythic person of Big Jerry, a French and Indian "half-breed" who befriends and protects the Ingallses in the dangerous railroad camp. Big Jerry is a gambler, and rumors (which Pa refuses to believe) suggest he is a horse thief. For Laura, who is having first thoughts of her own heterosexual future, he is the most compellingly romantic figure in this book, suggesting wide possibilities that her domesticated and law-abiding farmer father, who will never travel west again, can no longer enact. He rekindles the western images of "wild men" that first attracted Laura in Kansas. This is how she describes Big Jerry to her sister Mary, who is now blind:

> "Oh, Mary! The snow-white horse and the tall, brown man, with such a black head and a bright red shirt! The brown prairie all around—and they rode right into the sun as it was going down. They'll go on in the sun around the world."
>
> Mary thought a moment. Then she said, "Laura, you know he couldn't ride into the sun. He's just riding along on the ground like anybody."
>
> Laura did not feel that she had told a lie. What she had said was

true too. Somehow that moment when the beautiful, free pony and the wild man rode into the sun would last forever. (65)

As a man of mixed blood, Jerry opposes the "ideal" of fixed racial identity that Ma urges on her daughters when she warns them against the dread prospect of becoming "brown as an Indian." Laura's impatience with this restrictive ideal is suggested by the palette of beautifully mixed colors in her description—black, white, brown and red, the vocabulary of race in the nineteenth-century United States. Laura's vision of Big Jerry accommodates almost the full palette. As the girl sees him, this mysterious and powerful figure is bound to no fixed destination—unlike the Ingalls family, which must now, in the later novels of Laura's adolescence, follow roads and railroad tracks to towns.

In Laura's image of the "wild man" Jerry (with whom she never exchanges a word), her large dreams of *Little House on the Prairie* resurface, and those dreams are even more dangerous in a girl who is nearing sexual maturity. Mary seems to sense this; matter-of-factly, she rejects Laura's romantic picture. But Laura refuses to settle for her blind sister's safer literalism. Silently, she again makes a case for multiple languages and multiple visions; she thinks, "what she had said was true *too*," just as she earlier longed for a white *and* an Indian baby in her life. Earlier, Laura's spoken demand that her father get her an Indian baby had a deeply problematic sexual subtext, implying incestuous as well as interracial desire. By adolescence Laura's desire for multiplicity is even more taboo. She knows now that such desire cannot be spoken.

Thus, in the last three books, the possibilities of acculturation are less and less a part of the spoken agenda of the Little House series. An aged Indian appears in a store to predict the rigors of the Long Winter, and Pa heeds his warning; but Laura, sheltered at home, never sees the man. Finally, the next-to-last book, *Little Town on the Prairie*, returns to the pressing and repressed subject of acculturation in the debased and racist form of a minstrel show.

In the boredom and inertia of a winter spent in the raw new town of De Smet, the citizens entertain themselves with a series of increasingly elaborate "literaries"—public speaking, music, spelling bee, and the like. The culmination of this "whirl of gaiety" is the minstrel show, performed by five anonymous white townsmen in blackface. "The whole crowd was carried away by the pounding music, the grinning white-eyed faces, the wild dancing. . . . When the dancing stopped, the jokes began. . . . the big red mouths blabbed questions and answers that were the funniest ever heard." When the performance ends, the audience is "weak from excitement and laughing. The famous minstrel shows in New York surely could not be better than that minstrel show had been" (256–59).

According to Robert C. Toll, the minstrel show was "the first American popular entertainment form to become a national institution" (vi). Nowhere was it more effective than in small towns like De Smet. In the disparate population of a new western town, the minstrel show provided a "'national folklore' . . . that most white Americans could and did share. . . . Minstrelsy, in short, was one of the few comforting and reassuring experiences that nineteenth-century white Americans" had in common (Toll 271–72).

Minstrelsy had originated with northern whites, and "from the outset," it "unequivocally branded [blacks] as inferiors." However, it did appropriate elements of African American and Anglo-American folk culture.[24] Thus it is a form of acculturation—"intercultural borrowing"—but only as controlled and enacted by white men. Blackness, as portrayed by Wilder's minstrel men, does not imply the cooperative coexistence of *mutual* acculturation, in which disparate cultures retain some individual autonomy and maintain mutual respect. Here, instead, it is a cartoon-like mask of absolute difference that exaggerates contrasts with whitened eyes and reddened mouths. By their portrayal of difference, the painted "darkies" (as Laura calls them) forge a collective, monolithic racial identity for the bored, anxious, and hard-pressed white townspeople of De Smet. This, they agree, is the best their culture can offer—as good as New York.

Eric Lott, in his important recent work on minstrelsy, argues that it was underlaid by "a strong white fascination with black men and black culture" and that "an aura of illicit sexuality . . . shadowed the most chaste of minstrel shows" (25). The De Smet audience's response reflects such "white fascination" in a heady mixture of contempt, fear, and rapt, unbridled delight as they watch the blackface performers "blab" and dance "wildly" to "pounding," sexually arousing music. At the minstrel show, Laura's persistent and sometimes sexual curiosity about other races and cultures is enacted in a debased form approved by her fellow townspeople. But in such a performance Laura can take no active, speaking role. She is only a passive member of the audience, indulging her multicultural curiosity in a safe and sanctioned form. According to Lott, "blackface minstrelsy was based on small but significant crimes against settled ideas of racial demarcation, which indeed appear to be inevitable when white Americans enter the haunted realm of racial fantasy." Thus minstrelsy indicates "how precariously nineteenth-century white people lived their own whiteness" (23–24). As we have seen, Laura Ingalls has grown up among her Anglo-American family, Norwegians and other European immigrants, and Native Americans of many tribes. The only professional person she has ever met was an African American doctor. The facts of her life have been multiracial and multicultural, but those facts have been insistently ignored by much of her socialization. Thus, like many other Americans, she is ripe to enter the "haunted realm of racial fantasy" as projected by the minstrel show.

The minstrel show takes on another dimension for the Ingalls women when they realize that Pa, who is mysteriously absent from the family circle, must have been one of the blackface performers. But none of the performers had whiskers. "'Pa couldn't have cut off his whiskers, could he?' [Laura] asked Ma, and in horror Ma answered, 'Mercy, no! . . . I hope not'" (259). When Pa reappears at home with an innocent white face and whiskers intact, Laura pounces on him and searches until she finds a telltale speck of black in his beard. "He could not deny it. He had been the darky who rattled the bones" (260). Caroline Ingalls is horrified that her husband might sacrifice an important feature of his white male persona, his bristling, patriarchal, light brown beard, to achieve a blackface performance. For her his behavior is an unsettling reminder of how precariously his impersonation of a white patriarch is constructed, as Lott's analysis suggests. But Laura, who still sometimes chafes at the cultural fixity of the town, is sympathetic with her father's destabilizing experiments; "she really thought that, for such an evening, Pa would have sacrificed even his whiskers" (260).

As "the darky who rattled the bones," Charles Ingalls was one of the two endmen, Mr. Tambo and Mr. Bones, who provided much of the minstrel shows' comedy.[25] "With their seemingly endless store of riddles, puns and 'one-liners,' endmen made great impressions on audiences everywhere, but nowhere greater than in small towns" (Toll 54–55). Pa, self-styled as the storyteller, songman, and wit of his female family, seems perfectly cast as Mr. Bones. When he "blacks up" for the minstrel performance, he is exempted from the propriety that his wife enforces in his home performances and from the constricting outlines of his male role in "white settler" culture. Momentarily, Charles Ingalls slips out of the confines of his white skin, and then—like the wiliest of tricksters—he returns to his former identity with every whisker intact.[26] Even Ma admits the necessity, importance, and rarity of such a feat. "Such an evening came once in a lifetime, Ma said" (260).

The minstrel show is the last of the "literary" entertainments, and, typically, it offers no performing parts for girls or women.[27] Compared to the great possibilities of Kansas territory, where Indian cultures had variety and dignity and a black doctor was a valued and respected citizen, the minstrel show, Laura's last encounter with interracial acculturation, offers solidarity and release to whites through a debased parody of African American culture, and it tells a white girl that she cannot escape from her white skin and her white female position. Laura Ingalls can never hope to black up and to perform, as her father does, in a minstrel show.

Must we conclude, then, that although *Little House on the Prairie* may initiate a compelling romance of acculturation, an ongoing *process* of racial and cultural interaction is dismissed as impracticable and impossible in the Little House series?

I think not; Wilder and Lane's project is more complicated than such a formulation will admit. For example, as I've noted, revisionist western historians such as Glenda Riley have established that there was considerable interaction between Native American and settler women on the frontier, with much more flexibility than Ma's unchanging "hatred" of Indians would indicate, and that the roles of white settler women were more varied than those the Ingalls women enacted. As we have seen, the Little House series implies many telling cues to the *cost* of such a restrictive story of settlement. The "letdown" felt after the Indians' hieratic departure from Kansas, the unspeakable appeal of Big Jerry, the inadmissible poetry of a cow named "Wreath of Roses"—all suggest the cruel deprivations of a project that turns its back on the riches of acculturation. In the earliest Little House books, young Laura is eager to experience her own hereditary culture. As much as Mary does, Laura loves Ma's housekeeping and Pa's stories. She is equally eager to discover and delight in difference. Obviously, this child is a perfect candidate for acculturation. But by the time she attends the minstrel show as a young adolescent, Laura has become an accustomed spectator, consigned to watch as white men stage a cruel parody of black culture, a show that offers no role for her.

As I have argued in this chapter, the Little House books are, among other things, a narrative of the powerful impulses to and constraints against a multicultural life on the late nineteenth-century Great Plains. Wilder's life in the years before she began to write these books is full of clues to her continued interest and involvement in this subject—as is, more obviously, the peripatetic, adventurous life of Rose Wilder Lane. For example, in the years before they settled in Mansfield, Missouri, for the rest of their lives, Laura and Almanzo Wilder had, like their parents, moved halfway across the continental United States. They spent a year in the "piney woods" of Florida, where they found themselves very different from the local residents.[28] When they settled in Missouri, Wilder began to take notes about Ozark culture; according to Anderson, she "continually jotted down country folklore, tall tales, and music of the mountains." In a 1937 letter to her daughter, she passed on several pages of notes on Ozark culture, saying, "Perhaps you can use them as anecdotes or in some way. . . . They were written when Wilson was president and are true." One item from the notes is a menu from a capacious meal at a neighbor's house: "A dinner of 93 different dishes" (*Sampler* 148–49). Having come of age in the heyday of "local color" and regional U.S. fiction, Laura Ingalls thought of near-ethnological observation as "material" that might be grist for her writer-daughter's mill—and eventually for her own.[29] In fact, Wilder's sixty-some years of residence in Missouri were a long education in acculturation; her cooking, for example, as recorded in correspondence with her daughter, suggests that she adapted to the local style—although not to the extent of ninety-three-item menus!

When Rose Wilder Lane was living in San Francisco in 1915 as a young journalist and real estate agent, her mother made a visit of several months, eager to sample distant cultures in the commodified, packaged form that had become popular with so many Americans of her generation: the World Fair.[30] On this visit, too, one of Wilder's primary aims was to make her cultural investigations a subject of her *writing*. So the appearance of Wilder's "Indian juvenile," a troubled romance of American acculturation, had a long foreground in the events of the author's life.

The document that most tellingly predicts the concerns of *Little House on the Prairie* is Wilder's first extended prose writing, the diary she kept on the Wilders' trip from De Smet to Mansfield in 1894. This succinct private account—published posthumously, with a narrative "setting" by Lane, in 1962—has a remarkably assured voice and is full of trenchant observations. It is marked by Wilder's lively interest in the plural cultures that existed, and often thrived, on the Dakota, Nebraska, and Kansas prairies. According to Elizabeth Hampsten, such interest was not the norm; "The much-touted friendly and cooperative pioneer spirit does not often surface in private writings." More typically, "strangers are viewed with suspicion"

(1982, 8). In her 1894 diary, however, Wilder observes regional, ethnic, and racial differences with a pleased candor that is like the young fictional Laura of Indian territory. This is her typical description of a Kansas town: "Drove through St. Mary's. A pleasant town but strange, it is altogether Southern, and Catholic. There is a beautiful large church with a pure white marble Saint Mary. . . . The houses are neat and pretty. It is a clean town" (*On the Way Home* 48–49). Later, still in Kansas, she notes, "In all the towns now there are many colored people" (55).

The Wilders' 650-mile wagon trip from South Dakota was pleasant, relatively easy, and well-provisioned, as many westward migrations were not. They traveled with one other congenial family. And in many ways, Wilder's fledgling narrative presents their route, which included her first visit to Kansas since the Ingallses' Kansas experiment in her early childhood, as a panorama of multicultural riches, ripe for acculturation and enjoyment. For example, Laura and Almanzo Wilder are eager to visit and explore a semicommunal Russian settlement near Yankton, South Dakota. Although the two groups have little common language, they observe each other's dress, food, animals, and farming practices; at last, gifts are exchanged and Wilder writes, "We got to feel a little acquainted with the folks" (21–23). This promising encounter seems to suggest another way of writing the story of intercultural encounters on the Great Plains, and a far more positive version.

Yet, in the same passage, Wilder also describes an unforgettable incident that predicts the obstacles she would expand in *Little House on the Prairie*. As the Wilders and their traveling companions part from the friendly Russians, a Russian woman offers them a kindness. This is the published version of this passage: "When we were leaving a woman opened the front of her dress and took out a baking of cold biscuits from right against her bare skin and gave them to me. The man told me to put them in my *shirt*, but I carried them in Manly's clean handkerchief instead. The man said it was hard for people to cook when traveling. They are very kind people. A pity to waste the biscuits but we could not eat them" (22–23).

In U.S. writing, especially by women, food and foodways have probably been the most frequent signifiers of cultural exchange. Wilder earlier praised the Russians' cooking and pronounced their biscuits "light and very good" (21). But now, despite all the kindness and good will in the world, she cannot eat the Russians' bread. It would seem that Caroline Ingalls's priorities are suddenly being inscribed by her daughter Laura, even as she permanently turns her back on her parents' household in De Smet. This small but striking incident, punctuating the panorama of possibilities that unrolls on the Wilders' journey, suggests the deeply ingrained barriers to acculturation that Wilder will confront in the Little House books, and it suggests, too, that many of the most persistent of such barriers are preserved in domestic customs. Although the Laura Ingalls of the series grew up eating hand-shaped cornbread marked with the prints of her mother's bare hands and was taught that such marks were the best of "sweetening," bread that has touched the Russian woman's breasts is taboo, totally inedible. The result is *loss* and *waste,* the printed text acknowledges: "a pity to waste the biscuits." Yet she and Almanzo can think of no way to break through the conditioning that forbids eating them. In *Little House on the Prairie,* when Laura longs for the Indian child, she is also longing for a potential solution to this problem. For if the white child and the Indian child shared a life, they would also share a table, and the diets and lives of both would be expanded by acculturation. Already, in Wilder's earliest writing, we can see the longings for this commonality and the cultural barriers against it that were to be expressed with such intensity in the third Little House novel.

Yet another complicating and complicit presence in the published text of Wilder's journal is Rose Wilder Lane. Rose was seven when her family made its 1894 trip to Missouri, and her extended autobiographical "setting" for *On the Way Home* relates her memories of lively pleasure in the journey and the move. After Wilder's death, the travel journal was located among her papers and brought to Lane's attention; she supervised its publication. In *On the Way Home,* the published journal is preceded by these words from Lane: "My mother made daily notes of our journey in a little 5-cent memorandum book. . . . This is her record" (12). Lane never acknowledges in her "setting" that she made constant, usually small alterations in her mother's manuscript before it was published. Terse travel notations are extended to full sentences, repetitive diction is silently altered, and less explicable changes are made. (For example, Wilder regularly records morning departure times for the wagon train; sometimes Lane alters these times, making them earlier.) On 22 July Wilder wrote that everyone in the party bathed in the river except herself; "I am not feeling very well and cannot go in" (journal manuscript, published as *On the Way Home;* Western). Presumably, in the code of the late nineteenth century, she means to imply that she is menstruating and thus is "unable" to go in the river. Lane entirely deleted this reference, eliminating a telling and important reference to a woman's bodily experience on a journey of emigration.

When one compares Wilder's manuscript with the printed version, it is obvious that her daughter has made dozens of such changes, which subtly but significantly alter the nature of the journal. By 1962 the Little House series had been complete for nineteen years and Laura Ingalls Wilder was five years dead. Lane had no need to worry about the success of the Little House project or the reputation of her mother. Yet, as she had done with the books of the series, she continued to apply her ideas about propriety and quality to her mother's text, compromising its considerable potential value as a historical resource and an authentic emigrant narrative.

Lane's editing of *On the Way Home*, a project that (as far as I know) has not previously been acknowledged in print, indicates that, even after Wilder's death, the Little House story was a site of conflict for the collaborating mother and daughter. The most stunning evidence of this contest is in the account of the Russians' inedible gift of bread, which I quoted. In Wilder's manuscript, the Russian woman *does not* take bread out of her blouse, from against her bare skin. Instead, a man proffers the gift and suggests that Laura Wilder and her female traveling companion "put them in our *shirts*, but we put them in Manly's clean handkerchief instead." This account never says that the bread was inedible or uneaten, although the day's entry does end with the comment, "We baked bread today," absent from the printed version (manuscript published as *On the Way Home*; Sunday, 22 July 1894; Columbia).

What is Rose Wilder Lane doing here? Although her mother's account implied the traveling women's shock when a Russian man suggested that they carry bread within their blouses, it nowhere indicates that the Wilders were unable to eat the Russian bread. Lane, as an adult who had traveled around the world, was sometimes impatient with her parents' provincialities; has she elaborated this incident to underline their food prejudices and their resistance to unfamiliar cultural practices? Does she wish to make more emphatic the Wilders' refusal to observe a "dirty" custom? Is she drawing from her own memories as a seven-year-old—or from stories her parents may have told later—to provide what she considers a more accurate account of this incident? Or is she heightening and fictionalizing her mother's autobiographical manuscript, a practice that may have become almost second nature in the writing of the Little House books? Whatever motivations may have been involved in the reshaping of this passage, one of the most extended, vivid, and developed incidents in Wilder's manuscript, it indicates that the story of Great Plains acculturation was also a contested territory between the two authors of the Little House series, one that may have been among their most enduring tensions as daughter and mother. Some of the power of *Little House on the Prairie,* which was written when the two were living in close proximity on Rocky Ridge Farm, may have come from their mutual work on these potentially incendiary issues.

Finally, Wilder's 1894 journal is also pertinent to this chapter because here, in words almost unaltered by Lane, Wilder made her first predictive statement about a writing life to come. On the day after the Wilders left the Russian settlement behind, she wrote:

> July 23
> We started at 8. Hated to leave our camping place, it seems quite like home. We crossed the James River and in 20 minutes we reached the top of the bluffs on the other side. We all stopped and looked back at the scene and I wished for an artist's hand or a poet's brain or even to be able to tell in good plain prose how beautiful it was. If I had been the Indians I would have scalped more white folks before I ever would have left it. (*On the Way Home* 23–24)

Here Laura Ingalls Wilder seems to be claiming many of the great projects that she and her daughter elaborated in the Little House series. Already we see a delight in the experience of travel, at odds with an attachment to fixity and comfort (the "camping place" that "seems quite like home"). This writer longs to find the medium and the resources that will allow her to express the beauties of her journey, even if that medium is the one she finally chose, "good plain prose." Her wish to *write* the panorama of her emigration is tied to a sense of the land's rich resources and, simultaneously, to an image of cultures competing to the death for that land's possession. The "scalping Indians" are one of the few explicitly negative cultural stereotypes in this journal—and yet it is with the Indians' defense of a dear and beautiful homeland that Wilder herself identifies. In this passage, a twenty-seven-year-old author inscribes her largest ambitions for the first time. And from this beginning, we can see that the drama of acculturation that weaves through the Little House series is already a strong strand in Wilder's thought. For the fictionalized child who "wanted the other one too" grew up to write—in the guise of a family romance—one of our most disturbing and ambitious narratives about failures and experiments of acculturation in the American West.

Rose Wilder Lane as a successful and prosperous writer in Europe, about 1923. Two years later she would return to live with her parents on Rocky Ridge Farm in Missouri, where Wilder and Lane began their collaboration on the Little House series. Courtesy Herbert Hoover Presidential Library-Museum.

Chapter 3

Getting and Spending
Materialism and the Little House

When I was a child, *On the Banks of Plum Creek* (1937) was my favorite Little House book. My friends mostly agreed, even (for once) my younger sister. For this was the book we talked about the most. We debated the warfare between Laura and her schoolroom rival, Nellie Oleson; we envied Nellie's elaborate clothes and lifelike wax doll. Our mouths watered for a taste of Ma's vanity cakes, and we shared Laura's transcendent desire, as she longed for the fur cape that hung on the church Christmas tree (a cape that turned out—in the culmination of a perfect material romance—to have Laura's name on it). In *Little House on the Prairie,* Laura's desire for the Indian baby had been even stronger, but it was an unspeakable desire, one that her culture and her consciousness could not continue to acknowledge. *Plum Creek* was instead a story of speakable desires, of the conscious wishes that our culture was encouraging us girls to develop. And this book expanded into the new, sanctioned arenas beyond our houses that were beginning to open up for us, as they did for Laura: the schoolroom and the marketplace.

In *Plum Creek* the Ingalls family settles on a Minnesota farm, buying the land from a Norwegian immigrant who wants to move farther west. The farm is near a town with a school and a church. At the end of the previous book the family had no known destination; their dreamy, apparently aimless journey, however stressful it may have been for Ma and Pa, delighted Laura and challenged her imagination. But this new book begins with legal papers, transfer of property, and talk of money. Laura cries when she learns that Pa has traded Pet and Patty, the "Indian ponies" that love traveling, as she does, for oxen to pull his plow. But Pa explains, "with those big oxen I can break up a great big field.... A good crop of wheat will bring us more money than we've ever had, Laura. Then we'll have horses, and new dresses, and everything you can want" (7).

The previous Little House books (unlike *Farmer Boy*) have not indicated that the Ingallses had any money. Pa traded work or bartered the furs he had trapped for the few goods they needed and could not make themselves. But now Pa confronts Laura with one of the major myths of his capitalist culture: that *money* can buy "everything [she] can want." Obviously, then, the next step for Laura and Mary Ingalls will be an education in consuming: the choosing and buying of things, the spending of money.

Later in the book, when the family is preparing to move into the larger house Pa has built to replace the Norwegian dugout, Pa draws Laura and Mary aside to show them a secret: the new, large cast-iron stove he has purchased as a surprise for Ma. The girls are transfixed by the "marvellous stove," which is described in detail. Mary touches the writing on the stove "and spelled out, 'P A T. One seven seven ought.... What's that spell, Pa?'" He replies, "It spells Pat" (115). Next day, when Ma sees the stove, she is moved but dubious at all that her husband has purchased—on credit. She tells him, "Buying a stove—it's too much." But her excited daughters pull her away, instructing her in the delights and uses of "that wonderful stove" (120).

Soon after, Laura begins school and has her first reading lesson. The marvellous stove becomes her teacher:

> Just before dinner-time that first day, Laura was able to read, C A T, cat. Suddenly she remembered and said, P A T, Pat!"

Teacher was surprised.

"R A T, rat!" said Teacher. "M A T, mat!" And Laura was reading!
She could read the whole first row in the speller. (152)

These linked scenes are crucial to the Little House series, especially in
Plum Creek, as Laura and Mary learn to read, buy, and consume, thus becoming players and participants in postbellum, industrialized, nineteenth-
century U.S. culture. As they explore the stove, fingering it almost as Mary
will later finger her Braille texts, they are *reading a thing* and instructing their
mother, who is schooled in traditional, preindustrial household economy,
in fundamentals of contemporary consumerism. Although Ma sometimes
accompanies Pa on shopping trips, the series never depicts her independently entering a store, and most of her housekeeping practices, especially
in the first three books, are very traditional and untouched by the buyable
domestic innovations of the nineteenth century. Pa, although he makes sustained efforts at "modern" farming, is never very successful; his most reliably
lucrative work is in older craft traditions, as a carpenter and an agricultural
day laborer. It is the daughters who must learn the practices and vocabulary
of late nineteenth-century consumerism, female style; they must prove
themselves as virtuosos of the marketplace. In *Plum Creek* this process begins.

As Wilder and Lane corresponded before, during, and after the shared
composition of the Little House books, they often discussed commodities,
money, and anxiety about money. Like many mothers and daughters, they
frequently wrote (and presumably talked) about what they had bought or
might buy. Wilder, for example, wrote a detailed account of the "spring
styles" in a Missouri mail-order catalog; Lane sent descriptions of her latest
hats from Paris (including prices), and Wilder advised her daughter on
whether to put stoves or furnaces in the Connecticut house she was re-
modeling. However frugal (and Wilder, especially, was), they were both
zestful consumers, proud of their prowess.

For both women, the most traumatic periods of their lives were tied to
financial anxiety. In the decade after the 1929 crash, Lane's diaries are full of
worries about how she can maintain her income, continue a sporadically
extravagant lifestyle, and help support her parents; they are interspersed
with suicidal passages.[1] A somewhat more lighthearted verse that prefaces
a 1931–35 journal indicates that, for Lane, financial anxiety had become a
staple component of a writer's life:

Know, when passing this door that within
A writer is seated, pale and thin,

With nervous habits and thoughts sublime,
Wondering where she can borrow a dime. (Hoover)

Wilder, who had grown up with her parents' struggles to establish a profitable frontier farm, began another cycle of financial uncertainties and disasters when she married Almanzo Wilder; it was the disastrous Panic of 1893 that helped persuade them to leave South Dakota permanently, to try their fortunes in Missouri. In her setting for *On the Way Home*, Lane writes that the hundred dollars that was to be the Wilders' down payment on a farm was lost for several days after their arrival in Mansfield; that time was so terrible for Laura Wilder that, to the end of her life, she refused to speak of it. Lane reported that, fifty years later, when she casually mentioned the loss, her mother "stopped the words in my mouth with a fierce, 'I don't want to *think* of it!'" (75).

Wilder's career as a journalist roughly coincided with the era of scientific housekeeping (described by Laura Shapiro in *Perfection Salad*); during these years, the housekeeper was considered a "domestic counterpart of the professional man . . . responsible for the proper management of her household" (Gordon and McArthur 37–38). In her personal essays, Wilder often detailed consumer decisions by which she and other farm women could improve the lives of their families and empower themselves. For example, in a 1925 article for *Country Gentleman*, she described how she sold an outdated oak table and chairs for $11.00 and bought a new, simpler, fashionable set for $10.95. She explained why these changes in the dining room were so necessary to her: "My kitchen . . . was my workshop and office, the place where I conducted my business of canning and preserving and pickling, of counting and packing eggs, of preparing fruits and vegetables for market, of handling meat, and milk and cheese and butter. Like any other woman, I wanted to get away from my workshop and my job while I was eating" ("The Farm Dining Room," *Sampler* 142).[2] For Wilder, the purchase of dining room furniture was an important means of confirming the economic importance of her domestic work, which she frames as a "business" as significant as a man's. Here and elsewhere, the language of her journalism indicates that issues of income and consumption were often—and anxiously—on her mind.

In her seventies, Wilder gratefully wrote to her daughter that financial security, created by the success of the Little House books, had finally dispelled a lifelong, recurrent nightmare: "I haven't gone alone down that long, dark road, I used to dream of, for a long time. The last time I saw it stretching ahead of me, I said in my dream 'But I don't have to go through those dark woods, I don't have to go that way.' And I turned away from it. We are living inside our income and I don't have to worry about the bills" (17 March 1939, Hoover).[3] Worry about bills was a frequent theme of Wilder's correspondence with her daughter in the 1930s. Thus, when the Little House books turned to the subject of consumption, they were articulating issues that had long been at the center of these two hard-working authors' lives.

In *Plum Creek* the intense desires and large-scaled, mythic dreamwork of *Little House on the Prairie* are scaled down to a sequence of plots that a girl can complete. Such events include Laura and Mary's first solo purchase, Laura's competition with Nellie Oleson, and Laura's loss and rescue of her most prized possession, her rag doll. One reason this book is so affective for children is that it acknowledges how important things are to them and how urgently they need to have some understanding and control of their relation to things. In Laura Ingalls Wilder's Book Fair speech, delivered the year *Plum Creek* was published, she spoke of this as she explained her reasons for writing the series: "I wanted the children now to understand more about the beginnings of things, to know what is behind the things they see—what it is that made America as they know it" (*Sampler* 217). This project began, of course, in *Big Woods*, which often focused detailed attention on hand-made objects—Laura's doll, the log house, Ma's pats of yellow butter—and the processes by which they could be reproduced. As the Ingalls girls grow older, propelled toward literate, consuming adult lives in the late nineteenth- and twentieth-century United States, it becomes more necessary for the series to acknowledge what Eugene W. Metcalf has argued: "although we may feel uncomfortable admitting it, our behaviour as Americans indicates that the ownership of goods is a major goal in American life. Once this truth is acknowledged, we realize that the commercial matrix in which Americans live is not incidental" (202).

For the fictional Laura Ingalls, as for her parents, purchasing decisions are key life events, as they still are for most U.S. citizens. Beginning with *Plum Creek*, the Little House series becomes (among other things) one of our most complex and ambitious narratives of a U.S. child's relation to a material world. Wilder's fourth novel is neither a materialistic celebration of pure greed nor a simplistic moral tract, dismissive of commodities and the processes of buying and keeping them. Instead, it captures many facets of most children's complex relation to things, the material stuff of their lives.

According to Metcalf, "consumption can be seen as an important arena in which culture is negotiated, fixed and codified" (203). As the Ingalls girls attend school, church, and Sunday school, make purchases and participate in their first social events, they are becoming conscious members of an exogamous, temporal community unlike the timeless early childhood milieu of *Big Woods*.

In Minnesota the Ingalls family is starting over yet again. This is the third home for the fictional seven-year-old Laura (the actual Laura Ingalls had made more moves at an earlier age). Her parents, both veterans of a peripatetic frontier lifestyle, have made many more moves, and they are typical of their contemporaries; "frontier historians calculate that nineteenth-century westerners moved on an average of four to five times as adults" (Schlereth 13). According to Mihaly Csikszentmihalyi's trenchantly titled essay, "Why We Need Things," objects "stabilize" our sense of self and "give a permanent shape to our views of ourselves." Such stability is especially necessary in a mobile culture (23, 27), like the one the Ingalls family inhabits. They have settled on Plum Creek at Ma's insistence because she wants her daughters to attend community schools and to be imprinted with the cultural values she most respects. Thus, as in Laura's first reading lesson, it seems inevitable that schooling and buying become entwined in this book. According to Mary Douglas and Baron Isherwood, "consumption is the very arena in which culture is fought over and licked into shape" (57). As I have indicated in the previous chapter, frontier environments where acculturation is possible are often the scenes of intense cultural warfare; we have observed Ma's fierce defenses as she denigrates Indians and renames the family cow. Charles and Caroline Ingalls seemed anxious and disoriented as they packed up and headed for nowhere at the end of *Little House on the Prairie*. Those recent anxieties help to explain the energy with which they throw themselves into the relatively settled and secure life of the little Minnesota community where they next settle.

Collectivity and confirmation are the cultural benefits of life near a town. After the family attends church together for the first time, in Minnesota, Pa—who characteristically loves change and wandering—nevertheless affirms these benefits; he says, "Well, Caroline, it's pleasant to be with a crowd of people all trying to do the right thing, same as we are" (187). Later, Pa confirms his commitment to town values in the vocabulary of consumption, offering his daughters an important lesson: he contributes his last three dollars, saved to buy himself a much-needed pair of boots, to purchase a bell for the new church. For Pa the boots mean precious mobility and the ability to work comfortably and independently. But the church bell, which broadcasts the voice of Christian community values to a scattered rural congregation, has become a more important priority to independent, adventurous Charles Ingalls, now playing the role of a farmer and settled family man. According to Csikszentmihalyi, consumer decisions can provide the material reinforcement of stability that the Ingalls family—and perhaps especially Pa and Laura—will need if they are going to make a success of their farming-community life. Materialism is often "in large part due to a paradoxical need to transform the precariousness of consciousness into the solidity of things" (28).

As a very young child, Laura Ingalls did not much worry about the dangerous "precariousness of consciousness." In fact, she delighted in borderland places and borderline states, between consciousness and sleep—as when, being sung to sleep by her father on the prairie, she felt that the very stars were singing to her and were close enough for her to reach out and touch. Initially, many of *Plum Creek's* lessons in solidity and stability are difficult for Laura to accept.

An early chapter of *Plum Creek,* "Straw-Stack," dramatizes the new conflict between Pa and Laura about the "solidity of things." In the first fall on the new farm, after threshing, Pa rakes together all the wheat straw into one stack, to serve as necessary food for the stock in the coming winter. Laura and Mary are enchanted by the fragrant, "beautiful golden straw-stack. . . . tall and shining bright" (53). They climb to the top and blissfully jump and slide, again and again. Laura sings, "I'm flying! I'm flying!" When Pa discovers that the girls have scattered the stack, he instructs them, "You girls mustn't slide down the straw-stack any more." But the next day, the gold straw is again sensuously irresistible, and the girls (led by Laura) play in the stack again, climbing and *rolling* down ("Pa didn't say we can't roll!"). That night, when Pa sternly confronts them with the fact that the straw stack is again dispersed and asks, "DID YOU SLIDE DOWN THE STRAW-STACK?" Laura explains that, technically at least, they obeyed his orders. "We did not slide, Pa. . . . But we did roll" (53–60).

This is an important dispute over a stack of precious gold (again and again, gold imagery is used to describe the straw stack). To Laura, the straw's value is its immediate sensory appeal and the opportunity it offers to escape the materiality of solid flesh in the blissful experience of "flying." Although Laura does not acknowledge this to herself, her play in the straw stack is also an unaccustomed opportunity to demolish a solid, traditional, phallic structure erected by a patriarch. Laura uses her new facility with language to prolong the delightful, liberating experience of playing in the stack, although she actually knows that Pa meant to prohibit any kind of play that would disarrange the straw.

Obviously Pa has considerable sympathy for Laura's strategy, for when she explains that she did not *slide* but *rolled*, he has to conceal irrepressible laughter. Again, Laura is resisting fixity—as earlier, she preferred swift Indian ponies to a farmer's oxen and preferred not to sleep in the dugout: "she would rather sleep outdoors, even if she heard wolves, than be so safe in this house dug under the ground" (17). Laura's perception of the dugout is remarkably like the ultimate fixed human habitation: a grave. The enticing gold straw stack promises the opposite of deathlike immobility. For this lively girl, gold means mobility, pleasure, and expanded, "flying" consciousness.

Charles Ingalls loves these same intangible states. But now he is a farmer and a father who must worry about preserving food for the coming winter in an unknown territory. For him the golden straw must be a fixed asset, a stable investment in security and a safe future. He ends the straw-stack controversy by insisting that his children understand and share his responsibilities and his view of the straw as a commodity.

> "I want you girls to stay away from that straw-stack. Pete and Bright and Spot will . . . need every bite of it. You don't want them to be hungry, do you?"
>
> "Oh no, Pa!" they said.
>
> "Well, if that straw's to be fit to feed them, it MUST—STAY—STACKED. Do you understand?"
>
> "Yes, Pa," said Laura and Mary.
>
> That was the end of their playing on the straw-stack. (60)

However reluctantly, Charles Ingalls lays down the laws of fixity and stability to his daughters. By risking the animals' food supply, they have threatened the safety of the family.

The straw, a natural product, has been processed by men and (threshing) machine to become a cultural commodity. In *Plum Creek* for the first time, Laura is explicitly warned that the unprocessed natural world is a threat to her life; it could kill her. Newly adventurous, Laura is eager to explore the varied prairie and nearby Plum Creek. There she finds the fast current inviting and enticing; she sits on the footbridge and "plumped both legs into the water. The creek ran strong against them and she kicked against it. That was fun!" (102). It is so exhilarating to test her strength against the current that she wanted to be really in the roaring, joyous creek. She clasped her hands together under the plank and rolled off it.

In that very instant, she knew the creek was not playing. It was strong and terrible. It seized her whole body and pulled it under the plank. . . .

This was not like wolves or cattle. The creek was not alive. It was only strong and terrible and never stopping. It would pull her down and whirl her away, rolling and tossing her like a willow branch. It would not care. (102, 104)

Eventually, in a desperate, solitary effort, Laura does manage to climb out of the creek and to save her own life. But she can no longer revel in "flying" and the delights of the free fall, knowing that the straw will protect and cushion her. The flooding creek could reduce her to a lifeless thing without a will, like a broken willow branch.

I remember this grimly deterministic scene vividly from my childhood reading, for it painfully forced me to acknowledge mortality and the limits of human strength. "Laura knew now that there were things stronger than anybody. But the creek had not got her. It had not made her scream and it could not make her cry" (106). To preserve her life, Laura now recognizes that she must keep her distance from certain natural forces. And *Plum Creek* restates this lesson, again and again. The fast current and deep water of the creek, a fierce badger, crop-eating grasshoppers, stampeding cattle—all threaten her and the security of the Little House. It becomes essential that Laura know where the boundaries are—where is the water *too* deep for a girl? In *Little House on the Prairie,* when he took Laura and Mary to the Indian camp, Pa deemphasized boundaries and encouraged the girls to venture across the prairie with him. But on Plum Creek he instructs Laura in the importance of recognizing and respecting boundaries. For example, when they swim in the creek, he ducks her when she enters the deep water to teach her a lesson. (However, Laura is delighted—not properly scared—by her ducking.)

Many chapter titles in *Plum Creek* also emphasize the natural forces that threaten the Ingalls family and their farm and Little House, such as "Grasshopper Eggs," "Wheels of Fire," and "The Long Blizzard." Newly and clearly, lines are being drawn between nature and culture—and Laura has no choice but to side with culture. Thus it is especially important that she learn to order things and to read them. According to Steven Lubar, it is objects that "form the boundaries between us and the natural world we inhabit. They mediate our experience of our environment" (197).

This becomes apparent when Laura and Mary take their next step into the local community culture, starting school for the first time. Ma helps them dress carefully in their Sunday dresses and then performs a rite of initiation:

> she knelt down by the box where she kept her best things, and she took out three books. They were the books she had studied when she was a little girl. One was a speller, and one was a reader, and one was a 'rithmetic.
>
> She looked solemnly at Mary and Laura, and they were solemn, too.
>
> "I am giving you these books for your very own, Mary and Laura," Ma said. "I know you will take care of them and study them faithfully."
>
> "Yes, Ma," they said. (141)

Ma's ritual teaches her daughters that school will require a heritage of things, things that must be preserved with near-religious care. But when they arrive at school, it is clear that the things they have are not enough. First, their "Sunday dresses" seem newly inadequate, skimpy and shabby; Nellie Oleson wrinkles her nose and calls the two "Country girls!" (148). Then Teacher informs them that they must have a slate; "You cannot learn to write without a slate" (151).

To write—and to become the *writer* Laura Ingalls Wilder, whose book we are reading—Laura must buy a slate; she and Mary must ask Pa for a quarter, although the family is nearly out of money, and enter the store, a world of commodities, to get what they need. Pa gives them the money and tells them to buy the slate from Mr. Oleson. At Oleson's Store, making their first solo purchase, the girls find themselves surrounded by unaccustomed abundance. Items that are once-a-year treats for them—crackers, pickles, and "Christmas candy"—are available in everyday profusion, and Nellie Oleson and her brother stuff their mouths with candy and taunt Mary and Laura. The girls' quarter buys the slate, but Mr. Oleson informs them,

> "You'll want a slate pencil, too. Here it is. One penny."
> Nellie said, "They haven't got a penny." (155)

Although Mr. Oleson kindly offers to sell them the pencil on their father's credit, the Ingalls girls refuse; they are reluctant to ask for more money. Then they remember their own financial assets, the Christmas pennies that

Santa Claus left in their stockings. "They decided that Mary would spend her penny for the pencil, and after that she would own half of Laura's penny" (156). Next morning they go to the other store, "where Teacher lived," buy the pencil, and walk to school with their much-admired teacher.

This is an key victory for Mary and Laura. Making their first purchase with their own money, they hold their own in a bewildering world of tempting goods that they cannot buy, where they are taunted for their lack of money. Through the transaction, they begin learning to think abstractly about material assets (Mary now owns *half* of an indivisible penny), and they use their opportunity to choose between the two stores where they might buy the pencil to express their independence and their personal preferences and priorities. Mary and Laura have begun to be intelligent, discerning consumers. True, they do not question the received wisdom of their culture; they accede that a writing student *must* have a slate. In some ways, they resemble the consumers in Janice Radway's ground-breaking study of women who buy romance novels. Like Radway's book, the Little House series explores the commodity market as an arena where girls may be confined by the choices that are proffered to them by a restrictive social order but where they also have considerable opportunity for independence and growth through consumer decisions that express their own priorities.

Supported by the "right" things (books, slate, pencil, and even the instructive patent stove), Laura begins to read and to write with alacrity and aptitude. Soon she has friends and enough influence to override Nellie Oleson's dictatorial choice of schoolyard games. Laura's strong will makes her Nellie's natural rival, and the rivalry escalates to a new level when Nellie invites the schoolgirls to a Saturday party.

It is Mary and Laura's first party, and they are shy and curious. Ma sends them off with a validation in terms of the natural world: "You look sweet and pretty as posies" (161). Dressed in their same worn Sunday dresses, freshly ironed, the girls go to the Olesons' apartment behind the store. It is as if they are stepping into a showroom of late nineteenth-century domestic merchandise, all the machine-made goods desired by upwardly mobile Americans who are aiming for a secure place in the middle class. "Laura had never seen such a fine room. . . . The whole floor was covered with some kind of heavy cloth that felt rough under Laura's bare feet. It was brown and green, with red and yellow scrolls all over it. . . . The table and chairs were of a yellow wood that shone like glass, and their legs were perfectly round. There were colored pictures on the walls" (161).

Accustomed to the bare floors and handmade furniture of her own home, Laura is awed by ingrain carpet, machine-turned furniture, and chromo-lithographs, as well as the "china" washbowl set and lace curtains that she sees in other rooms. The only familiar thing she sees is a duplicate of the Ingalls family's most "modern" possession: "a cookstove . . . like Ma's new one." Like an awed spectator at an elaborate show, Laura wants only "to be still and look at things" (161–62).

But Mrs. Oleson, presiding over the party, insists that the children must *engage* with things: "Now, Nellie, bring out your playthings" (162). Nellie withholds her own precious toys, saying that the guests can play with her brother's toys instead. All the girls are delighted by Willie's tin soldiers, jumping jack, and, especially, a Noah's ark. It "was the most wonderful thing that Laura had ever seen. . . . There were zebras and elephants and tigers and horses; all kinds of animals, just as if the picture had come out of the paper-covered Bible at home" (163). Again Laura makes connections between books and objects, texts for her to read. But, reading these toys, she can find no representations of herself; Willie's playthings comprise a world of animals and men.

"Then Nellie walked among them, saying, 'You can look at my doll'" (163). Nellie displays first a porcelain-headed doll and then a newer, more fashionable wax doll of extraordinary verisimilitude. With "real" hair, "tiny white teeth" and eyes that "opened wide," this doll even speaks at Nellie's cruel command: "She punched the doll's stomach hard with her fist, and the poor doll cried out, 'Mamma!'" In the wax doll, beautifully dressed in blue silk with "real little panties" and "real little blue leather slippers," Laura sees a representation of a female child, like herself, in this bewildering, rich new world of merchandise. Involuntarily, she makes a gesture toward this wonderful thing:

> All this time Laura had not said a word. She couldn't. She did not think of actually touching that marvellous doll, but without meaning to, her finger reached out toward the blue silk.
>
> "Don't you touch her!" Nellie screeched. "You keep your hands off my doll, Laura Ingalls!"
>
> She snatched the doll against her and turned her back. (166–67)

Laura has been seduced into a world of buyable things; the Olesons, a storekeeping family, have what must seem to Laura unlimited access to goods. In the doll, she reads a story she knows well: that of a girl responding to her mother's command. Laura makes a tentative gesture to intervene, to take her place in that story of women and merchandise—a story that the Little House series, as it continues, will inscribe.

But Nellie reminds Laura of the boundaries that commodities enforce. Laura is a "country girl," as Nellie insistently reminds her; she and Mary play with homemade rag dolls. Nellie's wax doll, by contrast, is an object of urban fashion, designed to introduce little girls to a vast vocabulary of wearable goods that they may aspire to possess—but only if they can pay for the merchandise. At Nellie's outburst, Laura is so humiliated that she leaves the group to sit alone.

When Mrs. Oleson finds the solitary child, she offers her more objects: two books. One is "a little magazine, all for children"; the other is an illustrated Mother Goose. "Laura had not known there were such wonderful books in the world. On every page of that book there was a picture and a rhyme. Laura could read some of them. She forgot all about the party" (167).

For me and my childhood peers, this party scene was one of the most memorable in the Little House series. (For years I desired a doll like Nellie Oleson's—perhaps I still do.) For the first time, the Ingalls sisters glimpse the full, proliferating panoply of *goods* available in their time. They are urged to touch, to play, to eat (later, Mrs. Oleson serves frosted birthday cake and lemonade, new and luxurious foods to Laura and Mary). But simultaneously and paradoxically, they are reminded of the absolute privilege of private ownership; however intense her desire, Laura cannot even touch Nellie's doll.

Children's books and magazines are the only commodity in the Oleson household that Laura can wholeheartedly enjoy. For a child reader especially, Laura's absorbed immersion in the Mother Goose book may resemble her or his own experience of being absorbed in *On the Banks of Plum Creek*. We are reminded, too, of something Wilder and Lane knew very well: that publications for children are an increasingly important item on the commodity market (and the most lucrative commodity that Laura Ingalls Wilder ever marketed).

When Ma hears "all about the party" from her daughters, she plans a counterritual, instructing Laura and Mary to invite "Nellie Oleson and the others to a party here" (168). As opposed to the ostentatious town party, the Ingallses' equally instructive country party emphasizes preconsumer values. Ma's housekeeping is spotless; her "pink-edged curtains," handmade from recycled fabric, "were freshly crisp and white" (169). Wildflowers adorn the table, and the didactic refreshments are fresh milk and crisp, unsweetened "vanity cakes" prepared by Ma.[4] When Nellie asks, "Where are your dolls?" Laura withholds her handmade toy, "darling rag Charlotte" (172). Instead, determined to "get even" with her rival, Laura leads Nellie, resplendent in new town clothes, to her own country playground: the creek.

Wading in the creek, Nellie enters the natural realm Laura has been learning about since they moved to Minnesota. Just as Nellie withheld her possessions from Laura, Laura refuses to share her knowledge of the creek with Nellie. Instead, she deceives her, taunting her with the spectre of a fierce crab that lives under a rock, and maneuvers Nellie into the muddy water where leeches lurk. (Laura knows this from experience; she once had a disgusting but harmless encounter with the leeches herself.) Cowering, wet and bedraggled, Nellie emerges from Plum Creek with leeches on her legs. Laura and her girlfriends laugh as Nellie jumps up and down in disgust and fury. At the creek Nellie's property is irrelevant, perhaps even an impediment; her elaborate clothes make her less mobile than the other girls. She has no experience reading the natural world, so she is dependent on Laura's duplicitous instructions. Like anyone else, she is vulnerable to indignity and danger, in this case the bloodsuckers. Laura is deeply gratified by this outcome; on her own grounds she has triumphed over Nellie. "Deep down inside her Laura felt satisfied" (176). This too is a memorable scene for children, who usually find Nellie's humiliation unilaterally gratifying.

The "Town Party" and "Country Party" chapters are like parables, laying out two opposing and separate sets of values. On one level, the country values seem to triumph. But for a late-nineteenth-century child and for twentieth-century authors and readers, it cannot be that simple. In a mode more complex than the parable, Laura Ingalls must work out her own relations to the world of merchandise; she cannot permanently choose the natural world of the creek over the convolutions of an increasingly materialistic contemporary culture. Even Ma, whose very cooking is a warning against the "vanity" of the marketplace, will also teach her daughters how to buy things. And increasingly, the Ingalls daughters will become *both* country and town girls. For them as for twentieth-century rural Americans like Laura Ingalls Wilder, much of their relation to an increasingly urbanized national culture will be facilitated by the new techniques of mass marketing and by their reading—books, magazines, and catalogs will introduce them to new customs and products and will help them to buy.[5] Thus Nellie Oleson does not disappear from the Little House series after her humiliation on the banks of Plum Creek. Instead, she becomes a recurring character, right through the last book. To the end, she speaks for greed and competition. By the last book, however, her preferred commodities are men, and she is Laura Ingalls's major would-be rival for Almanzo Wilder.

As Laura's new experiences indicate, in many ways *Plum Creek* and the four following Little House books comprise an anecdotal history of domestic consumption behavior on the nineteenth-century frontier. Jean Gordon and Jan McArthur have written about the changes in U.S. women's habits of domestic consumption from 1800 to 1920, a period that spans the lives of several generations of Ingalls and Wilder women. Before 1830, they argue, most Americans practiced "traditional consumption," which "has as its goal the preservation of a stable way of life" and "takes place within clearly defined, stable classes and communities of people. Families seek to acquire what is appropriate for their class and group." In accordance with such goals, when Ma Ingalls hears about the egregious display at Nellie Oleson's birthday party, she does not attempt to produce a similar profusion of goods for her daughters' guests. Instead, she sets forth the things the Ingalls family can afford, which are mostly homemade. Ma has taken little part in choosing the purchased domestic goods that the Ingallses own. Like the stove, they have been chosen by Pa alone, and he has made the decisions about how he will pay for them. This was typical, Gordon and McArthur say: "The most important fact concerning women's consumption behavior within a traditional context was that it was severely restricted. . . . If a wife had any influence in what was bought it was usually through persuasion rather than by exercising what was an acknowledged right. . . . [Usually, a married woman's] consumption choices were confined to her personal clothing" (29–30).

In the first Little House book, Charles Ingalls teases his wife by threatening to strip her of the right to make these crucial decisions about clothing for herself. At the store, he insists that she have fabric for a new apron, although she protests that she doesn't "really need it." "But Pa laughed and said she must pick it out, or he would get her the turkey red piece with the big yellow pattern. Ma smiled and flushed pink, and she picked out a pattern of rosebuds and leaves on a soft, fawn-colored ground" (LHBW 170). Clearly a complicated dynamic is at work here. Although he is strapped for funds and can afford only enough inexpensive cloth to make an apron—not a dress—for his wife, Charles Ingalls makes the purchase into a major opportunity to exercise *his* will publicly. He allows Caroline Ingalls no say in decisions about how the funds will be spent (perhaps she would prefer knitting wool, or a favorite food?), and he playfully threatens to intrude into the one area where she is allowed to make consumer decisions, the choice of the fabrics she will sew and wear. Even from young Laura's perspective, the fawn-colored calico is an important expression of her mother's taste and character.

The historic period of traditional consumption was followed—in the 1870s and 1880s, the time in which the Little House books are set—by accelerated and expanded consumption, facilitated by such marketing innovations as mail order catalogs and widely available credit. During this period of "conspicuous consumption" first described by Thorstein Veblen, the ideal occupation of middle-class women was often considered to be the purchase and display of domestic objects that would elevate and/or confirm their social status and that of their families.[6]

In *Plum Creek* the Olesons are clearly attempting to establish themselves by this sort of consumption. The dangerous consequences of such behavior are apparent when the family reappears in a later book; they have lost the store and all their money, and Nellie's pretty clothes are now contributed by charities. As we have seen, Ma cautions her daughters against such behavior. Yet she displays some understandable vestiges of it herself. She fears her husband's willingness to enter into crushing credit arrangements, as when he buys the machine-made materials for a new house on Plum Creek, as well as the "marvellous stove," on the promise of a wheat crop that never actually materializes. But she is always eager for the domestic improvements that will increase the status, as well as the comfort, of the rudimentary dwellings her husband erects. Ma wants glass windows, painted walls, and multiple rooms in her Little Houses. As a married woman born before 1850, she is the most vulnerable consumer in the Ingalls family, committed to traditional consumption patterns and yet constrained by them. In the later books, as she gains access to contemporary women's periodicals of the 1870s and 1880s, she is exposed to the status-seeking consumer behavior of other U.S. women and must feel some desire to emulate it. In the next-to-last book, Ma encourages Laura to buy a set of decorated calling cards (the latest fad), saying, "we want you to have the pleasures of other girls of your age" (LTP 196)—and to practice consumer behavior that will confirm the family's social class.[7] The character of Ma is closely modeled on the actual Caroline Quiner Ingalls, who imperiled her own social class when she "married down" to Charles Ingalls. This "fashionable" young woman was the daughter of a Connecticut dressmaker who later emigrated west and a man who attended Yale University. Ma Ingalls's occasions for buying are precious and few; they are important opportunities to preserve her own class identity for herself and her daughters.

Another constant influence on the writing of the Little House books was the economic pressure of the Great Depression. The Depression made radical changes in the spending patterns of many U.S. families, including the Wilders and their daughter. (During this period Grace Ingalls Dow, Wilder's youngest sister, wrote from South Dakota that she and her farmer husband were destitute; Wilder and Lane did what they could to assist them.) In the early twentieth century, women consumers had been encouraged to invest in new household technology, such as electrical appliances. Now they revived earlier consumption practices. "The old saying 'Use it up, wear it out, make it do, or do without' " was taken up by many middle-class women in the 1930s, according to historian Susan Ware (2).[8] The saying well describes Ma Ingalls's housekeeping practices, which must have seemed newly sensible and pertinent to 1930s readers, and her modest buying habits and resistance of overextended credit. Steven Mintz and Susan Kellogg note that many 1930s-era families "sought to cope by adopting more labor-intensive household practices, including planting gardens, canning foods, making clothing, and doing their own household repairs" (137)—all practices that were familiar to the Ingalls family, especially Ma. Mintz and Kellogg also suggest that the configuration of much U.S. family life was altered by the changes in consumption habits enforced by the Depression:

> The depression sharply curtailed activities outside the home and forced families to pool their resources and find comfort in each other. Divorce rates actually declined during the depression, and in popular magazines a new emphasis on familial "comradeship, understanding, affection, sympathy, facilitation, accommodation, integration [and] cooperation" was apparent. Families began to play new games like Monopoly together and to listen to the radio or to go to the movies together. As a Muncie, Indiana, newspaper editorialized, "Many a family that has lost its car has found its soul." (136)

In such a climate, it is easy to see why the Little House books immediately found enthusiastic readers and buyers among adults as well as children. They reinforced and promoted the consumption patterns that many families were compelled to practice: minimal buying, limited travel, family entertainment at home. But the books did not make the mistake of dismissing or minimalizing the importance of things and consumption—and thus they met the needs of buyers who were also purchasing another 1930s product that was shared by parents and children: the Monopoly game, which—like the Little House books—allowed players of all ages to share in the romance and adventure of buying.

With *Plum Creek* the Little House series began to be a narrative of girls who were players in a compelling and pervasive game of things. Now Laura and Mary are actively reading and choosing, getting and spending, within the parameters of a white settlers' culture on the Great Plains. Telling that story, Wilder and Lane—veteran consumers themselves—drew on more than a century of U.S. women's consumption history.

For example, Laura's first visit to a store occurs in *Big Woods,* when Ma and the girls accompany Pa when he goes to town to barter his furs. This is a scene of traditional consumption; Laura, who has never been to town before, is overwhelmed by the store's profusion ("she had not known there were so many things in the world"). When Ma makes a modest selection of fabrics, Laura cannot imagine participating in such a demanding pursuit: "there were so many of them! Laura did not know how Ma could ever choose" (168–69). The storekeeper gives Mary and Laura each a heart-shaped piece of candy with "printing" on it; Ma must read the mottoes to the girls. Obviously, buying requires reading skills, and Laura will not learn to read for three more years. She is not yet ready to negotiate the world of the store, and this is confirmed later that day when, waiting for Pa, she crams her pocket so full of pretty lake pebbles that it rips out of her dress. Even at five, she is presented with a small, telling parable about the dangers of trying to take home more things than she can carry. Traditional, conservative consumption is still the major mode of the Ingalls family's stable life in the Big Woods.

On Plum Creek the Ingallses are no richer than they were in the Big Woods, but they are much more concerned with confirming their status as settled and successful farmers (which they never fully are) by their buying decisions, such as a new house with glass windows, china doorknobs, and a cast-iron stove. The girls are included in this; the slate, for example, was not a part of their mother's traditional equipment for learning to write but is a new pedagogical innovation that they must have if they are to hold their own in classroom culture. In fact, *Plum Creek* includes more scenes of instruction in stores than in schools.

As much recent scholarship has confirmed, textiles were a major arena of expression for nineteenth-century U.S. women, as well as objects of constant, ongoing labor.[9] Ma Ingalls knits and sews; she makes all her family's clothing and such household items as bedding and curtains; in the Big Woods she even weaves straw hats. But in the years after 1870 that the Little House series spans, she *does not* grow and prepare fibers or spin, dye, and weave her own cloth (as Almanzo Wilder's mother did in *Farmer Boy*). By the 1870s a profusion of inexpensive, sometimes durable machine-made fabrics had flooded U.S. markets, reaching even small frontier stores like those the Ingalls family patronizes. As Betty J. Mills observes, "it was no longer necessary or prudent to spend time with hand weaving. Yard goods were increasingly available at village mercantiles" (43). Choosing from this new profusion of goods became a key skill for women, especially those who did their own sewing, like Caroline Ingalls (and later, her daughters). Thus the choice of fabrics and the skills and aesthetic decisions involved in making them up into clothes become major motifs of the Little House series. Through such decisions, girls and women could maintain their links to the traditional textile skills by which nineteenth-century women had confirmed their domestic faculty and could also qualify themselves as practiced, discerning household consumers. Additionally, they could affirm and even raise their class status; thus Mary's college wardrobe and Laura's trousseau are freighted subjects. At best, these purchases were also opportunities for personal gratification. Later, as a young schoolteacher, Laura chooses stylish hats that give her such pleasure, as well as gifts for her family.

Since the beginning of *Plum Creek*, Pa has been promising Laura "new dresses" when the wheat crop succeeds. However, two seasons pass and Pa has to spend several months laboring in another state before he and Ma can afford to take their girls to the store for modest replenishing of their wardrobes. They make the most of this event as a scene of instruction, and the girls learn to think of consumption as a multileveled experience of enormous excitement and import. This time they are not just onlookers. When it is time to choose fabric for their first new dresses in years, Ma includes the girls in the decision-making process:

> "What do you think of this golden-brown flannel, Laura?" Ma asked.
> Laura could not speak. Mr. Fitch [the storekeeper] said, "I guarantee it will wear well."

Ma laid some narrow red braid across the golden brown, saying, "I think three rows of this braid. . . . What do you think, Laura? Would that be pretty?"

"Oh yes, Ma!" Laura said. She looked up, and her eyes and Pa's bright blue eyes danced together.

"Get it, Caroline," said Pa. . . .

Then Mary must have a new dress, but she did not like anything there. So they all crossed the street to Mr. Oleson's store. There they found dark blue flannel and narrow gilt braid, which was just what Mary wanted. (242)

Combining fabrics and trimmings, with their mother's guidance, the girls are learning to use the marketplace as a scene of aesthetic decisions ("Would that be pretty?") as they begin to package themselves in clothes they have helped to design. Mary, the older girl, also learns how to survey the range of choices in more than one store and to participate in the dynamics of supply and demand by her discriminating choice. The selection of gilt braid trim for a dress the child will wear to school suggests that display is important to her, as well, and her parents confirm that choice. Also, this buying perpetuates the romance between Laura and her father; the intense look that passes between them confirms that they both delight in Pa's purchasing power, which can fulfill Laura's desires.

One of the great appeals of the Little House books, especially for young readers, is that they frankly acknowledge what all children know: that such buying occasions are *not* trivial. Instead, these books take seriously the shopping decisions by which most of us work out the relation between our cultures' prescriptions about what we *must* buy and our sense of self-determination and individual expression.

Beginning with *Plum Creek* the Little House series explores the Ingalls daughters' educations as female consumers in relation to the Ingallses' three major domestic purchases in the series, which are also arguably three of the most importantly life-altering items offered for sale to housekeeping women in the nineteenth-century United States: a cast-iron stove, a sewing machine, and a parlor organ. These three purchases allow Wilder and Lane to explore the Ingalls women's relation to late nineteenth century advances of technology and marketing. Getting and spending, Laura discovers the difficulties of maintaining her self-possession and self-determination while exercising the pressures and pleasures of consumption.

Ruth Schwartz Cowan writes that the cast-iron stove was probably "the single most important domestic symbol of the nineteenth century" (54). In the course of the century, most U.S. women, like Caroline Ingalls, shifted from hearth cooking to stove cooking. An open, visible hearth fire had long been the traditional symbol of home and domesticity. In the stove, fire was contained and semiconcealed. Many observers of nineteenth-century U.S. culture found this change portentous. Nathaniel Hawthorne, for example, bemoaned the coming of the cast-iron stove as a major upheaval in "social intercourse" that threatened the very existence of "domestic life" ("Fire Worship," quoted in Brewer 47). As Priscilla J. Brewer has observed, the stove raised important questions: "Once stoves had become commonplace, observers began to ask what they symbolized. Was the cookstove a sign that the ideological barrier between home and world [an underlying premise of the separate spheres paradigm that flourished at mid-century] was more permeable than Americans had thought?" (35).

Despite conservative (male) misgivings such as Hawthorne's, most nineteenth-century U.S. women were eager to buy and use cast-iron stoves; they significantly eased the labor of preparing food, formerly done at "large and often dangerous open fireplaces" (Brewer 35). Stove designs were constantly changed and updated throughout the century; those changes were registered and patented. The patent number Mary read when she first saw Ma's new cookstove emphasizes the market importance of the new stove in the Little House; it brings the process of U.S. government regulation to the private domestic practices of Ma's cooking. As Brewer has noted, "the stove . . . symbolizes the tension that persisted between home and world throughout the nineteenth century" (54).

Ma is the most conservative member of the Ingalls family. As we have seen, she is rooted in the home labor economy of earlier nineteenth-century housekeeping and is the family's most reluctant consumer. Thus she is dubious at first about the new stove, seeming to sense that it puts her household in a newly close relation with the outside world of government and goods. Although normally a confident cook, she says, "My! . . . I don't know if I dare try to get dinner on such a big, beautiful stove!" Since Pa made Laura and Mary his accomplices in the surprise of the stove, they become, in an unusual reversal, their mother's teachers; Ma "lifted the lids as Laura showed her, she watched while Mary worked the draught" (120).

This important scene in *Plum Creek* clearly suggests that the Ingalls daughters will eventually outdistance their mother as consumers in the late nineteenth century. They will come of age in a world where the doctrine of separate spheres no longer prevails and will have to work out a more mobile, flexible, permeable relation between "home" and "world." In fact, for Wilder and Lane, the writing and marketing of the Little House books was a way of working out that relationship. In *Plum Creek* these issues are broached when the Ingalls family buys a cast-iron stove.

The next major purchase, the sewing machine, occurs nearly ten years later, when the Ingallses are homesteading in Dakota Territory. Before the Civil War, the stove had been the "one prevalent 'consumer durable'" in most U.S. households, as it was in the Ingalls household, and it "cost very little compared to a sewing machine, with its many precisely made moving parts." The sewing machine was marketed through the first "patent pool" and became one of the great marketing successes of the later nineteenth century because Singer and Clark invented the installment plan as a means to sell it (Strasser 1982, 138–39).

The Ingallses' "shiny new" sewing machine is another of Pa's surprises. Again he casts himself as an emissary between his wife and daughters' needs and the offerings of the marketplace. "A long time ago . . . a tone in Ma's voice when she spoke of a sewing machine had made Laura think that she wanted one. Pa had remembered that." Both husband and daughter have caught Ma's subtle signal of desire. But only Pa has the means and mobility to act on that signal. Again he heartily enjoys his purchase, and when Ma asks vaguely, "But how could you?" he replies, "I had to sell a cow anyway" (THGY 241). (Most sewing machines were bought on credit, so it is possible that Pa has again entered into a credit arrangement.)

Ma presumably learned to sew by personal, intimate instruction and example, as she taught her own daughters. (The actual Caroline Quiner Ingalls's mother was a professional dressmaker.)[10] Once the "beautiful" new sewing machine is in the house, she becomes a pupil in a less traditional medium, studying the instruction book for a week to learn to "run the machine" (250) before beginning a dress for Laura. However conservative her values may otherwise seem, Ma displays no nostalgia for the old skills of hand sewing. The style she chooses for Laura's dress spotlights machine stitching, instead of concealing it, with row after row of tucking. Ma is delighted with the results: "I don't know how we ever got along without that sewing machine. It does the work so easily. . . . And such beautiful stitching. The best of seamstresses could not possibly equal it by hand"

(251). Later, when Laura proposes to save time and tedium by stitching her wedding sheets on the machine, Ma acquiesces: "Our grandmothers would turn in their graves, but after all, these are modern times" (275).

In a 1919 *Missouri Ruralist* essay, Wilder looked back on her own life as a farm housekeeper and noted the differences from her mother's life and work. Relaxing after dinner, she "looked down at the magazine in my hand and remembered how my mother was always sewing or knitting by the evening lamp. I realized that I had never done so except now and then in cases of emergency" ("It Depends on How You Look at It," *Sampler* 112). Purchases of household technology undoubtedly facilitated Wilder's reading and writing; eventually they may have helped to make the writing of the Little House series possible. An important premise of the Country Life movement that flourished in the early twentieth century was that both farm men's and women's work would be eased by modern equipment. However, "most women did not yet possess the appropriate equipment," although male members of their families often did (Jellison 1). By valorizing Charles Ingalls's purchase of a stove and sewing machine, Wilder and Lane emphasized the necessity of technological support for women's work, a key issue for twentieth-century rural women. The important purchase of the sewing machine, which was widely and affordably marketed to modest-income households like that of the Ingalls family, brings some of the benefits of "modern times" to Laura and her mother, who despise the painstaking work of hand sewing. But it is still Pa who negotiates for them in the marketplace and brings the benefits of technology inside their domestic circle.

A third important purchase, a hundred-dollar parlor organ, requires Laura's entire salary—seventy-five dollars—from her second and last term of teaching. In this case, because of her new earning capacity, Laura has more say. But Pa still surveys the marketplace, learns that the organ is available, tries it out, and proposes the purchase to Laura, who gladly agrees to it, sight unseen.[11] The organ is for Mary, now blind and away at college in Iowa, so that she may "keep up her music" at home.

This purchase, unlike the others, makes no major alterations in the domestic work of the Ingalls women, although its elaborate fretwork probably requires tedious dusting. No one but Mary plays the organ, and she is home only a few weeks a year. Instead, this organ is an investment in "feminized" U.S. culture and in white, middle-class notions of the "feminine" that were being exported from the East to Dakota Territory. According to Kenneth Ames, playing such an organ was considered especially prestigious by upwardly mobile Americans in the middle and lower classes, as an indication of affluence, "an attribute of ladydom" and a "means for the display of feminine accomplishments." The organ "became a virtual symbol of civilization and community for . . . Americans at the edge of the frontier." It was also a triumph of packaging inexpensive works in an ornate, elaborate case, selling for less than half the cost of a piano. With its high back, ornamental shelves, brackets, and machine-executed decorative woodwork, the organ was an opportunity for "those with limited means and small spaces" to combine "musical and display functions" (1984, 29–32, 41). Such was the case with the Ingalls instrument; Wilder devotes two paragraphs of densely detailed description to the "beautiful organ."

Ames argues that the acquisition of a parlor organ, a large item of heavy cultural baggage, was likely to be a transforming event in the owners' lives. "The purchase of such a major item facilitated . . . a redefinition of self" and brought "a change in status" and "a whole range of new opportunities" (Ames 1992; 159). Such changes seem to occur for the Ingalls family. Pa builds a new room onto the claim shanty to accommodate the organ, and the new room raises the status of the family's dwelling, Ma decrees: "We must not call this a claim shanty any more. . . . It is a real house now, with four rooms" (THGY, 162–63). Organs performed this certifying function for many American families in the West; they frequently appear in formally posed commemorative family portraits, and in one famous Solomon Butcher photograph, the organ has been dragged outside to prove that, although this Nebraska family still inhabited an ignominious sod dwelling, they possessed an essential accoutrement of middle-class feminine values.[12]

Through the acquisition of the cast-iron stove, sewing machine, and parlor organ—as well as other purchases—the Ingalls sisters develop their sense of cultural possibility; they learn about what girls and women can buy and do and be on the Great Plains frontier. Purchasing is a complex and necessary part of their education. Douglas and Isherwood propose, "instead of supposing that goods are primarily needed for subsistence plus competitive display, let us assume that they are needed for making visible and stable the categories of culture" (59). The stove, sewing machine, and organ all confirm—and perhaps elevate—the Ingallses' cultural situation. Since Laura was a small child, Ma has been trying to keep her skin pale and her head covered with a sunbonnet or hat so that she will not appear "brown as an Indian" and slip into a cultural/racial category that Ma considers taboo. As the four Ingalls daughters grow older and begin to leave home for school, jobs, college, and marriage, it seems increasingly important that they be connected to the correct things, which will place them in the "right" cultural categories even when they are far from the confirming influence of the Little House. The perils of this process are first and especially apparent in the story of the oldest daughter, Mary.

In "Grandpa's Fiddle," Rose Wilder Lane summarized the life of her Aunt Mary Ingalls, whom she knew well as a young child, before the Wilder family left De Smet for Mansfield.

> Aunt Mary. . . . had scarlet fever as a child, and it left her blind. Grandpa and Grandma never quite got over it. She was their oldest, and so beautiful and so smart. They'd had great hopes for her. They wanted her to be a school teacher. She was the smartest of the family, everyone said so, and she loved books and studying and even as a little child she had great ambitions and they were all ambitious for her. But she went blind, and that ended everything. In a way, it was an ending for Grandpa and Grandma, too. Mama told me once that they were never quite the same after Mary went blind. (*Sampler* 61)

Interestingly, this account (never published in Wilder's and Lane's lifetimes) is *not* the story of Mary that Wilder and Lane wrote in the Little House books. Certainly Mary's blindness (which came on in Minnesota, after the ending of *Plum Creek* and before the next book begins) was a grief for the fictional Ingalls family, and certainly the fictional Mary is a bright girl, like Laura, and far more docile and studious than her younger sister. Mary's "good girl" qualities often infuriate Laura. In *Big Woods*, after the girls' exciting first trip to town, Laura is dirty and tear-stained, with a torn dress and a lap full of pebbles. She thinks, with chagrin,

> Nothing like that ever happened to Mary. Mary was a good little girl who always kept her dress clean and neat and minded her manners. Mary had lovely golden curls. . . .
>
> Mary looked very good and sweet, unrumpled and clean, sitting on the board beside Laura. Laura did not think it was fair.
>
> But it had been a wonderful day, the most wonderful day in her whole life. She thought about the beautiful lake, and the town she had seen, and the big store full of so many things. (175)

Mary is presented, from Laura's point of view, as the child who always follows the rules. We do not know from the Little House books how such a child might feel or what she might want. From the reader's point of view, Laura must seem the gifted child here, for—with her energy, appetite, and curiosity—she has made the trip to town into "a wonderful day." Inscrutable Mary, on the other hand, always seems to respect cultural boundaries. In *Plum Creek*, for instance, when Pa tries to teach the girls to keep out of the deep creek water by ducking them, "Mary was a good girl after one ducking," although "Laura was ducked many times" (26). Later, when the girls must wear corsets to mold their bodies into fashionable forms, Mary follows Ma's advice and wears hers all night, but Laura cannot. "Always before she could get to sleep, she had to take off her corsets" (LTP 94). Obviously, Laura has the desire and capacity for "boundary flexibility" that Jean Wyatt discusses as an essential component of creative process (17–18); this foreshadows Wilder's adult life as a writer. If Mary has any such capacity, it is seldom indicated by Wilder and Lane's narrative, especially in the earlier books. The Little House series was Laura Ingalls Wilder's opportunity to make her fictional self the center of the Ingalls family romance. In some ways Mary is the casualty of that project; the first five novels give us little hint of the intelligent, ambitious, energetic girl that Lane's account suggests. Instead, Mary is presented as a girl who always does, has, and is the predictable *right thing*. Even before the sad accident of her blinding, Mary is becoming a female who cannot see for herself.

Of all the Ingalls daughters, Mary is most endangered by the process of commodification. As an adolescent, unlike her mobile, seeing sister Laura, she cannot earn and buy. Instead, she becomes the Ingalls family's single largest and most strapping investment, as they struggle to find the means to send her to a college for the blind, in Iowa, for seven years.[13]

In *Little Town on the Prairie*, Laura's first worries about her own earning powers are connected to her sense that she should be contributing financially to Mary's needs. Laura's entire salary from her first job, nine dollars for six weeks of sewing shirts, goes for materials for one "best" dress and hat for Mary. Every item of Mary's wardrobe, from the hand-stitched underwear to the knitted silk mitts, is described in careful detail, in a passage that extends over eight pages. The "best" dress is the climax of Ma and Laura's work. At its final fitting, the bodice, which fitted perfectly the previous week, is suddenly too tight. " 'Don't breathe, Mary! Don't breathe!' Laura said frantically, and quickly she unbuttoned the straining buttons." The concern here is for the *dress*. Somehow, breathing or not, Mary must be fitted into it. This is accomplished by further tightening Mary's corset strings. "When Mary held her breath again and Laura pulled tight the corset strings, the bodice buttoned, and it fitted beautifully" (LTP 93).

When Laura sees Mary in the finished dress, handstitched by Ma, she is overcome by her "stylish" appearance. " 'Oh Mary,' Laura said, 'You look exactly as if you'd stepped out of a fashion plate' " (LTP 96). Laura sees her sister as a living embodiment of a commercial medium, the magazine "fashion plate" that sold current clothing styles to farflung consumers like the Ingalls women. For a moment, at least, Mary has become a function of the marketplace. Carefully, anxiously, her mother and sister have shopped for the materials from which they have made her wardrobe, gleaning fashion tips from dressmakers, merchants, and the single year-old *Godey's Lady's Book* to which they have access. Somehow, Mary's living, breathing body *must* fit within the boundaries of this dress, in which so much has been invested.

At the climax of this final fitting of a woolen dress on a hot summer day, every detail of Mary's "best" ensemble is in place, and her mother and sisters take a long (two pages) look:

> They all stood back to admire. The gored skirt of brown cashmere was smooth and rather tight in front, but gathered full around the sides and back, so that it would be ample for hoops. In front it touched the floor evenly, in back it swept into a graceful short train that swished when Mary turned. . . .
>
> The overskirt was of the brown-and-blue plaid. It was shirred in front, it was draped up at the sides to show more of the skirt beneath, and at the back it fell in rich, full puffs, caught up above the flounced train.
>
> Above all this, Mary's waist rose slim in the tight, smooth bodice. The neat little buttons ran up to the soft white lace cascading under Mary's chin. The brown cashmere was smooth as paint over her sloping shoulders. . . . A shirring of the plaid curved around them, and the wide wrists fell open, showing a lining of white lace ruffles that set off Mary's slender hands.
>
> Mary was beautiful in that beautiful dress. Her hair was silkier and more golden than the golden silk threads in the plaid. Her blind eyes were bluer than the blue in it. Her cheeks were pink, and her figure was so stylish. (94–96)

I have quoted this passage at length because its language is so extraordinary, especially in a book for children. First, the dense terminology of clothing construction assumes considerable knowledge of sewing, as well as of women's clothing and underclothing. Lane and Wilder, who both sewed from early childhood and all through their adult lives, assumed that readers would know the meaning of "shirring," "gores," "flounce," and other such specialized terms, *and* that they would be interested in every detail of this startlingly elaborate costume.[14] Wilder said that she wrote to help children understand "the meaning of things," and clearly Mary's dress is one of the significant things she intends to explicate.

As a child reading the Little House books, I was well hooked by the time I got to this and other long descriptions of clothing in the last two volumes. Furthermore, I liked clothes, my mother sewed for me, and I was laboriously learning simple sewing myself in a 4-H class, so I was better versed than most children would be today in the terminology of dressmaking. Nevertheless, when I read the description of Mary in her best dress, I felt deeply uneasy and uncertain, in ways that I tried to dismiss as plain (and unaccustomed) boredom. Are clothes really *that* important, I wondered. And what has happened to Mary? In all this long passage, the dress seems to have more volition than Mary does. *It* touches the floor, *it* sweeps back; *buttons* run and *lace* cascades. All Mary can do is turn, like an unseeing mannequin. She is anatomized into body parts: waist, chin, hands, hair, and "blind eyes." The smooth cashmere adheres to her shoulders like *paint* on an object. All of this adds up to an admirable image of fashion, "so stylish." But the long description offers no indication that intelligent Mary, who is leaving the security of her home because she wants to learn and to grow, has a mind or a will. Even Laura, who has been Mary's closest companion since her birth, sees her sister as a "fashion plate" whose flawlessly conventionalized appearance will confirm her family's taste and status: "there just can't be, one single girl in college who can hold a candle to you" (96).

Mary, who is normally adept at verbal sparring with Laura, is nearly overcome by this unaccustomed praise. Unable to see and judge and think for herself, she turns to her mother for help:

> "Do I really look so well, Ma?" Mary asked timidly, and she flushed pinker.
>
> For once Ma did not guard against vanity. "Yes, Mary, you do," she said. "You are not only as stylish as can be, you are beautiful. No matter where you go, you will be a pleasure to every eye that sees you. And, I am thankful to say, you may be sure your clothes are equal to any occasion."
>
> They could not look at her longer. She was almost fainting from the heat, in that woolen dress. They laid it carefully away, done at last, and a great success. (96)

Ma's usual practice is to emphasize conduct above appearance, admonishing her daughters that "pretty is as pretty does." But now she too conspires in the objectification of her beloved eldest daughter, with whom she has always had a special bond. Mary is "stylish" and "beautiful," her mother confirms. And she is the ultimate object of a gaze she cannot return, "a pleasure to every eye." Whether or not Mary *herself* is "equal to any occasion," Ma assures her that her *clothes* are. And the constant emphasis on sight and appearances devalues blind Mary's own perceptions, further dehumanizing her. Through all the intense work of buying, designing, and sewing for Mary, work that requires almost slavish attention to the ever-changing nuances of fashion, Ma has arrived at a state where she can only validate her needy child as an object. No wonder that this scene ends with Mary's "almost fainting." Her very consciousness is in grave danger. Wilder and Lane's text never acknowledges that danger directly; for now, it seems to take for granted the inevitability of Mary's plight. A great material "success" has been achieved in the triumphal dress; Mary's sole function is to provide a suitable form for its display.

Much of the remaining story of Mary is played out on the distant stage of the school for the blind in Vinton, Iowa, where Ma and Pa take her when she is about seventeen. Once her clothes are packed in the new trunk, Mary is complexly portrayed in the hours before her departure. She is plausibly sensitive, thoughtful, and worried about the drain of her needs on the family's resources. She's also eager and curious about what lies ahead of her: "I wonder if the sky and the sunsets are different in Iowa?" And she admits to her sister, "'Oh, Laura, I have never been away from home before. I don't know what I'll do.' . . . She was trembling all over. . . . 'I'm not scared. I won't *be* scared,' Mary insisted. 'But I will be lonesome'" (LTP 112–13). It seems almost impossible to reconcile this determined, perceptive young woman with the barely conscious, "stylish" figure in the best dress.

Such a reconciliation does occur, but we learn of it only obliquely, on the two brief visits home that Mary makes over the next three years, before the series ends. If I could add another volume to the Little House series, I would make it an elaboration of Mary's story (a no more unlikely project than *Farmer Boy!*), which would explore her seven years at college and her return to live out her life in her parents' house in De Smet. (The actual Mary Ingalls died at 63, in 1928.) As a subtext, that story is only lightly indicated in the Little House series. Away from the Little House, Mary is apparently able to work out an intelligent, active relationship with the world of things.

On one level, the actual Ingalls family may have despaired when Mary became blind, and thus projected the message that Rose Wilder picked up in early childhood: that Mary's blindness "ended everything." But in the writing of the Little House books, Wilder and Lane suggested the outlines of a more complicated, continuing story. In that version, even before going to college, Mary seems to have experienced a spiritual awakening that allows her to look back on her childhood "good girl" persona as self-absorbed and trivial. She tells Laura, "I wasn't really wanting to be good. I was showing off." Now, she says, "I don't believe we ought to think so much about ourselves, about whether we are good or bad. . . . I don't know how to say what I mean very well. But—it isn't so much thinking, as—as just knowing. Just being sure of the goodness of God" (13). In her hesitant efforts to explain this new perception to her sister, Mary also quotes from the many biblical texts she memorized as a child. She is groping for a language that can express her expanding consciousness.

It is apparent that Mary is finding that language at college. She learns to read both raised print and Braille and conceives a new ambition to write a book. On her first visit home, she moves "easily around the house, instead of sitting quiet in her chair," and when Carrie asks if she was afraid to travel alone on the train, Mary replies, "Oh, no. . . . I had no trouble. We learn to do things by ourselves, at college. It is part of our education" (124). When she opens her trunk, managing the locks easily, the objects she removes indicate her new poise, skill, and self-possession. Employing the beadwork she has learned, she has made pretty gifts. For Ma there is a decorative lamp mat; for the two adolescent sisters, beaded jewelry, and for little Grace, a delicate doll chair. The gifts show Mary's discrimination as well as her skill; for each female in her family, she has *created* an object of desire. Then she takes out a gift for her father:

> "This is for you, Pa," Mary said, as she gave him a blue silk handkerchief. . . . "I didn't make this, but I chose it myself. Blanche and I . . . Blanche is my roommate. We went downtown to find something for you. She can see colors if they are bright, but the clerk didn't know it. We thought it would be fun to mystify him, so Blanche signaled the colors to me, and he thought we could tell them by touch. I knew by the feeling it was good silk. My, we did fool that clerk!" and, remembering, Mary laughed.
>
> Mary had often smiled, but it was a long time since they had heard her laugh out, as she used to when she was a little girl. All that it

had cost to send Mary to college was more than repaid by seeing her so gay and confident. (THGY 129–30)

This crucial scene presents Mary as the self-possessed protagonist of a total success story. The eldest Ingalls daughter is returned to the market-place not as an immobile fashion plate (although she is still well dressed) but as an informed, empowered consumer, using the traditional feminine skills of judging fabrics that Ma taught her. She joins forces with a female ally, Blanche, and together they win a battle of wits with a male clerk. And Mary is not only a buyer; she is also a producer of objects of value and usefulness. Furthermore, once the gifts are distributed, she takes out another object— her Braille slate—and begins to write to friends and teacher. Although blind, Mary Ingalls is now confidently fluent in multiple languages and is obvi-ously, radiantly happy. She has a complex, productive relationship with the material world, and her family's great investment is repaid in full.

In fact, by the last book, Mary is developing a critical intelligence that allows her to interrogate the cultural scripts that govern her "seeing" sisters' lives. She is the only family member who openly questions Laura's decision to marry Almanzo Wilder when she is barely eighteen. And when the time comes for her second summer vacation, she chooses to spend it with her roommate, taking an opportunity to explore a new world instead of returning to the Little House in Dakota, where (unbeknownst to Mary) the new organ is waiting for her to play it. The following summer Mary is delighted to discover the organ, and she plays it with pleasure and grati-tude. But she does not become an adjunct of this valued instrument, an objectified organist who plays out the feminine ideal that her culture pro-motes. Whatever Mary's experiences at school (and the series tells us al-most nothing of them), they have given her back her selfhood and a rich vocabulary of words and things in which to express it.[15]

From the first, the character of Laura—the incipient writer—has been drawn to both these vocabularies, words and things. But the Little House series provides a far more complex elaboration of her story, and that story is often complicated by readers' knowledge that we are reading a *kunstlerroman*, the story of a female writer's development. (When I was a child reading the Lit-tle House series, I would occasionally stop at the end of some particularly satisfying chapter to look at the gratifying words on the spine of my book: LAURA INGALLS WILDER. And I would think, That's Laura! This little girl grew up to be a writer.) From *Big Woods* on, Laura often finds that when she is overwhelmed by a compelling object, she is robbed of speech, of the words that a writer needs. Her Christmas doll has that effect on her, as do the enticing goods in the general store. In some ways, as we will see in the next chapter, both the fictional Laura and Laura Ingalls Wilder's response to this dilemma is to make *things* into a language, one that gives Laura a voice. Certainly this was a ploy of nineteenth-century U.S. women's domestic culture, in which objects—often handmade—spoke eloquently and emphatically. Ma often uses this ploy. For example, instead of telling her daughters stories of her childhood, as Pa does, she lets her best delaine dress speak for her past, and she teaches Mary and Laura to understand its language:

> The delaine was kept wrapped in paper and laid away. Laura and Mary had never seen Ma wear it, but she had shown it to them once. She had let them touch the beautiful dark red buttons that buttoned the basque up the front, and she had shown them how neatly the whalebones were put in the seams, inside, with hundreds of little criss-cross stitches.
>
> It showed how important a dance was, if Ma was going to wear the beautiful delaine dress. Laura and Mary were excited. (LHBW 128–29)

The dress (which I have never forgotten) wordlessly but eloquently introduces the girls to a cluster of values that are enduringly associated with their mother: preservation, handwork, "stylishness," and the molded (by whalebone) female form. If an occasion merits the delaine dress, it *must* be "important," just as these values are. Ma does what Laura Ingalls Wilder would eventually identify as her own purpose in writing the Little House books: she helps children "to know what is behind the things they see."

For me, as a child growing up white, middle-class, and Christian in the Midwest, every year brought an annual crash course in the language of things: *Christmas*. Like many other readers, one of the things I loved best about the Little House books was the Christmas scenes that occurred at least once in each book. And perhaps another reason why *Plum Creek* was my favorite book was that it had the largest number of Christmases: three! This book is pivotal, too, in that each of these Christmases adds another facet to Laura and Mary's material education. In *Big Woods* they were simply delighted recipients, the center of an extended family celebration, with cousins, uncle, aunt, and parents. Except for ubiquitous store-bought Christmas candy, all the gifts were handmade. In *Little House on the Prairie*, they began to learn the delights of merchandise, as Santa Claus (via Mr. Edwards) showered them with tin cups, pennies, peppermints, and cakes made with white sugar and flour.

In the first two books, the girls' faith in Santa Claus was fostered by their parents. They were devout believers in a beneficent patriarch who could grant all their material wishes. But just before the first Plum Creek Christmas, when the family is still struggling without horses after their move to Minnesota, Ma tells Mary and Laura a new story about Santa Claus:

> "The older you are, the more you know about Santa Claus. You are so big now, you know he can't be just one man, don't you?" . . .
> Then Ma told them something else about Santa Claus. He was every-where, and besides that, he was all the time.
> Whenever anyone was unselfish, that was Santa Claus. (86–87)

Then Ma makes her pitch to her older daughters: if *they* ask Santa for what *Pa* desires, the Ingalls family will collectively receive horses for Christmas, not the clothes, toys, and candy that the girls have individually wished for. Through such "unselfishness," the girls will be empowered; they will *become* Santa instead of simply being his beneficiaries.

Initially, Laura doesn't like this idea; it brings into uncomfortable proximity the fantasy world of unlimited gifts and the mundane world of the Ingalls family's limited money and the necessities it must buy. She thinks, "Horses were everyday; they were not Christmas. If Pa got horses, he would trade for them. Laura could not think of Santa Claus and horses at the same time" (85).

Although Santa does come through with six pieces of "beautiful" hard candy for each girl's stocking, the only other gift is the "Christmas horses," and on Christmas morning, Laura finds herself delighted by the powerful animals and her father's obvious pleasure. The lesson of this Christmas is complex. Laura and Mary have become active consumers in the world of everyday transactions where horses are bought and sold, exercising their wills instead of waiting passively (as they did in the first two books) to see what Santa Claus will bring. But they are also taught that being mature females means suppressing their own desires to grant a beloved man's wish. This Christmas Laura is not *quite* made speechless by her present. When she sees the horses, she can "only say, 'Oh, Pa!'" (98). Laura has followed Ma's advice, and now the name of the father is all she can say.

Such mixed messages of self-empowerment and self-abnegation through consumption were standard fare for late nineteenth-century U.S. females. By "unselfishly" facilitating Pa's purchase of the horses he wants, Laura becomes the conventional "daughter of sentiment" that Linda Zwinger sees in many middle-class Western family stories, the daughter who facilitates her father's story of desire. According to Zwinger, such a "sentimental daughter is a dutiful acolyte to her father, with a loving heart, an innocent mind, and a positive lust for self-abnegation" (5). In *Plum Creek* this scene is surrounded with all the aura of familial bliss with which Wilder always invests her fictional Christmases. Nevertheless, Laura's near speechlessness suggests subtly that such behavior is a danger to her voice and her future vocation as a writer and teller of a *girl's* story.

The second *Plum Creek* Christmas sets forth a very different scenario. By now the Ingallses are members of a new church that has been built in the town, and one winter night (the girls do not realize Christmas is near), Pa and Ma take their daughters on an unprecedented night visit to town. When they enter the lighted church, they see a "wonderful" sight: a leafless tree thickly hung with an entrancing variety of seductive merchandise: candy, clothes, toys, farming and housework implements and "the most wonderful thing of all. . . . a little fur cape, and a muff to match!" Although a service is conducted and Reverend Alden, whom Laura adores, "preached about Christmas . . . Laura was looking at that tree and she could not hear what he said." Nor can she speak or sing. Like the tree of knowledge, the Christmas tree has taken root in the town's place of worship, heavy with the fruits of the townspeople's desires, the things they want and need. This Christmas, Laura and Mary need not suppress their desires in favor of their father's; instead, they simply stand and wait, raptly, while the tree's bounty is distributed to them, their family, and everyone around. The small pieces of china—a gilded box and a dog—that Laura and Carrie receive from their teachers will become touchstones of the Little House series, freighted objects that will be displayed and preserved and moved and displayed again, to the very last pages. There is also a doll for Carrie, warm clothing for Ma, Pa, and Mary, and at last, for Laura, the thing she has wanted most: the fur cape and muff. The child is overcome with sensuous, romantic joy. Everything else is wiped out by the joy of possession: "Laura knew only the softness of those furs" (251–55). The furs are all the sweeter because Nellie Oleson has been taunting Laura with her fur cape.

This scene, as I have recounted it, may seem like a celebration of unmitigated greed, as the Ingalls girls receive and receive without feeling any desire or obligation to give. But the experience of the scene may be very different for readers, especially children. Laura's bliss and wonder are contagious, and Wilder and Lane have captured the hypnotic aura that a desired, contested object may exert on a child. Furthermore, Laura needs the furs; her only coat is skimpy and inadequate. In fact, except for a few toys and ornaments and the children's candy, all the Ingallses' gifts are much-needed warm winter clothing. And most of the large gifts around the tree are similarly necessary merchandise: a washboard, a pitchfork, a churn. What is the source of these gifts? There is no indication that Ma and Pa have paid money for any of the things given to the Ingalls family. Instead, their major gifts have been contributed by a church "back East"; "they all gave things they had" and no longer needed. Thus this Christmas celebration is not simply an exercise in consumption. Instead, goods are redistributed and reused through the medium of a large, noncommercial institution, the church. The town's extremes of prosperity and poverty, as illustrated by the Olesons' opulent party and the Ingallses' modest one, are ameliorated by this festive redistribution of goods. The bags of candy are equally filled, and every child receives one. And Nellie and Laura's clothing is equalized. Laura feels no stigma because her furs are secondhand and a charitable gift. Instead, the resentment and dislike she always feels for Nellie are almost subdued.

> No wickedness boiled up in Laura now; she only felt a little bit of mean gladness.
>
> "Merry Christmas, Nellie," Laura said. Nellie stared, while Laura walked quietly on, with her hands snuggled deep in the soft muff. Her cape was prettier than Nellie's, and Nellie had no muff. (257–58)

Now Laura has regained her voice and (as in the scene with Nellie) is pursuing her own passions and conflicts.

In this Christmas celebration, the only communal one in the Little House series, Wilder and Lane suggest another kind of relation to the world of commodities, more communistic than capitalistic. For a moment, Laura glimpses what it might be like for her family to live in an egalitarian community. Even before she has received her furs, the child thinks: "There had never been such a Christmas as this. It was such a large, rich Christmas, the whole church full of Christmas. There were so many lamps, so much noise and laughter, and so many happinesses in it. Laura felt full and bursting, as if that whole big rich Christmas were inside her, and her mittens and her beautiful jewel-box . . . and her candy and her popcorn ball" (255). This is a new thought for Laura: that the "rich" joy of possessing material things can be experienced communally, in a celebration that reaches beyond the boundaries of her nuclear family. The new joy is nourishing and sustaining, as if she has ingested "that whole big rich Christmas."

A third Christmas ends *Plum Creek*. This time, in an unusually severe winter, Pa goes to town a few days before Christmas to buy tobacco and get news, against the advice of Ma, who emphasizes that she needs nothing from the stores in town. On his way home, Pa is caught in a blizzard and burrows under the creek bank for three days. Luckily, he has spent the enormous sum of ten dollars to buy himself a warm buffalo coat in town, and he eats the candy and crackers he was bringing home for a Christmas treat. When he arrives home, he still has canned oysters for Christmas dinner. His wife and daughters are relieved and overjoyed. On the last pages of *Plum Creek*, Laura has these "happy" thoughts: "Everything was so good. Grasshoppers were gone [the blizzards will prevent their return], and next year Pa could harvest the wheat. Tomorrow was Christmas, with oyster stew for dinner. There would be no presents and no candy, but Laura could not think of anything she wanted and she was so glad that the Christmas candy had helped to bring Pa safe home again" (338).

In such weather, the Ingallses are too far from town to attend school or church services, although they can hear the church bell pealing. The liberating expansions of the previous Christmas cannot happen this year. In many ways Laura is where she was when the book began: still waiting for Pa to harvest a wheat crop so the family can enjoy unaccustomed prosperity. She has returned to a self-abnegating mode, deferring to Pa's pressing needs. Since the patriarch alone can move freely between the markets and the Little House, he must have the best goods. Almost all the resources that could have made a materially "rich" Christmas for Ma and the girls are lavished on Pa: the fur coat and most of the festive food. But Laura does not think of complaining. The "unselfishness" Ma urged two Christmases ago has become second nature. Now she has internalized both her parents' values: "good" means a profitable crop and a united family. Although this book has indicated the intensity of Laura's material desires—for the furs, the new dress, Nellie's doll—those desires are nowhere apparent in the beatific final scene; "Laura could not think of any*thing* she wanted."

The Little House books have traditionally been read as an antidote to post–World War II U.S. materialism. Marcia Dalphin, surveying Little House Christmas scenes in 1953, argued that, as Ma said, *happiness* makes Christmas, and thus "it really *was* Christmas all the time in the Ingalls home. . . . in spite of this pioneer family's precarious economic situation, with a lack of this world's goods that would to many of us seem an impossible handicap" (41). Certainly Christmas did provide Wilder and Lane with serial opportunities to underline the solidarity of Ingalls family bonds. But, as I have tried to indicate in my reading of *Plum Creek*, Christmas is also for the Ingalls family what it has been for many other Americans: an occasion to work out the problems and possibilities of their complex relations with commodities.

On all of the *Plum Creek* Christmases, Laura is negotiating such relations: looking for ways that she can have her desires and sublimate them too. Each singular Christmas, however blissful, raises problems that attend the desire for things. Every Christmas Laura has problems with her voice; it is silenced or severely restricted by the mesmerizing powers of commodities— or their absence. Her relieved and happy thoughts on Pa's Christmas return at the book's end are never *voiced* (although, of course, they are written). Instead, the book's final conversation is between Pa and Ma, on Christmas Eve:

> "Supper is ready," Ma said in her gentle voice.
> Pa laid the fiddle in its box. He stood up and looked around at them all. His blue eyes shone at them.
> "Look, Caroline," he said, "how Laura's eyes are shining." (338–39)

Here the two parents voice scripts that are a refrain of the Little House series—Ma with her customary "gentle" domestic call to supper and Pa with the fiddle tunes and lyrics by which he customarily expresses the preoccupations of contemporary popular culture. Silent Laura, radiating a sense of contented well-being, is the object of her parents' gratified gaze. And she is particularly gratifying to Pa because *her* blue eyes shine like his own. On one level, Laura has become her father's confirming mirror, wordlessly reflecting the image of a patriarch. This is Jean Wyatt's assessment of the *Little House in the Big Woods* and *Little House on the Prairie;* she says that "Laura occupies a peripheral position in her own story. . . . Attributing agency to the father and deriving self-esteem from his affection and praise prepare a girl to depend for self-esteem on a man's approval rather than drawing satisfaction directly from a sense of work well done" (211).

I agree that such moments recur in the Little House series, especially in the early books. But in this chapter's discussion of consumption issues, I have intended to suggest that the books undertake a far more complex and ongoing contemplation of these issues and what they can mean to a girl's volition and her voice. The differing agendas of the three *Plum Creek* Christmases are one striking indication of this. Another occurs in a chapter called "Keeping House," near the end of *Plum Creek*. On a mild winter day, Pa and Ma walk to town, leaving Mary and Laura alone with Carrie for the first time. The girls try to play; first they attempt a game of "school," but Carrie refuses to be a cooperative pupil. Then they discover that the premise of their favorite game has changed:

> "Well," said Laura, "Let's play keeping house."
>
> "We *are* keeping house," said Mary. "What is the use of playing it?" (285)

Suddenly a blizzard blows in, and (remembering a story of children who froze to death in such a storm), the girls labor to bring in firewood—the one thing that will keep them safe. Despite the hazardous weather, they lug the entire woodpile indoors. Even tiny Carrie helps. They are disobeying their parents' orders to "stay in the house if it stormed" (287), relying instead on their own assessment of their needs in this situation. When Pa and Ma burst in, running from town, they are amazed and ultimately approving:

> Pa's great laugh rang out, and Ma's gentle smile shone warm on Mary and Laura. They knew they were forgiven for disobeying, because they had been wise to bring in wood, though perhaps not quite so much wood.
>
> Sometime soon they would be old enough not to make any mistakes, and then they could always decide what to do. They would not have to obey Pa and Ma any more. (291)

This scene interestingly broaches the close relation between the girls' play and their present and future work of *keeping house* and *teaching school*, both jobs held by their mother. Pa is often away from the house, sometimes for days at a time, but Ma has never been gone before and without her, "the house was empty and still" (285). With Ma gone, the girls must transform their "play" into her work, as they have been prepared to do. But they must also cast off their unthinking, unspeaking obedience to their parents' rules, which Pa usually lays down in an authoritative voice. Assessing the weather, Laura and Mary conclude that they need a particular "commodity"—wood— and they find a way to get it, even though they must disobey parental orders. This scene is tellingly double: it encourages the girls to look forward to a future as self-determining adults with judgment and volition—but it also indicates how thoroughly they are programmed to continue the work and the priorities of their mother.

Such complexity is typical of the Little House series and particularly of *Plum Creek*. Unlike the two previous novels about the Ingalls family, each of which spanned a year in the family's life, this one covers more time and expresses more abrupt alternations in their frontier life: some chapters, like those concentrating on school and church, are intensely social and reinforce community values, while others stress the isolation of the small Ingalls family or even of Laura alone, as when she wages solitary combat with the flooding creek. These alternations may make this novel less coherent and less sustainedly poetic than the previous books. But they are also one of the features that made this book a childhood favorite for me; they acknowledge contradictions that were very much a part of my own life as a girl.

In the Wordsworth sonnet from which I borrowed part of my title for this chapter, "getting" things and "spending" money are depicted negatively:

> Getting and spending, we lay waste our powers:
> Little we see in Nature that is ours;
> We have given our hearts away, a sordid boon!

According to Walter Benn Michaels, such a "fundamentally critical" attitude toward "consumer capitalism" has also characterized most of the printed texts that are "the most powerful works of American culture" (14–15). As we have seen, one of the striking features of the Little House series is its assumption of a more complex, ambivalent attitude toward "getting and spending." As Laura and Mary learn to choose and buy, they are both endangered and empowered. They have not simply alienated themselves from Nature and from genuine human feeling, giving their "hearts away" for the "sordid boon" of commodities. They have also begun to discover that things can be a potent language through which their hearts, minds, and wills can find expression. "Getting and spending," these girls begin to *discover* their powers. By acknowledging the complexities of this process, Wilder and Lane described the workings of U.S. culture far more fully and less dogmatically than most other contemporary books for children or adults.

As I said at the beginning of this chapter, when Laura and her sisters begin to want the commodities their culture offers—whether clothes, books, toys, or technology—the Little House series becomes a narrative of conscious, sanctioned desires. But Jean Wyatt also makes an important and pertinent point. She observes that vivid "descriptions of concrete objects" often characterize fiction for children, such books as *Heidi*, *The Wizard of Oz*, or *Little Women*. While "secondary processes, primarily verbal and obedient to the rules of logic and language, will be dominant in processing abstract explanations," the recurrent objects "will trigger primary processes" and tap *unconscious* desires. In this discussion, Wyatt adopts the version of the "unconscious" proposed by French theorists (specifically Cixous and Lacan), as being "composed of signifiers attached to drive energies that language cannot accommodate," which "escape . . . cultural constraints" (43–45).

Such unconscious dynamics are obviously at work through certain key objects in the Little House books. For example, in Laura's rivalry with Nellie Oleson, Ma counsels restraint and decorum; she never openly acknowledges the power struggle between the girls. But the forceful depiction of Nellie's luxurious doll and the equally luxurious gratification of Laura's Christmas furs vividly acknowledge the deep-seated struggle between the two girls and the naked desire for confirming things that Ma counsels Laura to repress. According to Wyatt, "in some novels that have been popular through many generations of child readers, vivid images of female power in action contradict set speeches that repeat lessons in feminine decorum" (43). Later in the series, the focused, extended description of the sewing machine and its powers allows both Laura and Ma covertly to acknowledge their hatred for the confining and tedious work of hand sewing, however "feminine" and "decorous" it may be. Yet another reason for the extraordinary power of *things* in the Little House books is that they become a language that taps both conscious and unconscious desire, extending the restricted vocabularies of girls and women.

Most fans of Laura Ingalls Wilder's fiction—whether children or adults—have seemed to apprehend that reading the Little House books is also an experience of reading things. At the museums that have mushroomed at sites where the actual Ingalls/Wilder family lived, visitors pore over the smallest material fragments of their lives—a few dishes, documents, textiles, remnants of unremarkable furniture—with near-religious intensity.[16] When the Children's Literature Association planned an expedition for scholars to the Mansfield Museum, its brochure advertised the *objects* there before mentioning the museum's extensive collection of handwritten Wilder manuscripts, which would presumably be of particular interest to scholars.

Obviously, in these novels certain things are not merely mentioned, noted, or described. Somehow they are *evoked*, so that the objects become continuous with the page. Of course, not every object has this power. Most things come and go, without much notice. Most of the Ingalls furniture, for example, seems expendable; it is often left behind when they move. Even such a central possession as Pa's fiddle, perhaps the single most consistent motif in the series, has little power as an *object*. When Pa is away and Laura misses him desperately, she never clings to the fiddle he has left behind. It is not even mentioned until his return. The fiddle is an instrument, meant for Pa's use. Ma's decorative china figure of a shepherdess has no such use; it is solely an ornament. Yet, unlike the fiddle, it *is* evoked, powerfully, memorably, and repeatedly. At the Ingalls/Wilder museums, the shepherdess is the missing object that visitors ask for again and again.[17]

I cannot end this chapter without confessing that I own a small, motley collection of objects, gathered over the past thirty years. A rag doll and a nine-patch quilt (*Big Woods*), a string of trade beads (*Little House on the Prairie*), a chipped porcelain "jewel box," a small Staffordshire dog, a few old buttons, and a copy of Mary Jane Holmes's *Millbank* (*Plum Creek*), a stack of decorated calling cards (*Little Town on the Prairie*), a glass bread plate (*The First Four Years*). I have plucked these things from flea markets, garage sales, and antique stores—sometimes paying more than their market value and more than I could afford—because I remembered them from my readings and rereadings of the Little House books. None of the other books I loved as a child, such as *Little Women*, has spawned such a collection. And it's not yet complete. I am still looking, hopelessly, for a china shepherdess. The experience of the Little House books has taken me back to the market, where I choose, buy, and read not only books but things.

Most of these things I have bought are domestic, with "feminine" associations. Assembling them, I have also acquired an elementary education in conventional nineteenth-century U.S. female culture. And as I read the thing-text of the Little House series, I also enter into an intense and sometimes problematic kinship with the fictional Ma Ingalls. The china shepherdess speaks to me in *her* "gentle," insistent voice, as perpetuated on the page by her daughter and granddaughter. The shepherdess urges me to choose stable, "civilized" domestic felicity over the fast-moving, transient frontier lifestyle preferred by Charles Ingalls.

In this chapter, I have argued that the Little House series is a complex commentary on the Ingalls family's relations with the U.S. culture of commodities. As the Ingalls daughters learn to read the stove, the clothes, the doll, and the parlor organ, as well as their books, they confront the texts that define and prescribe the prevailing paradigms of gender in their culture. In the books after *Plum Creek*, Laura Ingalls will discover that those texts point her toward pressing, disturbing choices. Ultimately, she will be pushed to choose between her allegiance to her mother and her alliance with her father.

From left, Carrie, Mary, and Laura Ingalls, in Dakota Territory, about 1880. This is the earliest known photograph of the Ingalls sisters. Photo courtesy of Laura Ingalls Wilder Memorial Society, Mansfield, Missouri.

Chapter 4

The Little House That Gender Built

The Novels of Adolescence

With *By the Shores of Silver Lake* (1939), the Little House books began to *look* different. The earlier books were large and squarish, with generous illustrations. But the last four took on the standard shape, thickness, and print size of novels for adults. When I read *Silver Lake* and the following volume, *The Long Winter* (1940), I had the exhilarating feeling that I was leaving "baby books" (however beloved) behind to become a grown-up reader.

Wilder and Lane debated this change in the series. Many of the most durably popular and lucrative U.S. series for children, such as Nancy Drew, the Rover Boys, and the Bobbsey Twins, had kept their protagonists at approximately the same ages over many decades, thus continuing to tap the same age market through generations of readers.[1] Perhaps with these facts in mind, Lane and the editors at Harpers seem to have been alarmed when the Little House protagonist, Laura, who was eight at the beginning of *Plum Creek*, suddenly appeared as a twelve-year-old adolescent on the first pages of *Silver Lake*. But Wilder was adamant about the necessity of such changes. She wrote to Lane,

> Just a word more about Silver Lake. You fear it is to [*sic*] adult. But adult stuff must begin to be mixed in, for Laura was growing up. . . .
>
> I thought I showed that Laura was rather spotted at the time, grown up enough to understand and appreciate grown up things. But at times quite childish. . . . Mary's blindness added to Laura's age. Laura had to step up and take Mary's place as the eldest. . . .
>
> I believe children who have read the other books will demand this one. That they will understand and love it. . . .
>
> We can't spoil this story by making it childish! Not and keep Laura as the heroine. And we can't change heroines in the middle of the stream and use Carrie in the place of Laura. (LIW to RWL, 26 Jan. 1938, Hoover)

In this dispute, Wilder entirely (and unusually) had her way. Laura Ingalls remained the "heroine" of the series, and, unlike Nancy Drew, she was allowed to grow up. *Silver Lake*, which spans less than a year, is marked by the mercurial "spotted" quality of early adolescence.

All the last four books, in fact, are sequential novels of adolescence, ending with Laura's early adult experiences as a schoolteacher and a bride. Thus gender issues intensify in these books. In the earlier books, despite her mother's scruples and care, young Laura is allowed many freedoms. She runs, shouts, and plays uproariously in the creek; her father takes her fishing, swimming, and exploring and allows her to shadow him when he works near the house. In "American Girlhood in the Nineteenth Century: Caddie Woodlawn's Sisters,"[2] Anne Scott MacLeod concludes, on the basis of a study of U.S. women's autobiographies, that the distinctions between the "treatment of girls and boys. . . . insisted upon in nineteenth-century America may have been fewer and less strict than we commonly suppose while children were preadolescent" (8). MacLeod continues,

> But this "free, joyous life" described again and again in American women's autobiographies came to an end for them . . . when they crossed the fateful line that marked the end of childhood and the beginning of young womanhood. Timing varied, but not the outcome.

For some, the doors closed at thirteen; for others not until fifteen or even later, but close it inevitably did once the claims and constraints of nineteenth-century womanhood were laid upon the growing girl. (12)

Silver Lake, in particular, is loud with the sounds of doors opening—to sexuality, independence, self-determination—and closing. Laura Ingalls is not immune to MacLeod's conclusion that, at adolescence, "a nineteenth-century girl could not but realize . . . that after childhood, gender (to paraphrase Freud) was inexorably destiny" (29).

In addition to the newly pressing problems of gender, there is a potentially problematic time lapse between *Plum Creek* and *Silver Lake*, the longest lapse in the series. The action of *Plum Creek* covers two years and several months; *Silver Lake* begins almost two years later. During this period, the actual Ingalls family left Walnut Grove, Minnesota (the townsite of *Plum Creek*, never mentioned by name in the novel). Their attempts to raise a profitable wheat crop had been foiled by grasshopper plagues and weather; another experiment in farming had failed. The family turned back east. They stopped for a long visit with Peter and Eliza Quiner Ingalls in South Troy, Minnesota; while they were there, the fourth and youngest child, nine-month-old Frederick, sickened and died. They went farther east to Burr Oak, Iowa, where they joined friends from Walnut Grove in the hotel business. During two years in the Iowa town, both Charles and Caroline Ingalls worked in the hotel, and Laura and Mary attended school. The last Ingalls child, Grace, was born in Burr Oak in 1877.

Burr Oak was yet another financial disaster for the Ingalls family. Wilder explained to Lane that her parents' partner in the hotel

handled the money and someway beat Pa out of his share. I don't suppose there was much.

Then we were out of that with rent to pay and Dr. bills. Grace was born there and we all had measels. . . . Pa worked catchely here and there but never enough to pay expenses. When we left there [in 1878] there was not money enough to pay the last month's rent and feed us on the way back to Walnut Grove. (LIW to RWL, 23 March 1937, Hoover).

Back in Walnut Grove after this failed excursion, the family did not even attempt to farm again. Instead, Charles Ingalls worked as a carpenter and miller and in a butcher shop. In 1879 Mary Ingalls contracted spinal meningitis, which left her blind.

Illness, debt, death, retreat to the east; failures of farming and of business. For Laura Ingalls Wilder, these were painful, charged, and *unnarratable* subjects. Yet they were integral parts of the autobiographical story she had set herself to tell. By this point in the project, January 1938, she and her collaborator were living far apart; most of Lane's work on *Silver Lake* was done in New York City. Because they worked through an exchange of drafts and letters, we can now examine a fuller written record of their collaboration, especially for this book. It is obvious that they often disagreed; Wilder referred more than once to their working process as "arguing it out" (LIW to RWL, 23 May 1939, Hoover). Perhaps their most vehement disagreement was about how to begin *Silver Lake*.

As published, the book begins on the Plum Creek farm. All the Ingalls family members but Laura and Pa have been gravely ill with scarlet fever; Mary is now blind. Suddenly Pa's sister, Docia, arrives. She offers her brother a job, working with her husband on the railroad in Dakota Territory, where he can take up a homestead. Despite Ma's reservations, they decide to accept the offer. Pa sells the farm to pay his debts and leaves immediately with Docia; several months later, when Mary is well enough to travel, Ma and the four daughters go by train (a morning's journey) to join him.

This is the opening for which Lane argued. Wilder emphatically opposed it. She preferred to fill in recent events, sketchily, through Laura's "dreamy" reverie as the women waited for Pa to join them in a Dakota hotel. Arguing her case, Wilder wrote Lane one of her bluntest letters:

> I like your idea for the beginning less and less the more I think of it. . . .
>
> It made to [*sic*] much of Plum Creek. We don't want to go back there. . . .
>
> It made an unpleasant beginning, a tale of sickness and failure and death.
>
> We don't want to tell of [the dog] Jack's dying. Nor of Mary's sickness.
>
> Nor of Pa's failure so that it was necessary for him to make a new start because he hadn't gained anything by all his hard work.
>
> The readers must know all that but they should not be made to think about it. . . . It is, and will be passed over lightly by the reader in the interest of the new adventure which is already begun.
>
> I am afraid I am going to insist that the story starts as I started it. (LIW to RWL, 28 Jan. 1938, Hoover)

Wilder has arrived at a point where her accumulated memories, fully perceived, seem almost unbearable: a weighty "tale of sickness and failure and death." Although the Little House project was clearly enormously satisfying for her, it was also a real threat to her mental well-being. In 1937 she had written to Lane, "I can't work on my book in the evening, because, if I do, I can't sleep. My brain goes right on remembering and it's H---" (LIW to RWL, 5 Feb. 1937, Hoover). Her memories of the Walnut Grove/ Burr Oak years pointed to conclusions that must have seemed hellish. The blithe adventure of "going West," proposed by Pa at the beginning of *Little House on the Prairie,* had become a disastrous series of failures of circumstance and judgment, especially for Charles Ingalls, the father whom Wilder had especially intended to celebrate in her series.

In her 1937 "Book Fair Speech," Wilder had represented her personal history—the basis of her series—as a smoothly sequential process: "I had seen and lived it all—all the successive phases of the frontier, first the frontiersman, then the pioneer, then the farmers, and the towns" (*Sampler* 217). But the full record of her family's wanderings from Wisconsin to Kansas, Missouri, Minnesota, and Iowa—and back and forth, again and again—is no such story. Instead, it is full of discontinuities, fits and starts, and contradictions that Wilder found difficult to remember, much less to celebrate.

Furthermore, Wilder and Lane may have discovered that their female protagonist did not facilitate a seamless sequential narrative. According to Jean Bethke Elshtain, "the social order" is likely to provide a boy with a "syntonic medium for his development," a medium that encourages a coherent life narrative. In *Farmer Boy* Almanzo Wilder enjoyed such circumstances. But, according to Elshtain, such a narrative of development is far less possible if the protagonist is a girl:[3] "Little girls . . . experience discontinuities, conflicts, ambiguities, and ambivalence as they encounter sex-appropriate games, toys, and activities. . . . 'Ladylike' behavior . . . is the preferred social norm for young women. The social medium for girls, then, has sharp breaks, roads that turn back upon themselves, and deep valleys that girls crawl out of with increasing difficulty" (294).

In the unnarrated years between *Plum Creek* and *Silver Lake,* Laura Ingalls seems to have encountered just such a course of "sharp breaks" and "deep valleys." All that she was learning of self-determination (and its limits) in her new experiences as a consumer and a reader was abruptly countered by her family's experience of "sickness and failure and death," circumstances that neither of her hardworking parents could change or control.

Laura Ingalls Wilder had aspired to work more independently on the manuscript of *Silver Lake*. She had hoped that "I had profited enough by your [Lane's] teachings that my copy could go to the publishers, with perhaps a little pointing up of the high lights [by Lane]. If it could, then perhaps I could do the following two without being such a bother to you" (LIW to RWL, 28 Jan. 1938, Hoover). But the beginning of this fifth novel became more than she could deal with alone. The new pressures of Laura's adolescence, the nadir of Pa's failure, Mary's illness, "Freddy's" death, and the problematic discontinuities of writing a western girl's narrative made it seem almost impossible to begin the new book, for which an eager audience (and market) was waiting. Finally she capitulated to Lane in an uncharacteristic letter: "Change the beginning of the story if you want. Do anything you please with the dam. stuff if you will fix it up" (LIW to RWL, undated [Feb. 1938], Hoover).

To "fix up" the series, it was necessary to jump-start the story of western expansion again and to give the Ingalls family a viable place within its conventions of frontier, farm, and town. Thus—despite Ma's wishes—Pa must be sprung from Plum Creek and set moving again, with a historically sanctioned goal: proving up on a Dakota homestead. Just as importantly, Laura must be separated from her father, who has always been her closest ally and the family member with whom she has most affinity. As an adolescent, she must (her parents assert) live within the parameters of a socially permissible *female* story.

One of the persistent strengths of the Little House series has been its capacity to reinforce the stories many U.S. readers have most wanted to hear. A typical early review suggested that the series was an invaluable (postwar) national resource:[4] "If our country can . . . work earnestly to solve its own problems at the same time that it carries its share of world responsibilities, it will be through vision of our children, their integrity and idealism, gained in homes like the home in the 'Little House' books" (quoted on flyleaf, SSL [1971]; unpaged). Again and again, reviewers and critics have repeated such sentiments, praising Wilder's perpetuation of a domestic ideal that, in the Depression and World War II years when the books were published, was already changing rapidly. Their approval has done much to make the series a long-running, best-selling success and a cultural icon.

But readers, children and adults, have also valued these books because of the sometimes-subtle ways they acknowledge complications, contradictions, and complexities, especially the "sharp breaks" and "deep valleys" that tend to characterize girls' stories. Nowhere is this more apparent than at the long-debated beginning of *Silver Lake*. The Ingallses have failed as farmers on Plum Creek, and Pa is tired of the settled, domesticated Minnesota country. Dakota territory offers free land and a fresh start; as Lillian Schlissel writes, frontiers have frequently "offered the space to separate from failure and the place to escape domestic despair" (1989, 240). As *Silver Lake* opens, Laura is experiencing such despair; she is mired in a valley of domestic routine and depression from which there seems no possible escape. "Washing the dishes one morning," she sees an buggy approaching Plum Creek.

> "Ma," she said, "it's a strange woman coming."
> Ma sighed. She was ashamed of the untidy house, and so was Laura. But Ma was too weak and Laura was too tired and they were too sad to care very much. (1)

The strange woman is Aunt Docia, who made a brief appearance as a young, single woman at the dance in *Big Woods*. Now, grown up and married, she is doing what Laura has not known that a woman could do, "driving alone in the buggy, all the way from Wisconsin to . . . Dakota Territory" (2). Within a few minutes, Docia has set this novel going: she offers her brother a well-paying job and a new start in the right direction (west); she lends her energies to help Laura with the housework; and she dispenses two dense paragraphs of family news, which links this volume with the Ingalls family characters who populated the first book in the Little House series. The next day Aunt Docia is gone; she has ridden west, taking Pa with her. And the Ingalls family is on the move again. Thus *Silver Lake* begins by acknowledging the transforming powers of an energetic, unconventional *woman*, who disrupts domestic stability and makes the argument for moving west. And, significantly, Laura is closely related to this woman by ties of gender and of blood. Docia's independence, mobility, and power were obviously attractive to Lane; they were qualities she admired and possessed herself, and she underlined them in her opening scene for *Silver Lake*. But Wilder resisted; she seemed to see Docia (and other Ingalls relatives) as threats to the myth of the self-sufficiency of the nuclear Little House family. She instructed Lane, "Don't bring Aunt Docia, Uncle Henry and the cousins into the story more than necessary. . . . The story is of the [nuclear] family and the family life. . . . Our interests all centered at home" (LIW to RWL, 8 Oct. 1938, Hoover). In *Silver Lake*, almost against Wilder's wishes, another strong woman, a relative, joins Ma as an adult female model for the

Ingalls daughters. Mobile, assertive and combative, Docia enlarges the female possibilities of the Little House series—and she threatens the family at its core, with its domestic ethos and its clearcut models of gender.

The changes of *Silver Lake* are intensified by the death of the dog Jack, another event that Wilder was reluctant to dramatize. On the day of Pa's departure, Jack dies in his sleep, of old age. In the entire series, this is the only acknowledged death of an elder, and the first cue that Laura's adult caretakers could weaken and fail. Jack has been Pa's protective male surrogate: "Whenever Pa had gone away, Jack had always stayed with Laura to take care of her and the family. He was especially Laura's own dog" (11). With Pa gone and Jack dead, Laura has no framework of male protection. In fact, she feels guilty that, because she was so busy caring for her mother and sisters in their illness, she neglected the old dog in his last days. At twelve, Laura is already expecting herself to give what she has received from her mother: constant domestic care. In Pa's absence, she cannot simply rely on Ma to take charge: "Laura knew then that she was not a little girl any more. Now she was alone; she must take care of herself. When you must do that, then you do it and you are grown up. Laura was not very big, but she was almost thirteen years old, and no one was there to depend on. Pa and Jack had gone, and Ma needed help to take care of Mary and the little girls" (14). To Laura, being grown up now means "taking care"—and it makes her the primary ally of her mother, whom she newly sees as an overburdened collaborator who "needs help."

Furthermore, Laura soon discovers that her parents expect her to take up her mother's profession, since Mary will be unable to. Pa says,

> "You know Ma was a teacher, and her mother before her. Ma's heart is set on one of you girls teaching school, and I guess it will have to be you. . . . "
>
> "Oh, I won't! I won't!" Laura thought. "I don't want to! I can't."
> Then she said to herself, "You must."
> She could not disappoint Ma. She must do as Pa said. (127)

Laura's emerging sense of maturity—her capacity to take care of herself and others—comes with a crushing sense of responsibility to a *female* tradition. Now and in the future, Laura thinks, she must share and perpetuate her mother's work. All through *Silver Lake* and *The Long Winter,* Laura exhibits the "spotted" energies and enthusiasms of early adolescence, as she begins to feel the range and power of her mature will. But when she thinks of her own future, she almost always does so with dread and despair. For she can imagine no way out: she "must" become the woman that her mother was and is.

When the Ingalls family settles in Dakota, near what will become the new town of De Smet, they have made their last westward move. (The actual Charles and Caroline Ingalls remained in De Smet until their deaths.) Although the phrase does not appear in the titles of the last four books, by now the entire series was beginning to be k :own (and marketed) as "the Little House books," and the *House* was more and more pressingly the container and the context of the series. Laura Ingalls will never spend another night in a wagon, under the stars, as she had loved to do as a child. Instead, she must live under the roofs of little houses, and this increasingly domestic context, combined with the conditions of her adolescence, pushes her to "choose" between her parents' gendered practices and priorities. But—does she really have a choice? As a dutiful daughter in a patriarchal household, she seems to have no option but to become her mother.

Although these issues are newly intense in *Silver Lake*, they have been important to the series from its beginning. They are implicit in the very figure of the Little House.

All these Little Houses are built by Pa. Constructing them, he also constructs himself as a citizen in a prevailing patriarchal tradition. The Ingalls houses epitomize the "detached dwellings in the countryside" that, as Gwendolyn Wright has written, signified "certain key national virtues" in the nineteenth-century United States: "personal independence. . . . democratic freedom of choice. . . . and private enterprise" (1983, 89). These "virtues" all matter enormously to Charles Ingalls, as they did to Wilder and Lane in the New Deal years, when they considered such values to be at risk. Pa's "freestanding single-family dwelling" is to him, in terms that Marilyn R. Chandler says still prevail in U.S. culture, "the most significant measure of the cultural enfranchisement that comes with being an independent, self-sufficient (traditionally male) individual in full possession and control of home and family. The seldom-realized ideal is for the householder to have designed and built this house with his own hands" (1–2), as Charles Ingalls *does* build the Little Houses. Furthermore, he always builds with wood, perpetuating Anglo-Saxon and Northern European traditions, even in situations where other modes (sod, adobe, dugout?) might be more affordable and appropriate. By the houses he builds in the West, Pa advertises to the world that he is a regular U.S. male, a member in good standing of Anglo-American, middle-class culture.

Even in the 1990s, architecture and building are still among the most male-dominated professions in the United States. And it is clear that Charles Ingalls's building is men's work. Once, in Kansas, he enlists his wife to help with lifting. A log falls on Ma and nearly crushes her foot, frightening the whole family. Pa says, "I blame myself. . . . I should have used skids" (61). Obviously, a woman who participates in building courts disaster; Ma never helps Pa again in raising a house. Instead, he finds other men with whom to trade work. Laura, however, is permitted to stay close by as her father builds the Kansas house. She considers herself his helper and proudly hands him tools and materials. Through her intent eyes, the processes of Pa's building are narrated in precise detail. Both Wilder and Lane were much interested in the processes of building themselves, and *Little House on the Prairie* sometimes reads like a manual for the construction of a log dwelling. Even today, it would seem possible to construct a wooden door latch, for example, from its careful instructions.

But after the Ingallses leave Kansas, Laura is distanced more and more from her father's work as a builder. At Plum Creek he erects an English-style, two-room-and-attic dwelling with manufactured materials bought on credit: machine-sawed boards, tar paper, shingles, latches, locks, and china door knobs. As Pa hauls his new supplies, "his face was one big shining of joy" (109). This house will demonstrate his purchasing power and his middle-class economic credentials. Caroline Ingalls and her daughters have no say in what he buys or how he builds; Ma apparently does not even see the "wonderful house," as Laura calls it, until the day they move in. Again Pa has promised his family that, when his wheat crop is harvested and sold, they will live "like kings." In the West, he seems to say, self-made men crown themselves kings by building castles. But the unspoken question for Laura is—how can a *girl* participate in that process? Apparently not by building; the series offers no example of a female builder.

In *Silver Lake* the Ingalls women find themselves shuttled from one house to another—in less than a year, they inhabit five dwellings. Some are makeshift, some are borrowed—such as the substantial surveyors' house in which they spend their first Dakota winter. But all are built by men. Pa puts up a store building in the new town, hoping to turn a profit. Eventually, the family lives in the store until, at the book's very end, he builds a tiny shanty on the claim. For Pa and other Dakota men, it is apparent that the *serial process* of building—Little House after Little House—matters far more than any single permanent edifice. Pa erects the shanty in a day, and the family moves in the next day; while he is cutting a window in the wall, Ma and

Laura are placing furniture under that very window.[5] Pa expounds, "That's what it takes to build up a country. . . . Building over your head and under your feet, but building" (253). He almost exactly echoes an 1859 *Pocket Manual of Rural Architecture*, which declares, "We are proud of the flimsy, insubstantial structures . . . which dot the whole face of the country. They are the homes of the people, who will by-and-by build better ones" (Daniel Harrison Jacques, quoted in Wright 1983, 86). Pa's near-constant building (when he has nothing more pressing to build, he hires out as a carpenter), which sometimes seems slapdash and frantic, is an important political process. He is helping to "build up a country," one where the only full-fledged citizens will be men.

More than any of the other Little House novels, *Silver Lake* seems to be shaped overtly by male values. It is sprawling and linear; the family moves frequently, as Pa loves to do, and they are always loading the wagon and heading farther west: first to Dakota, then to the railroad camp, then to De Smet and the new homestead site. All around her Laura sees men working, moving, and "building up a country." As I mentioned in Chapter 2, the "half-breed" Big Jerry is especially compelling to the girl. He protects the Ingalls family from a possible robbery on the road and helps to deflect a potential riot that endangers Pa's authority as railroad storekeeper. Bareback on his white horse, Jerry rides straight into the setting sun—the ultimate west. Laura's first romantic attraction outside her family is to this man, who seems to negotiate with ease the proliferating boundaries that control her life: between races, between law and individual freedom, between mobility and community.

Now Laura is fascinated not just with her father's carpenter work but with the other kinds of work she sees men doing. In the Dakota shanty, Ma's traditional domestic routine, established in *Big Woods*, is soon reinstated: "All the days went by, one like another. On Mondays Laura helped Ma do the washing. . . . On Tuesdays she sprinkled . . . and helped Ma iron. . . . On Wednesdays she did her task of mending and sewing though she did not like to" (91). This inescapable routine becomes almost unbearable for the adolescent Laura. Desperately, she wants "to go somewhere. She did not know where. She only wanted to go." When the railroad workers and other Ingalls relatives prepare to break camp, Laura pleads with her father, "Oh, Pa, let's go on West!" (126).

Pa understands this outburst very well; "kindly," he tells Laura, "You and I want to fly like the birds." But he has promised Ma that the move to Dakota will be their last. "You can't go to school and go West. . . . I'm going to get a homestead, Laura, and you girls are going to school" (126). For Charles Ingalls and his equally restless daughter, the flying days are over.

Silver Lake, where they first settle in Dakota, is alive with men working on the railroad and with thousands of flying birds. Some of Wilder's most lush and successful description is lavished on the birds and men.[6] The thronging flocks and work teams fill the air with their cries and songs, and Laura looks on, entranced. Collectivity and commonality are especially attractive to her—when she first sees the workmen, all dressed alike, they seem "like a little army coming across the vast land . . . and the song was their banner" (75). For months Laura has been shut inside Little Houses, first caring for the sick family and now helping her mother. When she was a little girl on Plum Creek, the worst punishment her parents could devise for her was to stay indoors for a day with Ma, being *watched*. Now that punishment is her daily life. Laura is bored and lonely, and the soaring birds and working men indicate another way of life, one she longs to share.

Thus, for Laura, "The Wonderful Afternoon" (Chapter 10) is one when Pa takes her to see the men working. Pa explains the process, while Laura watches entranced, as men and teams of horses prepare a smooth, graded surface for the railroad. For both Laura and her father, the men's supervised, synchronized labor is "pretty work"; they "keep time just like they were playing a tune" (104). Wilder and Lane devote ten pages of careful description to railroad building; Pa and Laura spend the whole afternoon watching. When Laura asks, "Why can't the trains just run over the prairie swells?" she receives a lesson in the economy of collective male labor.

> "It saves work, later on," Pa said. "You ought to be able to see that, Laura, without being told." . . . [Locomotives burn coal and] "Coal has to be mined, and that's work. An engine burns less coal running on a level. . . . So you see it takes more work and costs more money now to make a level grade, but later on there'll be a saving in work and money, so they'll be used for building something else."
>
> "What, Pa? What else?" Laura asked.
>
> "More railroads," said Pa. (101)

The railroad is a project of capitalism and industrialism; the men who build it are devoting their energies to an enterprise that seems much larger than the day-to-day domestic routine that Laura has known and been required to follow all her life. Pa expects Laura to understand and appreciate the logic and the beauty of the railroad project. But it is equally clear that Laura can never *participate* in railroad building. Her "wonderful after-noon" of watching with Pa is a once-only expedition, not approved by Ma, and when she returns to the family shanty and tries to tell Mary what she has seen, her sister is uninterested. As she says, Mary prefers to "stay here in the nice clean shanty. I've finished another quilt patch while you've been idling" (107). Mary, despite the impediments of her blindness, has retained the shelter of domestic space and domestic time, completing her stint of sewing. To her, anything else a girl might explore is simply "idling" and waste.

As Wilder and Lane drafted *Silver Lake*, the "Wonderful Afternoon" chapter was another debated point. The incident was a partial invention, Wilder reminded Lane:

> As I told you, I stretched a point to have Pa take Laura to see the work. I did it to not have Pa tell it but to have Laura see it first hand and get her reaction of the time they kept, playing a tune with their promptness. . . .
>
> There was a big crowd of men. There was no place at all where one could step out of sight. . . . If a man wanted to do his jobs [urinate or defecate] he dropped out and did them publicly. So Manly says. That would be reason enough that we would not go and watch them at work.
>
> Put sex and all relating to it out of your mind and think of the crowd as rough and vulgar and truculent, in camp and out, chewing and drinking and swearing and fighting. Not fit company for girls. But not degenerate. Not at all. (LIW to RWL, 25 Jan. 1938, Hoover)

Wilder's ambivalence about the working men is clear. The collectivity of their lifestyle, the openness with which they performed even the most private of bodily functions (functions that are never mentioned in the Little House series), made it taboo for the actual Ingalls daughters to watch them work. Yet it is apparent that Wilder too, like her youthful fictionalized self, is drawn to the railroad men's rhythmic work, and she resists the idea that these men, however "rough and vulgar and truculent," might have posed a sexual threat to herself and her sisters. Furthermore, both Wilder and Lane clearly bought into the romance of the railroads' transformation of the nineteenth-century United States. At the end of the "Wonderful After-noon" chapter, Laura is intellectually stimulated to ask her father important questions:

"Are there railroads because people think of them first when they aren't there?"

Pa thought a minute. "That's right," he said. "Yes, that's what makes things happen, people think of them first. If enough people think of a thing and work hard enough at it, I guess it's pretty nearly bound to happen, wind and weather permitting." (106)

Pa's assumptions about collaboration and progress are typical of popular male culture in the nineteenth-century United States. Such ideas could be expressed in a traditional linear plot in which conflict and complication advance toward resolution and completion, just as railroad tracks would eventually span the continent. Laura and her father choose to emphasize the importance of *individual* conception and volition in such projects— "things" happen because "people think of them." Their language suggests that "people" may be both male and female, and Pa mentions only as an afterthought that "wind and weather" can impede such human projects, even though he never made a successful wheat crop in several years in Minnesota because of just such natural impediments.

Adolescent Laura sees the railroad as a way to use one's physical and intellectual energies in a transformative project, one much more obviously ambitious than the static, endogamous housekeeping in which she is expected to participate as a growing girl. The railroad's scope is not unlike that of the Little House series itself, which the adult Wilder found such an engrossing project. In her "Book Fair Speech," she wrote that a multivolume historical novel for children was "a thing [that] had never been done before" (*Sampler* 217). Once launched, she said, the project "completely filled my mind" ("My Work," *Sampler* 176).

The railroad also posed a problem for Wilder and Lane because it was a threat to the stable family farm that they wished to promote. When the railroad workers have finished their work and are ready to go farther west, Laura, as I have said, is eager to take Pa's railroad earnings and also move west, to Montana or Oregon, but Pa has made a reluctant commitment to the domestic stability of a homestead farm, which seems by contrast a very prosaic, landlocked project.

The Little House series is ostensibly committed to the ideals of individual enterprise and the "free and independent" life that Pa often espouses to Laura. The collectivity of the railroad and the "Eastern" monopoly that controls it are both a necessity and an anathema to the Ingalls family. Like other Dakota settlers, they depend heavily on the staple foods, lumber, and manufactured supplies brought in by trains. But it seems almost impossible for ordinary individuals to make significant profits from railroad work. Aunt Docia and her husband, Uncle Hi, illustrate this. Hi is a railroad contractor, and Docia works closely with him. He is continually cheated of his earnings by the railroad company and thus is compelled to take on new contracts. Finally, in *Silver Lake*, Hi, Docia, and their children take off for parts unknown with railroad property that they consider to be theirs by rights. Caught up in a large capitalist enterprise, a small-scale individual contractor is forced to become an outlaw, at odds with the government that supports big business. Lane wanted to "leave out Aunt and Uncle's stealing. . . . I believe it's a better notion to give children the idea that honesty is the best policy" (RWL to LIW, 21 Jan. 1938, Hoover). Again, Wilder disagreed; such "stealing" was a routine and expected part of the railroad-building process, she said.

> Couldn't it be made *not* to approve of it, but that was the way they built R.R.'s. That after all "honesty" *was* "the best policy" and maybe that was why contractors on the R.R. never got rich. And leave it in.
>
> After all even though these books must be made fit for children to read, they must also be true to history and that was the expected, accepted thing. That *was* the way the R.R. was built. (LIW to RWL, 25 Jan. 1938, Hoover)

The published novel did, of course, "leave it in" as Wilder urged. But Wilder's letter, with its atypically convoluted syntax, indicates how strong and conflicted her feelings were on this issue. The compelling presence of the railroad complicated the morality of the Little House series in ways that Wilder considered herself obligated to acknowledge. A composite "Letter from Laura" compiled from Wilder's letters to Harper about herself and her books places honesty first in its credo: "the real things haven't changed. It is still best to be honest and truthful" ("A Letter from Laura"). Working for the railroad necessitated dishonesty and illegality—yet railroad contractors couldn't have *actually* been dishonest, Wilder argues, for they didn't get rich. The convolutions of such (historically accurate) reasoning are written into *Silver Lake*, and they are a part of the culture that Laura is slowly beginning to recognize as she strains to extend her vision outside the Little House.

As paymaster, Pa has the task of dispensing the railroad's funds, and the men's anger is directed against him when their salaries are withheld for two weeks while time checks are issued. The disputed money is hidden in the Ingalls home; Ma buries it in her sack of flour. Then she forces her daughters to wait quietly with her while Pa faces down an angry mob in the nearby store. (In another camp, the paymaster was dangerously tortured by such a mob.) As the women listen to the ominous shouting, Laura longs to join forces with her father against the mob:

> Laura ducked under Ma's arm, but Ma's hand clenched on her shoulder and pulled her back.
> "Oh, let me go! They'll hurt Pa!". . . Laura screamed in a whisper.
> "Be still!" Ma told her in a voice Laura had never heard before.
> (115)

With physical and psychic force, Ma shows her daughter where the gendered boundaries lie. Even when their beloved husband and father's life is endangered, they cannot rush to his defense. The men's discourse is even conducted in language unfamiliar to Laura: "rough language. . . . all mixed with swear words and with other words she had never heard" (115). Yet the boundaries are as arbitrarily constructed (and as flimsy) as the insubstantial shanty walls. The very subject of the men's dispute is inside the house, with the women: the money in the flour sack. Here and elsewhere, the Little House story seems to confirm Gillian Brown's reading of nineteenth-century U.S. culture, which argues that the "possessive individualism" exercised through the "market activities generally available only to white men" came "to be associated with the feminine sphere of domesticity" (2).

Through such events as the railroad payroll dispute, Wilder and Lane indicate how intractably strong and constricting the prerogatives of gender have become for their adolescent protagonist. The "rough railroad camp" is a border zone in rapid transition; Ma stresses that "it would be some time before this country was civilized" (96). It is these transitional qualities that attract Laura.

When the dispute about the payroll is resolved, through the effective intervention of Pa's ally, Big Jerry, Mary still longs to go back to the relative safety of Plum Creek. But Laura's feelings are different. "Her heart beat strong and fast; she could hear in her mind again the savage fierce sound of the crowd's growl. . . . And she remembered the sweating men and sweating horses moving strongly through clouds of dust, building the railroad in a kind of song. She did not want ever to go back to Plum Creek" (122).

Laura's body is growing stronger and she is approaching sexual maturity. Her will is strengthening too. And it is the world of *men* that seems to offer an outlet for such energies: their work, their bodies, their language, their violent intensities and contradictory morality. In the railroad camp, it is obvious that order and law are men's arbitrary inventions. Pa does not intervene when Hi and Docia ride away with railroad property, even though Ma thinks he should. And when a male friend needs help collecting a debt, he concocts fake legal papers and pockets the fake "court costs." Such audacity and power seem intoxicating to Laura; no wonder that she desires to leave the stuffy shanty and join her father, where the action, the danger, and the men are.

Thus, *Silver Lake* is the book in which Laura Ingalls most visibly recoils from identification with her mother. For example, when Pa tells a story of how rioters strung up the paymaster at another camp and made him capitulate to their demands, Ma approves of the capitulation. She says, "I'm thankful the paymaster was sensible. Better a live dog than a dead lion." But Laura protests vehemently, "Oh, no, Ma! You don't mean that!" (121). Although she has been trained not to contradict her parents, she cannot accept the conciliatory stance her mother typically assumes. Laura and Ma differ sharply over the male adventure stories Laura has heard from Pa all her life and has always loved. Ma has no patience with displays of heroics, and Laura is not satisfied by the peaceable survival tactics that her mother's maxims urge. Ma advocates the "maternal thinking" influentially described by Sara Ruddick, an "essentially preservative attitude" that Josephine Donovan says is typical of traditional domestic women's culture (104). Conversely, as Laura can observe, her father is happiest when participating in a "progressive" plot supported by male culture. The Ingalls family has moved west, as many other families did, because of a man's ambitions and desires. Pa's regrets are for the flights he will never make, the Oregon territory he will never explore, although he and Laura long to go there. Ma's regrets are for the households left behind. Like Mary, she longs to return east to the "civilization" of Plum Creek.

Laura, now clearly at odds with her mother and closest sister, seems particularly attracted to the rival female models presented by her Aunt Docia and Docia's stepdaughter, fourteen-year-old Lena. Both are vigorous women who ride the prairies alone as Ma never does. Energetic, slangy Lena is Laura's favorite companion in the early Dakota days. With Lena, Laura discovers new pleasures: bareback rides on swift black ponies and a new repertoire of slightly racy songs that repudiate the life of a farmer's wife and daughter. Loudly they sing together:

> I wouldn't marry a farmer . . .
> He's always in the dirt,
> I'd rather marry a railroad man,
> Who wears a striped shirt! (48)

When the two girls learn that the laundress's daughter has just married, at the age of thirteen, they are shocked and sobered. For them, marriage means the end of "good times" and the beginning of heavy responsibilities. Lena says defiantly, "I don't want to settle down. . . . I'm not ever going to get married, or if I do, I'm going to marry a railroader and keep on moving west as long as I live" (50).

The life that Lena wants for herself is the very one that Pa seems to desire—"moving west as long as I live"—and that Ma has vetoed for her daughters. No wonder that Ma disapproves of the girls' close friendship. When Laura and Lena come in disheveled after an afternoon on the ponies, Ma is "shocked" and says, "Really, Docia, I don't know when Laura's looked so like a wild Indian." The phrase "wild Indian," revived from *Little House on the Prairie*, signals that Laura is again at risk in her mother's eyes, liable to transgress boundaries of gender and propriety with Lena. The two girls "are a pair," Docia says (55); such a match is exactly what Ma aims to prevent. Lena is "boisterous," she says, "and Docia has not curbed her as much as she might" (96). Obliquely, this comment expresses Ma's philosophy of rearing adolescent daughters. They must be kept quiet and contained, and their liveliest impulses must be held back—"curbed." Especially in this new world of "rough men," Ma tells Laura, she must restrain her lively curiosity and her impulses to *act*. Instead, she must be quiet, "well-behaved and ladylike, and remember that a lady never did anything that could attract attention" (96).

By the middle of *Silver Lake*, Lena has made her final appearance, riding west with Hi and Docia. This is her last word to Laura:

> "Gosh!" Lena spoke that wicked word boldly. "I'm glad this sum-
> mer's over! I hate houses." She swung the milk pail and chanted. "No
> more cooking, no more dishes, no more washing, no more scrubbing!
> Whoop-ee!" Then she said, "Well, good-by. I guess you're going to
> stay right here as long as you live."
>
> "I guess so," Laura said miserably. She was sure that Lena was
> going out West. Maybe even to Oregon. "Well, good-by." (130–31)

Lena is such a threatening character that Wilder and Lane *must* dispose of her if the Little House narrative is to survive. She boldly claims men's "rough language" for herself, exuberantly planning a westbound life of mobility and exploration—the very life Laura intensely desires but cannot have. Lena repudiates the whole domestic routine and says what is unthinkable in this series, that she *"hates houses."* Such a girl threatens a central principle of the series, which is built on the assumption that "Little Houses" will have a compelling attraction for readers, especially girls. Lena is clearly a girl, like Laura. But she blurs the line between "men's" and "women's" culture. And that line is already under seige in an "unsettled" country where women—even Ma—often do tasks traditionally assigned to men. Lillian Schlissel, in her study of frontier women's diaries, finds that "the women suggest that the frontier, in a profound manner, threatened their sense of social role and sexual identity" (1982, 85). Ma's "curbs" on Laura express such anxiety, focused on her most dangerously adventurous daughter. Lena is a special threat because—*within* the Ingalls family circle—she shows Laura, as the Indian children did in *Little House on the Prairie,* that there might be another way to be an American girl, one that would appropriate some of the freedoms and prerogatives of men's culture. Wilder seems to have been aware of Lena and Docia's potential to deflect the Little House project; she directed Lane, "don't stress them, don't play them up" (LIW to RWL, 8 Oct. 1938, Hoover). Although Lane protested the deemphasis of relatives in the books after *Big Woods,* Docia and Lena are never again mentioned in a Little House book—and no girls or women who resemble them are allowed to surface again in Laura Ingalls's life (with the possible exception of the problematic Eliza Jane Wilder).

The Wilder-Lane papers include an undated fragment of a letter to Wilder from Mrs. Lena E. Heikes, who wrote of reading *Silver Lake.* Discovering remembered names, she concluded,

> "I do believe this writer is my own cousin. If it tells of Mary's blindness I'll be sure of it" Well it did and of the black ponies . . . and my own name Lena. . . . Dear Mrs. Wilder If you are my dear cousin Laura Ingalls—Please write me just a line and I can then write to you in a more personal manner.
>
> Please address me thus
Mrs. Lena E. Heikes
Dakota City
Nebraska
>
> P.S. This is a farming community and my husband is a fairly prosperous farmer—[Hoover]

There is no record of any further correspondence between Wilder and Heikes. This moving letter seems to confirm that Laura Ingalls Wilder had completely lost touch with her dashing cousin Lena—and that the lively girl had become exactly what she avowed she would not be: a farmer's wife, on the Great Plains, *east* of Dakota. Janet Spaeth's observation about the fictional Lena is acute: "When she has the chance to move from the work of the woman's world to the play of the child's, she does so almost fiercely, as if to . . . conserve whatever liberty she has left" (44). Although Lena may seem uninhibited to her younger cousin Laura, she is actually *more* tied to housework, cooking, and cleaning with Docia for the railroad men, and is closer to the pressures of an early marriage. In *Silver Lake* Wilder makes her cousin Lena a gender-bending figure of rebellious energy, so vivid that she must be repudiated—perhaps for life.

Charles Ingalls shares the ambivalence that plagues his daughter Laura in *Silver Lake*. Although establishing a homestead has been his major purpose in moving to Dakota, and although he often boasts to his family about the advantage of having "the pick of the land" as an early settler (61), he puts off choosing and filing for a homestead. The Ingalls family arrives in Dakota in summer, and Pa does not file until the "spring rush" in the following year. By this time, men—many of them "rough"—have flooded into the new townsite. By the time Pa gets to the claim office in distant Brookings, his chosen claim site is "the only piece left vacant" near De Smet (235). Pa's peaceable tactic for assuring that he gets his choice is to be first in line when the office opens; he spends the night waiting outside the door. But the Darwinian brawl of competing claimants (here depicted as all male) cannot be won by such tactics alone. Pa is ambushed by his rivals for the claim, and he wins only with the help of a "rough man," his old friend Edwards from Kansas, who conveniently surfaces just when Pa needs an ally.

Even with the homestead claim safely filed, Pa is in no hurry to turn his energies toward establishing a home and farm there; instead, he puts up a store building in town, for profit. Only another outbreak of violence spurs him to move his family to the claim. When a nearby homesteader is murdered by a claim jumper, Pa is indignant and aroused; he says, "I think we'd better get onto our claim before somebody jumps it. . . . I'll go get a load of lumber and a man to help and put up the shanty this afternoon. We'll move tomorrow" (257).

Clearly, Charles Ingalls is in no hurry to commit himself to the homestead life. Homesteading was an exercise in stability, fixity, and farming;

homesteaders were required to cultivate land, erect dwellings, and to inhabit the claim for at least six months of the year. Stability and fixity do not excite Pa—but chance, change, drama, and uncertainty *do*. When he tells his wife and daughters the story of filing for his claim, he frames it (over Ma's protests) as a gamble between men: "Well, girls, I've bet Uncle Sam fourteen dollars against a hundred and sixty acres of land, that we can make out to live on the claim for five years. Going to help me win the bet?" (237). In the rush of men competing for "free" land, he resorts to the "rough" tactics that make Dakota an "uncivilized" place, according to Ma. To survive in Dakota, Pa depends on the help of Big Jerry, a gambler and suspected thief, and Edwards, who is adept in starting and winning brawls and (as an unpublished chapter confirms) at gambling and drinking.[7] Neither of these men has a wife or children, and for Laura (who is infatuated with both men) they epitomize the mobile, "free and independent" western male, unimpeded by law or convention. To get himself excited about the homestead, Pa frames it in the terms of such men: gambling, competition, danger, and even murder. Although the homestead has been planned for nearly a year, the Ingalls family moves to it in an impromptu one-day frenzy of building, which Pa finds stimulating.

All the Ingallses are glad to be moving to the claim—but for tellingly different reasons. "Ma and Mary were glad because this was the end of travelling; they were going to settle on the homestead and never move again. . . . Pa was glad because he always liked moving" (259–60). If Ma and Mary are to get what they desire and "never move again," Pa must give up the mobility he enjoys. Or vice versa.

In *Silver Lake* Charles Ingalls is obviously trying to keep his options open, as long as possible, in the fluid environment of this western territory. He is gambler, farmer, railroad man, builder, and entrepreneur, both inside and outside the law. If he is to commit himself totally to the life of a farmer, he must give up this exciting fluidity. Adolescent Laura watches intently as her father juggles these options and listens hard to his tales of adventures among men, for those tales are almost her only access to the stimulating world of frontiers*men*. As Glenda Riley has observed, the traditional ways in which U.S. historians have defined "frontier areas have been male in orientation. The very notion of a western region as a fur, farming, mineral, or lumber frontier reflects an overwhelming interest in the economic pursuits of its Euro-American male settlers" (1988, 4). Even though the homestead will absorb the full-time labors of all the Ingalls family members in coming years, it is clearly *"Pa's* claim," and the only option he offers his wife and daughters is to help him win his bet with the U.S. government, in which only men are enfranchised participants. The homestead claim offers Pa an officially sanctioned project and plot. According to William Holtz, through the 1862 Homestead Act, Pa's "private quest finds official sanction in the government's offer of a homestead" (1984, 83).

Laura sees no such options opening up for herself, only the prospect (which she dreads) of becoming a teacher and, later, a wife who facilitates a man's western plot. As men pour into De Smet—aspiring farmers, missionaries, and business entrepreneurs (including Almanzo Wilder, whom Laura will marry)—Laura finds herself serving them. With her mother and sisters, she prepares meals and beds for legions of unannounced male boarders. "The house was so full of strange men, strange eyes and strange voices and bulky coats and muddy boots, that she could hardly get through the crowd" (228). The "rough men" have excited Laura before, but now that they are inside of the Little House and turning their gaze on her, she is exhausted by the numbing, repetitive work of serving their needs. Her mobility and her volition seem almost gone. Although she hates confinement, Laura is glad to follow Ma's instructions and lock herself into her bedroom, with her sisters, on nights when the male boarders are in the house.

In *Silver Lake* Laura's escape from such confinement is the natural world, perhaps more compellingly beautiful here than in any of the other Little House books. Sent outside to get water, Laura lingers to see the sunrise and explains to Ma, "I just had to watch it" (72). Later, on an icy winter night, even dancing to Pa's fiddle cannot satisfy her:

> Beyond every window the white world stretched away . . . and the sky was a curve of light. Laura. . . . must move swiftly. She must be going somewhere.
>
> Suddenly she exclaimed, "Carrie! Let's go slide on the ice!" (163)

Laura's energies draw her into the white landscape of expanding horizons, a traditional lure of the West, and she desires a plot of her own, "going somewhere." Outdoors "she felt herself a part of the wide land, the far deep sky and the brilliant moonlight. She wanted to fly." The girls slide and run. "'On the moonpath, Carrie! Let's follow the moonpath,' Laura cried" (165).

Running at night with her sister, empowered with physical energy, attuned to nature and following the path of the moon, Laura seems allied with Artemis, the chaste moon goddess and female hunter, in this dreamlike, powerful scene. Then, suddenly, Laura looks up.

And there, dark against the moonlight, stood a great wolf!

He was looking toward her. The wind stirred his fur and the moonlight seemed to run in and out of it.

"Let's go back," Laura said quickly, as she turned, taking Carrie with her. (166)

At breathless speed, the girls run to the Little House, unpursued. The enormous male wolf patrols the boundaries of Laura's exhilarating freedom; like a fairy tale, this episode suggests that wolves wait for girls who venture into the wild world.

Laura and Carrie's adventure recalls the tale that enthralled Laura in *Big Woods*, Aunt Eliza's encounter with the predatory panther. But now that Laura is an adolescent, she is protagonist of her own story, which she tells to the family members who wait in the house. And this story is more romantic and mysterious. The wolf is *not* the moon's adversary; instead, with the moonlight in his fur, he seems a natural (and erotically suggestive) part of the great white land. It is his gaze that frightens Laura—and what she knows of his power to devour her and Carrie. But the wolf does not exercise that power.

The next day Pa takes up Laura's story. He tracks the wolf and concludes that it had returned, with its mate, for a last visit to an old den. Following the moonpath, Laura has entered a mythic, archaic realm where an adolescent girl might face a great male power unharmed, emerging with her selfhood and her freedom intact. But the great wolf is "pretty nearly the last," Pa says. "The railroads and settlements keep driving them farther west" (172). Then Pa makes an important announcement to his family: tracking the wolf, he has found the perfect homestead. When their final home on the Great Plains is built, it will be on the site of the wolves' den. Laura's moonlight adventure as a female hunter has led, once again, to a Little House. Such a juxtaposition is ambivalent in ways that are characteristic of this book. Has Pa appropriated Laura and Carrie's female adventure and grafted it on to his own homesteading project? Must all female adventures, however wild and free, necessarily end at the site of a house?

As *Silver Lake* proceeds, Laura's intense outdoor interludes continue, but they are increasingly fraught with such questions. Near the book's end, she still runs in the wind and ecstatically rolls in the "flowery grass . . . like a colt." But her pleasure is interrupted with anxiety about her appearance; sure enough, she discovers a grass stain on her calico dress and hurries off "to the little dark tar-paper shanty" to help Ma, as she knows she should (271). More and more, Laura's moments of physical, outdoor ecstasy are becoming a guilty secret.

Annis Pratt has observed that fictions of female adolescence are often marked by the young woman's special attraction to the natural world: "taking possession of nature, she possesses *herself*." As we have seen in *Silver Lake*, Laura has exhilarating moments in such a supportive natural world, which Pratt calls "the green-world archetype." Within this archetype, however, the girl's "appreciation of nature" is typically "retrospective, a look backwards over her shoulder as she confronts . . . her future submission within a male culture" (16–17).

Laura confronts such a situation at the ending of *Silver Lake*. Fulfilling Ma's wish, Pa hauls wild cottonwood saplings to plant on the treeless prairie so that the Ingallses' Dakota homestead will more resemble the partially wooded terrain where Ma feels most at home. The tree planting signals the co-opting of nature, as well as the Ingalls daughters, in the project of establishing a farm. Suddenly the youngest girl, four-year-old Grace, makes her escape; she disappears. After a terrifying search, Laura intuitively finds her sister in an enchanting hollow filled with fragrant wild violets. As a little girl, Grace can enter a green-world retreat of enveloping sweetness, but Laura can only admire the womblike sanctuary with a backward look. She says, "Come Grace. . . . We must go home" (281)—to the omnipresent Little House.

Despite its energy and exuberance, *Silver Lake* is shadowed throughout with such intimations of loss. Early in the book, when she first sees Dakota, Laura notices "old Indian trails and buffalo paths . . . grassed over." The buffalo are gone, she knows; "they had been the Indians' cattle and white men had slaughtered them all" (61–62). By the end of the book, Laura has seen the last wolf, driven away by the railroad men, and the new town that white men are building has frightened the beautiful birds from Silver Lake. She also learns that Grace's retreat, which she calls a "fairy ring," is really an old buffalo wallow, a poignant reminder of all that has been lost from this Great Plains environment. The novel ends with Laura's rueful thoughts of the Dakota landscape. Her conclusions emphasize historical progression, enforced largely by white men. The green world is superseded—as are the boundless possibilities of her own adolescence—by claims, agriculture, towns, and white settlers' "civilization," with its gender prescriptions. Laura concludes soberly, "The buffalo are gone. . . . And now we're homesteaders" (285). The novel's last words suggest that Pa, too, has been co-opted by the

Little House homesteading project. He sings the nineteenth century's most popular U.S. hymn to domestic stability: "Home, Sweet Home."

The next book looks more closely at the dark side of "Home, Sweet Home," taking domestic stability to near-fatal extremes. *The Long Winter* (1940) is the grimmest and most intense of the Little House books, and it covers the shortest span of time, a single legendary seven-month winter.[8] Wilder seemed unsure about the marketability of such a book; she wrote to Lane, "I am sending you today by registered mail 'The Hard Winter' mss. . . . It is rather a dark picture, not so much sweetness and light as the other books, but the next one will be different so perhaps the contrast will not be bad" (LIW to RWL, 3 June 1939, Hoover). Apparently her publisher shared some of her misgivings about this "dark" book; Harper insisted that Wilder's original title, "The Hard Winter," the name by which this legendary season was still known in De Smet, be changed.

Long Winter also makes significant changes in the gender orientation of the series. As a narrative of confinement and the extremes of domestic survival, it is *Ma*'s book. In this novel, the dynamics of the series change. Pa's weaknesses begin to be apparent, and Laura is pushed to recognize that, as a young woman, her primary affinities must be with her mother, not her father. Although Pa does his best, it is primarily Ma who finds the resources of endurance and culture that keep her family alive, fed, and sane through the months of unremitting confinement, when they are huddled in one heated room of Pa's store and, after the railroad has discontinued service, must subsist on wheat and tea.

This increased emphasis on Ma forced Wilder to confront new problems of narration. She found herself engaged with issues that Rachel Blau du Plessis says have faced most twentieth-century women who have tried to write fiction: "To compose a work is to negotiate these questions: What stories can be told? How can plots be resolved? What is felt to be narratable by both literary and social conventions?" (3). It was her father's male adventures that Wilder initially considered the material of fiction and that shaped her ideas about plot. Although the inset stories of *Big Woods* had disappeared from the series, as late as *Silver Lake* Wilder was still insisting that Pa's storytelling be a major, ongoing part of the Little House narrative. When they were working on the episodes of the railroad camp riots, she directed Lane, "Absolutely, you must let Pa tell the story. Pa tells stories in every one of the books" (LIW to RWL, 25 Jan. 1938, Hoover). Most of Lane's proposals for presenting male-oriented events from Laura's point of view were vetoed by Wilder, who seemed to feel that certain kinds of stories *must* be told in a male voice, even though the character of the adolescent Laura Ingalls was straining against such gender strictures. On one evening at Silver Lake, Ma and Laura wait for Pa to come home from what they fear may be a dangerous riot.

> "Ma, let me go out and find Pa," Laura whispered.
>
> "Be quiet," Ma answered. . . . "let Pa take care of himself."
>
> "I want to do something. I'd rather do something," Laura said.
>
> "So would I," said Ma. In the dark her hand began softly to stroke Laura's head. "The sun and the wind are drying your hair, Laura," Ma said. "You must brush it more. . . . I had lovely long hair when your Pa and I were married. . . ."
>
> She did not say any more. She went on stroking Laura's rough hair while they listened for the sound of shooting. (88–89)

Here Ma lays out narrative possibilities she approves for her adolescent daughter: Stay inside, distant from the sphere of male action. Stay quiet and groom yourself for a patriarchal marriage. This scene is extraordinarily intimate and sensuous. Although she hates waiting indoors, Laura also feels the sensory pull of her mother's agenda and of the close physical and emotional bond between them. And Ma makes an admission that is unique for her: she too hates waiting and would rather be active. When Pa does come in, he tells only fragments of a tale about horse thieves and averted violence; Laura will never know the whole story.

In *Long Winter* Wilder and Lane decided to foreground the world of Caroline Ingalls and her daughters, waiting indoors in confined intimacy and knowing only fragments of the male stories that take place outside the Little House.[9] This fifth book was their most sustained effort to make a *narrative*—not just descriptive passages—out of what must have previously seemed unnarratable. As du Plessis says, many twentieth-century women writers have essayed this "untold story, the other side of a well-known tale, the elements of women's existence that have never been revealed" in fiction (3). As Wilder turned to these largely unstoried elements of women's traditional culture, she found herself suddenly blocked and uncertain, as she confessed to Lane in a crucial letter:

Here is what is bothering me and holding me up. I can't seem to find a plot, or pattern as you call it.

There seems to be nothing to it only the struggle to live, through the winter. . . . This of course they all did. But is it strong enough . . . to supply the necessary thread running all through the book.

I could make a book with the plot being Laura's struggles to be, and success in becoming a teacher. . . . That would be a plot. . . . But it seems to weaken it. To be a sort of anti-climax. . . . I don't like it. But where is the plot in Hard Winter? (LIW to RWL, 19 Feb. 1938, Hoover)

This author is struggling to narrate a constricted domestic life. Laura's efforts to establish herself as a teacher would make a more conventional, completable plot—but obviously that isn't what Wilder wants here; she rejects that strategy. "Plot" in *Silver Lake* meant progress toward an achievable goal; that book ends with the Ingalls family establishing a residence on the new homestead. But in *Long Winter* the only goal is to stay alive today—and then to take up the same effort tomorrow. Such a domestic struggle has properties that Kathryn Allen Rabuzzi says are characteristic of housework, "so obviously circular that . . . completion scarcely can be experienced" (149). Typically—as in *Big Woods*—repetitive domestic work is inscribed, if at all, as the background for more conventional plots, usually executed by men. Although Caroline Ingalls is a constant and influential force in her daughters' lives, she is usually a silent one compared to her voluble husband.

In fact, even before *Long Winter*, a subtle but important subtext of the Little House series has been to establish Laura's connection to Ma and Ma's work. One means of accomplishing this is the ongoing story of Laura's rag doll, Charlotte. The rag doll first appears in *Big Woods* as a gift for Laura's fifth Christmas. As the little girl scrutinizes this beloved toy for the first time, every detail evokes a process and a craft: "A black pencil had made her eyebrows, and her cheeks were red with the ink made from pokeberries. Her hair was black yarn that had been knit and raveled, so that it was curly" (74–75). Knitting and sewing and drawing and even making ink—all these tasks, and more, are involved in the making of a simple rag doll. From watching her mother, Laura must already know that Charlotte is the product of a woman's work; her father does none of these tasks. Yet her thoughts suppress the maker's identity, making it possible for the child to believe in a male benefactor, Santa Claus. Such suppression also protects Laura, in her early childhood, from perceiving the overwhelming *extent* of women's work. Yet Laura's and Mary's rag dolls are a means of preparing themselves to assume such work. According to Karin Calvert, after 1850

> childlike dolls gained rapid popularity in America, where many established residents feared that the influx of eastern and southern European immigrants . . . would eventually overwhelm the established American culture unless something was done. With declining birthrates among middle-class women. . . . little girls had to be convinced of the joys of motherhood so that they might ensure the survival of their way of life. (118–19)

By presenting their daughters with dolls, Ma and Pa are teaching them to perpetuate a conservative, ethnocentric "way of life" and its gender prescriptions. The choice of a homemade rag doll, in addition to reflecting the Ingallses' limited economic options, also reflects values that Ma supports. According to Miriam Formanek-Brunell, late nineteenth-century women's periodicals "extolled the virtues" of "cloth dolls that taught virtue and understanding" instead of fashion affectations (3). Making dolls like Charlotte, "women used textiles in part because of life-long domestic familiarity with their properties" (68).

On Christmas Day, Laura is mesmerized by her new fabric doll, which she names Charlotte.[10] "She just held her tight and forgot everything else. She did not know that everyone was looking at her" (76). The new doll initiates Laura into the world of child care and sewing. Tellingly, Laura is voiceless as she cradles Charlotte. This puts her into the position that, according to Josephine Donovan, typified most traditional women in a patriarchal culture; they were "silenced" and confined, as Caroline Ingalls is, to a "domestic or private sphere." Their work was "non-progressive, repetitive, and static," and they created objects "for use rather than for exchange" (100, 103). On Christmas Day, the very young Laura assumes with Charlotte the posture that her culture will urge on her again and again. Silently she preserves a precious object (or surrogate child) and will produce more objects (doll clothes, dolls—and children). In this position, she is in danger of being objectified herself; the surrounding relatives turn their gaze on her.

Charlotte is one of the most popular figures in the Little House pantheon; the doll is one of the four or five ongoing threads that Lane advised Wilder she *must* retain throughout the series to reinforce continuity. Cloth

"Charlottes" are best-selling items in the shops at the Little House sites. I still have my own Charlotte, hand-stitched by a Mansfield woman, and her black button eyes seem to reproach me for the stern views of Charlotte that I have just written. Like the young Laura, many little girls (and some women) understand very well what it means to be passionately attached to a "darling rag Charlotte," and they cherish that attachment. In fact, Charlotte epitomizes the cultural efficacy of the Little House books. She marks a crucial spot where play, pleasure, education, and gender indoctrination meet. And although the doll may school Laura in domestic submission, she also encourages sewing skills that will become a significant source of income for Laura during her adolescence and young womanhood.[11]

Charlotte becomes an important figure in Laura's life, and in *Plum Creek* she is at the center of another memorable episode, a special favorite of girls. When the Nelsons' visiting daughter cries for Charlotte, Ma forces Laura to give away her doll: "For shame, Laura. . . . Anna's little and she's company. You are too big to play with dolls." Later, Laura finds Charlotte abandoned in the Nelson barnyard. Defiantly, she turns outlaw and "steals" back her battered doll. This is one of the series' harshest scenes of violation; in the ice and mud, Charlotte is terribly displaced and mistreated—as is Laura—and it is the fault of Ma.

However, the episode reveals another side of Ma and another aspect of Laura's relation to her mother's domestic culture. Ma's prescriptions and priorities have sometimes seemed to violate Laura's desires and to silence her voice. But now Ma *apologizes* to Laura: "I wouldn't have given away your doll if I'd known you care so much," she says (233). Devotion to and preservation of a beloved object/icon/child is something Ma can understand. She helps her daughter to revise patriarchal Mosaic law—"Thou shalt not steal"—to honor Laura's priorities. "They decided that it had not been wrong for Laura to take back Charlotte. It had been a terrible experience for Charlotte, but Laura had rescued her and Ma promised to make her as good as new." Ma also creates a new story for her daughter, in which preserving things can be a daring, heroic act—as in the "rescue" of Charlotte. As she repairs the doll, the processes of dollmaking are cataloged again, as they were on the original Christmas. But now *Ma*, not Santa, is the acknowledged maker—and *Laura* is her assistant. "They thawed Charlotte and wrung her out, and Ma washed her thoroughly clean and starched and ironed her while Laura chose from the scrap-bag a new, pale pink face for her and new button eyes" (236). Laura is still being indoctrinated in a domestic script. But now she can also see that script as one that facilitates her own desires and allows her to enact powerful, important stories—saving Charlotte's life and her own.[12]

Significantly, the rescue of Charlotte occurs when Pa is away for several weeks, working in the eastern harvest. In the first four books, it is during such absences that the Ingalls daughters are most fully aware of their mother's powers. But in *Long Winter* Wilder and Lane emphasized those powers in Pa's *presence*. In his earlier explanation to Laura of "how things [such as the railroad] happen," Pa dismissed weather as a breezy afterthought. But in this book of blizzards, weather is a central, relentless fact that no man's plot can circumvent. The concerns of *Long Winter* are those of the most traditional domestic culture: food, clothing, shelter. And the book's rhythms are those that dominate housework, the repetitive tasks of maintenance and waiting.

However, the book begins, as the Ingalls family's first summer on their claim ends, with Laura's intuitions about how arbitrary the distinctions between men's and women's tasks are. At fourteen, a healthy adolescent, she feels newly large and powerful, ready to reject conventional myths. In Pa's hayfield, she encounters a little garter snake in the grass: "Laura felt suddenly as big as a mountain when the snake curved up its head and stared at the high wall of her calico skirt" (3). In this grassy Eden, the serpent is no wily tempter but a gentle companion, and it makes Laura aware of her own strength. Now she has a new idea: since no man is available to help Pa with the haying, she will help him herself. Ma is doubtful; "only foreigners did that" (4). Laura's working in the fields threatens Ma's construction of civilization. Nevertheless, Pa needs the help and Laura learns to make hay. Although she does "women's work" regularly—cooking, cleaning, sewing—Laura expresses no satisfaction in such domestic chores. But haying, although painfully strenuous, is deeply gratifying: "Laura was proud. . . . She liked to see the stacks that she helped to make" (9). Like the railroad builders, she is making a mark on the land—as well as providing hay that will be food and fuel for the family and their stock during the coming hard winter.

After this success, when Pa sends Laura on her first solo errand to town, she has an exhilarating sense of her own capabilities and options; on the road to town, she and Carrie feel "free and independent and comfortable together" (19). But soon they are lost in the tall slough grass, and the "green world" turns against them. At last they come upon a strange boy who, high on a hay wagon, can see Pa in the distance and gives Laura directions. (This is her first encounter with Almanzo Wilder.) Miserably, Laura confronts the limits of her powers. The boy can see far because he is doing a man's work. But Laura, who feels like a shy, helpless rabbit, must ask for male help; she cannot manage on the prairie alone. Her fantasy of being "free and independent" is destroyed, and she feels gallingly dependent.

Pa has encouraged Laura's fantasy of independence. When the two are haying, they find an extra-sturdy muskrat house, which is their first indication that the coming winter will be severe. "God tells" the muskrats of coming extremity, Pa says.

> "Then why doesn't God tell us?" Laura wanted to know.
>
> "Because," said Pa, "we're not animals. We're humans, and, like it says in the Declaration of Independence, God created us free. That means we got to take care of ourselves."
>
> Laura said faintly, "I thought God takes care of us."

For Laura, the ideal of independence is as frightening as it is exhilarating, and now Pa tells her that she cannot rely on the omnipotent care of a benign, patriarchal God. Pa goes on, trying to explain free will: "Look at that muskrat house. Muskrats have to build that kind of house. . . . But a man can build any kind of house he can think of. . . . he's free and independent" (39). Although the discussion began in terms of "us humans," Pa has switched to male pronouns. And Laura is perplexed: is she included in or excluded from the state of being "free and independent" that is guaranteed by the U.S. government? Again, Pa uses the conventions of building and architecture to proclaim his powers: a *man* builds *his* own house. As an adolescent girl, Laura must find *her* place in the prevailing culture. To succeed as a westerner, she must live an active, inventive, pioneering life. But just as she begins to feel the new strength and energy that could launch such an independent life, she is pushed to confine and efface herself by assuming a feminine role. On her first day at school in town, she athletically leaps to catch a ball tossed a boy. "A great shout went up from the other boys. 'Hey. . . . Girls don't play ball!'" Acting according to her healthy body's strengths and impulses, Laura has broken a powerful taboo, and she feel "ashamed, fearful" (78). In town it is unthinkable that she work with Pa in hauling the hay, even though he could use her help. Someone might see her exercising her strength.

Laura again finds herself in the position that Annis Pratt says is typical of adolescent girls in much fiction by women. For such girls, being "'adult' means learning to be dependent, submissive, or 'non-adult.' As a result of this conflict, an imagery of entrapment or fear of psychological invasion introduces a nightmare element into texts that also, at the opposite extreme, manifest yearnings for an integration of childhood hopes with adult social possibilities" (16). *Long Winter* plays images of a protracted series of debilitating storms against images of Ma's preservative housekeeping, which strictly observes gender roles. Both sets of imagery are charged with the nightmarish potential Pratt describes (and which Wilder suggests in her description of this novel as "dark"), as Laura is forced to acknowledge that her place, as a woman, will almost certainly be *in* the Little House.

As the long winter approaches, Ma and Pa seem to vie with each other to demonstrate their mastery of traditionally gendered skills, showing their growing daughters how a Euro-American man and woman can act out a western life. Pa brings in the meager first-year harvest; Ma, with her girls' help, transforms it into pickles and preserves. Even inedibles—such as the smallest green tomatoes—are made edible. Ma, usually modest, boasts triumphantly, "gloating" over her tomato pickles. It is such domestic feats in which she takes greatest pride, and she teaches her girls to admire and emulate them. According to Mintz and Kellogg, within the prevailing model of the nineteenth-century "democratic" U.S. family, "the ideal wife and mother devoted her life exclusively to domestic tasks" (53). The fictional Caroline Ingalls enacts that role flawlessly.

In the fall rains, Pa goes out to hunt meat. Although Laura hates staying in the cabin, there is no possibility that she could accompany her father; he never takes his daughters hunting or teaches them to shoot.[13] When he hunts, Charles Ingalls comes and goes as he pleases. Alone in a world storied in the male mythology of his tales, he can ignore regular mealtimes and the scheduled, civilizing domesticity that his wife's housekeeping upholds.

Left indoors, Laura sits sewing with her mother and sisters. While Pa is stalking on the boundless prairie, she is stuck making sheets, stitching together two breadths of cloth.

> Sewing made Laura feel like flying to pieces. She wanted to scream. The back of her neck ached and the thread twisted and knotted. She had to pick out almost as many stitches as she put in.
>
> "Blankets are wide enough to cover a bed," she said fretfully. "Why can't sheets be made wide enough?"
>
> "Because sheets are muslin," said Mary. "And muslin isn't wide enough for a sheet."
>
> The eye of Laura's needle slipped through a tiny hole in her thimble and ran into her finger. She shut her mouth hard and did not say a word. (33)

Silently, Laura must contend with confined spaces, predictable tasks. According to Mary, muslin will always be the same width, so Laura will always have to sew sheets. Yet this is the same century in which, through new technology and the cooperative work of men, the railroad is being put in place. Laura longs for an invention that will change her domestic work—as the sewing machine will do, in the last Little House book.

On this very day, Ma chooses to show her girls how women can invent even in the most traditional domestic space: the kitchen. She concocts a never-before-made pie from slices of green pumpkin. Laura is doubtful; she says, "I never heard of such a thing, Ma." And Ma replies, "Neither did I. . . . But we wouldn't do much if we didn't do things that nobody heard of before" (32). Pa returns home empty-handed; he could find no game. But Ma's unique pie is a delicious success. Her invention creates its own climate in the shanty, transforming confinement to content: "That was such a happy supper that Laura wanted it never to end" (36).

For Ma life is not simply a matter of acceding to the outer weather. Instead, she invents her own domestic weather. For example, on the first day Laura works with Pa, Ma flavors their drinking water with ginger. "Such a treat made that ordinary day into a special day, the first day that Laura helped in the haying" (8). By such kitchen magic, Ma controls the life of her family and reminds them of domestic priorities, even when a daughter has temporarily entered a male world. Ma's housekeeping is an enormous and life-enhancing power, yet its cost is the confinement and circumscription of her own life—and those of her daughters.

In the first blizzard, the most horrifying occurrence, for Laura, is seeing a herd of cattle "terribly still," with great white heads frozen to the ground. "She felt that somehow, in the wild night and storm, the stillness that was underneath all sounds on the prairie had seized the cattle" (50). The image of the cattle touches Laura's own deepest fears—fears of being stilled, immobilized, silenced. Always before, Laura has connected such fears with *indoor* life in Ma's sphere. But now, in the most extreme weather of her life, she apprehends that she might be stilled by the great natural forces *outside*, where she has longed to be.

At school Laura also has to acknowledge that the authority of her young, female teacher is unreliable, for "Teacher," a prairie novice, knows nothing of weather. When a storm hits the schoolhouse, Laura thinks, " 'I ought to tell her what to do.'. . . But she could not think what to do. It was not safe to leave the schoolhouse and it was not safe to stay there" (85–86). The man who arrives to lead the school to shelter is a novice too; disoriented in the swirling storm, he leads the children toward death on the open prairie. Laura's intuition rebels; she "felt that they were going in the wrong direction." But "Teacher had told them to follow. . . . There was nothing to go by—no sun, no sky, no direction" (89–90). Significantly, Pa does not come to the rescue, as he might have in an earlier book. Laura finds herself enveloped by a nightmare of obliterating storm, where all signs and all authority are blotted out—even her own, for she fears to trust her (correct) intuition. No wonder that, when she is reinstated by the family stove, drinking Ma's warming ginger tea, Laura feels that she is in heaven with all the household gods. Soon after this close call, school is closed, the railroads shut down, and coal and food run out. The life of the Ingalls family shrinks to one room, where they huddle near the hay-burning stove, eating only two meals each short, dark day.

Pa still goes out every day, feeding the stock, hauling hay, and visiting with other men in the town stores. But the girls and Ma must stay in. And Ma is most confined of all; in their seven months in town, she is depicted outdoors only once, hanging laundry. Yet Ma clearly rules the roost during the long winter. She preserves her family's life through her control of the smallest details of housekeeping. For example, when the kerosene runs out, she contrives a "button lamp" from a scrap of cloth, axle grease, and a button—"only a little light, but it makes all the difference." Pa says, "you're a wonder, Caroline" (197).

Pa himself is attentive to natural phenomena; the thick muskrat house and early animal hibernations spurred him to accelerate winter preparations. But he repeatedly praises Ma in terms of something that flouts the usual laws of nature: she is "a wonder."[14] Characteristically, from inside her kitchen, Caroline Ingalls combats unbridled nature with prediction, denial, routine, and domestic magic. She teaches her girls how to manage time, encouraging them to ration their small pleasures (food and stories) and to observe daily routine even when they are totally isolated in the frozen village. Lillian Schlissel, studying diaries of Oregon pioneer women, concluded that Ma's impulses were nearly universal among western women; they "tried to weave a fabric of accustomed design, a semblance of their usual domestic circle. . . . The women created and held onto some order and routine" (15–16).

During the long winter, Laura emulates Ma more than she ever has before. At Christmas, for example, she gives her mother and sisters embroidery and fine knitted lace that she had been making for herself, just as Ma gave her own best handkerchief as a gift to an unexpected guest the pre-

vious Christmas. Laura begins to be her mother's confidante and collaborator in the rituals that stitch the Little House series together, and a producer
and preserver of the cherished domestic objects that anchor the family's
peripatetic life. In the Ingalls family, Ma has been the keeper of objects, and
her things reinforce her goals of "schooling and . . . a civilized life" (SSL
209) for her daughters. She preserves books, fabrics, buttons, scraps of
paper, and her pearl-handled pen for writing to the "folks" left behind.
Ritual, stability, and literacy are Ma's realm, even in the long winter.

All these values are expressed by Ma's dearest object, a fragile porcelain figure of a shepherdess. The shepherdess is determinedly unrealistic.
She is impractically garbed in a white dress, pink apron, and gold shoes,
and her perfect blonde curls are never disarranged by western weather.
Although the Ingallses' efforts at farming are assailed by droughts, plagues,
and blizzards, the shepherdess's gilding, glaze, and delicate pigments in-
voke a pastoral ideal and a perennially civilized tradition. Since *Big Woods*
this venerated figure has been beautiful and important to Laura; it is the
oldest object in her home, "older than Laura could remember" (LTP 18).
Unlike the Ingalls daughters, the shepherdess does not change, grow, or
suffer from disease or blindness. In each dwelling that Ma deems worthy as
a family home (some of them, like the railroad shanty, are *un*worthy), she
deliberately, artfully places this bit of china. Again and again, when the
shepherdess is placed, she is described—at least five passages, dispersed
throughout the series, restate, in fugal repetitions, the same details of color,
glaze, form. For readers as for the maturing Laura, meaning accrues with
each reappearance of the shepherdess. Always, placing the shepherdess is
the climax of "moving in":

> The last thing, Pa hung the bracket . . . and Ma stood the little
> china shepherdess on it. . . .
> That was the same smiling little shepherdess . . . her little china
> bodice laced with china-gold ribbons and her little china apron and
> her little china shoes. She had travelled from the Big Woods all the
> way to Indian territory, and all the way to Plum Creek in Minnesota,
> and there she stood smiling. She was not broken. She was not nicked
> nor even scratched. She was the same little shepherdess, smiling the
> same smile. (BPC 123)

Ma's shepherdess establishes the Ingalls family in an enduring continuum
of "civilized life." Repeatedly, she provides a triumphantly female ideological center for the rudimentary houses Pa hastily builds, connecting the

Ingallses' hard manual labor to establish a farm with a more elevated, affluent, and leisurely pastoral tradition. In the face of such daunting obstacles as the long winter, this figure of an imperishable, unchanging agricultural woman becomes even more preciously meaningful. On the frontier, according to Sally I. Helvensten, "the vigorous labor, involved in establishing a homestead so dramatically altered [Euro-American settler] women's physical condition and appearance that their perceptions of themselves as attractive ornaments were effectively changed" (37). But although Ma may be unable to keep her daughters or herself safely sunbonneted and securely sheltered in a Little House, her porcelain ornament is an indispensable stand-in for her ideal, always "the same."

As the series proceeds, Wilder and Lane make it more obvious that, as much as Pa, Ma is the conceptual architect of the Little Houses. Inside the amorphous spaces he constructs, she intensely, rigorously articulates space, and she teaches her daughters to do the same. For Ma is very aware that, as Daphne Spain says, "houses are the spatial context within which the social order is reproduced" (140). In the last three books, shuttling between the store building in De Smet and the shanty on Pa's claim, the Ingalls family moves at least twice a year. Thus "home" for them is no one dwelling but rather the stable idea of a house that (unlike any actual structure) is portable and imperishable. The *signifier,* the word "house," becomes more and more distant from any literal, physical *signified.* Schooled by Ma, Laura learns to think of the structures her father builds in reference to this conceptual house. Thus the Ingalls women see the minuscule new claim shanty as *half* a house; the other half exists in their minds. When Pa adds more rooms, years later, Laura says, "Pa built the missing half of the claim shanty" (LTP 16).

Wherever the family lives, Ma supervises the arrangement of their necessities, including her essential vocabulary of cultural signifiers, such as the shepherdess, curtains, quilts, books, and a red-checked tablecloth. The continuities of *home* are created by these arrangements and their combinations of variables and constants, so that even a blind daughter has the security of a stable shelter. Mary says, after a move, "The cupboard is in a different place, but Ma put all the dishes in the same places in the cupboard, so I find them just as easily as ever" (73). In the earlier books, Ma sometimes seems cowed by her husband's egocentric feats of building and buying. But now her confidence and powers of invention are more apparent. Faced with the problem of fitting six people and all their possessions into a tiny claim shanty, Pa is perplexed. But Ma replies confidently,

"Where there's a will there's a way." Laura, by now a moving veteran herself, comes to her mother's aid, proposing an ingenious arrangement of furniture and curtains. Ma's response is the most explicit praise she ever gives Laura: "That's my smart girl!" (SSL 268).

Laura is praised because she is following her mother's example, controlling space as she has seen Ma do, and inventively using textiles such as quilts, curtains, and sheets—traditional appurtenances of women's culture—as her medium. Thus the women "build" rooms in the frame Pa has constructed, expressing the preoccupation with differentiated space that was so important to the domestic literature of the second half of the nineteenth century.[15] Ma reads domestic literature whenever it is available on the frontier: a sentimental novel by Mary Jane Holmes,[16] *Godey's Lady's Book* (which published monthly house plans, as well as illustrated reports on interior decoration and fashion), and Protestant women's "church papers." Through such reading, she would have been at least indirectly touched by the most influential housekeeping manual of the times, Catharine Beecher and Harriet Beecher Stowe's *American Woman's Home*, published in 1869.

The Beecher sisters began their discussion of houses with these words: "In the Divine Word it is written, 'The wise woman buildeth her house'" (23). Pivotally, this text claims "Divine" approval for women's appropriation of the prerogatives of *building*, and especially as Ma does so, by the articulation of interior space. Beecher and Stowe offer instructions for "the close packing of conveniences" in "small and economical houses" and they advocate the use of home-constructed movable storage screens to define space. With their quilts, curtains, and recycled packing boxes, Laura and her mother accomplish these same ends. The Ingalls family's practice confirms what Angel Kwolek-Folland has argued: in the late nineteenth-century United States, "the home environment essentially was a woman's creation even though the physical shell was designed or built by males" (1983, 72). Especially on the frontier, such work was often an assertive act of *creation*, as Kwolek-Folland says, and of invention; according to Glenda Riley, in the West "an individual woman's creativity was often the key to the successful conversion of a primitive structure into a comfortable home" (1988, 56).

Ma's increasing power in the Little House constellation is partly a function of Laura's growing sense of alliance with her mother. But it may also be related to the fact that Ma's isolation is lessening somewhat. By *Long Winter* De Smet is beginning to be a town. Pa estimates that seventy-five or eighty people are wintering in the new community, and a significant number of them are girls and women. Ma seldom sees these women, but their presence is a support. Also, the Ingalls family has more contact with newspapers and periodicals; Ma's "paper" for churchwomen and her occasional glimpses of *Godey's Lady's Book,* as well as the girls' *Youth's Companions,* forge supportive connections with a network of women elsewhere. Wilder and Lane, who both wrote for and avidly read women's magazines, knew how important such connections could be, especially for farm women.

According to Donovan, a traditional woman who has been "silenced" in a patriarchal culture must, in order to create art, "be in communication with others of her group in order that a collective 'social construction of reality' be articulated" (100). When "quiet" Ma speaks, she often does so in proverbs and maxims, such as her litany of "Wash on Monday. . . . " Such utterances have made her seem narrow and priggish to many readers. But on isolated farms where she could go for months without seeing another woman, such conventionalized expressions of traditional female wisdom provide Ma with a buttressing sense of "communication with others of her group," necessary if she is to work and create effectively on the frontier. By the later books, her adolescent daughters, Mary and Laura, are also beginning to be her peers, and the Little House is itself becoming a self-perpetuating community of women.

In *Silver Lake* Docia and Lena enact versions of female possibility that Ma cannot endorse. But later in that book, a new female character appears who reinforces Ma's values and serves as a catalyst for the increasing female influence in the Little House series. Ellie Boast, a seventeen-year-old from "the East" (Iowa), is a homesteader's bride; she becomes Ma's one close female friend and a staple presence in the series who need not, like Lena and Docia, be banished. Besides admiring and emulating Ma's traditional skills, Mrs. Boast exposes the Ingalls girls to contemporary trends in domestic culture. Ma's youth was presumably dominated by the ideology of "separate spheres" that was influential in the midcentury United States, and she passed much of that ideology on to her daughters, born in the 1860s and 1870s. But by the late seventies and eighties, the high point of "separate spheres" had passed and the emphasis on "order and hierarchy in domestic life" was giving way to "new stress on individual talents, the display of material possessions and the equality of household members" (Clark 108).

Merry, energetic, sociable Mrs. Boast provides a female model that both Laura and her mother can like and admire. Her frequent visits to the Ingalls house are a foundation for the first alliances of female power in the new town of De Smet. As Julie Roy Jeffrey has noted, such "visiting . . .

created a female support system and assisted women in their attempts to regulate society" in frontier settlements (85). And, as an "Easterner," Ellie Boast brings the resources of popular culture to the Ingalls women, in the form of a "tall stack. . . . of New York Ledgers from Iowa" (207), which introduce the girls to the delights of serial fiction and stories with female protagonists. (Such continuing narratives may be forerunners of the Little House series.) Despite the dimensions of her excruciatingly small shanty, the determined bride invents a furniture arrangement that allows her to invite the Ingallses to a "fashionable" dinner party—even if the door won't close! To Laura, Mrs. Boast's novel housekeeping is entrancingly "odd and new," as stylish and contemporary as something from *Godey's Lady's Book* (204). In a pivotal episode, Mrs. Boast instructs the Ingallses in constructing an Iowa (and national) fad, a whatnot. With this task, the architecture and building that have been Pa's realm become a female project. Pa does the basic construction while Mrs. Boast acts as architect, issuing commands, and the Ingalls women do the fine finishing work. At last the shelves are in place:

> "So that's a whatnot," Pa said.
> "Yes," said Ma. "Isn't it pretty?"
> "Mrs. Boast says they're all the rage in Iowa," she told him.
> "Well, she ought to know," Pa agreed. "And there's nothing in
> Iowa too good for you, Caroline." (SSL 211)

Pa's responses are newly equivocal; he accedes to the cultural authority of his wife and Mrs. Boast.

The whatnot (which becomes a staple object of the remaining books in the series) is a homemade adaptation of a Gothic Revival furniture style and an important signifier. According to Kwolek-Folland, "the what-not cabinet or its equivalent appeared in all homes with any pretension to culture." It duplicates the Little House, presenting "a small replica of the rooms themselves" (1983, 73). Like a little temple, the whatnot becomes a tableau as telling as any altar. When Pa later builds "two tiny bedrooms" onto the homestead shanty, his labors are summarized in only two paragraphs, although *Little House on the Prairie* previously devoted several chapters to the processes of Pa's carpentry. However, eight paragraphs describe the women's arrangement of the shanty's "front room," newly spacious with the bedsteads removed. The crucial separation of public and private space is finally accomplished. The chapter culminates in a minutely detailed description of the whatnot:

> The afternoon light made plain the gilded titles of the books on the whatnot's lower shelf, and glittered in the three glass boxes on the shelf above. . . . above them, on the next shelf, the gilt flowers shone on the glass face of the clock and its brass pendulum glinted, swinging to and fro. Higher still, on the very top shelf, was Laura's white china jewel box with the wee gold cup and saucer on its lid, and beside it, watching over it, was Carrie's brown and white china dog. . . . It was a beautiful room. (LTP 18)

The whatnot orders and summarizes the values that Ma (and now also Mrs. Boast) would impress on the Ingalls daughters: literacy, socialized time, amenities, and preservation.[17] It also functions as a narrative device, for each of the objects it holds evokes an earlier episode in the series. Like the shepherdess, it provides coherence for a series of Little Houses and of Little House books. The whatnot speaks for women's capacities to invent, to build, to survive, and to perpetuate culture, even in a community where houses are built and owned by men.

In *The Long Winter* the Ingalls daughters' education in buying and consuming comes to an almost complete stop.[18] In snowed-in De Smet, cut off from the railroad that has brought in manufactured commodities, there is virtually nothing to buy. As I observed in Chapter 3, Ma is less invested in the market than the other family members; thus it is not surprising that she comes into her own during the hard winter. Conserving, reusing, and recycling are second nature to Caroline Ingalls. She personifies the principles of a very popular nineteenth-century housekeeping manual, Lydia Maria Child's *The American Frugal Housewife*, which begins: "The true economy of housekeeping is simply the art of gathering up all the fragments, so that nothing be lost. I mean fragments of *time*, as well as *materials*" (1). Again and again, Ma's resources are her scrap bag and her button box. They provide the materials for Charlotte, for the button lamp, for the crisp curtains that hang in every Little House,[19] and for the many other textile projects that "civilize" the Little House and facilitate its rituals.

The actual Ingalls family was "poor," Wilder reminded Lane,[20] and so are their fictional counterparts. Ma's recycling is an economic necessity, as it was for many Depression families who were the first readers of the Little House books. For example, Laura's Big Woods calico dress is remade for Baby Carrie, and then turns up, volumes later, as edging for Ma's *new* curtains, sewn from *old* sheets. At Christmas in Dakota, gift bedshoes are cut from a worn-out blanket, and bits of mismatched yarn become striped mittens. As little girls on Plum Creek, Laura and Mary were allowed to make a Christmas button string for Baby Carrie out of Ma's hoarded button box:

> Ma had saved buttons since she was smaller than Laura, and she had buttons her mother had saved when her mother was a little girl. There were blue buttons and red buttons, silvery and goldy buttons, curved-in buttons with tiny raised castles and trees on them, and twinkling jet buttons, painted china buttons, striped buttons, buttons like juicy blackberries, and even one tiny dog-head button. Laura squealed when she saw it. (BPC 90)

Ma's button box is like a tiny catalog of the proliferating visual resources of nineteenth-century popular culture, preserved and augmented for at least three generations and then restrung to beguile a baby girl and to teach her the value and meanings of preserved things.

The prototypical scrap bag, which almost every housekeeper possessed, became an emblem of the resources of women's domestic culture for many nineteenth-century female readers and writers; for example, Louisa May Alcott published a series of collections called *Aunt Jo's Scrap Bag*. Ma is visibly proudest of her daughters when they begin to utilize the resources of her scrap bag themselves. As Ma makes a Christmas apron for Laura from one old curtain, Laura secretly makes a matching apron for her mother from the other curtain of the pair. Such projects were a major part of Laura's education in aesthetics as well as household economy. Like most nineteenth-century daughters, she was taught knitting, simple sewing, and patchwork at an early age, long before she learned to read.[21] The actual Laura Ingalls Wilder also sewed all her life; she was still making quilts years after the writing of her series was completed. Lane, too, was an accomplished and prolific needlewoman and author of a popular study of U.S. women's needlework.

When Wilder and Lane looked for ways to give coherence to an ambitious serial of eight volumes, they drew from the button box/scrap bag aesthetic practiced by Ma Ingalls. Recycled textiles, such as the dress-curtain-apron fabric, often provide a shorthand reminder of continuities of plot and values, as do the repeated references to arrangement and rearrangement of significant domestic objects. In particular, pieced quilts, which were a constant element in Wilder's and Lane's personal lives, offered a model for the Little House sequence of novels. Quilts are a constant background presence in the books: they are warmth, comfort, protection, privacy, decoration, a baby's pallet, a temporary door, and a constant task for girls and women. Quiltmaking, widely practiced by nineteenth-century U.S. women, is an art of choice and placement and often of salvage, in which scraps of things are given new meaning and use. The series mentions only *pieced* quilts in classic geometric patterns—such as the nine patch and bear's track, with which Mary and Laura began—all based on a grid. Jonathan Holstein argues that the grid form was invented by nineteenth-century women in response to the technological advances of the century (22, 26). Caroline Ingalls, although she can be very conservative, does not romanticize the laborious handwork of preindustrial women's crafts; as we have seen, she buys fabrics and uses the sewing machine with enthusiasm. The grid quilts designed and assembled by Ma and her daughters illustrate their commitment to both tradition and innovation within women's domestic culture, values that were extremely important to both Wilder and Lane. Elaine Showalter has written suggestively about the importance of the grid to nineteenth-century women's art: "While the discipline of the pieced quilt itself represents women's confinement within the grid of nineteenth-century feminine domestic morality, it also offers the potential creative freedom of textuality and design" (233).

In *Long Winter* particularly, as we have seen, Wilder worried about finding a "plot" in a life of exacerbated confinement. During those seven months, the entire Ingalls family labors at the most basic tasks of maintenance, grinding wheat for bread and twisting hay to feed the fire. They survive not because of the technological innovations of the late nineteenth century but because of preindustrial skills. Ma makes sourdough; Pa twists hay; Laura knits lace. Both Pa and Ma rail against the linear nineteenth-century plot of *progress*: "These times are too progressive. . . . Railroads and telegraph and kerosene and coal stoves—they're good things to have but the trouble is, folks get to depend on 'em" (192–93). Progress was the plot of *Silver Lake*, but the "pattern" of *Long Winter* must be different. It is telling that Wilder wrote of her struggles with this book in terms of fabric and sewing: she was searching for "the necessary thread."

Here, and throughout the series, the resources of Caroline Ingalls's domestic culture offered essential aesthetic support. The grid quilts that Laura Ingalls was taught to make as a child lack Aristotelean plot; they do not encourage the eye to follow a linear course across a surface and to complete a motion. Instead, their geometric figures advance and recede, with duplications and reversions of the same forms and configurations, again and again. The nine-patch pattern, with its infinite possibilities of variation within one simple form, is an obvious illustration, and it is the pattern with which the Ingalls daughters, like other nineteenth-century girls, traditionally began. Pieced quilts are made of duplicate blocks; each block may have a separate identity. (Indeed, as in the Little House books, some blocks are preserved for many years before they are assembled and quilted.) The volumes of Wilder and Lane's innovative "multi-volume novel" thus resemble the blocks of a grid quilt, which were assembled to create a unified, functional whole that expressed both the preservationist and innovative values of domestic women's culture. Within the Little House series, Ma's expressive things—Charlotte, the shepherdess, the quilts themselves—appear and reappear much as a particular motif or fabric might recur in a pieced quilt top.

Long Winter employs this domestic aesthetic more completely than any of the other Little House books; *waiting* is the central fact and problem of this novel. Wilder and Lane's fictional portrait of their mother and maternal grandmother shows how Caroline Ingalls marshaled her considerable resources to deal with this stressful period in the Ingalls family history, a period that is in many ways simply an exacerbated version of her entire adult life as a wife, mother, and housekeeper. As Lydia Maria Child advised, she manipulates the smallest fragments of conserved physical and intellectual food to nourish her family. For example, on one rare clear day she seizes the opportunity to do backed-up laundry (young Mrs. Boast, totally alone in an isolated shanty, does the same, refusing the opportunity to join her husband on a trip to town). Ma hoards bits of food, such as a fragment of a frozen codfish, to give her family treats and surprises, and encourages the girls to save a much-anticipated bundle of *Youth's Companion* stories to make a barren Christmas Day special. When Laura and her sisters fall to "moping" during the long days inside, Ma—the former schoolteacher—contrives "entertainments" for them, with the girls reciting "pieces" from their schoolbooks. Thus words and the stirring history of human civilization are pitted against the inhuman howl of storm, and the girls are rescued from awful stillness. But the most invigorating words are about warlike men: "The Speech of Regulus," "Old Tubal Cain," "The Midnight Ride of Paul Revere." There are no such active, exciting images of women. Instead, Laura and Carrie "repeat, in concert, 'Little Ellie sits alone'" (231). Throughout the winter, the girls know only examples of immobilized women. Ma's skilled efforts are clearly heroic, but they cannot stop the blizzards or shorten the confinement of the long, hard winter.

Both weather and gender seem to argue against a completable plot for Laura, as Wilder perceived in her letter to Lane. When blizzards close the schools, Laura wails, "Oh Ma! How can I ever teach school and help send Mary to college? How can I ever amount to anything when I can only get one day of school at a time?" (139). Entirely confined to a static and circular domestic routine, Laura cannot reconcile her ideas of accomplishment and achievement with the facts of dailiness, living only "one day . . . at a time." To this thoughtful adolescent, completed achievement, "amounting to something," seems a male imperative, like the work of the men who completed the local railroad and moved on. Men, Laura thinks, accomplish plots. Yet she does not turn to her father, who has often advised her in the past, with these problems. Instead, her anxious question is directed at Ma, to whom she is newly close. Clearly, the girl is confused about conjunctions of gender and power.

More than the other Little House books, *Long Winter* makes occasional forays into male consciousness, especially that of young Almanzo Wilder, who, with his brother Royal, is also waiting out the winter in De Smet, comfortably well provisioned. His wider options throw Laura's confinement into sharper relief. When other townspeople run out of supplies, he is pressured to surrender his precious seed wheat for food. Almanzo must mediate between the immediate domestic imperatives of "daily bread" and the farmer's future-oriented project of spring planting. So he and another intrepid young bachelor set out on a forty-mile trek toward a rumored source of wheat, transforming the unmarked, frozen prairie into a route and a destination. They come back with the life-saving grain, barely beating the next storm. In her letters to Lane, Wilder underlined the heroic qualities of this trip; she wrote of her future husband's "risking his life for his seed wheat" (LIW to RWL, 7 March 1938, Hoover). Another letter emphasizes how exceptional such daring was: "In the Hard Winter. . . . people became numbed and dumb with the awfulness of those storms and terrible cold. There were only a few who kept normal and very much alive. Pa and the Wilder boys did. They were the only ones who would go to haul hay or hunt or anything" (LIW to RWL, 20 March 1937, Hoover). Clearly, Wilder associates keeping alive with going out, as only Pa and the Wilder boys did. And thus being fully alive and articulate (not "dumb") seems, like completion of a plot, to be an option open only to men.

Although he is a man, Charles Ingalls cannot fully exercise this option. In *Long Winter* it has become apparent that Pa's strength is finite. He needed Laura's help with the haying, and now, suffering from malnutrition and fatigue, he is gaunt, with shaking hands that cannot play the fiddle. Nevertheless, Pa would like to attempt the journey for the wheat. It is just

the sort of male western gamble that stirs his imagination, a chance to wrest
a goal and a plot out of the blizzard's oblivion. But Ma vetoes such a plan:

> "No!" said Ma. . . . "I say, No. You don't take such a chance. . . .
> This time I put my foot down."
> "All right, that settles it," Pa agreed.
> Laura and Carrie . . . felt as if thunder and lightning had come
> down on them suddenly, and suddenly gone. Ma poured the tea with a
> trembling hand. (244–45)

Although she may be individually frail—her hand trembles as she pours the
tea—Ma's vehement defense of domestic culture is such a powerful force
that no member of her family dares to contradict it. Pa's commitment to his
female household draws him into their confinement. Unlike the unmarried
Almanzo, he is no longer free to choose risks and distances, conventions of
masculine plots.

Ma tells Laura that the family will not starve without wheat; if necessary, Pa will kill their cow and calf. Laura protests, "Oh, no! No!" To kill the
stock would be to kill the future, to obliterate everything but day-to-day
continuance of meals and routine. When Almanzo feels the same threat to
his future crop, he acts in response, setting out on a journey to save his seed
wheat. When Pa goes out to learn if the journey was successful, Laura must
remain by the stove with the other females. "They all sat in the dark, and as
if in a dream, they heard Pa's steps coming heavily the length of the front
room, and the kitchen door opening. . . . 'The boys got back!' he said,
breathing hard. 'Here's some of the wheat they brought, Caroline!' " (308).

Such passive, dreamlike helplessness and stasis are, for Laura, the
nightmare of the long winter. Lifesaving adventures outside, where one can
be *alive*, are for "the boys," who are not yet tied to families and domestic
routine. The Ingalls family members, who must subsist for weeks on a
single sack of wheat, exist—despite Ma's most valiant efforts—at the lowest
common denominator, laboring constantly at the most basic maintenance
tasks: twisting hay, grinding wheat. Wilder and Lane's powerful style conveys the stark rhythms of this minimal life: "The coffee mill's handle ground
round and round, it must not stop. It seemed to make her [Laura] part of the
whirling winds driving the snow round and round over the earth and in the
air, whirling and beating at Pa on his way to the stable, whirling and
shrieking at the lonely houses, whirling . . . forever on the endless prairie"
(254). The peculiar horror of this passage is that the howl of the storm is
indistinguishable from the saving sound of domestic routine, the grinding

mill. The wind has got inside the house and inside Laura's self: there is no safety. The nightmare imagery described by Pratt, signaling the gender dilemma of the adolescent female protagonist, here reaches a peak of intensity. It must appear to Laura that there is no way out. As she does her domestic task, turning the mill, she seems to become a "part of the whirling winds" that attack the house. Within her female self, Laura is both the defender of the house and its foe.

Neither Ma nor Pa nor Almanzo can resolve this ambivalence for Laura. Nor can they bring the blizzards to an end. Finally, in late April, Laura is awakened by a telling sound: the Chinook wind, signaling the coming of spring. The long winter is over, and weather permits the men and trains to move again. The trains bring ample supplies, even a long-promised Christmas barrel, full of gifts for the Ingallses. There are clothes, food, children's books for Grace, and Laura is entirely happy to receive a quintessentially feminine gift of embroidery materials. The prize gift, a fine silk shawl, goes by acclamation to Ma, whose household survival skills have been the saving "wonder" of the excruciating winter. In earlier books, Laura identified with Pa, longing to share his male adventures. But in this book, Laura's oblique accolade is for her mother, and she frames it in terms of the textiles that have long been associated with domestic culture: "Such a beautiful shawl was for Ma, of course. . . . it was like her, so soft and yet firm and well-wearing, with the fine, bright colors in it." Ma reminds her daughters that the shawl is also their heritage; she says, "We will all take turns wearing it" (324). This important passage is Laura's acknowledgment that, within the limits of her cultural powers as a traditional woman, her mother has exercised endurance, grace, and wisdom. The shawl is an adornment and a protection from weather, but it is also a muffling veil, and now—educated by the long winter—Laura cannot deny that she will wear it someday, too, becoming an iconic figure in a domestic language.

As *Plum Creek* did, *Long Winter* ends with the celebration of Christmas. The Christmas barrel contains a large turkey, and Ma decides that, with the Boasts, the Ingalls family will "celebrate the springtime with a Christmas dinner" (325). The dinner is Ma's project, executed with the help of her well-trained daughters. With replenished supplies, she runs through the repertoire of her domestic faculty. "When night came the cupboard held large brown-crusted loaves of white bread, a sugar-frosted loaf of cake, three crisp-crusted pies, and the jellied cranberries"—far more than the family could *need*. The dinner is a triumphant ritual demonstration. Ma's preparations are a form of art, and when she sets the glass bowl of "glowing cranberry jelly" in the center of a white cloth, "they all admired the effect" (327, 328). Mrs. Boast adds her own artful contribution, a ball of butter.

After the winter's lessons, Laura identifies more closely with her mother and is newly aware of all that Ma does to create and order this great domestic occasion. Her view of the banquet emphasizes Ma's constant, unspoken direction: "Ma looked at Pa and every head bowed. . . . Ma poured the coffee and Pa's tea. She passed the bread and the butter and reminded Pa to refill the plates" (332). Laura now has a far more acute and anxious awareness of how a woman must keep things going, especially this most basic life-giving activity, the serving of food, and of the cost of such control. At the table, she is Ma's chief assistant. The winter has taught her that this gendered role is something, like Ma's shawl, that she too must wear.

The dinner reminds its celebrants of the triumph of the version of "civilized life" that is so important to Ma. Celebrating Christmas, they have restored their traditional calendar and affirmed their family and cultural priorities.[22] But Laura is also giddy with disorientation, for now she knows how arbitrary a human construction that calendar is, and how vulnerable it is to insurmountable natural forces. A *Christmas* in *May* reminds her of all that humans can and cannot do, for even with all her resources of skill and determination, Ma could not produce this beautiful celebratory dinner on the twenty-fifth of December.

To conclude the celebration, Pa returns to his fiddle, and they all sing a new song, which ends the book:

> "Then what is the use of repining,
> For where there's a will, there's a way.
> And tomorrow the sun may be shining,
> Although it is cloudy today."

> And as they sang, the fear and the suffering of the long winter seemed to rise like a dark cloud and float away on the music. Spring had come. The sun was shining warm, the winds were soft, and the green grass growing. (334)

Pa's homiletic and aggressively cheerful ditty, "Where There's a Will There's a Way,"[23] seems to resume his celebration of the "free and independent" will with which this book began. But even the song admits what Laura has been forced to acknowledge: finally, the weather is in charge. "Tomorrow the sun *may* be shining"; no human will, however heroic, can change that uncertain forecast. At last, all this novel can do is to honor the human ordeal of the winter by unflinchingly naming it: "the fear and the suffering of the long winter." The suffering has stopped, at least briefly, because spring has come. But the weather is still in control.

The Long Winter explores what that inexorable fact can mean to a spirited girl, eager to invent herself a plot and a life. With *Silver Lake*, it offers responses to Laura's earlier question about what "makes things happen." In the earlier book, Laura saw how Pa and other men build railroads, establish towns, take up claims. In *Long Winter* she has become more fully conscious of what her mother, like many other women, has been doing all along: keeping the bread rising and the fire burning, every day. For the Ingalls family, these are clearly important matters of life and death. But Laura's very consciousness, the spark of her selfhood, is threatened by the necessary domestic routine, the "women's work" that she has helped to do. As a female adolescent, newly aware of the twin pressures of gender and weather, where can she go? What can she do? *Long Winter* offers no answers to these pressing questions, but it states them starkly, with a force unsurpassed in the Little House series.

The Long Winter was the first of the two Laura Ingalls Wilder books I owned as a child, a sturdy hardbound volume (no paperbacks, then), with the original illustrations, claustrophobic oval vignettes by Helen Sewell and Mildred Boyle. The book still feels familiar in my hands. My name is penciled on the flyleaf in my best, tilted nine-year-old printing. I read this book at least once every winter, for many years; I probably read it more often than any other Little House book—indoors, absorbed, and always (it seems) eating. On nearly every page there are brown stains—cocoa? apple seeds? what? The book makes me think about food. As a child, I longed to taste the ground-wheat bread that was the Ingalls family's only fare; I fantasized about grinding some wheat in my mother's "antique" coffee grinder. (I still do.)[24]

I lived in a household of daughters, with a father who went out to do his work and a housekeeping mother who stayed in to do hers—a constellation very like the Ingalls family. Somehow, *Long Winter* seemed to distill what was most satisfying *and* most confining about such domestic arrangements. As a girl reading, I ate it up, and the eating was both a means of nourishment and an act of furious aggression. I devoured the Little House, Laura's and my own.

Among twentieth-century U.S. women writers, Laura Ingalls Wilder and Rose Wilder Lane seem uniquely qualified to probe the issues that came to a head in *Long Winter*. They are collaborating authors, both with long professional careers behind them. They are daughter and mother, with all the tensions, obligations, and ineradicable attachments that that relation can imply.[25] As their efforts to narrate fictionalized versions of the lives of Charles Ingalls and Almanzo Wilder indicate, they have strong commitments to patriarchal projects and a deep interest in how nineteenth-century men worked. They were also both working housekeepers, practiced in traditional domestic skills. Wilder cooked, sewed, and did housework all her life. Her *Missouri Ruralist* and other magazine articles discussed a wide range of domestic practices, and her correspondence with Lane often includes recipes, sewing and fashion notes, and menus. Lane's diaries are also full of notations about cooking, and her papers include extensive collections of recipes and needlework patterns (some inherited from her mother). Lane's ambitious *Woman's Day Book of American Needlework* (1963) is voluminously knowledgeable and deeply respectful of domestic arts. The first chapter begins, "Needlework is the art that tells the truth about the real life of people in their time and place." In this book, based on a very popular series in a mass-market magazine sold primarily at grocery stores, Lane found in the needlework she had known all her life what was perhaps her most accessible vehicle for her libertarian political philosophy. "American needlework tells you . . . that Americans live in the only classless society," she claims (10). Lane always presents herself as a practitioner of the needlework about which she writes. Crocheting, for example, is something she has done all her life; as a girl, she recalls, "for a petticoat I had made nine yards of a star pattern" lace (144), and among the photographs of fine examples of crocheted work she includes "one of a pair of cuffs made and worn by the writer's grandmother, Caroline Quiner Ingalls, about 1870" (147).

In Wilder's and Lane's long careers, their writing and their familial, domestic practices were closely linked. Both women were deeply qualified by their own experience to write about an adolescent girl's ambivalent ties to a domestic caretaking tradition, as expressed by her mother and her grandmother. The domestic aesthetic traditions, such as quilting, that were a constant presence in their lives became a natural and effective resource of the Little House books.

Wilder and Lane also collaborated on another ambivalent fiction, that of Wilder as the sole and independent author of the Little House books. This fiction seems to draw more from the (largely male) myth of the freestanding "independent" individual author than from the more collaborative traditions of women's domestic culture. To sustain such a fiction, Lane had to deny some of her own best and most demanding work, that which she did on the Little House books. This story of self-fulfillment and simultaneous self-loss through a daughter's collaboration with her mother is replicated, in some ways, through the narrative of Laura's collaboration with Ma in *The Long Winter* and may be yet another reason for this book's extraordinary power.

By the Shores of Silver Lake and *The Long Winter* are compelling because they are serious, probing examinations of questions that matter deeply to young people. As an adolescent, Laura looks around her and wonders what "makes things happen." Is it weather? Gender? The will of a "free and independent" person? Her middle-class, Euro-American culture insists that she acknowledge both the masculine and feminine traditions of work and behavior that her parents enact; those gendered traditions have made it possible for the Ingalls family to endure the long winter. But within such paradigms, how can a girl plot her own story? The problems of a plot for Laura Ingalls will become the central issue of the last two Little House books.

The Ingalls family in De Smet, South Dakota, soon before Laura Ingalls Wilder moved to Missouri in 1894 with her husband and daughter. *Standing:* Carrie Ingalls, Laura Ingalls Wilder, Grace Ingalls. *Seated:* Caroline, Charles, and Mary Ingalls. Photo courtesy of Laura Ingalls Wilder Memorial Society, Mansfield, Missouri.

Chapter 5

Laura's Plots
Ending the Little House

Recently I told my mother (who is now eighty-two) that I planned to begin this book with an account of my trip with Grandmother to see Laura Ingalls Wilder. "What do you remember about that day?" she asked. So I told her about my birthday gift, *These Happy Golden Years*, and my memories of admiration, awe, and total silence before my favorite author.

"But you *weren't* silent," she replied. "I asked Mom what you said to Mrs. Wilder, and she said you asked her if she was going to write another book. And Mrs. Wilder said no."

Do I remember that? Perhaps I do; through a fog of repression I hear the thin, cracking sound of my own frightened voice. In 1952 I knew, of course, that the "newest" Little House book was already nine years old, almost as old as I was. I knew that the book Mrs. Wilder inscribed for me was probably her last—and in another day, unable to stop myself, I would have read to its end. I knew—but what I knew I could not bear to remember. So I have no memory of her voice, telling me the stories have stopped.

At eighty-five, Laura Ingalls Wilder must have been thoroughly tired of the question I asked her. Adults and children had been repeating it for twenty years. Typically, Marjorie Vitense, an Iowa fourth-grader, had written in 1933, after finishing *Big Woods*: "I would like to know if you have any more books like it for I enjoyed the book very much. I wish it would never come to an end for it was so good" (22 Feb. 1933, Western). Greta Walker wrote a similarly intense letter: "My teacher just finished 'These Happy Golden Years' and when she put it up we all just stared without a sound as if there were more. You could never guess unless I told you that I'm always dreaming about you. And I even talk about you in my sleep" (undated letter to LIW, Hoover). Katherine Afonin also wrote from elementary school about the Little House books as a dream space where she could escape the physical and economic constrictions of a post–World War II childhood: "I wish I lived when you did. I would like to live on the prairie because you didn't have to be fenced in a little yard. You had free things to do on the prairie" (To LIW, 28 May 1949, Hoover).

In the eight volumes of their serial, Wilder and Lane had created a liminal space for continuities and exploration, a space where a female childhood might be rendered with a weight and attention unusual in U.S. writing for children. And children responded with a barrage of questions about what happened to whom, next: Did Laura marry Almanzo? Did she teach school? Did Mary go to college? Did the cat Black Susan, left behind in Wisconsin, manage to produce descendants in Dakota, ten years later? (*No*, Wilder said emphatically.)[1] As practiced, socialized readers, they asked for completed plots. But, like me, they also resisted endings, even though *These Happy Golden Years* definitively closed with the words, "The End of the Little House Books." From within a well-regulated childhood, an unfenced place with "free things to do" seemed enormously desirable. I felt the way Marjorie Vitense did: I wished "it would never come to an end." And yet, plot-hungry, I read faster and faster, to the very last page.

As Wilder and Lane worked on the Little House narrative, they kept extending it, from Wilder's initial 1920s draft of a first-person account of her childhood and adolescence (the unpublished "Pioneer Girl") to the series that expanded in length as the authors' audience and ambitions grew.

Initially, Wilder intended to follow *The Long Winter* with one concluding volume, "Prairie Girl," which would end with Laura and Almanzo's engagement. She wrote to Lane:

> If we could skip from June Christmas [the concluding scene of *Long Winter*] to beginning school then Mary could go to college the following summer and Laura and Manly could be engaged in the fall when Laura would be 17 in the coming winter. Let the book end with the engagement which can be supposed to last a couple of years before the wedding not to have a horred [*sic*] child marriage.
>
> I don't know how else to handle the last book. . . . Unless we make the story cover two years and it is hardly worth it.
>
> We can have Manly say at the end "And while we wait I'll build us a little house on the claim. . . . "
>
> I will block it out as soon as I can and let you see it. (LIW to RWL, 7 March 1938, Hoover)

In the following months of work, these plans were drafted and revised again and again by both authors, and intensely debated. Eventually, "Prairie Girl," renamed *Little Town on the Prairie,* became the penultimate volume of the series, which concluded with *These Happy Golden Years.* In the process, the authors wrestled with important problems that are suggested by Wilder's letter. Wilder's initial plan seems to have been to privilege the courtship plot that culminates in Laura's engagement to Almanzo, but she is also intent on writing the story of Laura's teaching career and of Mary's going to college. The conclusion she first proposes for Laura's story emphasizes *Almanzo's* work ("I'll build us a house"), not Laura's. Wilder seems unsure about her material and her audience. Of the multiple possibilities offered by the three years between Laura's first teaching job and her marriage, which are "worth it?"

At the same time, Wilder was compiling lists of characters who would continue or reappear in the last books and arguing with Lane about how to create the connections that would bind the volumes of the series together. Lane considered plotting to be her mother's weakest point as a writer; as a practiced author of successful commercial fiction, she proposed a series of consolidating strategies, reintroducing and conflating characters—for example, she recommended substituting a cousin for Mr. Boast. Wilder often opposed such suggestions vehemently, and the printed books indicate that she usually won these arguments. Again and again, Lane argued for continuity and coherence, with knots neatly tied. Wilder proposed more fluid arrangements, looser plotting that reflected the frontier family dynamics described by Schlissel, Gibbens, and Hampsten, who have observed that "behind the Victorian ideal of the well-ordered home, American families were unruly assortments of comings and goings, as men and women tried to fit their lives into a rapidly changing society" (107). Similarly, Wilder said of the relatives and friends who turn up (or don't) unpredictably in the last two volumes, "I think their appearing and disappearing as I have them do gives a feeling of the march westward, of the passing on of people and of their appearing unexpectedly. Also they make a contrast to the family left behind with clipped wings" (LIW to RWL, 7 March 1938, Hoover). Wilder argued successfully for this disorderly cast of characters because, "They come and go, pass in and out of the story as they really do. . . . I think to bring the characters along as you [Lane] suggest is unnecessary. I know it is unnatural and untrue of the times" (LIW to RWL, 7 August 1938, Hoover).

These ongoing controversies suggest that ending the Little House series was at least as complex and ambivalent a process for Wilder and Lane as it was for their young readers. In her early seventies, Wilder feared that her memory was deteriorating; "That's why the sooner I write my stuff the better," she explained (LIW to RWL, 5 Feb. 1937, Hoover). Yet Wilder resisted many of the conventions of closure that her daughter urged. Eventually, the series ended with Laura's marriage, not her engagement, and another volume was required to articulate an extended story. By expanding their original plans and narrating the events of the months that preceded Laura's first teaching job and the year of Laura and Almanzo's engagement, Wilder and Lane complicated their narrative and interwove multiple strands of plot, exploring Laura's various experiences earning and spending money, her changing relations with her parents, and her subtle growth as a recipient and arbiter of gendered culture. These important additions make Laura Ingalls a far more complex and active adult protagonist, one who cannot be contained by the conventions of the courtship plot that remains the nominal frame of the final volume. In letters from this period, Wilder wrote to Lane with new confidence about her efforts to sustain multiple plots that would project the fluid, open-ended qualities of frontier experience she wanted to convey. On learning that many children were most curious about "whether Laura ever got to be a teacher," she told Lane, "I have kept that idea working" (LIW to RWL, 23 May 1939, Hoover), and she also made plans for such unpredictable frontier characters as Mr. Edwards in the last volumes; "I have a use for him," she claimed (LIW to RWI

7 March 1938; Hoover). Such comments suggest that Wilder had developed an ongoing sense of multiple, interwoven plots.

Peter Brooks, one of the most influential recent theorists of plot, argues that plot has been a persistent habit of thought for Western cultures in the past two hundred years, providing—through the patterns of conflict, complication, and climax defined by Aristotle—a *"form* of thinking" about "human memory and desire" (xii, 319; emphasis mine), usually by working through one issue—one primary plot—at a time. As a narrative principle, such plotting has worked better as an instrument for telling men's stories than women's, as feminist critics have often noted. Marianne Hirsch argues that Brooks's phallic formulation of plot precludes female protagonists; it is "predicated on woman's quiet participation as an object of desire" (52).In the Little House books, Laura Ingalls *is* conceived by a patriarchal economy as an object of desire—as consumer, wife, daughter, teacher, and future mother. But she is also, and emphatically, the protagonist of the series. In Wilder's letters about the books, her most troubled moments occur when Laura seems most objectified and thus immobilized, as in the helpless insensibility of the long winter or in the early plans for the last book, when it looked as if Almanzo would assume the acting-out of the Little House plot. As Wilder sees it, she *needs* plot as an instrument for thinking through important issues of her books and her life.

I see the multiple plots of the Little House series as a strategy for claiming an active, self-possessed, thinking life for a young female protagonist and her authors while still acknowledging their patriarchal commitments. This multiplicity is especially apparent in the last two books, which are marked by several kinds of simultaneous female plots. As protagonist, Laura is implicated in a courtship narrative, in multiple narratives of women's work, in a mother-daughter plot, in a kunstlerroman plot that traces the emergence of a female writer, and in a U.S. Western plot. These competing, complementary, separate, and simultaneous plots weave through the last volumes, both compelling and resisting closure. They indicate the multiple agendas of the series, its simultaneous intentions to replicate and to undermine patriarchal arrangements. Such proliferation, I suggest, is one of the strongest reasons for the Little House series' continuing appeal, especially for female readers. These books evoke the rhythms of simultaneity and competition among the multiple plots of many U.S. girls' and women's lives.

As they elaborated the Little House plots, Wilder and Lane drew on a wide range of cultural precedents that proffered insistent cues about how girls' and women's stories could—and could not—be told. Some of the most important of these cues were autobiographical. The series' multiple, competing fictional plots resemble those of Wilder and Lane's own lives. After her marriage at eighteen to Almanzo Wilder, Laura Ingalls Wilder worked variously—and sometimes simultaneously—as housekeeper, hired seamstress, farmer, cook, egg and chicken producer, administrator of a farm-loan program, and writer. Rose Wilder Lane constantly and flamboyantly reinvented herself, personally and professionally.

In addition, both women were constant readers. The turn-of-the-century farmhouse that the Wilders built on Rocky Ridge Farm included a shelf-lined library, an unusual feature for an Ozark home. As a girl and young woman, Wilder almost certainly read staples of nineteenth-century popular fiction written by and for women, and Lane probably read many of these same books. For example, Lane's journals mention an early autobiographical fiction by a woman writer, Caroline Kirkland's 1839 *A New Home, Who'll Follow?* And in 1939 mother and daughter corresponded about another staple text, one of the earliest and most influential works of U.S. women's fiction, Susanna Rowson's 1799 best-selling novel of seduction, *Charlotte Temple.*[2] The authors' experiences as female readers became a significant influence on the plotting of the female narrative at the center of the Little House books.

In the series, reading is a decisively gendered activity. The family Bible is jointly owned, but the other two repeatedly mentioned texts are Pa's book, a "big green *Wonders of the Animal World*" that illustrates and describes a jungle world, reflecting Charles Ingalls's delight in "unsettled" places with plenty of uncultivated land and undomesticated animals, and Ma's book, "the novel named *Millbank*" (BPC 122). Since Wilder insisted that the series be accurate about titles and texts, it is probable that the few books in the actual Ingalls household did include this 1871 novel by Mary Jane Holmes, which is mentioned in the first volumes as the fictional Ingalls family's only novel and which Ma read aloud so often that Laura memorized the first sentences—suggesting that the book was a significant influence on both the fictional and actual Laura Ingalls, who would have been encouraged to think of the reading and writing of fiction as female activities.

Holmes was one of the most popular U.S. women novelists of the nineteenth century, and *Millbank* has interesting affinities with the concerns of the Little House project. It replicates many features of the prototypical plot of sentimental "woman's fiction" described by Nina Baym, in which a motherless girl, thrown back on her own resources, develops a successfully individuated will before contracting an engagement or marriage, which ends the book. (The fictional Laura, although not motherless, otherwise enacts a similar plot.) But *Millbank's* plot also has some *un*prototypical features. Magdalen, its young female protagonist, uses her paternal inheritance at the novel's end to buy the ancestral house—Millbank—that was lost by the man she loves; thus she is in a position of power that comes from money and ownership of real estate. It is Magdalen who proposes the marriage that ends the book: she tells her lover that she has "come here to bring you Millbank and—and, myself, if you will take me. Will you, Roger?" (331). Thus Holmes's novel suggests means by which even this most conventional of protagonists can claim some of the traditional prerogatives of patriarchy, owning real estate and proposing marriage, and can openly make arrangements and decisions that facilitate her own desires. Such issues are clearly on the minds of the authors of the Little House books. Although the Ingalls houses of the series are built and owned by Pa, Wilder and Lane complicated this patriarchal condition by raising questions about female ownership and female voice, especially in the multiple plots of the last books.

In the later Little House books, the Ingalls girls and women also read "story papers" and the girls are introduced to the delicious suspense of serial fiction. (In *The Long Winter*, a bundle of hoarded stories is almost the only treat that Ma can contrive for her daughters on Christmas Day.) With these stories, Laura begins to learn the ambiguous satisfactions of rushing toward and delaying closure, the same satisfactions that Wilder and Lane manipulated so skillfully as they crafted their series in the 1930s. The Ingalls daughters devour *The Youth's Companion* as well as Mrs. Boast's stack of *New York Ledgers*. It was estimated that each issue of the phenomenally successful *Ledger* was read by a million persons (Coultrap-McQuin 51), and the many women fiction writers under contract to editor Robert Bonner included E.D.E.N. Southworth, whose brilliantly audacious novel *The Hidden Hand*— a wild play with and within the boundaries of conventional sentimental female plot—was serialized in the *Ledger* three times between 1859 and 1883.[3] It is quite possible that the actual Ingalls daughters encountered it.

Laura disagrees with Ma and Mary about *how* to read the story papers. They propose reading only one installment a day, so the stories will "last longer. . . . Laura did not say that she would rather read as fast as she could. . . . Every day she read [aloud] one part of the story, and then they wondered until next day what would happen next to the beautiful lady" protagonist (SSL 208). By rationing the stories, Ma teaches her daughters that pleasure—and the enjoyment of female agency—must be contained and deferred, not devoured in a frenzy of immediate, private gratification. Furthermore, since Mary is blind, she cannot enjoy the stories unless Laura reads them aloud. Inside the cramped Little Houses, silent reading is one of Laura's few opportunities to experience a rich *private* life. But such reading must also seem a betrayal of Mary and of the familial ties and obligations that are expressed in the communal sessions of reading aloud.

In Lane's life, too, reading was a constant motif; her fiction reading was more eclectic than her mother's and ranged from Jane Austen and Walter Scott to such contemporaries as Theodore Dreiser, Dorothy Richardson, Lewis Lewisohn, Virginia Woolf, Sigrid Undset, and many others, including stories in such popular magazines as *McCalls* and *Cosmopolitan.* Lane regarded her reading as an important professional discipline; she even urged her mother to follow her own practice and copy an entire novel by hand, attending to the style. Her 1923 diary comment on *Babbitt* suggests her uncertainties about the formal problems that would be posed by the Little House project: "Sinclair Lewis does a new thing, the plotless novel. It's ugly, but is it art, the devil whispers behind the leaves" (RWL diary, 17 Feb. 1923, Box 20, item 12, Hoover). But at the same time that Lane worked at her writing through such reflective reading, she excoriated herself for the kind of unregulated reading that tempts the fictional Laura Ingalls. Lane wrote in her diary, "In June, 1930, I resolve to fight my lifelong habit of constant and indiscriminate reading, which in my case has been little more than a drug habit." The next entry in that diary was "August, 1930—Have continued to read steadily—" (RWL Diary, Hoover).

In *The Woman Reader* Kate Flint argues that "the study of reading . . . involves examining a fulcrum: the meeting-place of discourses of subjectivity and socialization." Reading has traditionally been "a prime tool in socialization" and is "centrally bound in with questions of authority" (43). With Wilder and Lane, those questions of authority are also closely linked with questions of authorship, the strategy by which both women extended their agency and achieved financial security. By the end of the Little House series, Laura Ingalls is a very anxious reader,[4] torn between the priorities of "subjectivity and socialization," and both she and Mary have developed ambitions to become authors themselves.

The issues and texts of Wilder's and Lane's own reading are a little-noted but important subtext of the Little House series. By the time Laura is fifteen, a new book found in her mother's underwear drawer exerts forces of eroticism and luxury:

> under the red flannels she felt something hard. She put in her hand and drew out. . . . a perfectly new book, beautifully bound in green cloth with a gilded pattern. . . . The . . . gilt edges of the pages looked like solid gold. . . . the fresh, untouched pages lay spread, each exciting with unread words printed upon it in clear, fine type. Straight, thin red lines enclosed each oblong of printing, like the treasure it was.

The page is headed by a title, "THE LOTOS-EATERS. . . . [B]reathlessly Laura read" (LTP 139–40). Eight lines of Tennyson's poem follow.

Intensely, Laura desires to read on—but she realizes that the book is a hidden Christmas gift, probably for her. She has "no right to read it" or to ask her parents about it and spoil their pleasure in the surprise. "It was almost more than she could do, not to read just one word more, just to the end of that one line. But she knew that she must not yield one tiny bit of temptation" (141). Laura desires the private, sensuous pleasure of consuming this rich text to the end, through the convolutions of what she probably imagines will be a climactic plot like those she has encountered in the story papers. But her desire is in direct conflict with the institutional values she is pledged to honor—those of her family and the ritual of Christmas gift-giving—and Laura's socialized conscience forbids her to continue reading. This story of reading—or of *not* reading—restates the conflicts between private gratification and communal commitments that recur throughout Laura's adolescence. Furthermore, when she finally receives the book as a Christmas gift and can give it her sanctioned attention, "The Lotus Eaters" is "a disappointment. . . . the sailors turned out to be no good. . . . and lie around complaining. When they thought about bestirring themselves, they only whined, 'Why should we ever labor . . . ?' Why indeed! Laura thought indignantly. Wasn't that a sailor's job? But no, they wanted dreamful ease. . . . Laura slammed the book shut" (235). Laura has done *her* "job" and waited until the proper time to read her book—only to find that the drugged sailors are incapable of such discipline. Their langour cannot satisfy her desire. This is Laura's first narrated encounter with a canonical male-authored and male-centered text, and it expresses her dissatisfaction with the plot proposed by Tennyson. By extension, this incident also suggests the disappointments that tales of male adventure may hold for an eager female reader. We may read it, in fact, as Wilder and Lane's critique of the canonical texts that competed for the attention of their readers. Whatever else it may be, the Little House series is certainly *not* a narrative of "dreamful ease," and Tennyson's langorous men—too fatigued to complete an active plot—offer no satisfaction to Wilder and Lane's vigorous and desiring female protagonist.

The books that Wilder found most satisfying in her later years offered plots of physical action, usually with male protagonists. She was a prodigious reader of popular Western fiction, as Nava Austin, the Mansfield librarian in Wilder's last years, confirmed: "In her later years, she read mostly westerns. They were paperbacks. She said, 'People probably wonder why this is my type of reading, but they are easy to hold, and I just enjoy them.' And she was a horse lover, a lover of the outdoors. . . . Luke Short was one of her favorite western writers. . . . Zane Grey was another favorite" (Hines 120). Western fiction was also a staple of the magazines in which Lane published in the 1920s and 1930s; Lane's *Let the Hurricane Roar* and *Free Land*, which were serialized before book publication, were her major (and somewhat revisionist) Western projects. Clearly, both authors were well grounded in the conventions of this enormously popular genre. In fact, Wilder more than once used Western fiction as a confirming standard of authority and authenticity.[5]

Jane Tompkins has recently argued that the Western form developed in response to the "feminization" of late nineteenth-century U.S. culture; it intentionally suppresses women's language and authority, valorizing the "strong, silent" male whose authority comes from physical force and discredits words. For Wilder and Lane, Westerns meant market success and satisfying reading. But, on the level Tompkins discusses, they also meant limitations on the possibilities for action and powerful expression that were available to girls and women. In the writing of the Little House series (especially the later novels of adolescence), as the two women authors plotted an autobiographical narrative of a budding woman writer, they contended with a vocabulary of Western conventions that devalued and suppressed such female-centered plots. In the later books, as Laura attains more mobility and some modest financial resources, such conventions become more obviously problematic for her development, and Wilder and Lane found themselves at odds with the active, male-centered Western plots that had, in some ways, served them both.

Yet another precedent that importantly influenced the plotting of the series was the fact that Wilder considered herself to be writing *history* in the Little House books. John E. Miller has provided a useful discussion of what history probably meant to Wilder. Her "method of studying history as a schoolgirl had helped her cultivate her memory and thus aided her in recalling" events of her youth, Miller says. "Rote memory was the principal tool for learning" when Laura Ingalls Wilder attended U.S. common schools, and "history textbooks encouraged this approach by highlighting important names, dates, and facts and by including . . . time lines and lists of historical events and dates to be memorized" (98).[6] Wanting to make her books as attractive and useful as possible in elementary classrooms, Wilder placed a high premium on such factual precision.[7] Lane shared this preoccupation; she wrote to William T. Anderson after Wilder's death, "If my mother's books are not absolutely accurate, she will be dis-credited as a person and as a writer" (quoted in Anderson 1983, 288).

According to Frances Fitzgerald, "American-history texts gained general currency in the schools only in the eighteen-nineties." Previously, public grade schools, such as those attended and taught by Laura Ingalls in the 1870s and 1880s, "had very little history of any kind in their curricula" (48). But in the classroom scenes depicted by Wilder and Lane, no subject is more elaborated than U.S. history. This fact probably expresses the authors' shared preoccupation with perpetuating a particular version of western history that privileged the "settlement" efforts of "free and independent" white families, a version that they thought was endangered by the New Deal. It may also reflect their belief that the elementary history classroom could provide an important audience and a market for their series.

Little Town on the Prairie culminates with a public school exhibition in which Laura takes the "principal part," reciting American history from its "beginnings" with Columbus through the administration of John Quincy Adams.[8] This is an important scene of public initiation, a rite of passage in which Laura proves herself as a mouthpiece and enforcer of prevailing U.S. culture through her recitation of sanctioned history. She performs before an overflow audience in the "sacred" space of the community church, hung with schoolroom portraits of U.S. presidents. After the other exercises and performances,

> Laura stood up. She did not know how she got to the platform. Somehow she was there, and her voice began. "America was discovered by Christopher Columbus in 1492. . . ." Her voice was shaking a little. She steadied it and went carefully on. It did not seem real that she was standing there, in her blue cashmere . . . with Ma's pearl pin. . . .

> She told of the Spanish and the French explorers . . . of the
> English . . . of the Dutch. . . .
>
> At first she spoke into a blur, then she began to see faces. Pa's
> stood out from all the others. His eyes met hers and they were shining
> as slowly he nodded his head.
>
> Then she was really launched upon the great history of Amer-
> ica. She told of the new vision of freedom and equality in the New
> World . . . the war. . . the Constitution. . . . Then, taking up the pointer,
> she pointed to George Washington.
>
> There was not a sound except her voice. (291–92)

Wielding the male teacher's pointer, Laura narrates the career and administration of Washington and the five succeeding presidents; these years of
expansion and growth are her favorite part of her favorite subject. She ends
with the opening of lands west of the Mississippi for settlement: "Then the
first wagon wheels rolled into Kansas. Laura had finished" (293). She receives thunderous applause.

Laura is applauded because she has given voice to the collective
dreams and beliefs of her fellow white settlers. Before her performance, she
was "stiff with dread" and fragments "raced madly through her mind. . . .
Give me liberty or give me death. . . . We hold these truths to be self-
evident. . . . Their feet left bloody tracks upon the snow" (289). But as she
brandishes the teacher's pointer, Laura imposes sequence, order, and plot on
this chaotic and controversial material. The very next day, a member of the
audience comes to the Ingalls house and offers Laura a job, teaching a newly
organized school for a salary beyond her imagining ("Forty dollars!"). She is
quickly examined by the school superintendent and, at fifteen, awarded
a coveted third-grade teaching certificate. Thus *teaching history* becomes
Laura's route to acceptance and compensation as an authoritative adult. It
links the girl to the mature woman who, readers know, will take on some of
the functions of a historian in the writing of the Little House books.

Laura's performance at the school exhibition is by all accounts a triumph. Yet it also contains elements of female self-loss. At the beginning,
her recital is described almost as an act of (male-controlled) ventriloquism;
"her voice began" without volition, and her public appearance in her best
dress and Ma's jewelry "did not seem real." Laura's performance takes off
and becomes actual and exciting to her only when her eyes meet Pa's shining eyes; his nod confirms the *history* she is telling. Laura has become the

voice for white patriarchy, tied to its priorities and mythology by her passionate, romantic bond with her father. Her recital ends exactly where her
father's story as a westerner began: with wagons rolling into Kansas, as narrated in *Little House on the Prairie*. The story she tells mentions not a single female actor; instead it glorifies such males as Columbus, Washington, Jackson. Yet her last sentence sets the stage for Laura's own western experience.

According to Susan Armitage and Elizabeth Jameson, "the crucial
step in women's history is to see women as actors, not as onlookers in
history" (7). The Little House books come down on both sides of this
ongoing endeavor of "women's history," which of course was not yet officially launched when Lane and Wilder wrote. Laura's recitation, the product of the public education that she is expected to replicate as a teacher,
presents women largely as onlookers who give voice to the deeds of men.
But the plotting of the Little House series, which places a girl's developing
will and sensibility at the center of western events, resembles a project in
women's history because it focuses on Laura as an *actor* in her own life story.

The final event of the Little House series—with Laura's marriage, in
1885—almost exactly coincides with the closing of the frontier, as plotted
by Frederick Jackson Turner, and Wilder and Lane were obviously much
affected by the male-oriented, settler-valorizing "frontier" version of Ingalls
family history that Turner's pervasive influence would have urged. Fred
Erisman, in his recent survey of critical comment on Wilder, suggests that
an approach to the series as "part of the literature of the American West
provides perhaps the most satisfying approach to the works" (1994, 43),
and he cites several commentators who have persuasively read Wilder and
Lane's books as expressions of a Turnerian frontier perspective.[9] Yet the
story of Laura Ingalls that I am examining in this book—a story that both
expresses and challenges white settlers' patriarchal frontier culture—is
more complex and controversial than most of these commentators have
acknowledged. Peggy Pascoe has recently urged that western historians
abandon the previously prevalent concept "of the frontier [as] . . . a road
that stretches from east to west, a one-way thruway for white settlers" (45).
Instead, she proposes a more culturally and racially inclusive approach to
the "West" and specifically to women's experience there. Today, Pascoe
says, "we have to build our histories on intercultural relations as well as on
multicultural diversity" (53). In the Little House series, we see Wilder and
Lane wrestling with their priorities as self-appointed historians. Within the
Turnerian framework established by settler culture and enacted by her fa-

ther, Laura Ingalls also struggles with other priorities—both "intercultural" and "multicultural"—that are linked to some of her strongest desires: to possess an Indian baby, to see how men work, to taste the freedom and release that white men experience performing as "blacks" in a minstrel show. In the last books, as Laura nears sexual and professional maturity, she becomes a hot property in the culture of De Smet. Her teaching job establishes her as a valuable commodity, partly because of her potential to promote a particular version of U.S. history. And the historical orientation that was important to both Wilder and Lane becomes yet another site of conflict in the plotting of the final Little House books.

The altered priorities of these last two books are indicated by the first words of *Little Town on the Prairie:*

> One evening at supper, Pa asked, "How would you like to work in town, Laura?"
>
> Laura could not say a word. Neither could any of the others [Laura's mother and sisters]. They all sat as if they were frozen. . . .
>
> "A job? For a girl? In town?" Ma said. (1)

This is the first of the books to begin with a proposed change to which *Laura,* not her parents, must respond, prodding herself out of "frozen" silence into speech, action, and earning. It is late spring on the claim, after the confinement and deprivation of the Long Winter, and Laura is enjoying the uninflected routines of the house and farm. For her, "perhaps the best part was knowing that tomorrow would be like today" (34). Routine will be radically altered if Laura accepts the offered job, sewing shirts in town. Both final books are marked by Laura's ambivalence about change and by her simultaneous efforts to resist *and* to make alliances with the plots that her culture offers to girls and women. If Wilder and Lane's projected plots are to be set into motion, completing the Little House series, Laura must make money and both she and Mary must grow and move outside the Little House constructed by their parents.

In *Little Town* the primary site of such transformative change is the town of De Smet. The climate of the new community is pluralistic, almost carnivalesque, in ways that both frighten and exhilarate Laura. As the girl begins her first job, she sits by a store window, basting shirts for the single men who have flooded the new town. She hears the constant "racketing hum" of the sewing machine (the first she has seen) and the unaccustomed bickering of her employer and the storekeeper, and she has a view of the street, where one day she witnesses a pair of comical drunk men marching from one saloon to the other, singing and kicking in screen doors on their way. Laura laughs uncontrollably, even when reprimanded by her employer, Mrs. White, who says, "Think of the cost of all those screen doors. . . . I'm surprised at you." At home, Ma adds, "Goodness gracious, Laura. How could you laugh at drunken men?" (54). Both Pa and Ma oppose drinking and regret the presence of the saloons in town, but Pa surreptitiously shares Laura's amusement, while Ma says, "It's a crying shame that such things can happen before Laura's very eyes." Ma intimates, for the first time, that women may need to take an active part in the regulation of town life: "I begin to believe that if there isn't a stop put to the liquor traffic, women must bestir themselves and have something to say about it" (55). Clearly, this bespeaks Ma's support of the temperance movement, perhaps nineteenth-century U.S. women's most successful project in social reform.

Lillian Schlissel has suggested that newly settled western territories were often the sites of carnivalesque "irreverent dramas," places for "breaking bounds" where "one wore different faces and lived different lives that needed no accounting" (Schlissel, Gibbens, and Hampsten 234). I propose that this carnival tradition was another strong precedent for the complex plotting of the last Little House books. In the earlier volumes, only Pa ventured into the "carnival frontier" that Schlissel describes. His experiences in the claim office brawl, among the all-male railroad gangs and itinerant harvest workers, and in the saloons he visited with Edwards were shared with his womenfolk only in (presumably) highly censored stories. Previously, when the Ingalls family lived near places where standards of law, order, propriety, and rationality were flouted in carnivalesque style, Ma kept her daughters strictly contained in the Little House, as she did in the railroad camp on Silver Lake.

But now, since Laura can no longer be entirely confined, the new town becomes an intensely contested site, for if Laura is to have freedom and even limited mobility, the values of the Little House must prevail in the Little Town as well.[10] When Laura laughs at drunk men's destruction of private property, she is enjoying and confirming carnival values, and her mother is motivated to consider regulatory civic action, using means that were typical of the historic West, where, according to Julie Roy Jeffrey, "saloons were a threat to the whole structure of domesticity which women tried to create on the . . . frontier and, at times, even a threat to their physical well-being" (135).

In De Smet, Ma has new opportunities to join other women in organizing to control community life. For example, with other members of the Ladies' Aid, she plans a communal Thanksgiving celebration, a "New England Supper" to help pay for the new church building. The supper is very much in the spirit of the Colonial Revival events that were popular in the years after the 1876 centennial, and Ma prepares traditional New England foods, pumpkin pie and baked beans. (The actual Caroline Quiner Ingalls was of New England ancestry.) When Pa compliments her on the "great success" of her "Aid Society sociable," her snappish response is unprecedented: "it wasn't a sociable. It was a New England Supper" (232–33). Reinforced by the new support of other women workers, Ma is intent on getting the vocabulary and Puritan values of this exemplary event *right*. With its emphasis on tradition, civic responsibility, and paying debts, the New England Supper is an anticarnival and perhaps an antiwestern event, and Pa requires instruction in its proprieties.

Soon after, when Laura attends another Ladies Aid event, the first "dime sociable," she is confused and disappointed. It is her first adult party, and she dresses with care, even cutting a new "lunatic fringe" of bangs that befits a carnival celebration. Leaving her parents' house alone, "Laura went out into the dark and starry night. Her heart was beating fast with anticipation" (205). However, her passionate expectations are met by only tepid conversation and meager refreshments. Laura concludes,

> "You should have gone, Ma, instead of me."
>
> "This is only the first sociable," Ma made excuse. "No doubt when folks are better acquainted, the sociables will be more interesting. I know from reading *The Advance* that church sociables are greatly enjoyed." (208)

The Advance, a "church paper," links Ma to a larger community of Protestant women and powerfully influences her sense of the social possibilities of the new town. For the first time, we can clearly see the structures of "feminized" institutional support behind Ma's vision of community. However, it is also apparent that Ma's anticarnival values are not satisfying Laura, whose heart is pounding with anticipation for something she cannot yet name.

With Mary gone to college, the Ingalls family again moves to town for the winter. There Laura's predictable student life seems stymied in safety and sameness, and suddenly she cannot bear the routine.

> Tomorrow would be the same as today, and in all her life, Laura felt, there would never be anything but studying and teaching school. . . . She . . . slammed her book shut. . . . "I don't care!" she cried out. "I don't want to study! I don't want to learn! I don't want to teach school, *ever*! . . . I want—I want something to happen. I want to go West. I guess I want to just play, and I know I am too old," she almost sobbed.

All the comfort that Ma can offer is an unread story in the *Youth's Companion*, and that cannot mollify Laura. "She did not know what she wanted, but she knew she could not have it, whatever it was" (211–12).

What Laura desires is what carnival offers. As summarized by Dale Bauer, Bakhtinian "carnival is the realm of desire unmasked, taken out of the law of culture. . . . carnivalized discourse renders invalid any codes, conventions, or laws which govern or reduce the individual to an object of control" (679). As a pubescent girl in town, Laura is living entirely within "the law of culture"; she is so thoroughly an "object of control" that she cannot even identify her overpowering desire—she is only sure that she wants to "go West," where there will be no towns, no schools, fewer constraints. Ma, who has vetoed further western moves for the Ingalls family, can only offer Laura the vicarious, sublimated gratification of a continued story in a Christian periodical.

The townspeople decide to allay such winter malaise, which is epidemic in De Smet, by organizing a "literary society." For the rest of the winter, led by Pa, they devise a series of weekly entertainments, each more lively and inventive than the last. Suddenly Laura is caught up in "Madcap Days,"[11] a "Whirl of Gaiety." The literaries seem intended to make some of the excitements of a carnivalesque West available to everyone in town, even a girl like Laura. Rejecting the cruel and divisive isolation of the previous Long Winter, the citizens of De Smet cooperate to provide for themselves the entertainment that professional performers would bring to a more established community.[12] Even the first impromptu "literary," a community spelling bee, is exciting and satisfying. The bee illustrates the modified version of carnival offered to Laura: the usual hierarchy of school is dismantled and Laura can compete with adult women and men; in fact, she outspells Ma. The contest is punctuated with shouts, applause, and "breathless silence," very unlike everyday schoolroom lessons. Yet the same (male) teacher presides, familiar textbook in hand, and everyone observes

the schoolroom ritual of spelling out words syllable by syllable. Pa triumphs, spelling down the whole town. Laura finds the bee thrilling; it
transforms the most ordinary townspeople into actors in a dramatic contest. Nevertheless, Pa's victory reinforces his patriarchal dominion even in
an arena where Ma has dominated, and the whole contest validates the
very schoolroom values that Laura found so unbearably tedious.[13]

Later literaries reinforce these mixed messages. In an evening of cha-
rades, Pa wins again with a sly literary joke. On another occasion, men debate about historical male greatness: "Resolved: That Lincoln was a greater
man than Washington" (233). One entertainment purports to portray a
woman on top—it is "Mrs. Jarley's Wax Works," where "waxen" figures of
historic personages obey the commands of their mistress, Mrs. Jarley:

> In a deep voice she said, "George Washington, I command thee! Live
> and move!" and with the pointer she touched one of the figures.
>   The figure moved! (237)

Washington is followed by Daniel Boone, Elizabeth I, Sir Walter Raleigh—
"history" appears before Laura's eyes, to do the bidding of a tall, fate-like,
powerful woman, in a carnivalesque reversal. But at the performance's end,
patriarchal order is restored; "Mrs. Jarley took off her bonnet and was
Gerald Fuller," a Main Street merchant, and every other historical personage is revealed as a man. Ma can imagine no more audacious entertainment;
"This is the climax, surely," she says (238). But in fact there is one more
"literary," the minstrel show. As I argued in Chapter 2, this final entertainment definitively claims the satisfactions of carnival performance for *white
men*, who are allowed an evening's release from the specificities and constraints of their civic identities in a newly lawful western community. At
such a performance, a girl like Laura can only take the part of a spectator.[14]

The literaries feature only one actual female performer, Mrs. Bradley,
who sings to the accompaniment of her precious organ:

> Backward, turn backward,
>   Oh Time in thy flight.
> Make me a child again,
>   Just for tonight.

> Laura could hardly bear the sadness of it. . . . All the women
> were wiping their eyes, and the men were clearing their throats and
> blowing their noses. (223)

Mrs. Bradley's enormously popular song, "Rock Me to Sleep," was published in 1860; its woman-authored lyric is a hymn of longing for an absent,
long-dead mother voiced by a middle-aged female persona.[15] In fact, the
song's last words (not quoted by Wilder and Lane) express a desire for stasis
that ends as a death wish for a maternal embrace in which "never hereafter
to wake or to weep." Mrs. Bradley's performance, which points *backward* toward a maternal figure, describes a totally enveloping mother-child union
that is very unlike the carnival "whirl" of "madcap" desires. It also points
back East, where the mothers of the tearful De Smet adults presumably
reside or are buried. Schlissel points out that the inhabitants of such western communities, "living precariously, sometimes desperately, on the pe-
rimeters of change . . . [frequently] longed for an image of home outside
time" (Schlissel, Gibbens, and Hampsten 242). The omnivorous maternal
embrace described in this affective nineteenth-century song is a vivid image of such a home place, simultaneously cradle and grave. And the image
of the Little House itself, as a portable domestic/psychic construct sanctioned by Ma Ingalls, implies another such (maternal) "home outside time,"
one that must have seemed compelling and necessary to Wilder and Lane,
both of whom lived much of their adult lives far from their families and
dwellings of origin, as was typical for their generations of Americans.

The exciting sequence of the literaries and other community events
in *Little Town on the Prairie* dramatizes the institutional competition for Laura's
allegiances as she approaches adulthood. Such events as the New England
Supper, the dime sociable, and Mrs. Bradley's performance make the case
for stable, "feminized" values through female-authored institutions. Other
events, such as the minstrel show and wild rides on the schoolboys' sleds,
allow more of the heady release and exhilarating reversals associated with
carnival; such events tend to be authored by men. Laura is drawn to both
kinds of events, and a major problem of Wilder and Lane's last books is how
to devise plots that will express and facilitate her desires. As I have suggested, the image of the *Little House*, which gradually emerged as a leitmotif,
expresses stability in a narrative of mobility, change, and frequent disaster
and disruption. At the same time, the *series* form allows more fluidity and
multiplicity than would be possible in any single novel. The series creates a
space where protagonist and authors can experiment, at least, with some of
the liberating strategies of carnival. One of the most striking ways in which
the Little House books do this is through the proliferating plots enacted by
their protagonist, especially in the last two books. Through these plots,

Laura Ingalls can begin to enact her multiple and sometimes disruptive desires, even within the often-rigid parameters of propriety and patriarchy.

One of the most singular features of the plotting of *Little Town on the Prairie* and *These Happy Golden Years* is their emphasis on women's wage-earning work. According to Joan M. Jensen, "the 1920's and 1930's," when Wilder and Lane conceived and largely wrote their series, "were important decades in the transition of women from household production to wage labor" (203). Those transitions were also important to the lives of Wilder and Lane. The Little House books are part of an ongoing debate between mother and daughter about how rural women could earn money. While Lane often encouraged her mother's writing projects, as we have seen, she also had other suggestions, such as these in an (early) undated letter:

> go up to Springfield [the nearest city to Mansfield], see the managers of the two hotels there, and close with one of them a contract to supply all his eggs and milk at market prices . . . on condition that he will feature the name of the farm on his menu cards, with the line—"All our eggs are new laid from Rocky Ridge Farm." . . . Pretty soon . . . send milk and cream up to the hotel. . . . Next fall buy [and cure] all the hams from all the country round. . . . Take up a sample of your homemade vinegar . . . have labels printed. "Rocky Ridge Farm Pure Cider Vinegar. Made the way Grandma and the girls used to do it." . . .
>
> Why, there's no limit to what can be done there if you will go at it like a business woman. (RWL to LIW, n.d., Hoover)

Such advice indicates what sweeping business ambitions Lane urged on her mother and how she rooted them in rural skills and traditions—her mother's knowledge of how "Grandma and the girls used to do it." But Lane was dismissive of Wilder's more modestly "modern" ambitions: "Nonsense, honey, you don't want to go into any little dinky office as a stenographer. You want to keep up and employ your own stenographer before so very long" (RWL to LIW, n.d., Hoover). The most successful money-earning scheme that Lane negotiated with her mother was, of course, the Little House series itself, and, as the two women collaborated throughout the Depression and early World War II years, it is not surprising that they emphasized the issues of occupation and earning that they shared with so many female U.S. readers. One of the satisfactions for me, in my years of reading and rereading these books, has been that they inscribe the little-mentioned and almost-forgotten ways my grandmothers made money in the rural Midwest— teaching common schools, taking boarders, selling eggs, butter, and cream—and also dramatize some of the issues I anticipated and then confronted as I began to earn money myself as a young woman.

As we have seen, it is Laura's first paid job that sets the plots of *Little Town on the Prairie* in motion. Her wage earning is various and ongoing; it expands her mobility and transforms her life. After a few jobs, no matter how pleasant the routine of domestic work at home with Ma and her sisters, Laura says,

> "I don't know why, but I feel I ought to be earning something."
>
> "That is the way it is, once you begin to earn," Pa said.
> (THGY 134)

In fact, the various ways that Laura and other women earn money in the Little House series constitute a near-comprehensive survey of the major rural U.S. women's paid occupations in the nineteenth century.[16] Teaching, of course, is Ma's past and Laura's future profession. But many other possibilities exist as well. For example, women also work at making and selling butter in the series; in *Farmer Boy* Mother Wilder prides herself on the price her butter brings from the New York City buyer, and she passes on her expertise to her daughters. According to Jensen, in the mid-Atlantic region where the Wilders lived, women had dominated butter making since the late eighteenth century, and by the nineteenth century butter was "a stable, reliable source of income." In fact, "butter became more profitable as agricultural commodities traditionally produced by men, especially grain and livestock, became less valuable" (171).[17] Thus, early in the Little House project, as we saw in Chapter 1, *Farmer Boy* emphasized the importance of women's financial contributions to a successful farm. One of Jensen's aims as a historian is to attend to kinds of work done by women that have received little attention from historians and are "usually omitted from descriptions of wage work and housework—that is, work done in the household in addition to producing goods and services for use" (187). Wilder and Lane shared this aim; as with the butter making, they brought such overlooked labor onto the page—and into their plots.

Another major way women earned money was by taking in boarders; "boarding was widespread among both native born and immigrant households until the 1930s" (Jensen 197). As I noted in Chapter 4, boarding figures prominent!y in *On the Shores of Silver Lake*, as new male homesteaders flood into De Smet before hotel accommodations are available. The brunt of the work—cooking, dishwashing, cleaning—is done by Ma and Laura, with occasional help from Mrs. Boast. "Pa did not like to charge folks for shelter and a meal"; it is Ma who "firmly" says, "We can charge them for it, Charles" (226–27). Thus it is Caroline Ingalls who first teaches her daughters the economic value of their labor and its products. (The income from boarders, much of it accumulated while Pa is away, becomes the nucleus of family savings that eventually make it possible for Mary to attend college.) Later, it is also Ma whom Laura asks for permission when she is offered paid employment, and it is Ma who approves the salary offered for Laura's first teaching job. Quintessentially domestic though she may often appear, Caroline Ingalls is presented as a woman who understands and promotes the monetary worth of women's work.

Jensen also notes that, in the late nineteenth century, "some [rural] women began to turn their attention to other farm commodities ignored by males, such as poultry raising" (171). In *Little Town on the Prairie* the Ingalls family gets its start in poultry raising—thanks to Ma's closest woman friend, Mrs. Boast, who "sets a hen" for the Ingalls—and the growth of their flock becomes a significant strand of plot. Mrs. Boast sends the baby chicks on the very day that Laura's first sewing job ends, leaving her disconsolate that she has "only earned nine dollars" (58). The possibilities represented by the chickens offset the stringent limits of Laura's earning powers—in ways that were no doubt very telling to Laura Ingalls Wilder, who prided herself on her expertise with poultry and made her chickens into a significant source of income for much of her adult life. (Indeed, her work as an agricultural clubwoman and a writer for the *Missouri Ruralist* was spurred by her reputation as one of Missouri's top egg producers.)[18] The fictional Ingalls daughters know that chickens can mean economic success and a comfortable, satisfying life. They understand the significance of Mrs. Boast's "generous" gift:

> ". . . a whole setting of eggs—It saves us a year in starting a flock."
>
> If they could raise the chicks, if hawks or weasels or foxes did not get them, some would be pullets that summer. Next year the pullets would begin laying, then there would be eggs to set. Year after next, there would be cockerels to fry, and more pullets to increase the flock. Then there would be eggs to eat, and when the hens grew too old to lay eggs, Ma could make them into chicken pie.
>
> "And if next spring Pa can buy a young pig," said Mary, "then in a

couple of years we'll have fried ham and eggs. And lard and sausages
and spareribs and headcheese!" (30)

Such a passage, written from the point of view of the older daughters,
indicates how specifically they have learned to translate the facts of farm
economy into the staples of everyday life, the foods on their table.

As was typical on farms, the chickens represent an important female
occupational tradition and are entirely Ma's responsibility.[19] She mixes
their feed and supervises their care, assigning tasks to her two younger
daughters: "it would be Carrie's task to feed them often and to keep their
water pan filled. . . . it would be Grace's part to keep a sharp lookout for
hawks" (60). Through such tasks, even "baby" Grace can begin to contrib-
ute to the family finances and to understand the economic significance of
her work.

On the night that the chickens arrive, Ma and Laura meet in the dark
chicken coop, both checking on the vulnerable sleeping chicks. Ma shares
with Laura, for the first time, her own economic vision of the homestead
project:

> "The place begins to look like a farm," she said. The oatfield and
> the cornfield were shadowy pale in the darkness, and the garden [also
> Ma's responsibility, with her daughters' help] was bumpy with lumps
> of dark leaves. Like pools of faint star-shine among them spread the
> cucumber vines and the pumpkins. The low sod stable could hardly be
> seen, but from the house window a warm yellow light shone out.
>
> Suddenly, without thinking at all, Laura said, "Oh Ma, I do wish
> Mary could go to college this fall."
>
> Unexpectedly Ma replied, "It may be that she can. Your Pa and I
> have been talking of it." (61)

Throughout the Little House series, Laura has shared romantic visions of
the possibilities of western life with her father. But here she is her mother's
collaborator; together they envision the risky gamble of the homestead
transformed into beautiful and productive real estate, a fertile *farm* that they
are helping to create. This new vision of empowerment makes it possible
for Laura to voice her most economically ambitious desire—a college education for Mary. And Ma includes Laura in the adult plans for that project,
reminding her that she has already made a significant contribution to it, by
wage earning: "Your nine dollars are a great help, Laura. I have been planning, and I do believe that with nine dollars I can buy the goods for Mary's

best dress, and perhaps the velvet to make her a hat" (62). Laura's increasing involvement in the Ingallses' major economic commitments—the education of Mary and the development of the farm—becomes a major plot of the last two Little House books, *Little Town on the Prairie* and *These Happy Golden Years*.

Throughout those two books, women's labor, paid and not, is represented as ongoing and various, and increasingly Laura is involved in it. She continues to attend school and to share in the domestic work of the Ingalls household; she also becomes involved in several business enterprises launched by women who have emigrated to De Smet. One such enterprise is the shirt-sewing venture started by Mrs. White; it takes advantage of the newly available boon of the sewing machine and the new "rush" of single male settlers, all in need of work shirts. Then Laura is hired by a married dressmaker, Mrs. McKee, and by a single milliner, Miss Bell. Through the wages she earns for this work, Laura contributes to Ingalls family expenses and to Mary's school expenses; for herself she buys only clothes (and later, trousseau linens). Her work with hats and fabrics makes her a more informed and discriminating consumer.

Later, Laura also earns money by claim sitting; she joins Mrs. McKee and her young daughter summering on their claim because Mr. McKee cannot afford to give up his town job as a clerk to fulfill the legal requirement that homesteaders live on their claim. Mrs. McKee bitterly criticizes the Homestead Act:

> "Whoever makes these laws ought to know that a man that's got enough money to farm, has got enough to buy a farm. If he hasn't got money, he's got to earn it, so why do they make a law that he's got to stay on a claim, when he can't? All it means is, his wife and family have got to sit idle on it, seven months of the year. I could be earning something, dressmaking, to help buy tools and seeds, if somebody didn't have to sit on this claim. I declare to goodness, I don't know but sometimes I believe in woman's rights. If women were voting and making laws, I believe they'd have better sense." (THGY 118–19)

The dressmaker, prevented from exercising her own marketable skills, opposes a male-devised economy that ignores the importance and value of a woman's business. The entire Little House series, both as a narrative and as an enormously successful economic project executed by women, reinforces Mrs. McKee's argument for legislation that recognizes the economic contributions of female workers. (Appropriately, this argument appears in the last novel, published in 1943, when World War II was bringing large numbers of women into the labor market.) By the time this final volume is complete, the Little House series has presented a significant gallery of occupations for women. Many, as I have indicated, are practiced by Laura; Wilder and Lane also provide glimpses of other kinds of female occupations, such as hotel keeper, maid, and even writer—the minister's wife, Mrs. Brown, is paid for her contributions to "church papers."

The most elaborated of these occupational plots involves Laura's brief but important career as a teacher. *Little Town*, which began with Laura's first paid employment, ends with her first teacher's examination and her employment to teach the newly established two-month Brewster School. *Golden Years* begins on the road, as Pa delivers Laura to the Brewster neighborhood, where she will board and teach. The first hundred pages of this final Little House novel are almost entirely dominated by Laura's first teaching experiences.

By the mid-1870s, when Laura Ingalls began school in Minnesota at the age of eight, the national campaign to provide qualified female teachers for western schools, led by Catharine Beecher, had successfully encouraged "Americans to shift their image of 'teacher' from second rate young man to exemplary woman" (Hoffman 11). Although the one- or two-room "common schools" that the Ingalls sisters attended could be taught by anyone who had attained the age of sixteen, passed an examination (usually administered by a county superintendent of schools), and been hired by a school board, female teachers were the norm. (Of the five of Laura's teachers mentioned in the series, three are women.) They commanded considerable prestige, and their work was more lucrative than any of the other available jobs that Laura's parents considered respectable for a single woman. In fact, the community of De Smet encourages Laura to take up teaching; as I have already argued, her public recital of history makes her very marketable as a conduit of sanctioned values, despite her young age (fifteen). According to Mary Hurlbut Cordier, this was a typical situation on the Great Plains in the later nineteenth century; "because the teachers were members of the settler families, their motivation to teach was part of the ambiance of the time and place as they brought to the schoolhouses the moral, ethical life-styles demanded by their communities" (38–39).[20] Thus Laura, an apparently exemplary daughter of the oldest "settler family" in De Smet, never needs to apply for a teaching position; offers come to her from the all-male school boards of three small new schools.

As a child, Mary Ingalls aspired to be a teacher; Laura did not. But after Mary was blinded, Pa told Laura, "You know Ma was a teacher, and her mother before her. Ma's heart is set on one of you girls teaching school, and I guess it will have to be you" (SSL 127). Teaching is an Ingalls-Quiner female heritage, enforced by maternal expectations. When Laura is only fourteen, Ma installs her as teacher in a home school for Carrie and two little neighbor girls. Laura finds teaching just as tedious and boring as she had feared—worse than housework—and when her reluctant pupils stop coming to school, she is "so glad to be free from teaching that she began to sing while she swept the floor." Mary says, consolingly, "Anyway, you have taught the first school in De Smet" (255–56), suggesting that teaching is one of the few means by which a young woman can insert herself into the history of the settlers' town. But the young Laura has no interest in distinguishing herself thus; she knows that she has "got to be a teacher" (256), but only to fulfill Ma's desires and Mary's need for college money.

At fourteen, Laura is more sympathetic to her father's desires. Because of his wife's insistence on his daughters' need for "schooling," Charles Ingalls has permanently tabled his persistent ambitions to move farther west, ambitions that are restated in all the last four Little House books and shared by Laura. For Laura, school comes to represent confinement and stability, properties that became problematic in the original Little House in the Big Woods and launched the Ingalls family on their western wanderings. In other words—for both Laura and her father, the schoolhouse appears *anti-West*.

Throughout the Little House series, the presence and possibility of the West has raised issues of freedom and confinement, property and mobility, borders and boundaries, acquiescence and will. Once the Ingalls family settles in De Smet, Laura will never make any further forays into the geographic west. As the possibilities of western immigration recede in her life (if not in her imagination), schoolroom experiences increasingly dominate Laura's adolescent life, and the schoolroom becomes the stage on which a young woman works out the issues of expansion and control that were often enacted by Laura's young male contemporaries in the Turnerian drama of the frontier.

All Laura's life, a significant portion of her mother's authority has come from the fact that she was once a teacher. Laura has been taught that the figure of the female teacher represents propriety and mastery and has been instructed to give her teachers—female or male—unquestioning respect and obedience. But as she begins to realize that teaching must be her own future, the adolescent Laura turns more evaluative attention to her teachers and begins to ponder the various ways they fail as well as succeed. In the last books, schoolroom scenes are more frequent, more elaborated, and more integral to plot. In *Long Winter*, as I indicated in Chapter 4, Miss Garland's uncertainty about where to lead her pupils in a blizzard endangered all their lives. As Laura dutifully followed her teacher onto the open prairie, she had to ignore her own prairie experience and her intuitive sense of direction; thus she imperiled Carrie's safety as well as her own. Clearly, a teacher may be fallible, and her error of judgment may be a matter of life and death.

Next, in *Little Town*, Laura's teacher is Eliza Jane Wilder, Almanzo's sister. At first, when other pupils question the new teacher's methods, Laura argues for the cultural authority conveyed by the patriarchal certification process, saying that Miss Wilder *must* know "how to teach. She has a certificate" (125). But the new teacher commits blunder after disastrous blunder, and the De Smet school becomes a circus of pranks and disorder. Laura concludes, rebelliously, that the new teacher is "unfair" and lacks "good judgment" (153). If she is to expand and grow into an authoritative and self-sufficient woman and teacher, Laura must learn to make such evaluations and to act on them. When Carrie is humiliated by being forced to continue rocking the loose desk she was unconsciously moving while she studied, Laura is overcome by "fury" at the teacher. She assumes the desk-rocking herself, and the sound of her enraged movement fills the classroom. "THUMP, THUMP! THUMP, THUMP! No one could study now" (162). Like an insistent heartbeat, the sound of Laura's angry energy fills the room, and the school is destroyed by her will.

> Loudly Miss Wilder said, "Laura, you and Carrie are excused from school. You may go home for the rest of the day."
>
> "THUMP!" Laura made the seat say. Then there was dead silence.
>
> Everyone had heard of being sent home from school. No one there had seen it done before. It was a punishment worse than whipping with a whip. (162–63)

Fueled by anger and physical strength, Laura has found a commanding voice in which she enters an assertive dialogue with her teacher, challenging everything she has been taught about respecting female authority. When Miss Wilder invokes her official power, imposing a severe punishment, Laura does not allow herself to be entirely silenced; she replies with a last emphatic THUMP! In one sense Laura has won—but the cost of her victory is expulsion from the school and from the education that is the only means by which she can become a teacher herself.

Next day the Ingalls girls return anxiously to school. Although Laura suppresses her rebellious voice, the unruly younger boys now look to her to authorize their own rebellion; she finds that she can egg them on or subdue them with just a smile or frown. Furthermore, when Laura uses her writing skills to revise a secret schoolroom verse maligning the teacher, she learns that she cannot control the dissemination of her words; horrified, she hears the jeering "anonymous" rhyme—"lazy, lousy Lizy Jane"—sung all over town. And Miss Wilder obviously recognizes Laura as a powerful rival; when the school board (including Pa) makes a disciplinary classroom visit, she tells them that "It is Laura Ingalls who makes all the trouble in this school" (180).

Laura is caught in a cruelly instructive paradigm. In Miss Wilder's school, she has won authoritative language and pervasive influence, especially over males. But as a girl who wants to retain her position as a sanctioned patriarchal daughter and to qualify for a teacher's authority, she must curb, hide, and deny the very powers she has discovered. The episode ends when Ma asks for Laura's autograph album and ceremoniously writes, in a teacher's copybook hand, this verse:

> If wisdom's ways you wisely seek,
> Five things observe with care,
> To whom you speak,
> Of whom you speak,
> And how, and when, and where.
> [Signed] Your loving mother
> C. Q. Ingalls (184)

Ma's homiletic verse reasserts the authority of the ultimate female teacher—herself—and reminds Laura of the power of language. Words must be rigorously controlled and sometimes repressed, the verse says; anger must be *contained*. Once Laura *wrote* the words "lazy, lousy Lizy Jane," although she intended them as a private joke, they became common language, chanted by children on the street. A teacher, as Ma is and Laura aspires to be, dictates language to children. Ma's careful, impeccable verse reminds Laura that those words must be chosen with extreme, almost paralyzing care; it urges repression on a voluble daughter. Ma's verse is almost certainly not an original composition, as Laura's racy rhyme was.

Instead, it passes on conventional wisdom that helped to define Victorian womanhood, in the ritualized medium of an inscription in an autograph book (a nineteenth-century girls' fad). In the text of *Little Town*, Ma's verse is reproduced not in print but as a facsimile, in "her own" handwriting. The facsimile gives maternal inscription a heightened, iconic power, and the handwriting recalls a teacher's instructive pen(wo)manship. Ma has the last word; her verse concludes the chapter and the narrative never returns to Miss Wilder's schoolroom.

On another, almost subliminal level, however, the facsimile resumes the dialogue that Laura began in the schoolroom. For the few lines of Ma's "handwriting" are surrounded by a sea of print, print that represents her *daughter*'s mature voice and often broaches subjects (such as anger) that Ma would censor. Print makes Laura Ingalls Wilder's words into widely circulated cultural capital. And on the page, it is the contrasting surround of print that *conveys* much of the iconic power of Ma's verse. In these ways, the schoolroom controversy between Laura and Miss Wilder is linked to the large issues of language, authority, and repression that are at the center of a twentieth-century woman writer's career.

Another striking feature of this episode is its merciless portrayal of an actual woman—Eliza Jane Wilder, a significant and sometimes very helpful figure in the lives of Almanzo, Laura, and Rose Wilder. The Little House series tells that the "bossy" sister of *Farmer Boy* became a strong-willed woman; in *Golden Years* Almanzo describes his sister as being "for women's rights" (Laura is not) (269), and he persuades Laura to marry unceremoniously, earlier than they had planned, to deflect Eliza Jane's plans "to take charge of our wedding" (268). The characterization of Eliza Jane Wilder as a vindictive, failing teacher is horrific, and it suggests yet another way that Wilder and Lane used the power of their written language to continue an apparently lifelong battle of wills that began in a classroom. In the classroom story, expulsion is a trump card, and Miss Wilder plays it. But Laura Ingalls Wilder trumps that trump when she *publishes* her version of her sister-in-law as teacher.

After Miss Wilder disappears at the end of one term, Laura's last two teachers are competent men whom she never defies. But she cannot return to unreflective acquiescence. The case she ponders most deeply is that of Willie Oleson, a "bright enough" boy who simulated retardation to tease Miss Wilder, who was taken in and "required nothing of him." The next teacher followed suit. Now Willie habitually lapses into his act, and Laura fears it is no longer an act. Then the new teacher, Mr. Owen, whips Willie thoroughly and informs him that he will be expected to learn with the others. Intimidated by discipline, Willie begins to "try . . . to think. . . . Laura often wondered whether he could pull his mind together after he had let it go to pieces so" (LTP 270), and she cannot decide what to think of Mr. Owen's punishment of the boy. Willie's case spurs her to think about teachers and pupils in broader and more reflective ways. The case's most alarming implication is that a child can regress in the classroom, perhaps permanently. Whatever later teachers do, they may not be able to reverse the pattern of debilitation that Miss Wilder allowed to begin. Laura wonders whether Mr. Owen's vigorous physical punishment is a salutary corrective or mere brutality. The case of Willie Oleson emphasizes how much is at stake in the classroom and how irrevocable a teacher's influence can be.

Laura's ongoing reflections on the uses and misuses of a teacher's authority turn the attention of the Little House series to another series of rooms in which most children and adolescents find themselves contained—the classrooms where they spend large portions of their lives. The demands of the classroom were especially intense for nineteenth-century girls; they attended common schools more regularly than boys, who might be kept out of school to do agricultural work (as Almanzo was, in *Farmer Boy*). Even in school, boys would be boys—they were allowed more latitude for enjoying inversions of authority and order. In Miss Wilder's classroom, most of the disorder came from boys, and even the male school board members could not contain their amusement at the boys' subversive antics. But daughters were allowed no such latitude; Pa said, "I cannot have my girls making trouble in school" (LTP 165). Propriety became a female duty that girls must assume. And if, like Laura, they planned to be teachers themselves, the sometimes oppressive power dynamics of the classroom were their future as well as their present dilemma. To assume the teacher's role in the nineteenth-century West meant that a young woman must transmit a stable version of "civilization" to her frontier pupils, embodying and enforcing a propriety that put her at odds with the open-ended, carnivalesque possibilities of the West that Laura Ingalls (like her father) found most attractive. No wonder that, on her first day at Brewster School, when Laura opens the schoolhouse door and surveys the scene, she is terrified. "In the corner . . . stood a small table and a chair. 'That is the teacher's table,' Laura thought, and then, 'Oh my; I am the teacher'" (THGY 16).

Always before, Laura has worked under another woman's direction. When she takes her place at the teacher's table, she faces her first experience in independently creating and maintaining order out of the raw materials of her own insight and will. The first third of *Golden Years* is dominated by the rhythms and the plot of Laura's first eight-week term of school. Anxiously, Laura counts days, hours, and minutes. When she meets her pupils and discovers what they know, she immediately invents a pattern for the days. The worst specter of Laura's schoolroom past is Miss Wilder, who could not *keep order*, so she acts to defend herself and her five pupils against chaos and failure.

However, Laura's plans must contend with powerful forces. One is weather; in midwinter, she must find a way to maintain discipline in an uninsulated room so cold that students must leave their seats to huddle near the stove. Even the school superintendent, Laura's supervisor, emphasizes this force. His address to the school is one sentence: "Whatever else you do, *keep your feet warm*" (80). Laura must also avoid the errors of Miss Garland, who nearly lost her scholars to blizzard weather.

An even more difficult problem is maintaining distance from her students. Laura is a homesick girl away from home for the first time. Her pupils are her only peers and potential friends; some are as old as she, and taller. With them physical discipline would be impossible, and moreover (remembering Willie Oleson), Laura is not sure she approves of such punishment. So the students' friendliness is very tempting, and on the third day she joins in their snowball fight. The repercussions are immediate. "That very afternoon Clarence pulled Martha's hair" (27), and more misbehavior follows. Laura's invented order begins to fail. By the end of the second week, she is overwhelmed by "despair." "She was too little . . . she could not interest them . . . they were all against her, she could not discipline them" (48, 51). By the second week, time, order, and work have no meaning in her classroom.

In her first experience as a self-directed young working woman, Laura has discovered that her own resources are inadequate; to be "free and independent" is both insufficient and impossible. Miserably she identifies with her nemesis, Miss Wilder, who is emblematic, for Laura, of a failed woman. "'This is the way she felt,' Laura thought" (51). So on her second weekend visit, she breaks her silence and confesses her troubles to her sympathetic family.

Carrie, still a child, suggests that her sister ask a member of the school board to whip the most troublesome boy, Clarence. Laura is unwilling to defer to male authority and physical force; she protests, "How can I tell the school board that I can't manage the school?" Pa rejoins, "There you have it, Laura! . . . It's all in that word, 'manage'." "Managing" is the title of this key chapter, in which Laura's parents advise her on how to exert public power in her new job. The repeated word *"manage"* also subtly evokes issues of gender, for Ma and Pa employ very different vocabularies in which to instruct their needy daughter. Pa begins: "Brute force can't do much. Everybody's born free, you know, like it says in the Declaration of Independence." Though Pa rejects the physical coercion that his daughter is too small to exert over a large adolescent male, he evokes male-authored political precedents that assume a male electorate (in the Declaration of Independence, of course, "everybody" means white men). Pa recommends that Laura respect the authority of *Clarence's* independence: "Try to see things his way. . . . Better not try to make him do anything, because you can't." Such advice, however well meant, reinforces Laura's feelings of inadequacy; she concludes, "I guess I just don't know how to manage him" (54).

Ma advises next, in a very different style:

> "If I were you," Ma gently began, and Laura remembered that Ma had been a schoolteacher, "I'd give way to Clarence. . . . It's attention he wants; that's why he cuts up. Be pleasant and nice to him, but put all your attention on the others and straighten them out. Clarence'll come around."
>
> "That's right, Laura, listen to your Ma," said Pa. "Wise as a serpent and gentle as a dove."
>
> "Charles!" said Ma. Pa took up his fiddle and began saucily playing to her, "Can she make a cherry pie, Billy boy, Billy boy . . . ?" (54–55)

Ma's tactical advice is similar to Pa's but couched very differently. It is based in psychologically acute observation and attention to classroom dynamics, probably growing out of Ma's experience as teacher and mother. When Ma suggests that Laura refrain from disciplining Clarence, she presents the tactic not as an abnegation of Laura's power but an expression of it, a version of "managing" that would have been familiar to a nineteenth-century woman, who would probably have known a great deal about the exercise of covert power. Pa's response to his wife's advice (which is more practical and specific than his own) is to praise her in sanctioned biblical language that combines stereotypically masculine and feminine qualities—"wise as a serpent, gentle as a dove." But then he also puts her in her domestic place with a song that emphasizes the culinary skills of a woman (unlike Laura) who does not work outside her home—"Billy Boy's" sweetheart, who bakes a mean cherry pie and is too young to "leave her mother." The mixed language of Pa's response suggests that he both admires his wife's modest display of professional acuity and is slightly threatened by it.

Laura takes her lessons in "managing" back to her classroom and, benefiting from Ma's insight, begins to improve. She grows more attentive to her pupils' individual and collective needs and less obsessed with enacting her own rigid version of order. As the days pass, she becomes an effective and practical teacher. Even when her boarding circumstances become almost unbearable, she is determined to complete her term of work: "A teacher could not walk away and leave a term of school unfinished. If she did, she would not deserve another certificate, and no school board would hire her" (82). Now Laura is thinking of herself as a teacher, mindful of her responsibilities, her credentials, and her future employment.

On the last day of school, the teacher's table is no longer strange to her, and she has maintained a climate in which lessons are "well learned" and pupils are "well-behaved." At the end of the day, Laura presents each pupil with one of her treasured name cards, printed with her full name and a Victorian spray of flowers. On the back she has inscribed, "Presented to [pupil's name], by her teacher, with kind regards" (87). Through her successful teaching, Laura Elizabeth Ingalls has taken full possession of her own name and staked a claim to her continuing identity as a successful, independent woman. She has *managed* a successful school.

The story of Laura's first term of teaching is intimately interwoven with another important plot: that of her courtship with the "farmer boy" Almanzo Wilder, now a young homesteader in the De Smet community. Almanzo has begun to "see Laura home" from town events such as the literaries and has placed an anonymous gift on the church Christmas tree for her. Every week of her school term, he makes the round trip to Brewster school—twenty-four miles—in his elegant cutter, rescuing Laura from fear and homesickness and returning her briefly to the security of the Little House. However, despite all evidence to the contrary, Laura staunchly denies that Almanzo is courting her. Her friend Mary Power says,

"Laura's teaching school, and Almanzo Wilder's beauing her home."

"Oh, no! He isn't!" Laura cried out. "It isn't like that at all. He came for me as a favor to Pa. . . . I just don't want you to think Mr. Wilder's my beau, because he isn't." (THGY 38–39)

However, despite such protests, Laura never refuses an invitation from Almanzo.

Her conflicted response indicates her ambivalence at the onset of adulthood. On one level, it is easiest to think of herself as an adjunct to her patriarchal father, seeing Almanzo's attentions as "a favor to Pa" and herself only as a footnote to a primary, homosocial relationship between men. On another level, courtship, as represented by the conventions of much nineteenth-century women's fiction, offers new, challenging, and attractive (although usually self-limiting) opportunities for exploration and self-determination. Although Laura customarily asks her parents' permission when she is offered work and even consults them about such small personal matters as whether to keep her "Sunday dress" on after church, she never requests their permission to make dates with Almanzo. And Pa and Ma do not interfere with Laura's decisions about Almanzo. Although Ma fears his unruly horses, she says, " 'Of course Laura will go if she wishes.' . . . So Laura and Almanzo went" (THGY 249). Furthermore, Laura is never represented as discussing her relationship with Almanzo with another person, not even her mother, sisters, and female friends. She has grown to sexual maturity in the cramped physical spaces of Little Houses, usually sharing her bed with a sister. The developing courtship with Almanzo is largely conducted in the mobile space of his cutter, buggy, or sleigh, a space inhabited only by the two young people; it provides Laura's only extended experience of *privacy*. According to Karen Lystra, romantic love made a major contribution to the ethos of U.S. individualism that burgeoned in the nineteenth century and that Wilder and Lane promoted in the Little House story. Lystra argues that "the goal of American middle-class courtship was to create some special experience within an individual before marriage that was not shared by others" (8–9). With Almanzo, Laura begins to share such experience.

Laura has never wanted to teach, even though she feels obligated to do so, to fulfill Ma's wishes and to help pay for Mary's education. And although she finally succeeds with Brewster School, she never admits to *liking* her work there. As she tries to envision her future, she can imagine only two alternatives: being "an old maid schoolteacher, like Miss Wilder"

(THGY 136) and marriage. Before she begins to teach or to see Almanzo, Laura quizzes her mother:

> "How many terms of school did you teach, Ma?"
>
> "Two," said Ma.
>
> "What happened then?" Laura asked.
>
> "I met your Pa," Ma answered.
>
> "Oh," Laura said. Hopefully she thought that she might meet somebody. Maybe, after all, she would not have to be a schoolteacher always. (LTP 266)

Courtship was Ma's way out of the schoolroom, and at first Laura "hopefully" sees that plot as a way out for herself as well. But once she is teaching Brewster School, it becomes clear that Laura fears the courtship plot—a sequence that will inevitably end with a commitment to marriage—as much as she desires it. On Laura's first visit home, Carrie asks her, "Do you dreadfully hate to teach school?" "Yes I do," Laura replies. Attempting to console her sister, Carrie says, "Maybe you'll get married. Ma did." But Laura's response is now vehemently negative: "'I don't want to. . . . I'd rather stay home than anything. . . . always,' Laura said, and she meant it with her heart" (THGY 36).

Laura's new aversion to marriage is related to the circumstances of her life in the Brewster community. There she boards with Mr. and Mrs. Brewster and their baby son. Their claim shanty, although cramped, is weathertight and their food is "good"; what makes Laura's situation unbearable is the unrelenting antipathy of Mrs. Brewster. Not much older than Laura, this young wife and mother is trapped in dead winter in a community much smaller and more isolated than De Smet. She is never depicted outside her tiny shanty. Laura's friendly overtures are sullenly rejected. On her first night, she overhears Mrs. Brewster complaining to her husband: "suits you, but I keep a boarder!. . . . Schoolteacher, indeed! . . . been a teacher myself, if I hadn't married" (10). Suddenly Laura finds herself at a top level of the local female occupational hierarchy, at least in Mrs. Brewster's envious and desperate eyes. Like Ma Ingalls, Mrs. Brewster can only work within a confining domestic frame, keeping a boarder within her own house, and for no apparent personal profit. (By contrast, remember that Ma insisted on compensation for her and her daughters' labors when they kept boarders in *Silver Lake*.) But Laura, who is single and mobile, can earn a living wage as a teacher and thus can partially extricate herself from the interior of a Little House. In furious complaints that Laura is meant to overhear, Mrs. Brewster vents her anger and envy to her husband, refusing to "slave for a hoity-toity snip that had nothing to do but dress up and sit in a schoolhouse all day" (22). Nevertheless, Laura remains with the Brewsters—there is no other place for her to stay.

As the weeks of Laura's school term pass, Mrs. Brewster's condition worsens; she exhibits symptoms of clinical depression: "Mrs. Brewster let the housework go. She did not sweep out the snow that Mr. Brewster tracked in. . . . She did not make their bed nor even spread it up. Twice a day she cooked potatoes and salt pork and put them on the table. The rest of the time she sat brooding. She did not even comb her hair, and . . . Johnny squalled with temper" (46). Only once is this apathy broken; on one especially frigid morning, Mr. Brewster comes in with "half-frozen" feet and his wife tends him anxiously and lovingly. "She was so concerned and so kind that she seemed [to Laura] like another woman." Rubbing her husband's numb feet, she says, "Oh, Lewis, this dreadful country!" (63).

In some ways, Mrs. Brewster's narrative in *Golden Years* retells the story of the Long Winter, which Wilder and Lane presented in their sixth volume as a qualified triumph of survival for the Ingalls family and especially for Ma. Here the story is framed in terms of a homestead wife's furious resistance to her role as western housekeeper. As opposed to Ma's determined performance of sanity and control in even more extreme circumstances, Mrs. Brewster rages and sulks and threatens, acting out the behavioral extremes of a prairie madwoman in the attic. Yet her tender care of Mr. Brewster's frostbite makes it clear to Laura that the Brewsters do have a loving marriage.

On the night of the frostbite episode, Laura's terror comes to a head. She is wakened by a "wild" scream. In the moonlight, through a crack between the thin curtains that surround her sofa-bed,

> Laura saw Mrs. Brewster standing there. Her long white flannel nightgown trailed on the floor and her black hair fell loose over her shoulders. In her upraised hand she held the butcher knife. . . .
>
> "If I can't go home one way, I can another," said Mrs. Brewster.
>
> "Go put that knife back," said Mr. Brewster. He lay still, but tensed to spring.
>
> "Will you or won't you?" she demanded.
>
> "You'll catch your death of cold," he said. "I won't go over that again, this time of night. I've got you and Johnny to support, and nothing in the world but this claim. Go put up that knife and come to bed before you freeze."

Eventually, Mrs. Brewster replaces the knife in the kitchen and returns to bed. From then on, Laura "dared not sleep. Suppose she woke to see Mrs. Brewster standing over her with that knife? . . . What could she do?" (66).

This horrific scene forces Laura to witness the spectacle of a trapped housewife, miserably homesick (as Laura herself is), contemplating either suicide or a violent attack on her loved husband as her only escape from an untenable situation (confinement, isolation, poverty, vulnerability to extremes of weather) that is in fact the *usual* situation for prairie homesteaders, especially women, as depicted in the Little House books. Mr. Brewster's position is exactly that of Pa Ingalls or of Almanzo Wilder—he is tied to the claim as his sole economic asset, his only means of supporting a family. Finally, Mrs. Brewster is controlled by her husband's voice and will; she returns to their marital bed, unable to complete her violent threat. In the morning, "nothing was different; breakfast was the usual silent meal" (66).

Consciously, Laura fears Mrs. Brewster; she is afraid of waking to find the woman brandishing a knife over her. Yet it is clear that Mrs. Brewster's potential violence is directed only toward herself or her husband, who controls the circumstances of her homestead life. In frustration with her own powerlessness, Mrs. Brewster seizes the potentially powerful phallic knife; the midnight encounter that Laura witnesses through a curtain seems to be a contest about control of the phallus and control over the circumstances of the Brewsters' lives. Although Mr. Brewster never raises his voice and never enacts physical violence, he ultimately possesses the power that the phallus conveys in a patriarchal economy: his wife stays on the homestead, takes a boarder, and returns the knife to the kitchen—where it resumes the status of a domestic tool—because his word is law. Unconsciously, at least, Laura is receiving an education in the conjunction of sexual and gendered power, enacted in the dark by Mrs. and Mr. Brewster.

After the knife episode, Laura refuses to enter an unconscious state in the Brewster house; she resists sleep. Her parents observe her weight loss and fatigue with concern, but now she cannot reveal her anxieties in the familial rapport of the Little House, as she did when she needed advice about teaching. "She could not tell them about Mrs. Brewster and the knife. If they knew, they would not let her go back, and she must finish her school" (82). To function as a successful and independent adult and complete her school term, Laura must forfeit her most valuable resources: her family's support, restorative weeknight sleep, and access to the full depth and range of her own unconscious.

Laura's only rest is during her precious weekend visits home, and she is dependent on faithful Almanzo for transportation to and from De Smet. Yet her experience with the Brewsters makes her increasingly wary of any commitments to him. She rails against the language and conventions of courtship, furious when her students speak of "Teacher's beau" but grateful when Almanzo offers her an escape to De Smet. Finally she tells him, painfully and bluntly, "I am going with you only because I want to get home. When I am home to stay, I will not go with you any more" (62)— taking the terrible risk that he will leave her stranded with the Brewsters for the remaining weekends of her school term. (He does not.) Mrs. Brewster has provided a sobering lesson. Homesick and young, she resembles Laura. Alone with her husband and a child on a remote homestead, with no other financial or emotional resources, she is in the very position Laura would probably inhabit if she married an impecunious young homesteader like Almanzo Wilder.

For a child reader (or for me, anyway), Mrs. Brewster was a creation of near-gothic horror, nightmare fodder. When I reread *These Happy Golden Years* as an adult, I paged through my childhood copy (the one Grandmother bought me at Brown Bookstore) looking for the chilling illustration I remembered of Mrs. Brewster in the darkened bedroom, wielding her butcher knife. I couldn't find it. In fact, the pertinent chapter, "A Knife in the Dark," has no illustrations.[21] Finally I realized that the illustration I was remembering came from another book I had read in early adolescence, *Jane Eyre*. It is Fritz Eichenberg's frightening 1943 wood engraving depicting Bertha Mason Rochester, the prototypical Madwoman in the Attic, with wild hair and bestial features, leaning over the bed of another terrified young teacher, Jane Eyre. Bertha—trapped, desperate, and mad—is Jane Eyre's potential double, just as Mrs. Brewster is Laura's. My unconscious conflation of illustrations underlines the importantly archetypal qualities of Mrs. Brewster, who is an unforgettable figure for most girls and women who read this book. She is what Ma Ingalls will never allow herself to be. Mrs. Brewster brings the figure of the trapped, raging, and (presumably) doomed wife into the Little House series, in a specifically western form that Laura Ingalls Wilder and Rose Wilder Lane probably knew well.[22] And Mrs. Brewster is a figure that Laura Ingalls must painfully contemplate as she begins to conceive herself as an adult, a wage-earning woman and/or a wife.

In fact, before the courtship plot of *Golden Years* could proceed to the engagement of Laura and Almanzo, it was necessary for Wilder and Lane to counter some of the threatening implications of Laura's experiences at Brewster School. They did this, at least partly, by telling the story of Laura's second term of teaching as a tranquil, domesticated idyll. In the balmy months of spring and early summer, Laura teaches the Perry School. In the abbreviated (and far less interesting) narrative of this assignment, Pa (who was absent when the Brewster arrangements were made) takes charge of Laura's teaching career. He negotiates with the school board, which offers Laura a higher salary ("Why, Pa . . . that will be a little more than a dollar a day," Laura says wonderingly [149]), and contracts to build the schoolhouse himself, in the form of a Little House that is more refined and complete than he has been able to make the Ingalls home. When the "little schoolhouse" on the prairie is complete, Laura thinks

> There had never been a prettier, small schoolhouse.
>
> It stood snowy white on the green land, and its rows of windows shone brightly in the morning sunshine as Laura walked toward it across the short, new grass.
>
> Little Clyde Perry, seven years old. . . . put the key of the new door in Laura's hand and said solemnly, "My father sent you this.". . .
>
> Laura stood a moment in the doorway, looking at that fresh, bright expensive room. . . . Nothing could be more complete and perfect than this beautiful little schoolhouse. (150–51)

Teaching the Perry School, Laura lives comfortably and securely at home with her family, and she is well paid for instructing only three prepubescent pupils, who raise none of the problems of authority, discipline, and sexuality that she faced at Brewster School. This schoolhouse, constructed by her father, is a refined version of the Little House, and her term there is a new contract with patriarchy, sealed when the key is sent by little Clyde's father, the president of the school board. At Perry School she is confident that she can give "each little pupil the very best of schooling," keep up with her own lessons, and perform pleasant domestic tasks, knitting lace while the students play at recess. These are "happy days," untroubled by the isolation, cold, homesickness, and fears of violence and entrapment that shadowed the Brewster term. Laura's only worry is that she may be overpaid, but she concludes that "it must be right, since Pa said so" (152). Pa also disposes of the seventy-five dollars Laura earns; at his suggestion, she invests it (sight unseen) in an organ for Mary that Pa purchases.

The Perry School story seems to neutralize the threats of traumatic heterosexual relations that Laura was painfully aware of while she lived in the Brewsters' house; it allows Laura to continue working and earning without defying patriarchal authority or leaving the Little House. However, the entire school term is narrated in one brief, tension-free chapter, while the Brewster School narrative occupied almost a hundred pages, about a third of *Golden Years*, and was filled with conflict and suspense. As I can testify, it is the Brewster story that a reader is likely to remember.

There is only one hint that Laura is not entirely content at Perry School. During her term, she often gazes longingly at the "Wessington Hills, sixty miles away, looking like a blue cloud on the horizon. . . . Their shadowy outlines drew her with the lure of far places. . . . She wanted to travel on and on . . . and see what lay beyond the hills." But she knew "she must be content to stay where she was, to help with the work at home and teach school" (153). The hills contain the "essence of a dream" for Laura, and that dream is of "Wes . . . t," a word concealed in the name of the landmark. But now, contained in the security, content, and relative prosperity that the little white schoolhouse affords, Laura recognizes that she cannot travel to that dream. At least not alone.

In many ways it is *horses* and the speed, escape, excitement, and affluence that they promise that draw Laura Ingalls to Almanzo Wilder and confirm their courtship. When they become engaged, Ma says to Laura,

> "Sometimes I think it is the horses you care for, more than their master."
>
> "I couldn't have one without the other," Laura answered shakily.
> (216)

As *Farmer Boy* established, Almanzo's primary identity is as a horseman. In a De Smet Fourth of July race, lacking a buggy, he overcomes the disadvantage of a heavy peddler's cart to win through his superior horses and horsemanship. " 'He's an independent kind of a young cuss,' someone said. 'He'd rather lose with what he's got than win with a borrowed buggy' " (82). Almanzo embodies the values of the "free and independent" self-sufficient person, which Laura has been schooled to admire but is finding difficult to achieve for herself. Despite her fears at entering a courtship, Laura cannot resist the prospect of more rides after her Brewster School term is over, and when Almanzo invites her to join the other young people of the town in a sleigh ride, she eagerly accepts and then laughs, "I didn't intend to go with you any more but I forgot." He replies, "I thought maybe you'd change your mind after you watched the crowd go by" (92). Dating and courtship are clearly sanctioned by the "crowd" of Laura's contemporaries; not to join in courtship rituals is to be "left out" and forgotten.

Since the permanent departure of her cousin Lena in *Silver Lake*, Laura has not ridden horseback; she never will again in the series. The exhilarating, independent, eroticized pleasures of the girls' bareback rides are now replaced by a series of lengthening rides behind Almanzo's swift horses. Almanzo is also an enterprising salesman; his major financial successes are as a horse trader.[23] Naturally, he frequents the livery stable, which, according to Thomas J. Schlereth, "served as the hub of [a] horse-powered universe. . . . it provided covert arenas for boxing bouts, gambling, and cock fights, and . . . often doubled as a saloon." As a "male dominated environment," it also supplied boys and young men with sex education and initiated them into "the mores of drinking" (20–21). The occasional mentions of Almanzo's comings and goings to and from the livery stable (which Laura never enters) signal his easy familiarity with a culture of masculinity that Laura has always found interesting and attractive.

Almanzo's horses suggest freedom and physical expression to Laura, as well as the dynamics of subjection and control. Jane Tompkins's discussion of the importance of horses to western narratives describes some of Laura's responses:

> Horses are something people have close physical contact with. . . .
> Something that is alive . . . big, powerful, and fast-moving. Something
> not human but not beyond human control, dangerous, even poten
> tially lethal, but ductile to the human will. . . .
>   Horses express a need for connection to nature, to the wild. . . .
> More than any other single element in the [Western] genre, they sym
> bolize the desire to recuperate some lost connection to life. (94–95)

To Laura, Almanzo's fast, dangerous horses are both compelling and beautiful, and perhaps they do "symbolize," as Tompkins suggests, the desire for a "lost connection" that might allow full physical expression of her energy and desire. Certainly she is fascinated by the reins that are Almanzo's controlling connection to his powerful, intelligent team. The first time Almanzo makes a move to touch Laura erotically, placing an arm behind her shoulders, she makes her own move, touching the buggy whip to signal the horses.

> The colts jumped forward and broke into a run.
>   "You little devil!" Almanzo exclaimed, as he closed his hands on
> the lines. . . .
>   [Later,] "Suppose they had run away?" Almanzo then asked her
> indignantly. . . . "You're independent, aren't you?"
>   "Yes," said Laura. (167–68)

Laura's proud desire for independence and control over her own body is expressed by a bid for control of the horses. To Almanzo, admiring as he obviously is, such a bid makes her a "little devil" and perhaps increases her erotic attraction. Later, when Almanzo brings along an unwelcome third person—Nellie Oleson—on one of their drives, Laura again provokes the horses to frighten Nellie and express her displeasure to Almanzo. Then she lets "her eyes twinkle at" him. "She didn't care if he did know that she had frightened the colts . . . on purpose" (184). Through the horses, Laura begins to inform Almanzo that she wants a share of the power in their relationship. She becomes preoccupied with learning to control the horses; eventually, she begins to drive them, and she and Almanzo are especially proud when she is able (as Almanzo is not) to drive the rebellious colt Barnum, slowing him to a deliberate walk. "She loved the feel of Barnum's mouth coming to her hands through the lines" (200). *Barnum*, of course, bears the name of one of the most audacious and successful of nineteenth-century U.S. male entrepreneurs; controlling this definitively "masculine" horse indicates that Laura is holding her own in the public arena of gendered power—although it is important to remember that the horses are Almanzo's property and she drives them only when he gives her permission to do so. Also, in the vocabulary of the Little House series, which is very reticent about sexual feelings, the description of Laura's feelings about Barnum is remarkable for its erotic specificity, suggesting again that horses facilitate expression.

Laura began to admire Almanzo Wilder during the Long Winter, when he drove his team across the frozen prairie to get wheat for the starving town; he was willing to broach the undifferentiated space *outside* the relatively secure community of little houses when no one else in town would. On her first personal encounter with Almanzo, they discuss his unusual first name. He explains,

> "My folks have got a notion there always has to be an Almanzo in the family, because 'way back in the time of the Crusades there was a Wilder went to them, and an Arab or somebody saved his life. El Manzoor, the name was. They changed it after a while in England. . . ."
>
> "I think it is a very interesting name," said Laura honestly.
> (LTP 199)

Almanzo's name is an obscure link to the nonwhite, non-European cultures that *did* interest Laura Ingalls as a child; it gives him a metaphorically mixed ancestry and perhaps enhances his romantic appeal to Laura, whose first adolescent attraction was to the "half-breed" Big Jerry, whom she associated with forbidden and attractive western wandering and distances. The continuing importance of the name "Almanzo" to Laura Ingalls Wilder is underlined in a letter she wrote to a friend a few years after her husband's death: "There is no one in the family to carry on the name of Almanzo. I am very sorry and wish some Wilder family would so name a son" (LIW to Miss Weber, 11 Feb. 1952, Western). The name of Laura's first and only lover, "Almanzo James Wilder," with its combination of traditional English and appropriated Arab nomenclature and its accompanying tale of intercultural allegiance, is one of the very few hints in the last two volumes of the interest in intercultural relations that we observed in the earlier Little House books. Marrying Almanzo, Laura Ingalls will incorporate the heritage of his name into her own identity.

Thus, in several ways, Laura's horizons and vision are expanded by Almanzo and his horses. As they drive to local landmarks that Laura has never seen, commonly covering more than sixty miles on a Sunday afternoon, "the whole country seemed different to her. . . . She wondered what next Sunday would show" (172). Riding behind the spirited (and sometimes runaway) horses, Laura discovers an expanded sense of possibilities—within the country, herself, and this new, increasingly mutual relationship with Almanzo. When Almanzo invites her to accompany him to singing school, they begin a series of more specifically romantic night drives, and Laura begins to sing to Almanzo. Their favorite song is "In the Starlight," which ends with this refrain:

> Where the silv'ry waters murmur
> By the margin of the sea,
> In the starlight, in the starlight,
> We will wander gay and free. (214)[24]

This romantic picture of free nighttime *movement*, unhampered by daylight boundaries, strictures, and houses, is attractive (and presumably erotically suggestive) to both young people, who are already heavily burdened by commitments—Almanzo illegally took a homestead claim when he was only nineteen, and Laura has been working for wages to assist her family since she was fourteen. Their courtship is a rare opportunity to "wander gay and free."

Lystra, in her study of heterosexual romantic relationships in the Victorian United States, emphasizes the eloquent and expansive range of verbal expression enjoyed by many nineteenth-century lovers. The portrait of Almanzo and Laura during their courtship and engagement does not feature such verbal range and freedom; neither of them ever speaks of *loving* the other, and in her correspondence with Lane, Wilder repeatedly emphasizes that laconic language was typical of early Dakota and of her family. The actual Almanzo Wilder's taciturn style became a part of the Wilder family mythology; his wife and daughter called him an "oyster" in the 1930s. However, despite their verbal and physical restraint, the fictional Laura and Almanzo appear to share some of the satisfactions of romantic love that Lystra describes: "Among native-born middle-class Victorians, who were beginning to expect less gratification from social roles and all the supporting structures of custom and institutions and more fulfillment from the individual psyche, romantic love provided enormously satisfying and fulfilling support for and sharing of the burdens of the self" (54). Since early adolescence, Laura has been anticipating that soon "Pa and Ma will stop telling me what to do. . . . I will have to make myself be good. . . . That is what it means to be free" (LTP 76). Already she and Almanzo share a few secrets, and her relationship with him is her first intimation that, as Lystra says, the *burden* as well as the exhilaration of freedom might be shared with another person, with whom she might "wander gay and free."

Yet another attraction of the courtship period for Laura and Almanzo is the possibility—or illusion, at least—of freedom from time constraints. As young adults, both are contending with strict timetables. Almanzo is committed to proving up on his claim within the legal time limits, and as a novice teacher Laura is learning to schedule every minute of her workday. For both, it is novel and liberating to set aside hours every week for the pursuit of a courtship. This sense of space and leisure is one of the most attractive features of the middle chapters of *Golden Years*. Yet, at the same time, a courtship plot has its own insistent pace and momentum; it pushes toward the climax of engagement and marriage. In the very next chapter after Laura and Almanzo become officially engaged, Almanzo leaves abruptly to spend the winter with his family in Minnesota. "Laura was shocked. . . . It was shocking that the whole pattern of the days could be broken so suddenly. There would be no more Sunday drives" (219). The expansions of courtship and the leisurely, intense Sunday drives are lost when an engagement is contracted—and one of the striking features of this narrative is that it acknowledges Laura's alarm and sadness at this loss.

Although they are both homesteaders and like and respect each other, Charles Ingalls and Almanzo Wilder are very different men, and one of the most obvious differences is that Pa is voluble while Almanzo is not.

His relative silence—as talker and singer—gives Laura more space to develop verbally. In the Ingalls Little House, as we have seen, Laura repeatedly found herself speechless, especially on occasions of great emotion. But during her courtship with Almanzo, although she is emotionally reserved, she adopts her father's tactics and uses songs to expand her emotional vocabulary. Although he never joins in, Almanzo enjoys her singing and compliments her, "Your songs are like your father's! They always fit" (238). In her courtship, as in her teaching, Laura is becoming someone who deploys words with discrimination and skill.

Occasionally she is frustrated by the gendered conventions that control her expression; for example, she is chagrined, after a quarrel with Almanzo, that she must wait all week to see if he shows up for their regular Sunday drive. "If he didn't, he didn't; that was all. And she could only wait" (177). Laura's antithesis (and her aggressive rival for Almanzo) is her old foe, Nellie Oleson, who is a model of gushing volubility. " 'Why are you so quiet, Laura?' [Nellie] asked without stopping and went on, with a giggle, 'My tongue wasn't made to lie still. My tongue's made to go flippity-flop!' " (173). Such an uncontrolled tongue is an emblem of ineffectuality and indiscretion (as Ma indicated in the verse she inscribed in Laura's autograph book). In her last appearance in the Little House series, Nellie has no power: she lives on a poor, isolated claim with no job, no horses, no beau, and hand-me-down clothes. She exhibits the babbling that Jane Tompkins associates with the powerless female characters in Western films and fiction, while Laura—more like the male Western heroes that Tompkins observes—deploys her power by holding her tongue and manipulating physical action (she provokes the horses to run away, frightening Nellie).

A striking example of Laura's verbal control is her response to Almanzo's proposal of marriage. After singing "In the Starlight" at his request, she counters,

> "I've sung for you, now I'll give you a penny for your thoughts."
>
> "I was wondering . . ." Almanzo paused [taking Laura's hand for the first time]. . . . "I was wondering if you would like an engagement ring."
>
> "That would depend on who offered it to me," Laura told him.
>
> "If I should?" Almanzo asked.
>
> "Then it would depend on the ring," Laura answered and drew her hand away. (214)

On their next drive, Almanzo slips a ring on Laura's finger and tells her, "The set is a garnet, with a pearl on each side." . . . "It is a beautiful ring," Laura said. "I think . . . I would like to have it" (215).

Laura's language here seems extraordinarily calculated and self-protective. She places herself in the position of a discriminating, canny consumer, first "purchasing" Almanzo's thoughts for a penny, then choosing a piece of jewelry instead of accepting a husband. As we saw in Chapter 3, the Ingalls daughters were educated—by their parents and their culture—to use consumer decisions as a means of self-determination and self-discovery, just as they were cautioned to eschew emotional expression. Accepting Almanzo's proposal and ring, Laura's most impassioned declaration is in response to his promise to build a "little house" for them the next summer. "It will have to be a little house," he says. "Do you mind?" Laura replies ardently (for her): "I have always lived in little houses. I like them" (215). Her declaration of love—or at least of liking—is for the ethos and the culture in which she has come of age; for the Little House. For Laura Ingalls, and for her creators, romance resides in the continuation of the Little House. When Almanzo drives Laura home, they hear Pa singing a love song "that he often sang to Ma." It begins, "A beautiful castle I've built for thee," and ends, "We'll tell our time by the lovers' chime / That strikes the hour with kisses." It is the music of her parents' love, floating from the Little House, that gives Laura her first cues to a language of verbal and physical expression. She "held up her face . . . 'You may kiss me good night,' she said, and after their first kiss she went into the house while Almanzo drove away" (216).

When the engagement is effected, the courtship plot is complete, and, as I have said, this is where Wilder originally planned to end her series. However, about a fourth of *Golden Years* remains, and in these pages Wilder and Lane depict Laura making some crucial adjustments before her marriage. The free-floating preengagement period is over, and although Almanzo remains attentive, the tone of the relationship subtly changes. Almanzo makes abrupt, independent decisions, departing almost immediately for Minnesota, then returning unexpectedly at Christmas. There are fewer leisurely drives, for Almanzo is busy building a house and tending his crops. Furthermore, he urges Laura to set their wedding date earlier than they had planned, to fend off his mother and sister Eliza Jane, who plan to come West and take charge of the wedding. In fact, he says, there can be no formal wedding—for to hold one without Almanzo's mother would be insulting to her. So Laura agrees to be married hastily in the minister's parlor, in a new black dress instead of the wedding dress she had planned. She has little say in the plans; nor does Ma, who deeply desires a proper wedding for her daughter. Although none of them is present except Almanzo, the Wilders control the timing and circumstances of Laura's wedding, suggesting that marriage may require considerable abnegation of her developing selfhood.

With such developments, it is not surprising that Laura refuses to promise obedience in the marriage ceremony. She says, "I cannot make a promise that I will not keep, and, Almanzo, even if I tried, I do not think I could obey anybody against my better judgement." He replies, reassuringly, "I'd never expect you to" (270). Here Laura takes a stand for self-determination, putting her own "better judgement" first. But she also puts limits on her public powers of self-determination, for we learn, for the first time, that Laura is not "for woman's rights" and does "not want to vote" (269). Instead, Laura makes the paradoxical (and common) choice to exercise her "better judgement" within the determining framework of patriarchal government.

Furthermore, when Laura leaves school at the end of the term, her male teacher tells her, regretfully, that he held her back "because I had a foolish pride; I wanted to graduate the whole class together and some weren't ready. It was not fair to you." Although Laura claims that "it doesn't matter," obviously it *does* matter in a family that values education as much as the Ingallses do; she admits that she is "glad to know I could have graduated" (236), although she is denied that confirmation by a system that puts a male teacher's pride ahead of her individual achievement. Before her marriage, she teaches one more term of school, and the theme of this last teaching assignment is not a rapprochement with patriarchy like that of Perry School but female collaboration. Laura gets the job through the influence of a classmate she befriended, Florence Wilkins, and she boards with Florence's family, sharing her room. This last successful term reinforces the fact that *female* peers can provide valuable personal and professional support.

Given the conflicting signals that characterize the period of Laura's engagement, it is not surprising that she turns much of her attention back to the Little House, scrutinizing the power dynamics of her parents' marriage. In the last two books, Pa declines further in power. Although optimistic as ever, he is glad to take a portion of Laura's last teaching salary to "help" him "out of a pinch" (245), and it is apparent that such pinches are an economic and personal pattern that Charles Ingalls is not likely to change. As I noted in Chapter 4, the last three books pay less admiring attention to Pa's labors as Laura approaches womanhood. Mintz and Kellogg's description of the changing dynamics of U.S. families suggests that Pa's decline is historically apt.

> By the middle of the nineteenth century, the scope of the father's authority had . . . been constricted—a transition clearly evident in art, with family portraits, for the first time, showing all family members on the same plane, and in child-rearing manuals, which began to be addressed to mothers, not to fathers. . . . The father's authority, which had once rested on control of land and craft skills, had become increasingly symbolic. (54–55)

Some of these historical changes may be implied by a photograph of the actual Ingalls family taken in De Smet in the early 1890s. Charles Ingalls is seated at the exact center of this portrait, flanked by Caroline and Mary Ingalls, also seated. Standing behind them, in similar dark dresses, are Carrie, Laura, and Grace. As the father and only male of this portrait, Charles Ingalls is in a symbolically weighted position, and his posture might be construed to emphasize sexual potency—his knees are spread and his hands, relaxed on his upper thighs, point toward his crotch. Yet, in this picture, such conventions have little force. Slumped in his chair, Charles Ingalls seems to recede; his posture is slack and his gaze is blank. By contrast, the five women appear erect and self-possessed. Laura in particular, well tailored and sleekly corseted, has a confident and compelling (perhaps even seductive) gaze. Her hand rests proprietarily on her father's shoulder, and her figure vies with his for the central space in the picture. Another interesting feature of this 1890s portrait is the absence of Almanzo Wilder, to whom Laura had been married for several years. (None of the other sisters was yet married.) Was he considered an outsider in the Ingalls family? Or a rival to the paternal authority of his father-in-law, which required shoring up? Also absent is Rose Wilder, the only Ingalls grandchild, who had been born in 1886. (It is also possible that Almanzo was absent when the photo was taken, or that other poses were taken and have not survived.) Although such evidence is notoriously slippery, the photograph *may* suggest that the crisis of paternal authority in the nineteenth-century family was being complexly enacted within the actual Ingalls family in the years of Laura's engagement and early marriage, as we see it fictionally enacted in the later Little House books.

In the same period, the fictional Laura's allegiance with her mother intensifies. Together they buy fabrics, plan clothes and linens, and do Laura's "wedding sewing," spending hours together in the small rooms of the Little House. As I suggested in Chapter 4, Ma's competence now means more to Laura; it authorizes the daughter's future. Laura admires her mother's confident cutting of fabric and her use of the sewing machine, her skilled development of the garden and chickens that are transforming a raw claim into a promising farm, and her management of domestic work and workers (her daughters), as well as her effective teaching advice. As this admiration grows, Laura's romantic attachment to her father recedes.

In their claim shanty, the Ingallses are troubled by mice, and Pa wakes one night to find that a mouse is chewing off his hair. Shorn like Samson, he is embarrassed that he must attend a county meeting, a patriarchal occasion, with gnawed hair. Jokingly, he deflects blame onto Ma—"better just let them think this is the way my wife cuts my hair" (LTP 23)—recasting her as a power-hungry Delilah. Comically, this incident foreshadows the decline of Pa's authority. Later he brings home an effective solution to the mouse problem—in the form of a very young female, a kitten, whom Ma and her daughters raise to be a ferocious mouser. Predictively, the little cat tells Laura's story as she grows in skills and authority. Like Laura, the kitten is game, a survivor, and a fighter. But she is too young to be taken from her mother.

On the day of Laura's marriage, Pa helps her into the buggy for the last time and says to Almanzo, "You'll help her from now on, young man" (283). The implication is that Almanzo is replacing Pa as *the* man (and the patriarch) in Laura's life. However, marriage promises Laura no replacement for her mother. Thus, as the Little House series nears its end, the continuation of a mother-daughter plot becomes one of its most important issues. And this issue is heightened by the fact that the series is being written by an adult mother and daughter whose relationship is intense and volatile.

Marianne Hirsch's *The Mother/Daughter Plot* is helpful in understanding the bonds between the fictional Caroline and Laura Ingalls and the ways they structure the Little House series. Hirsch argues, as other feminist critics have, that nineteenth-century daughters' narratives usually start from the premise of motherlessness; in these stories "plot itself demands maternal absence" (67). Jane Eyre, for example, is typically a presumed orphan, as are the female protagonists of *Millbank* and other enormously popular U.S. "woman's fiction," such as *The Hidden Hand* and *The Wide, Wide World*, with which Wilder was probably familiar. However, the story of Laura Ingalls's nineteenth-century girlhood is told from a twentieth-century perspective and is characterized by near-constant maternal *presence*, not absence. Although Pa is often away from the Little House, sometimes for weeks, Ma never leaves until, in the last two books, four significant separations occur. First, Ma is gone for several days when she and Pa take Mary to Iowa to enter college; in her absence, Laura is left in charge of the house and her younger sisters, and she finds the work and the responsibility exhausting and stressful. Then Laura leaves home for three periods, claim-sitting with Mrs. McKee and teaching the Brewster and Wilkins schools. Although Laura never entirely loses her homesickness, her absences are significantly more bearable when she has the companionship and support of a competent woman—definitively absent at the Brewsters'. These separations trigger two kinds of anxiety in Laura—first, that she will not be able to muster the kinds of maternal and domestic competence that her mother exercises, and second, that she will be cut off from the forms of female support she has always received from her mother and sisters. As Laura prepares to move into a new Little House and live alone with Almanzo Wilder, both of these feared circumstances seem real possibilities.

In the Little House series, Wilder and Lane wrote the kind of mother-daughter plot that Hirsch terms *modernist* and associates with the period in which the series was written. Such plots, she says, reflect Freud's influential assertion that "when the girl abandons her mother as libidinal object she. . . . transfers her attachment to the father and represses her love for her mother" (99). (As we have seen, the Little House series begins at the moment when Laura, at four, would be negotiating this transfer.) But modernist mother-daughter plots also reflect the influence of women analysts of the twenties and thirties, such as Melanie Klein, who, according to Hirsch, affirms both "androgynous male identification" and "the pleasures and dangers of a primary femininity" for women and "tells the story of pre-oedipal mother-child attachment from the mother's own perspective." Implicitly, this complex approach questions conventional male-oriented plot, "the sequential, teleological narrative of development" (101). (Laura's recurrent adolescent flights from and returns to the Little House also question such teleological plot progression.)

Thus the model for the typical modernist mother-daughter plot, Hirsch says, is the story of Persephone, whose dual "allegiance is split between mother and husband." Persephone's plot is characterized by *"opposi-tion, interruption, and contradiction."* The "repeated cycle" she enacts, as she shuttles between Demeter and Orpheus, is not sustained by the "reconcilia-tion" of traditional male plots but by "continued opposition." This plot is based on the assumption that all women—even those "who bond and iden-tify with women—are implicated in heterosexual plots," as Laura Ingalls obviously and deeply is. Thus modernist mother-daughter plots are typ-ically situated "in the liminal space between a passionate maternal eroticism and the anxieties which shape the heterosexual plot" (102–4).

This sense of modernist oscillation marks the Little House books (which Hirsch does not discuss), especially the later ones. In the striking scene in *Silver Lake* during the railroad camp riots, for example, Laura sits in the "liminal space" of the darkened shanty with Ma, held by the sensuous and compelling touch of her mother's hands on her hair but, at the same moment, straining to join her father and the beckoning world of masculine romance and danger. Later, during her absences from her parents' home, Laura especially misses her mother and the order that Ma has labored to express through the Little House. At the same time, she is bored with that order and eagerly energized by (hetero)sexual curiosity and desire. Laura *is* a Persephone-like figure, and her anxiety about taking her first job in town, at the beginning of *Little Town*, is caused by her reluctance to leave the newly fruitful cycles of the farm, over which Ma (as Demeter) presides. The competition of concurrent plots that I have been describing in the last Little House books is clearly related to the characteristic *"opposition, interrup-tion, and contradiction"* of Hirsch's modernist mother-daughter plot.

A Demeter/Persephone-like pattern also emerges in the biographies of Wilder and Lane. Both women's earlier adult lives were marked by departures from and returns to their parents' homes. The writing of the autobiographical Little House books was itself an act of return (as well as reinvention) for Wilder, and the Wilder-Lane collaboration was an oppor-tunity for both women to reenter and reshape the confines of their own mother-daughter relationship.

In addition to the issues Hirsch describes, one of the important rea-sons why the fictional Laura's attachment to and identification with her mother must constantly be broken, and then reestablished, is the limita-tions of Ma's spoken and written language. As I have shown, Ma is typically quiet (especially in comparison with Pa) and often speaks in formulaic, constricting proverbs and sayings. Although she is the family letter writer, her epistolary style is terse; she is very concerned with conserving paper and fitting her words into a confined space. The one time Ma writes for Laura, in her autograph book, it is, as we saw, a verse about the importance of *controlling* language that seems intended to remind Laura of the danger of putting her feelings into words. This attitude seems reflected in the few pieces of correspondence from the actual Caroline Ingalls to Laura Ingalls Wilder that I have seen in the Wilder-Lane archives. An example is this very brief expression of thanks, in 1913: "Dear Laura/Your nice Christmas gifts received. Thank you for them. We are grateful indeed for the love that prompted" (Caroline Quiner Ingalls to LIW, 9 Jan. 1913, De Smet). I read this note, however affectionate, as restrained, vague, and formulaic in ways that could have been frustrating to the distant daughter, who probably longed for more specific reactions to the gifts she had laboriously mailed from Missouri to South Dakota. By contrast, the mother-daughter correspondence between Wilder and Lane is far more expansive and voluminous (although Lane's diaries indicate the many topics that she *did not* bring up in letters to her mother). Their letters often include thanks for gifts, which both women elaborate more specifically than Caroline Ingalls did in her note. Clearly the verbal style of the actual Caroline Ingalls was rejected by her daughter and granddaughter as a model for their personal correspondence and professional writing.

In fact, it is apparent that almost every phase of the Little House collaboration involved the negotiation of an oscillating mother-daughter plot enacted and written by Wilder and Lane. After the series was underway, Wilder insisted on keeping the figure of Laura as protagonist; she rejected suggestions that they switch to Carrie when Laura entered adolescence. This meant, of course, that the authors continued to focus on the figure of young Laura. Such an extended representation of her mother as daughter demothered Rose Wilder Lane. True, as we have seen in her correspondence, Lane often worked at altering the terms of her relations with Wilder, complaining that her mother still saw her as a child and flaunting her professional success and skills. Her advice to her mother is always authoritatively delivered and sometimes specifically maternal. But often, too, the anger Lane expresses in her private diaries seems to be about not having been properly mothered. In 1933 when Lane was living at Rocky Ridge, in sometimes uncomfortably close proximity to her parents, they went through a series of small financial negotiations that reminded Lane of her Depression-reduced circumstances and made her feel helpless and furious. She wrote in her diary,

It's amazing how my mother can make me suffer. . . . She made me so miserable when I was a child that I've never got over it. I'm morbid. I'm all raw nerves. I know I should be more robust. I shouldn't let her torture me this way, and always gain her own ends, thro implications that she hardly knows she's using. But I can't help it.(RWL Diary, 10 April 1933, Hoover)

Although the Little House books certainly authorize Laura as an independent person, they *deauthorize* Laura Ingalls Wilder as an effective mother. The series never represents her as a mother, and—although Laura shows some sisterly solicitude for Carrie—she does not behave maternally. It is Mary, the oldest sister, who becomes a surrogate parent for Grace, patiently holding the little girl in her lap for hours and telling her the stories that Pa told Laura and Mary when they were small children in *Big Woods*. By contrast, Laura is never shown administering any "maternal" nurturing to Baby Grace. (In this book, such tending of a very young child is represented as a maternal activity; Ma often holds Baby Grace and Baby Carrie, but Pa seldom does.) Thus, in some ways, the Little House books freed Rose Wilder Lane from her mother (Lane's original intention was that the series would secure financial independence for the Wilders, as it did) while, simultaneously, they robbed her of a mother.

The series also locked the two women into a twelve-year collaboration and an implicit public deception about Lane's large role in the books' authorship. When Wilder, apparently on her own, attempted an "adult" novel based on the early years of her marriage, she chose to write about herself as a mother and Rose as a daughter, as she told the story of Rose's birth and the experience of her own early motherhood. But Rose Wilder Lane did not encourage her mother to publish this story. After Wilder's death, Lane apparently never worked on revising it and did not choose to publish it during her lifetime. Instead, *The First Four Years*, which is—among other things—a story of Laura Ingalls Wilder as a good mother and Rose Wilder Lane as a happy young daughter, was suppressed until after both women's deaths.

As critics and biographers have begun in recent years to tell the story of the collaborative writing of the Little House books, we have often cast that story in the form of a mother-daughter plot. William Holtz's influential reading of the Wilder-Lane relationship, for example, fits the model that Marianne Hirsch calls the *postmodern* mother-daughter plot, which includes "preoedipal" experiences in which the mother is a prominent figure but views them only from the daughter's point of view. Holtz emphasizes Lane's anger and frustration (and exploitation) in her working and personal relationship with Wilder. Those feelings were primarily expressed in Lane's private diaries. As far as we know, Wilder kept no such diaries. Holtz's reading is valuable, as I have said, because it illuminates the complexity of Lane's persona and her career. But such a reading cannot access (and is not really interested in) *maternal* experience and expression. Thus Holtz concluded, in 1993, that the interest and value of the Little House series come from the *daughter*-author. According to Hirsch, the child's story is "the narrative of our culture," and its dominance necessitates the "othering" of the mother (168).

The Little House books also suggest a woman artist's plot. We may read them as a serial female kunstlerroman, noting—as I have—the constant emphasis on voice, silence, and expression and observing that the onset of Mary's blindness, which coincides with the onset of Laura's adolescence, brings Laura the responsibility of serving as her sister's "eyes" and verbalizing everything she sees. This constant early experience with description may well have been, as several critics have noted, a foundation of Laura Ingalls Wilder's adult writing skills. It was *description* that Rose Wilder Lane—a practiced judge of literary markets—considered her mother's strongest asset as a writer.

In the final Little House book, Mary Ingalls, home from college, speaks of her own ambitions:

> She talked of her studies in literature. "I am planning to write a book some day," she confided. Then she laughed. "But I planned to teach school, and you are doing that for me, so maybe you will write the book."
>
> "I, write a book?" Laura hooted. (136)

For the reader, the effect of this passage is pointedly ironic: obviously Laura Ingalls (Wilder) *did* "write the book." As a woman who was denied a high school diploma, the competitive younger sister of a college-educated woman, and later the ambitious but obscure mother of a widely known and highly paid U.S. writer in the 1920s, the fictional and actual Laura Ingalls

Wilder must have delighted in the confirming fact that she, too, could write—and publish—a book. The plot of Laura's becoming a writer is very much submerged in the last Little House books, but the reader's knowledge that "Laura" is the author "Laura Ingalls Wilder" keeps that plot constantly in mind. Such awareness was facilitated by Wilder's early decision to use actual names—most notably her own—in the series.

For example, Laura's saucy, original verse about "lazy, lousy Lizy Jane," which became a favorite of De Smet schoolboys, provides a lesson in the uncontrollable and unwelcome publicity that writing can bring, and Ma's verse in Laura's autograph album reminds her of the dangers of such publicity. (Much recent scholarship on nineteenth-century women writers has emphasized their problems of privacy and publicity; this is a major subject of Mary Kelley's much-cited *Private Woman, Public Stage: Literary Domesticity in Nineteenth-Century America*.) At the end of Brewster School, when Laura presents each pupil with a name card bearing her printed name on one side and a handwritten message on the other, she is obviously working on these same issues, in terms of professionalism and of writing.

When Brewster School is finished and Laura returns to her own De Smet classroom, she undergoes another writing test. Having studied diligently while away, she expects to maintain her position at the head of the class. But she discovers that the teacher has assigned a composition, on ambition, due that day. "Laura was in a panic. She had never written a composition, and now she must do in a few minutes what the others had been working at since yesterday. . . . Mrs. Brown had helped Ida write hers. Mrs. Brown wrote for the church papers, so Ida's composition would be good." At recess, Laura hurriedly drafts a text, relying heavily on the dictionary for inspiration. "She must not fail, she couldn't. She would not. But how did one write a composition?" When Laura reads her brief text aloud, the teacher says, "I would not have believed that anyone could do so well the first time. . . . There are no corrections. It grades one hundred." Laura is elated; "she felt confident now . . . and she looked forward happily to writing more compositions" (96–98).

Here writing is presented as a test on which Laura *must* perform successfully. She competes in a field that includes a professional woman writer, Mrs. Brown. She gives herself no leeway: it would make sense to ask for an extension, but instead Laura pushes herself to produce during a fifteen-minute recess. At the end of the episode, Laura's confidence is newly grounded in her *writing* skills, as she anticipates more compositions. Writing becomes a part of the future she imagines for herself as a competent, achieving young woman. One of the unanswered questions of *Golden Years* is what happens to such ambitions when Laura Ingalls leaves the classroom and marries Almanzo Wilder.

The Wilder-Lane museums and archives suggest some biographical answers to that question. In a Mansfield museum case, we can see the original 1883 text of "Ambition," an actual school composition, reproduced exactly in *Golden Years*. Through the upheavals of her early adulthood, which included several long migratory journeys, Wilder carefully preserved evidences of her prowess as a writer—the composition, a book of childhood poems, her 1894 journal of the South Dakota–Missouri journey and the account of that trip that she wrote for the De Smet newspaper. This suggests that "ambition," the subject of Laura's triumphant composition, may have been an important factor in Wilder's life as a young woman. At the same time, Laura is learning to subdue her aspirations in favor of Almanzo's, as a male homesteader. During their engagement, he says to her:

> "No buggy wheels of mine will ever rattle. I keep 'em tight and greased. But never mind. When the wheels roll around in this direction for three months more, you will be through teaching school, for good!"
>
> "I suppose you mean, for better or worse," Laura said demurely.
> "But it better be for good."
>
> "It will be," Almanzo said. (238)

Here Almanzo's assurance and his plans for his own achievement are evident, and Laura's giving up her paid work as a teacher is clearly an important part of his ambitious program. She accedes to that program "demurely" (*not* a word typically used to describe Laura) but with a mild reservation that tempers his assurance and issues a subtle challenge—"it *better be* for good."

In fact, the apparently "good" married life that the actual Laura and Almanzo Wilder achieved depended heavily on the force of Laura's (and later Rose's) ambition, which rehabilitated the family finances, primarily through writing. In the Little House series, the story of Laura Ingalls's beginnings as a productive writer and a money-earning woman are only lightly indicated, perhaps in deference to the patriarchal affiliations that the series at least nominally retains. But the woman writer's plot *is* clearly present, and it points toward the continuing plot of the actual Laura Ingalls Wilder as author, a complex story that critics and biographers are just beginning to tell.

Finally, the woman writer plot of the Little House series is also importantly revisionary in terms of the Western genre. As we have observed, the series, with its emphasis on western migration and frontier settlement, has many features of the "classic" Westerns that Laura Ingalls Wilder loved to read. In Jane Tompkins's recent analysis, which I have found very persuasive in the context of late nineteenth- and early twentieth-century U.S. gender politics, "the Western is at heart anti-language" (50), and women's linguistic skills mark them as ineffectual and inconsequential. Tompkins argues that the Western, as a literary form that developed at the turn of the century, was a response to the nineteenth-century proliferation of woman-authored texts and to women's movement into public life (phenomena in which both Wilder and Lane participated personally). Westerns aim at "the destruction of female authority" (39). "[I]n a reaction that looks very much like literary gender war," Tompkins says, classic Westerns "privilege the male realm of public power, physical ordeal, homosociality, and the rituals of the duel" (42).

For authors who are writing a girl's Western narrative, these conditions of *silenced, discredited women,* in an arena where the "authentic" language of physical action is available largely to men, pose very large problems, and we have seen Wilder and Lane struggling with them. They took strides toward reclaiming Western narrative as a female arena in the Little House series, significantly altering the gender dynamics of the traditional Western described by Tompkins. By making a *girl* who will become a *writer* their Western protagonist, they reclaimed wider powers of action and language for twentieth-century U.S. women. As I have tried to show throughout this chapter, those powers are expressed in Laura Ingalls's multiple plots.

The End of the Little House Books

Final page of the first edition of *These Happy Golden Years* (Harper, 1943). Drawing by Helen Sewell and Mildred Boyle. Courtesy HarperCollins.

Conclusion
"The End of the Little House Books"

Plots imply endings. But the plots that the Little House series sets in motion insist on continuation. Through them, as we have seen, Laura Ingalls learns to work and to love; to express and sometimes to repudiate the prevailing ethos of late Victorian U.S. culture. A series implies continuation. But the Little House series did end; *These Happy Golden Years*, the book I received from Laura Ingalls Wilder's hand, has no sequel. What she told me in 1952 (and I could not bear to remember) was true; she would write no more books for me to read.

Nevertheless, every year offers me a lengthening menu of Little House items. The Sunday newspaper supplement advertises a "poseable porcelain" Laura, "an heirloom-quality doll with excellent credentials," available for purchase in four easy payments. (Her eyes are the wrong color.) The travel section headlines "Pilgrim on the Prairie" and maps an extensive tour of Little House sites in midwestern towns, ready to accommodate "Laura fans" (Summers). HarperCollins has repackaged the first Wilder book, *Big Woods*, as a calendar, paper dolls (The Big Woods Collection), a songbook, and four separate "first" Little House books for very young readers. Presumably, each of the eight Little House books will generate its own set of products. And although the television series "Little House on the Prairie," which took very large liberties with its source, has finally receded into reruns, an advertisement in *Martha Stewart Living* invites me to "spend 10 days with America's best-loved family" and "relive every special moment" by ordering a $4.99 *Little House* video on approval from Time-Life.

These products, aimed at adults as well as children, suggest that large numbers of consumers are, like me, unwilling to let the Little House story end. That story bears rereading—and *reliving*, they imply. But at the same time, the story is obviously considered problematic, in need of revision and retelling. In the new "first" Little House books, for example, the lean and avid Pa of the first novel has disappeared, along with his woodsman's tales of predators and his game of "Mad Dog." Instead, in Renée Graef's placid color illustrations, Pa resembles a plump, composed young businessman, with smooth, pale hands.

Since 1952 I have stared repeatedly at the illustration on the last page of the book I received for my tenth birthday. A small, round drawing surrounded by white space, it depicts Laura and Almanzo on their wedding night, sitting on the doorstep of their first home, a prototypical Little House. Underneath are those inexorable words, "The End of the Little House Books."[1] The words insist on closure; the picture implies continuation—of the enduring, serial Little House.

Although *These Happy Golden Years* begins with Laura's departure for Brewster School, initiating the intense conflicts of professional validation and gender anxiety that she enacts there, it ends with the conventional conclusion of a nineteenth-century "woman's fiction"—Laura's marriage and her removal to the new Little House that Almanzo has independently and secretively prepared for her. The most intimate space in this house is not the bedroom but the pantry that Laura discovers behind "the last door." Almanzo's only question to her about the house is, "Like your pantry?" It is an intensely organized space with intricately fitted cabinetry, planned to facilitate housework, with "empty space for other things as they should come." Through his cabinetry, Almanzo shows how highly he values the work Laura will perform inside the house he has built. It is as if he has gotten inside her domestic consciousness, anticipating and controlling every move she will make as she works. The pantry cabinetry is an act of love—and it is also an act of patriarchal control, putting Laura in place.[2] This scene recalls the famous conclusion of one of the most popular of nineteenth-century sentimental novels, Susan Warner's *The Wide, Wide World* (1850), which ends with Ellen, the newly married female protagonist, being brought to a room that her husband has planned and furnished to contain her and to meet all her domestic, devotional, and sexual needs. In that novel's last words, Ellen nestles near her minister-spouse and murmurs, "I am satisfied. . . . I want no more" (583).

Although the circumstances of Warner's and Wilder's endings are strikingly similar, it their differences that are telling because they indicate the significant break Wilder and Lane are making from mid-nineteenth-century conventions. Although she is happy at the end of the series, Laura makes no claims to be entirely "satisfied." In her life, as in the pantry, there are empty spaces for "other things as they should come," and the precedents of the Little House series have established that Laura's energy and ambition will continue to demand and discover new things and new challenges. Unlike Ellen, she does not sink comfortably into the shelter of patriarchal dominance. Instead, in the first afternoon of her marriage, Laura begins to make the new pantry her own, taking cues from her mother.

That first afternoon is represented as a model of the companionate marriage ideal that, according to Lystra, "was a powerful counterbalance to male dominance in nineteenth-century male-female relationships" (233) and became more influential in the twentieth century. Laura and Almanzo spend hours "exploring" the small Edenic realm of their claim together. (Such exploration implies, but does not state, sexual consummation.) In the barn they see Laura's cow—a wedding gift from her parents[3]—stalled with Almanzo's horses. Then, in the novel's last image (repeated in the illustration), they sit on the doorstep:

> Laura's heart was full of happiness. She knew she need never be home-sick for the old home. It was so near that she could go to it whenever she wished, while she and Almanzo made the new home in their own little house.
>
>   All this was theirs; their own horses, their own cow, their own claim. (289)

Immediately, the married Laura assumes the mutual ownership that she has never presumed for her parents; despite Ma's labors, Laura always thinks and speaks of "Pa's house" and "Pa's claim." But in this passage, she provides a legal catalog of jointly held property; her cow and Almanzo's horses are now *theirs*, and it is "their own claim"—a claim on a mutual "free and independent" future.

By the time *These Happy Golden Years* was published in 1943, Wilder had probably already written the experimental and then unpublished *The First Four Years*. That book confirms that the actual early years of her marriage were very different from the idyll of continuity that Laura anticipated on her wedding night, in which the parental Little House remains near and accessible while the newlyweds make "the new home in their own little house." In the decade after their marriage, the Wilders lost their house (with its elaborate pantry) to fire; they lost a male child; they lost their claim. They tried living in Florida and Minnesota and spent long periods with both their sets of parents. Almanzo suffered a long illness that left him disabled for the rest of his life, and Laura worked as a seamstress to help pay their crippling debts. In 1894, after nine years of marriage, they moved to Missouri with their surviving child, Rose. In the following years, Laura and Almanzo returned to the Little House in De Smet (actually a new house in town, built by Charles Ingalls in 1887) only a very few times, and apparently Rose never returned.[4] The fictional Laura's ideal of adjacent, coexisting Little Houses to which she would have full and permanent access is a *fiction*; the only place it ever existed, for Laura Ingalls Wilder, was on the last page of *These Happy Golden Years*. And yet—what more permanent place to preserve such an ideal, in transient twentieth-century U.S. culture, than on a *page*? Wilder and Lane are dead, with no descendants, and all the dwellings about which they wrote in their series have disintegrated, leaving almost no traces.[5] But the Little House books are thriving, repackaged in a new edition. And my eyes—with many others—are trained on the page.

Since I have been an adult, I have lived in four cities, a modest total for a middle-aged academic. All those cities are far from the house in the Ozarks where I began, a place I still miss, although my family—and Laura Ingalls Wilder—no longer live there. The traumas of separation from the intricately articulated, intensely gendered domestic culture that formed me, and the exhilaration and danger of launching and living *other* lives, continue to be the most intimate stuff of my existence. As a ten-year-old in 1952, dimly anticipating the separations of my own future, I already understood very well Laura's hunger for continuity and her refusal to acknowledge that departure is inevitably attended by loss.[6] Like millions of other readers, I treasured the Little House books and wanted them to keep on coming, forever—because they told me that a girl could desire continuity and fear separation, at the same time developing a lively and exploratory independent selfhood. To have the series *end* when Laura is only eighteen— the age at which I was expected to leave home for college—seemed threatening and dangerous. Were there no stories worth writing about Laura's continuing life as a woman (or about mine)?

In Laura Ingalls's multiple plots, I have found implicitly affirmative answers to my question. For despite the determined tone of summary and fulfilled closure in the last chapter of *Golden Years*, these are vital female plots *without* the end-stops of climax and denouement. The plot initiated with Laura's courtship, for example, altered as she became an engaged woman, and it promises to change more as she takes on the project of sharing a house and a life with a husband. As Wilder's biography confirms, the plot of Laura as a working, wage-earning woman continued into the last decade of her long life. And the subtle plot of the woman writer in the Little House series is perpetuated for the reader by every page, each confirming that Laura Ingalls *did* grow up to write books. These continuities are one reason why we are so troubled by "The End of the Little House Books." In a series that has led us to expect innovative, continuing plots, the words are an unexpected termination. They imply an end to desire and to the objects of desire: the Little House books.

One reason why these books are so desirable is that they use the structure of the serial to propose that a *house*, an enduring cultural construct, can also be mobile and elastic—elastic enough to accommodate multiple, competing discourses. As I have tried to show in this book, Wilder and Lane's series explores a long agenda of pressing issues, rooted in the nineteenth century of Laura Ingalls's childhood, that have had important, sometimes painful, and sometimes liberating consequences for twentieth-century U.S. girls and boys, women and men. I have discussed the ways Lane and Wilder negotiated with patriarchy to claim authorship of a girl's story in their series, the problems of broaching intercultural and interracial contacts in these border texts, and how material culture and gender constructions shaped the Ingalls daughters' sense of possible plots that they might live and write. All these plots are part of the baggage that Laura Ingalls takes with her into her adult life; they are also a part of the cultural baggage of most U.S. readers at the end of the twentieth century.

Significantly, one of the last scenes in the Little House series is *about* baggage. In the penultimate chapter of *Golden Years*, on the day before her wedding, Laura packs her trunk for the move to her new home, with Ma's help. The objects she packs are a material reprise of the Little House series: "Charlotte, with all her clothes," the knitting and crochet needles that Laura has been taught to use, the quilt that she "pieced as a little girl," the new dresses and hat that Laura has bought with her earnings and Ma has sewn for her. Ma puts in a "red-and-white-checked tablecloth like those I have always had; I thought it might make the new home more homelike." She adds two fat pillows. "I want you to have these, Laura. . . . You helped me save the feathers from the geese that Pa shot on Silver Lake. . . . I have been saving them for you" (274–75). For the attentive reader, each of these things evokes a piece of narrative and adds to a collective plot. Silently, in the language of objects in which Ma is so fluent, they describe the culture that has produced Laura Ingalls. They are also a portable kit for reconstituting the Little House, elsewhere.

As Laura continues her packing,

> [Next,] Carrie brought Laura's glass box from the whatnot, saying, "I know you want this."
>
> Laura held the box in her hand, undecided. "I hate to take this box away from Mary's. They shouldn't be separated," she mused.
>
> "See, I've moved my box closer to Mary's," Carrie showed her. "It doesn't look lonesome." So Laura put her box carefully in the trunk. (274)

The glass box forces Laura to acknowledge that, when she removes her possessions and her presence from the Ingalls house, she creates an absence and a loss. Laura *must* choose between two places and two lives; separation is unavoidable. Although the glass box seems to belong with that of Mary, the single sister with whom Laura has shared a special closeness, now Laura takes it with her into a new, chosen intimacy with Almanzo Wilder. When Carrie moves her own box nearer to Mary's, she signals an important shift in the Ingalls family constellation, created by Laura's departure from the Little House. The material texts in Laura's baggage spell out the full import of Laura's departure—all the complexities of continuity, possibility, and loss.

These objects speak in Ma's language. But Pa also offers a reprise, through his music. On her last night at home, as Laura sits on the liminal doorstep, Pa's fiddle sang the songs that Laura knew in the Big Woods of Wisconsin, and the tunes that Pa had played by the campfires all across the plains of Kansas. . . . it remembered the days in the dugout on the banks of Plum Creek. . . . It sang of the Christmas on Silver Lake, and of springtime after the long, Hard Winter.

Then the fiddle sounded a sweeter note and Pa's deep voice joined its singing. . . .

> Still to us at twilight comes love's old song,
> Comes love's old sweet song. (277)

For the Ingalls family and for readers of the series, this music also evokes a remembered narrative. Pa's "old songs," a constant refrain of the Little House books, evoke archetypes that are expressed in popular culture. Finally and reassuringly, Pa places Laura's potentially disruptive marriage in the continuum of his music and locates it in an ongoing, patriarchal family plot. Like the other fiddle tunes, the intimacy that Laura will share with Almanzo is a familiar *old* song.[7]

In the first hours of her marriage, Laura at once unpacks the baggage of both her parents. With the food Ma has sent for the newlyweds' first supper, she begins to take possession of her new kitchen and her new work. Then, in the last words of the last novel, she sits on the doorstep with her husband and recalls Pa's music: "in memory she heard the voice of Pa's fiddle and the echo of a song, / 'Golden years are passing by, / These happy, golden years'" (289).[8] Laura is the heir of both her parents and both their gendered vocabularies. Now she and Almanzo, the two protagonists of the series, are in position to make "their own claim." It is the end—and the beginning—of the Little House story.

After the last volume appeared in 1943, Wilder and Lane and their publisher had to deal with an audience of fans, composed increasingly of adults as well as children. In her "composite letter," the corporate "Laura Ingalls Wilder" insisted to her fans that "the real things haven't changed" ("A Letter from Laura"). However, such U.S. institutions as the patriarchal family and the "frontier" West *had* changed radically in Wilder's lifetime. The Little House series has become an enduring fixture of many readers' lives because it acknowledges a human desire for enduring, sustaining "real things"—such as those contained in Laura Ingalls's precious baggage of objects, stories, and songs—and also takes on the task of acknowledging and articulating the historical and cultural changes that have proliferated in the twentieth century, and have continued to proliferate in the years since the last Little House book was published. Laura Ingalls's life, as narrated by the series, is hard and dangerous and sometimes marginal; it is often curtailed by cultural constructions of gender and race. Nevertheless, this *girl* is presented as someone with her own compelling, continuing claim: a claim to a life, and a claim to a story.

Many readers, like me, have made large investments in Laura Ingalls's claim; in some ways her story has become our own. For us, "The End of the Little House Books" is inevitably and deeply problematic. The proliferating cultural fallout of the series—television, rewrites, reruns, restorations, and merchandise—has become big business because it offers ways to *keep on reading*, and thus to keep on inhabiting the Little House. Perhaps I have written this book with the same motives—to postpone, for at least another chapter, "The End of the Little House Books."

Notes

Introduction: *The Voices from the Little House*

1. Louise Mowder also notes and discusses Laura's aphonia (15).
2. *Little House in Brookfield*, by Maria D. Wilkes, is a fictional account of Caroline Quiner Ingalls's girlhood, based loosely on letters to Laura Ingalls Wilder from her mother's sister, Martha Carpenter.
3. I am using Richard Brodhead's suggestive phrase.

Chapter 1: Preempting the Patriarchs: *Daughters in the House*

1. Rosa Ann Moore's three articles (1975–80) were, importantly, the first to suggest how profoundly Lane collaborated with Wilder on the series. William Holtz's 1993 autobiography of Lane discusses that collaboration most thoroughly of all commentators to date, although almost entirely from Lane's perspective.
2. Wilder refers to this book in a 1937 letter to Lane: "Looking through my desk yester-

day, I found a book Ma made of writing paper. When I put it there I couldn't bear to read it, but I am having to live over those days with Pa and Ma anyway, so I did. Ma had written some of her own poetry in it and copied some that she liked" (LIW to RWL, 5 Feb. 1937, Hoover).

3. Wilder's first composition, "Ambition," is preserved in the Mansfield Home and Museum and reproduced in the last Little House book, *These Happy Golden Years.*

4. Wilder's manuscript is in the Western Historical Collection at the University of Missouri; edited and revised by Lane, it was published as *On the Way Home.*

5. Wilder's account is collected in *Sampler* (87–88). According to editor William T. Anderson, Wilder preserved the clipping in her scrapbook with the notation, "First I ever had published" (87).

6. See Karen Blair and Theodora Penny Martin on the U.S. clubwomen's movement in Wilder's lifetime. According to Martin, such clubs "filled the gaps between society's formal institutions and the informal needs of individual women" and their "members developed—along with the stirrings of intellectual independence—an awareness of and confidence in themselves and in their sex which they had not been able to accomplish alone" (3).

7. Unless otherwise indicated, biographical information about Rose Wilder Lane comes from William Holtz (1993).

8. As of 1996, "Pioneer Girl" remains unpublished.

9. In a letter, Lane described this manuscript to her mother: "It is your father's stories, taken out of the long PIONEER GIRL manuscript, and strung together" (RWL to LIW, 16 Feb. 1931, Hoover).

10. "Mrs. Brown," wife of the local minister, appears in *Little Town on the Prairie* and *These Happy Golden Years* as the adoptive mother of Laura's close friend, Ida.

11. In a 1947 letter to a reader, Wilder confirmed, "I never saw Grandma Ingalls after the dance" (LIW to Ida Carson, 22 May 1947, Mansfield). This suggests that in the actual Ingalls family, contact with vigorous Grandma Ingalls was even more limited than in the Little House series, when Grandma makes a second brief appearance at the beginning of *Little House on the Prairie*, to say farewell to her son Charles and his family when they leave the Big Woods for Kansas Indian territory.

12. In response to a questionnaire from his daughter, Almanzo Wilder tersely recorded several pages of very specific memories of his homesteading days in Dakota Territory, to help with Lane's writing of *Free Land* ("Dakota Territory in the 1870s and Around 1880," *Sampler* 200–14).

13. An early manuscript of *Farmer Boy*, in Wilder's hand, ends with Father's trip to Minnesota and his subsequent decision to sell the New York farm and move there. Almost all the Wilders' property is sold before the move, including the colts Almanzo loves. Almanzo takes no part in the decision to move (Western).

14. In the actual Wilder family there were six children, not four, and Almanzo had a younger brother, Perley, as well as another sister, also (and confusingly) named Laura. Wilder and Lane's decision to portray only four Wilder children simplifies the family dynamics and makes Almanzo's decision to follow in his father's footsteps all the more important to his parents.

15. The version of nineteenth-century boyhood that Wilder and Lane inscribed in Almanzo's story would already have been old-fashioned when the actual Almanzo Wilder was nine, in 1866. By then "boy culture" was beginning to flourish for middle class U.S. boys, according to E. Anthony Rotundo. "This 'free nation' of boys was a distinct cultural world with its own rituals and its own symbols and values. As a social sphere it was separate both from the domestic world of women, girls, and small children, and from the public world of men and commerce" (31). But Almanzo, although he attends school, does not have close relationships with peers in a boys' world like that of Tom

Sawyer, whose adventures valorize "boy culture." Instead his life resembles the pattern that Rotundo describes for New England boys of the seventeenth and eighteenth centuries, who, after the age of six, were initiated into farm work by their fathers and typically worked alone or among men (32). Thus the fictional Almanzo's version of boyhood is a historical anachronism, probably intended to reinforce Lane and Wilder's ideal of agricultural self-sufficiency.

16. Before the thirties, the Wilders were "loyal Democrats" (Anderson 1992, 195). Rose Wilder Lane, who vehemently opposed the New Deal, may have influenced her parents' change. Lane eventually became a spokesperson for the Libertarian Party. For an account of her post–Little House political career, see Holtz 1993.

17. Fred Erisman observes that in *Farmer Boy*, "money in the larger society plays a central role, as the very affluence of the Wilders attests" (1993, 126).

18. According to Joan M. Jensen, nineteenth-century women's income from such work as butter making was usually "absorbed into the household economy to make it more productive, with any surplus reinvested in male-directed economic ventures" (202).

19. According to Francis Gervaise Thayer, Eliza Jane Wilder Thayer's grandson, "There was no real will ever written so the family [children from the husband's previous marriages] took everything, her wedding dress, her wedding ring. . . . Everything he acquired after they got married was sold at auction. She came out on the wrong end of the stick" (interview in Hines 1994, 230).

20. Holtz speculates that Eliza Jane perhaps "saw in Rose something of herself, a woman of high abilities not destined for the common fate of early marriage and a housewife's lot" (1993, 42).

21. On the way to Louisiana and just before their financial reverses, Almanzo's parents visited the Wilder family in Missouri; James Wilder bought the rented house where the Wilders were living in Mansfield while they developed Rocky Ridge Farm and "turned over the deed to his son." The younger Wilders lived in the house for several years; Almanzo worked as a drayman and Laura served meals to travelers and boarders (Anderson 1992, 162–64).

22. According to Anderson, Eliza Jane Wilder Thayer and the youngest Wilder brother, Perley, persuaded James Wilder to make his disastrous Louisiana investments (1992, 165).

23. For this account of the Wilder family, I have relied on Anderson, *A Wilder in the West* and *Laura Ingalls Wilder: A Biography*, and on Holtz, *The Ghost in the Little House*.

24. See Holtz on Lane's relationship with Thomas, which she found increasingly troubling (1993, especially 224–25).

25. "Bonny Doon" is a "traditional Scottish tune" with 1792 words by Robert Burns (Garson 124–25).

26. See especially LIW to Secretary, South Dakota State Historical Society, n.d., Hoover.

27. The pervasiveness of these traditional female roles is well indicated by Deborah Fink's recent book, *Agrarian Women: Wives and Mothers in Rural Nebraska, 1880–1940*. Fink's research indicates that "the vast majority of these women lived and worked within their families. . . . First and foremost they were wives and mothers." She finds little evidence of strong bonds between biological sisters or "sisterly solidarity with other women and men" (xiv). Interestingly, when Fink cites important influences on her book she mentions that, "Like many others, I have learned much from reading Laura Ingalls Wilder's books about family life on the plains" (xxi). Fink's work suggests that Wilder's and Lane's strong patriarchal allegiances were typical of Great Plains white women in their times, and her comment on reading Wilder's books suggests that the Little House books may have played a significant role in reinforcing Fink's conclusions about Great Plains women.

28. Caroline Fraser, in a review essay in *The New York Review of Books*, also differs decisively with Holtz. She argues that he based his conclusions exclusively on a comparison of

Wilder's handwritten drafts with published versions, ignoring her continuing participation (which I found clearly demonstrated in the Wilder-Lane papers) in the editing and revising of the Little House books. Fraser calls Holtz's conclusions "simplistic" and maintains that, while the Wilder-Lane collaboration clearly "combined their strengths and minimized their weaknesses. . . . it is also clear that, of the two, Wilder was the genuine writer" (45). Although I find Fraser's conclusions a valuable corrective, I resist the pressures that have been intensified by Holtz's biography to choose one of the two collaborators as more "genuine" than the other.

29. In this regard, Fred Erisman's conclusion seems pertinent: "It is enough that the books were written, and I am as comfortable speaking of 'Laura Ingalls Wilder' as of such other composite authors as . . . Ellery Queen" (1994, 130). It is important, however, that the composite author "Laura Ingalls Wilder" is very specifically gendered as a (married) woman, as "Ellery Queen" is not.

30. By 1918, Holtz writes, Lane had agreed to "revise" Frederick O'Brien's "manuscript about his South Seas adventures." Lane did substantial work on the book, eventually published as *White Shadows on the South Seas* under O'Brien's name alone, and she sued O'Brien for a share of the royalties (1993, 81, 116).

31. Apparently Wilder's assumption was correct; Martha Carpenter replied with a lengthy memoir, of which Wilder and Lane appear to have made little published use (Hoover).

32. She particularly cautions against "the tendency to an ahistorical essentialism of psychoanalytical theory as a description of (universal) parent-child relationships" (166).

Chapter 2: "Indians in the House": A Narrative of Acculturation

1. No such meeting is mentioned in any of the Little House books or in the Ingalls family documents I have examined.

2. Especially in recent years the anti-Indian views held by some characters in the Little House series (most notably Ma), and the tendency of some volumes to ignore the historical presence of Native Americans, have been noted by commentators; for example, see Dorris. In a 1990s children's book market that often places a high value on multiculturalism, Laura Ingalls Wilder's series (widely honored in previous decades) *is* problematic because of its central focus on the struggles of white settlers on the Great Plains. Hazel Rochman, writing about the deliberations of the committee that chose the recipient of the 1995 Newbery Medal for a distinguished book for children, implies that such a committee would be unlikely to honor the Little House series today: "let's face it, no story about a pioneer boy in the West has a hope of winning a prize today, especially if he doesn't have a 1990's consciousness about how his home was taken from the Indians."

3. Susan Naramore Maher writes that "the American West . . . has provided children's writers a wealth of border crossings" (130) and usefully discusses *Little House on the Prairie* in this context.

4. Elizabeth Hampsten's research on Great Plains settlers and their children suggests that Caroline Ingalls's insular stance was typical. Hampsten reports, "I read of few settlers initially wanting to understand Indians (let alone disturbed about having displaced them) or reaching out to other groups of settlers of backgrounds different from their own. Wanting their children to honor and not to forget their past, people diverted attention as best they could from 'new' forms around them, even as they considered themselves to be venturing into fresh territories" (1991, 8).

5. The Ingallses settled in what is now Rutland Township, Montgomery County, Kansas (Anderson 1992, 35).

6. The title was changed to *Little House on the Prairie* (Wilder's alternate suggestion) at the urging of the publisher. See letter from Ida Louise Raymond, Wilder's editor at Harper, to LIW (27 Aug. 1934, Hoover).

7. See Bosmajian for a useful discussion of the prairie's impact on Laura and of this novel's construction of prairie space. Also see Quantic for a view of the Little House novels as prairie texts.

8. This photograph is reproduced in Chapter 4. For the suggestion that Carrie's necklace, clearly visible, is made from the trade beads of *Little House on the Prairie* I am indebted to Wilma Kurtis and Anita Gold (17).

9. McAuliffe reads *Little House on the Prairie* as a major betrayal of Osage history, and he tends to conflate Ingalls family history, the Little House novels, and the 1970s television series. For example, he writes, "Osage writer John Joseph Mathews could have been staring at a family portrait of the Ingallses when he described the covered wagons filling up Osage land as being full of 'dirty-faced children peering out from the curtains, and weary, hard-faced women lolling in the seat beside evil-eyed, bearded men.' The actor Michael Landon was horribly miscast as Pa in the television series. . . . Landon was too sweet-faced, clean-shaven—and focused. The real Charles Ingalls wore a two-foot-long vinery of beard. His dark, narrow, hard, glassy, chilly, creepy eyes would, a century later, stare out of photos of Charles Manson, the Hollywood murderer. Pa's resume reads like that of a surfer bum in search of the perfect amber wave of grain" (111–12).

10. In her conclusions about male experience, Schlissel draws on work by Howard R. Lamar and Daniel J. Levinson.

11. Donald Zochert suggests in his biography of Wilder that Carrie Ingalls was born, with the assistance of neighbor Mrs. Scott, on the day when Pa, Mary, and Laura visited the Indian camp (42–43).

12. Louise Mowder sees Ma Ingalls's frontier housekeeping as depicted in the first three Little House books as an expression of the colonial imperatives implicit in "settlement" of the West. Mowder comments, "Colonialism here is the triumph of the domestic" (18).

13. Dr. George Tann (1825–1909) is buried in Independence, Kansas (Anderson and Kelly 12).

14. The height by which Laura designates "The Tall Indian" seems to have been characteristic of Osage men; early nineteenth-century non-Indian observers of the tribe typically commented that the men were "tall in stature, usually six feet or more" (Din and Nasatir 6).

15. Rose Wilder Lane studied classical Greek and Latin in high school, and as a young woman she worked hard to learn several modern languages, which afforded her mobility and facility while she was living in Europe. Her parents seem to have been monolingual, however, and small Ozark towns like Mansfield were typically stonily unreceptive to any spoken language but English. These differing attitudes toward languages are probably reflected in *Little House on the Prairie*'s mild critique of the Ingallses' monolingual insularity.

16. The song may also have had special importance for Wilder. As she wrote in a letter to Lane, it was one of two songs that Charles Ingalls inscribed in his wife's manuscript book of poetry. "He signed the songs and the date is 1860. . . . Blue Juniata is not much like the printed one we had when I used it, but it is as I remember hearing it" (LIW to RWL, 5 Feb. 1937, Hoover).

17. William Cronon, George Miles, and Jay Gitlin argue that the process of *"boundary setting"* is "the very essence of frontier life. Every activity contributed to this process. Ways of defining property . . . ways of planting fields, ways of building houses, ways of rearing children . . . all became symbols of difference between those who stood on opposite sides of frontier boundaries" (15).

18. According to Din and Nasatir, Osage "children usually wore no clothing until they reached the age of six or seven" (7).

19. Mowder offers a related but somewhat different reading of this scene; she says that the Indian "baby becomes the quintessence of the freedom of the Other, and Laura's outpouring surge of desire is for the emancipation that the baby embodies" (17).

20. Maher also discusses the importance of the Indians' "colorful procession" to Laura; she sees it as Laura's "greatest joy in the novel." To Maher, Laura's demand for the Indian baby is a "brief border crossing" that "penetrates the Indians' otherness [and] . . . reaches out to the entire 'long line of Indians'" (137). While I agree with Maher about the importance of this scene, I don't see that Laura successfully "penetrates the Indians' otherness," although she clearly *desires* to do so.

21. The circumstances under which the actual Ingalls family departed from Kansas were quite different—they left because the buyer of their farm in Wisconsin was unable to pay off his debt to them—and Laura Ingalls was too young to remember them. The fictionalized scenario that ends this novel probably reflects Lane and Wilder's anger at New Deal policies, which they saw as intruding into the lives of citizens, especially farmers.

22. In *Love and Theft* Eric Lott argues that Foster's phenomenally popular song, originally published in 1848, had by 1850 been transformed into "the national anthem of westward expansion." Originally the song was "a sentimental ditty about two black lovers probably separated by slavery and trying to find their way back to each other." But later revisions of the song, a staple of minstrel shows, "implicitly connected the North's westering impulse and its growing distaste for southern slavery, in the process turning 'Susanna' into a rather mordant comment on the desperate problem of American nationalism at midcentury" (206). Thus, for Charles Ingalls, this song may have been related to the Civil War issues raised by his other music of the evening and to his concerns about government interference in his personal independence. Also, in the postwar years in which *Little House on the Prairie* is set, Pa's version of "Oh, Susanna" is an ironic reversal of the 1850 promises of westward expansion.

23. This song was published in 1847, with music by A. F. Winnemore and lyrics by S. S. Steele (Garson 117–18).

24. According to Toll, "minstrelsy's borrowing of Afro-American culture is of great significance because it was the first indication of the powerful influence Afro-American culture would have on the performing arts in America." However, Toll warns, this "does not mean that early minstrels accurately portrayed Negro life or even the cultural elements they used. They did neither" (51).

25. See Wittke for an account of the evolution and importance of the endmen's roles (140–42).

26. The African American trickster tradition was often tapped by minstrel shows (Toll 140–42).

27. Minstrel shows always repudiated women's rights, according to Toll (163).

28. In Florida, the Wilders settled in the "backwoods" of the panhandle, near the village of Westville. Laura Wilder described this as a region of enormous insects, carnivorous plants, and alligators which to a "Yankee woman" like herself were a curiosity. The Wilders were not happy in Florida, where they remained for less than a year (Anderson 1992, 139–40). Lane's story about this period, "Innocence," addresses the racial and cultural tensions that the Wilders experienced in Florida.

29. Lane produced numerous stories and books that drew significantly from Ozark culture, such as *Cindy* and *Hill-Billy*.

30. Wilder's letters from San Francisco to her husband, who remained at home in Mansfield, record her eager curiosity. They are collected in *West from Home*.

Chapter 3: Getting and Spending: *Materialism and the Little House*

1. For example, on 9 May 1940, Lane wrote in a diary, "No argument against suicide has any reality now. Only I don't like to leave a mess, debts, a nuisance of funeral and probate, etc. that would only annoy people" (Hoover).

2. Since Lane advised her mother heavily on her articles for *Country Gentleman,* some of this language may have come from her.

3. In a related letter of 27 January 1939, Wilder wrote gratefully to her daughter, thanking her for the many comforts she had provided for the Wilders. The letter begins, "Yesterday I was thinking how unbelievable it is that we are so comfortably situated." And it ends, "Oh Rose my dear, we do thank you so much for being so good to us" (Hoover).

4. When Wilder wrote to her Aunt Martha Quiner Carpenter, requesting reminiscences and recipes from Quiner family history, she specifically recalled this food: "Mother [Caroline Quiner Ingalls] used to make what she called 'Vanity Cakes' years ago. They were mostly egg and they were fried in deep fat. When done they were simply bubbles . . . crisp around the edges. Perhaps you know how to make them. I would so much like to have the recipe" (22 June 1925, Hoover).

   Martha Carpenter replied, "Laura the vanity cake that you ask about is just made of one or two egg and flour a pinch of salt and pinch of [sic] in little pieces and rolled out as thin as you can in hot lard the same as fried cakes. They were called vanity cakes because there was nothing to them. . . . we used to make them for a change" (2 Sept. 1925, Hoover).

   Barbara M. Walker provides a recipe for vanity cakes (202–3).

5. In *Satisfaction Guaranteed: The Making of the American Mass Market,* Susan Strasser provides a useful and pertinent account of marketing development during these years.

6. In Veblen, see especially chapter 4, "Conspicuous Consumption," 68–101.

7. In *Death in the Dining Room,* Kenneth L. Ames discusses the elaborately ritualized importance of calling cards in the Victorian United States. Colorful, sentimental lithographed cards like those Laura buys for twenty-five cents a dozen "were seen as gauche by the dominant culture" and marked their owners as "not members of the ruling class." Almanzo Wilder's plain calling card indicates his social class may be above Laura's. Ames says that decorated cards like Laura's "mocked and subverted what struck many ordinary folks as the impersonality and austerity of ruling-class cards" (40). However, the Ingalls family seems to participate in no such conscious mockery. Laura wants "name cards" because she wishes to participate in the ritual of exchanging similar cards with her friends. The name cards emphasize how completely Laura's consumption behavior is bound up with issues of class.

8. Jeanne Westin's oral history of U.S. women in the 1930s takes its title—*Making Do*—from this common phrase. Westin's book usefully elaborates much of the cultural context in which the Little House books were written.

9. Representative recent works on the importance of textiles to nineteenth- and early twentieth-century U.S. women include Brackman, Kiracofe, and Lasansky.

10. Caroline Quiner Ingalls's mother's business card advertised her work thus: "Miss C. W. Tucker, Dress Maker, Corner of Union and Warren Streets, Roxbury [Conn.]" (De Smet).

11. Laura's willingness to give her income to her father to spend reflects conditions that Jellison says prevailed on U.S. farms through the Progressive Era: "Farm women performed their work under a patriarchal system in which their labor largely belonged to their husbands and fathers" (xx).

12. In Butcher's 1887 photograph of the David Hilton homestead, the parlor organ is at the exact center in the foreground of the photograph, in a barnyard full of hogs, cattle, horses, and mules. Six members of the Hilton household are symmetrically grouped around it. According to John Carter, Mrs. Hilton was embarrassed by her family's sod dwelling and "refused to be photographed in front of it. . . . Mr. Hilton and the photographer had to drag the pump organ out and away from the house so that she could show friends back east that she had one without revealing the condition of their dwelling" (55). This account vividly emphasizes the organ's signifying power.

13. The actual Mary Ingalls's tuition and boarding expenses were paid by Dakota Territory, which as yet had no school for the blind, as Wilder wrote in an early draft of *Little Town on the Prairie*. Mary's family bore only the expense (considerable, for them) of her travel, clothing, and other needs. However, after Lane's revisions, the published book included no references to the state's assistance, perhaps because Lane wanted further to emphasize the Ingalls family's independence and to oppose the tendency to rely on government aid that she saw developing through the New Deal. See Holtz's discussion of these changes (1993, 384).

14. In his 1953 illustrations for the Little House books, which are much more "realistic" in style than the original stylized illustrations by Helen Sewell and Mildred Boyle, Garth Williams made a concerted effort to be faithful to the material circumstances of the Ingallses' lives. (See Williams's account of this project, "Illustrating the Little House Books.") But his illustration of this scene depicts a much simplified version of Mary's dress (95). It is as if the prevailing illustrative vocabulary of 1950s' U.S. children's books could not accommodate the elaborate, proliferating detail that the print text lavishes on this crucial Victorian object. Smith and Bodmer have influenced my thinking on the Little House illustrations.

15. Rose Wilder Lane's reminiscences of her actual Aunt Mary in De Smet, after her return from college, confirm this complexity. She emphasizes the variety of her aunt's activities: housework, horticulture, writing in Braille (both personal correspondence and poems that were published in religious periodicals), beadwork. Mary also made Grace and Carrie Ingalls's clothes, fashioned a doll for Rose, pieced quilts, and netted everything from hammocks to hairnets. "Strangers never guessed that she was blind, she knew so well where everything was and did everything so confidently" ("Memories of Grandma's House," *Sampler* 56–58). This affectionate description emphasizes Mary Ingalls's skillful negotiation of a material world, through her housekeeping and other domestic work, and the fact that this work coexisted with her wide reading and writing.

16. A particularly powerful example of this intense relation with the Ingalls-Wilder things is found in *The Story Makes Them Whole*, Laura Jensen's sequence of poems chronicling her visit to the Wilder house and museum in Mansfield. The center of this series is a group of poems about objects in the museum: "Mary's Gloves—The Museum," "Pa's Fiddle," "Bread Plate—the Home," and "The Wedding Gift."

17. The newsletter *Laura Ingalls Wilder Lore* has continued to report on fans' intense interest in the "real" china shepherdess. The 1989 discovery of a porcelain figure among Carrie Ingalls Swanzey's belongings was "electrifying," and much evidence "points to" this figure as "THE ONE." Writing in response to schoolchildren's questions in 1943, Wilder said, "Sister Carrie has the china shepherdess" ("Sister Carrie Has the China Shepherdess").

Chapter 4: The Little House That Gender Built: *The Novels of Adolescence*

1. According to Paul Deane, in most of the enduringly popular twentieth-century U.S. series for children, "time is not an element of importance." Typically, Deane argues, such books do not respond promptly to cultural change; "values, ideals, and attitudes . . . remain unchanged essentially in the series from 1900 to the present" (12–13). Clearly, the Little House books differ significantly from most other serials for children in this regard.

2. Carol R. Brink's *Caddie Woodlawn* was published in 1935 and shares many of the concerns of the Little House series. On parallels between Brink's novel and *Little House on the Prairie*, see Maher. MacLeod's essay is collected in her *American Childhood*.

3. This conclusion was influenced by the work of Erik H. Erikson, who, according to Elshtain, outlines a suggestive "paradigm of human development" that "males alone can fully share" (292–93).

4. One indication that the books were perceived as such a resource is the fact that they were translated by the U.S. State Department into Japanese and German and distributed after World War II as part of a reeducation campaign in occupied Japan and Germany. They were also translated into many other languages.

5. The rapidity of this process was typical of the early settlement of South Dakota. Glenda Riley quotes an 1886 letter from a South Dakota woman to a friend: "It does beet all how fast this country is getting up. . . . Im looking round and see two new houses been put up since yesterday" (1988, 99).

6. According to Lane, such description was her mother's strong suit. She wrote to Wilder about Wilder's presumably first draft of *Silver Lake*, "Most of the writing is perfectly beautiful and I would not change one word of descriptive work" (RWL to LIW, 19 Dec. 1937, Hoover).

7. An unpublished manuscript chapter of *The Long Winter*, "Chapter 9—'Mr. Edwards Comes,'" chronicles Pa's encounter with Edwards in Volga, where both are working on the snowbound railroad. Edwards is portrayed as a wily, mythic figure of great powers. He wins eighteen hundred dollars at poker and (for another bet) outruns a train. Then he drinks whiskey in the saloon while "teetotaler" Pa drinks water. Pa takes Edwards home for dinner, where he is greeted warmly by Ma and the daughters; Ma says, "You always bring us good luck" (transcript of chapters in Detroit Public Library, typed by William Anderson; Hoover).

8. Virginia Wolf, in her Bachelardian reading of the Little House series, also considers *The Long Winter* "the darkest" of the books (169).

9. Peg Wherry cautions against a stereotypical view of a frontier woman who was almost entirely enclosed in an indoor domestic sphere; she notes that Great Plains frontier women habitually tended gardens and livestock and did other outdoor work, as well as visited neighbors (72). During the Long Winter, Ma Ingalls is cut off from all these outlets; thus this book is the most intensely and problematically domestic in the series.

10. "Charlotte" was the name of Laura Ingalls Wilder's actual maternal grandmother. Thus the doll's name is another link to a maternal tradition.

11. In *Made to Play House: Dolls and the Commercialization of American Girlhood, 1830–1930*, Miriam Formanek-Brunell argues that the manufacture of dolls, particularly fabric dolls, was a significant career option for U.S. women in the late nineteenth and early twentieth centuries, and that women's ideas about how dolls should be made and marketed were very different from those of men.

12. Laura Jensen writes about Charlotte in the last of her sequence of Little House poems, emphasizing the restorative power of Ma's domestic skills:

> Ma made the doll new eyes,
> new hair, new clothes. It represented hope,
> that needle that defied tragedy. (N.p.)

13. While working on *Silver Lake*, Lane suggested that Laura go with Pa on a hunt. Wilder vetoed her proposal: "Seems to me it would be very improbable to have Laura go with Pa on a hunt. . . . He wouldn't want to bother with Laura and he loved his solitary tramp and besides it was no place for a girl. So I don't see how she could go" (LIW to RWL, undated response to RWL's letter of 19 Dec. 1937, Hoover).

14. Western culture has more usually equated women with nature, men with culture. For a classic feminist examination of these issues, see Ortner.

15. According to Clifford Edward Clark, "by the middle of the nineteenth century such divisions [especially between "public and private spaces"] had become an obsession" (42).

16. One of Wilder's early drafts of *Big Woods* mentions a visit from Ma's brother, "Uncle Tom" Quiner. He brings gifts of candy for the girls and, for Ma, a copy of Mary Jane

Holmes's *Millbank*. "Ma said it was a novel and not for little girls, but Laura listened when Ma read it aloud to Pa at night" (Western).

17. Angel Kwolek-Folland argues that icons of "movable culture," such as the shepherdess and the whatnot, had special import for women who settled the Great Plains between 1870 and 1900, as Caroline Ingalls and Ellie Boast did (1984).

18. In the single exception, Ma and her daughters pool their financial resources to buy Pa a pair of twenty-five-cent, machine-embroidered suspenders for Christmas.

19. According to Glenda Riley, "curtains seemed to be a particular mark of civilization to thousands of plainswomen who took great pride in having them hanging at the few windows they had" (1988, 88).

20. Wilder made this observation in her description of the Iowa years (LIW, response to RWL's letter of 19 Dec. 1937, Hoover).

21. A crude sampler, red yarn embroidery on gray wool, is displayed in the Wilder-Lane museum in Mansfield. According to its label, it was made by Laura Ingalls in the Big Woods of Wisconsin, when she was about four.

22. Mintz and Kellogg argue that such family celebrations reinforced the centrality of the nuclear family in the nineteenth-century United States: "the Christmas tree, Christmas presents . . . were all manifestations of the reorientation of daily life around the family" (48). Many of Wilder's and Lane's decisions about the shaping of the Little House series, such as their decisions to omit persons in the Ingalls family history who were not members of the immediate family, reinforce such values.

23. The song was written by Harry Clifton in 1867 (Garson 52–54).

24. Barbara M. Walker's *Little House Cookbook* has been popular since its 1979 publication. Walker writes that her book got its start when she read the Little House series with her daughter Anna; she began by making the pancake men of *Big Woods* for Anna. "Laura Ingalls Wilder's way of describing her pioneer childhood seemed to compel participation. . . . As time went by, and Anna read and reread the series, we somehow acquired a coffee grinder in order to make 'Long Winter' bread. . . . From other mothers I learned that our impulses were far from unique" (xiii). Clearly, other child readers have shared my association of food with reading the Little House books, especially *Long Winter*.

25. Anita Clair Fellman has provided the most complete analysis of this working relationship, valuably concentrating on its political implications.

Chapter 5: Laura's Plots: *Ending the Little House*

1. "Leave Susan out," Wilder wrote to Lane as they were planning the last three books. "Don't bring her in at all" (LIW to RWL, 17 Aug. 1938, Hoover).

2. Wilder wrote to Lane, "I have handled over every book in the house this winter and spring and no where [sic] did I find Charlott [sic] Temple. I am sure now that it is not here" (LIW to RWL, 23 May 1939, Hoover).

3. According to Joanne Dobson, after the initial publication of *The Hidden Hand* in 1859, "constant demands for the story from the *Ledger*'s readers encouraged Bonner to reprint the serial in 1868 and . . . 1883." It was first published as a book in 1888 (xl).

4. Such anxiety obviously resembles the ambivalence about reading and writing described by Carol J. Singley and others in *Anxious Power: Reading, Writing, and Ambivalence in Narrative by Women*.

5. For example, defending her portrayal of the Ingalls family as unemotional and "stoic," Wilder wrote to Lane: "you will read of [such behavior] in *good* frontier stories" (LIW to RWL, 7 March 1938, Hoover).

6. John E. Miller has examined the history textbook Wilder used in her last years of formal schooling, Edward Taylor's 1878 *A Brief Account of the American People for Schools*, which Wilder gave to the Detroit Public Library along with manuscripts of two Little House

novels. As described by Miller, the Taylor text employs time charts, boldface type, and review sections to aid memorization. It attends less to military events than did many nineteenth-century texts; instead, it celebrates "national development" "within a basically chronological framework, using presidential administrations to organize the material" (101–2).

7. For instance, note her insistence on recalling and verifying the exact name of the Osage chief of *Little House on the Prairie* (Soldat du Chêne), because books "to be used in schools . . . must be right" ("My Work," *Sampler* 179).

8. Laura's friend Ida Wright follows her with a recitation of the "second half" of U.S. history, from J. Q. Adams to the 1880s present.

9. Among the most substantive of such discussions are William Holtz's "Closing the Circle: The American Optimism of Laura Ingalls Wilder" (1984) and John E. Miller's *Laura Ingalls Wilder's Little Town* (1994).

10. John E. Miller's book is based on the plausible premise that the last four Little House books are in fact the Little *Town* books, and he reads them as "stripped-down history," constituting "a record of the social history of the town" (5).

11. For readers familiar with nineteenth-century women's fiction after 1855, the designation "Madcap Days," a chapter title, might well recall E.D.E.N. Southworth's enormously popular novel, *The Hidden Hand, or Capitola the Madcap*, thrice serialized in the *New York Ledger* during the years when that story paper was read by the fictional (and presumably the actual) Ingalls women. Capitola (nicknamed Cap) was a phenomenally popular heroine, who lived in a constant atmosphere of carnival potential that befitted a "madcap."

12. John E. Miller records the building of an opera house in De Smet that would feature such professional entertainment; it opened in 1886, the year after the marriage of Laura Ingalls and Almanzo Wilder, which concludes the Little House series. See especially Miller's chapter 9, "Relaxing and Building Community at the Course Opera House" (131–32).

13. Mary Russo, in her discussion of the importance of carnival issues to feminist theory, describes the controversy about whether carnival has ultimately conservative functions, as described by Victor Turner, reinforcing "social structure, hierarchy, and order through inversion," or whether it may be seen as an innovative, "productive category, affirmative and celebratory," as argued by Mikhail Bakhtin (214–15). This controversy is relevant to the Little House books, and "carnival" scenes like the spelling bee seem to display both conservative and innovative functions.

14. Laura's female adolescence is another reason why carnival states are especially attractive *and* dangerous to her in the last two books. As described by Russo, the Bakhtinian concept of carnival places special emphasis on "the grotesque body . . . the open, protruding, extended, secreting body, the body of becoming, process, and change" (219). As an adolescent, Laura has begun to menstruate (a fact never mentioned explicitly in the series) and is now capable of sexual intercourse and childbearing; her body is potentially "grotesque." Her new, culturally determined strategies for shaping and controlling her body, subduing its "grotesque" possibilities, are emphasized—corsets, hoops, stylish dress—and they limit her participation in carnival.

15. "Rock Me to Sleep" has lyrics by Elizabeth Akers Allen (pseud. Florence Percy) and music by William Marton. For complete lyrics, see Garson 28–29.

16. Almost the only significant Little House omission from the roster of major occupations open to nineteenth-century western women is (for obvious reasons) prostitution. However, *Silver Lake* does include a brief image of a woman who may be a prostitute; on the train to the railroad town of Tracy, Laura observes, traveling alone, "a woman with bright yellow hair and, oh, Mary! the brightest red velvet hat with pink roses" (24).

17. Jensen's entire chapter on butter making (170–85) is illuminating and pertinent; she

concludes that "women developed butter making for the market, adopted the necessary skills and technology to increase production, and managed their own labor and the labor of children and hired assistants to facilitate the production of increasing amounts of butter. [Mother Wilder had five hundred pounds to sell annually.] In so doing women made possible the profitable commercialization of butter making" (185).

18. Wilder wrote about poultry raising for the first time in her 1894 diary of the journey from De Smet to Mansfield. Chickens traveled with the Wilders from South Dakota, and a week into the trip, Laura Ingalls Wilder noted, "The hens are laying yet" (*On the Way Home* 29).

19. This tradition of female responsibility for poultry still exists for some women. After I spoke about Wilder's career at a children's literature conference in South Dakota in 1993, a young teacher came up to me and said, shyly and privately, that she lived with her husband on a farm and performed some tasks very similar to Laura Ingalls Wilder's. "The chickens are my thing," she said. "I take care of them, and that's my money."

20. According to historian Sandra L. Myres, public schools were an important and early priority of new western communities. "Settlers were anxious that their children not only learn to read and write but that they be inculcated with the social, economic, and political values which represented civilized society. Schools were perceived as civilizing agencies" (182). Another useful source on this subject is Cordier.

21. In the 1953 second edition of *Golden Years*, Garth Williams did illustrate this scene, with a back view of Mrs. Brewster with loosened hair and trailing nightgown, arm upraised, pointing an enormous knife at her cowering husband while Laura peeks between her curtains (64). I never saw this edition as a child.

22. The Brewster episode in *Golden Years* was based on the actual Laura Ingalls's 1883 experience teaching Bouchie School and boarding with a Bouchie family. According to John E. Miller, an 1884 *De Smet News* carried an item about the death of an Isaac Bouchie, who may have been related to the family with whom Laura Ingalls boarded. "'Isaac Bouchie came to his death by result of a wound on the cheek willfully and feloniously made by a large bone thrown by [thirteen-year-old] Clarence Bouchie instigated and abetted by his mother, Elizabeth Bouchie'" (55). Such an instance of familial violence and death may have been part of the material from which Wilder and Lane shaped the story of the Brewsters. See Miller for a fuller account of the Bouchie affair (54–56).

23. In the 1930s, the actual Almanzo Wilder told his daughter in an interview that the two major extravagances he remembered from his youth were horse-related: "a top buggy" and "a $50 nickel-plated harness," both bought in 1882 ("Dakota Territory in the 1860s and around 1880," *Sampler* 215). Significantly, 1882 was the year that he started courting Laura Ingalls.

24. "In the Starlight," with words by J. E. Carpenter and music by Stephen Glover, was published in 1843. See Garson for complete text, 100–102.

Conclusion: "The End of the Little House Books"

1. This drawing, captioned with the words "The End of the Little House Books," appears only in the 1943 edition of *These Happy Golden Years*, which was illustrated by Helen Sewell and Mildred Boyle. In the current (1996) edition of the series, the list of "Little House books" includes *The First Four Years*, which was published after Wilder's and Lane's deaths, as well as the original eight books in the series.

2. *The First Four Years* begins with a less romanticized account of the Wilders' wedding day that also features the "beautiful" pantry cabinetry. However, in this text Almanzo is not the carpenter. Instead, he hires "a carpenter of the old days who though old and slow did beautiful work, and the pantry had been his pride and a labor of love to Manly" (13). This account represents the pantry as a transaction between men that passes a patriarchal tradition from an older man to a bridegroom. *Golden Years*, by making Almanzo

do the carpentry for his bride, emphasizes their intimate heterosexual relationship and also underlines Almanzo's resemblance (actually quite slight) to the former Little House patriarch, Pa, who is a capable carpenter.

3. Katherine Harris says that a milk cow was a typical "'going away' present" for young adults in the West (173).

4. William Holtz confirmed that, in his years of research on Lane's life, he never found any evidence of a return visit to De Smet after 1894 (conversation with William Holtz, April 1995).

5. There is one exception to this; the Surveyors' House, in which the fictional and actual Ingalls family spent their first winter near Silver Lake, still stands in De Smet. However, it is not in its original lakeside location; Silver Lake was drained in the 1920s and the house was moved into town (Anderson and Kelly 24).

6. Fraser observes these complexities in the Little House series; she calls it "one of the few profound explorations of familial relationships in American children's literature" (42).

7. Two useful essays discuss the importance of music in the Little House books. See Phillips and Susina.

8. "Golden Years Are Passing By," with words and music by Will L. Thompson, was published in 1879 (Garson 38–39). When Pa first plays the song for his family, he says, "Here is one for you girls." Then he sings a stanza that includes the injunction to "call back" the "golden years" "as they go by" (THGY 155–56). In the broadest sense, we might read this line as Pa's direction to his daughter Laura to "call back" the years of her childhood and youth by remembering and writing them in the form of the Little House books.

Works Cited

Adam, Kathryn. "Laura, Ma, Mary, Carrie, and Grace: Western Women as Portrayed by Laura Ingalls Wilder." Armitage and Jameson 95–110.

Ames, Kenneth L. 1992. *Death in the Dining Room and Other Tales of Victorian Culture.* Philadelphia: Temple UP.

———. 1984. "Material Culture as Non Verbal Communication: A Historical Study." *American Material Culture: The Shape of Things around Us.* Ed. Edith Mayo. Bowling Green, Ohio: Bowling Green State U Popular P. 25–47.

Anderson, William T. 1992. *Laura Ingalls Wilder: A Biography.* Rpt. New York: HarperTrophy, 1995.

———. 1986. "Laura Ingalls Wilder and Rose Wilder Lane: The Continuing Collaboration." *South Dakota History* 16 (Summer): 89–143.

———. 1983. "The Literary Apprenticeship of Laura Ingalls Wilder." *South Dakota History* 13 (Winter): 285–331.

——, ed. 1971. *A Wilder in the West.* De Smet, S.D.: Laura Ingalls Wilder Memorial Society.

Anderson, William T., and Leslie A. Kelly. 1989. *Little House Country: A Photo Guide to the Home Sites of Laura Ingalls Wilder.* Kansas City, Mo.: Terrell P.

Anzaldúa, Gloria. 1987. *Borderlands/La Frontera: The New Mestiza.* San Francisco: Spinsters/ Aunt Lute.

Armitage, Susan, and Elizabeth Jameson, eds. 1987. *The Women's West.* Norman: U of Oklahoma P.

Arpad, Susan S. "'Pretty Much to Suit Ourselves': Midwestern Women Naming Experience through Domestic Art." Motz and Browne 19–25.

Bauer, Dale. 1991. "Gender in Bakhtin's Carnival." *Feminisms.* Ed. Robyn R. Warhol and Diane Price Herndl. New Brunswick, N.J.: Rutgers UP. 671–84.

Baym, Nina. 1995. *Woman's Fiction: A Guide to Novels by and about Women in America, 1820–1870.* Ithaca, N.Y.: Cornell UP.

Beecher, Catharine E., and Harriet Beecher Stowe. 1869. *The American Woman's Home.* Rpt. Hartford: Stowe-Day Foundation, 1975.

Blair, Karen J. 1980. *The Clubwoman as Feminist: True Womanhood Redefined, 1868–1914.* New York: Holmes and Meier.

Bosmajian, Hamida. 1983. "Vastness and Contraction of Space in *Little House on the Prairie.*" *Children's Literature* 11: 49–63.

Brackman, Barbara. 1989. *Clues in the Calico: Guide to Identifying and Dating Antique Quilts.* McLean, Va.: EPM Publications.

Brewer, Priscilla J. 1990. "'We Have Got a Very Good Cooking Stove': Advertising, Design, and Consumer Response to the Cookstove, 1815–1880." *Winterthur Portfolio* 251 (Spring): 35–39.

Brodhead, Richard H. 1993. *Cultures of Letters: Scenes of Reading and Writing in Nineteenth-Century America.* Chicago: U of Chicago P.

Brooks, Peter. 1984. *Reading for the Plot: Design and Intention in Narative.* New York: Vintage. 1985.

Brown, Gillian. 1990. *Domestic Individualism: Imagining Self in Nineteenth-Century America.* Berkeley: U of California P.

Calvert, Karin. 1992. *Children in the House: The Material Culture of Early Childhood, 1600–1900.* Boston: Northeastern UP.

Carter, John E. 1985. *Solomon D. Butcher: Photographing the American Dream.* Lincoln: U of Nebraska P.

Chandler, Marilyn R. 1991. *Dwelling in the Text: Houses in American Fiction.* Berkeley: U of California P.

Child, Lydia Maria. 1832. *The American Frugal Housewife.* Rpt. Boston: Applewood Books, n.d.

Clark, Clifford Edward. 1986. *The American Family Home, 1800–1960.* Chapel Hill: U of North Carolina P.

Cordier, Mary Hurlbut. 1992. *Schoolwomen of the Prairies and Plains: Personal Narratives from Iowa, Kansas, and Nebraska, 1860s–1920s.* Albuquerque: U of New Mexico P.

Coultrap-McQuin, Susan. 1990. *Doing Literary Business: American Women Writers in the Nineteenth Century.* Chapel Hill: U of North Carolina P.

Cowan, Ruth Schwartz. 1983. *More Work for Mother: The Ironies of Household Technology from the Open Hearth to the Microwave.* New York: Basic Books.

Cronon, William, George Miles, and Jay Gitlin. 1992. "Becoming West: Toward a New

Meaning for Western History." *Under an Open Sky: Rethinking America's Western Past.* New York: W. W. Norton.

Csikszentmihalyi, Mihaly. "Why We Need Things." Lubar and Kingery 20–29.

Dalphin, Marcia A. 1953. "Christmas in the Little House Books." Rpt. *The Horn Book's Laura Ingalls Wilder.* Ed. William Anderson. Mansfield, Mo.: Rocky Ridge Shop, 1987. 41–45.

Deane, Paul. 1991. *Mirrors of American Culture: Children's Fiction Series in the Twentieth Century.* Metuchen, N.J.: Scarecrow P.

Derrida, Jacques. 1966. "Structure, Sign and Play in the Discourse of the Human Sciences." Rpt. *Contemporary Literary Criticism: Literary and Cultural Studies.* Ed. Robert Con Davis and Ronald Schliefer. 2nd ed. New York: Longman, 1989.

Deutsch, Sarah. "Landscape of Enclaves: Race Relations in the West, 1865–1990." Cronon, Miles, and Gitlin 110–31.

Din, Gilbert C., and A. P. Nasatir. 1983. *The Imperial Osages: Spanish-Indian Diplomacy in the Mississippi Valley.* Norman: U of Oklahoma P.

Dobson, Joanne. 1888. Introduction. *The Hidden Hand.* By E.D.E.N. Southworth. Rpt. New Brunswick, N.J.: Rutgers UP, 1988. xi–xli.

Donovan, Josephine. 1984. "Toward a Women's Poetics." *Tulsa Studies in Women's Literature* 3: 99–110.

Dorris, Michael. 1993. "Trusting the Words." *Booklist* 1–15 June: 1820–22.

Douglas, Mary, and Baron Isherwood. 1979. *The World of Goods.* New York: Basic Books.

du Plessis, Rachel Blau. 1985. *Writing Beyond the Ending: Narrative Strategies of Twentieth-Century Women Writers.* Bloomington: Indiana UP.

Elshtain, Jean Bethke. "'Thank Heaven for Little Girls': The Dialectics of Development." Elshtain 288–302.

——, ed. 1982. *The Family in Political Thought.* Amherst: U of Massachusetts P.

Erisman, Fred. 1994. *Laura Ingalls Wilder.* Boise, Idaho: Boise State U.

——. 1993. "*Farmer Boy:* The Forgotten 'Little House' Book." *Western American Literature* 28 (Summer): 123–30.

Farrow, Connie. 1988. "Museum Honors Guardian of 'Mrs. Wilder's' Heritage." *Springfield News Leader* 11 June.

Fellman, Anita Clair. 1990. "Laura Ingalls Wilder and Rose Wilder Lane: The Politics of a Mother-Daughter Relationship." *Signs* 15: 535–61.

Fink, Deborah. 1992. *Agrarian Women: Wives and Mothers in Rural Nebraska, 1880–1940.* Chapel Hill: U of North Carolina P.

Fitzgerald, Frances. 1979. *America Revised: History Schoolbooks in the Twentieth Century.* Boston: Little, Brown.

Flint, Kate. 1993. *The Woman Reader 1837–1914.* Oxford: Clarendon P.

Flynn, Elizabeth A., and Patrocinio P. Schweickart, eds. 1986. *Gender and Reading: Essays on Readers, Texts, and Contexts.* Baltimore: Johns Hopkins UP.

Formanek-Brunell, Miriam. 1993. *Made to Play House: Dolls and the Commercialization of American Girlhood, 1830–1930.* New Haven: Yale UP.

Fraser, Caroline. 1994. "The Prairie Queen." *New York Review of Books* 22 Dec.: 38–45.

Friedman, Susan Stanford. 1989. "Lyric Subversion of Narrative in Women's Writing: Virginia Woolf and the Tyranny of Plot." *Reading Narrative: Form, Ethics, Ideology.* Columbus: Ohio State UP. 162–85.

Garson, Eugenia, ed. 1968. *The Laura Ingalls Wilder Songbook*. New York: Harper and Row.

Gilbert, Sandra M., and Susan Gubar. 1987. *The War of the Words*. Vol. 1 of *No Man's Land: The Place of the Woman Writer in the Twentieth Century*. New Haven: Yale UP.

Glover, Vivian. 1990. Personal interview. August.

Gordon, Jean, and Jan McArthur. "American Women and Domestic Consumption, 1800–1920: Four Interpretive Themes." Motz and Browne 27–47.

Green, Rayna. 1975. "The Pocahontas Perplex: The Image of Indian Women in American Culture." *Massachusetts Review* 16 (Autumn): 698–714.

Hampsten, Elizabeth. 1991. *Settlers' Children: Growing Up on the Great Plains*. Norman: U of Olkahoma P.

———. 1982. *Read This Only to Yourself: The Private Writings of Midwestern Women*. Bloomington: UP of Indiana.

Handlin, David P. 1979. *The American Home: Architecture and Society, 1815–1915*. Boston: Little, Brown.

Harris, Katherine. "Homesteading in Northeastern Colorado, 1873–1920: Sex Roles and Women's Experience." Armitage and Jameson 165–78.

Helvensten, Sally I. 1986. "Ornament or Instrument? Proper Roles for Women on the Kansas Frontier." *Kansas Quarterly* 18 (Fall): 35–49.

Herring, Joseph B. 1990. *The Enduring Indians of Kansas: A Century and a Half of Acculturation*. Lawrence: UP of Kansas.

Hines, Stephen. 1994. *"I Remember Laura": Laura Ingalls Wilder*. Nashville: Thomas Nelson.

Hirsch, Marianne. 1989. *The Mother/Daughter Plot: Narrative, Psychoanalysis, Feminism*. Bloomington: Indiana UP.

Hoffman, Nancy. 1981. *Woman's "True" Profession: Voices from the History of Teaching*. Old Westbury, N.Y.: Feminist P.

Holmes, Mary Jane. [1871.] *Millbank*. Hurst and Company.

Holstein, Jonathan. "The American Block Quilt." Lasansky 1986, 16–27.

Holtz, William. 1993. *The Ghost in the Little House: A Life of Rose Wilder Lane*. Columbia: U of Missouri P, 1993.

———. 1984. "Closing the Circle: The American Optimism of Laura Ingalls Wilder." *Great Plains Quarterly* 4 (Spring): 79–90.

Jeffrey, Julie Roy. 1979. *Frontier Women: The Trans-Mississippi West 1840–1880*. New York: Hill and Wang.

Jellison, Katherine. 1993. *Entitled to Power: Farm Women and Technology, 1913–1963*. Chapel Hill: U of North Carolina P.

Jensen, Joan M. 1991. *Promise to the Land: Essays on Rural Women*. Albuquerque: U of New Mexico P.

Jensen, Laura. 1979. *The Story Makes Them Whole*. Tempe, Ariz.: Porch Publications. Inland Boat Pamphlet Series. Vol. 3.

Kaufman, Polly Welts. 1984. *Women Teachers on the Frontier*. New Haven: Yale UP.

Kelley, Mary. 1984. *Private Woman, Public Stage: Literary Domesticity in Nineteenth-Century America*. New York: Oxford UP.

Kiracofe, Roderick. 1993. *The American Quilt: A History of Cloth and Comfort 1750–1950*. New York: Clarkson Potter.

Kolodny, Annette. 1992. "Letting Go Our Grand Obsessions: Notes Toward a New Literary History of the American Frontiers." *American Literature* 64 (March): 1–18.

Kowaleski-Wallace, Beth. "Reading the Father Metaphorically." Yaeger and Kowaleski-Wallace 296–311.

Kurtis, Wilma, and Anita Gold. 1978. *Prairie Recipes and Kitchen Antiques*. Des Moines, Iowa: Wallace-Homestead Book Company.

Kwolek-Folland, Angel. 1984. "The Elegant Dugout: Domesticity and Movable Culture in the United States, 1870–1900." *American Studies* 25 (Fall): 21–37.

——. 1983. "The Useful Whatnot and the Ideal of Domestic Decoration." *Helicon Nine* 8 (Spring): 72–83.

Lane, Rose Wilder. 1963. *Woman's Day Book of American Needlework*. New York: Simon and Schuster.

——. 1938. *Free Land*. Rpt. Lincoln: U of Nebraska P, 1984.

——. 1935. *Old Home Town*. Rpt. Lincoln: U of Nebraska P, 1985.

——. 1933. *Let the Hurricane Roar*. New York: David McKay.

Lane, Rose Wilder, and Helen Dore Boylston. 1983. *Travels with Zenobia: Paris to Albania by Model T Ford*. Ed. William Holtz. Columbia: U of Missouri P.

Lasansky, Jeanette, ed. 1988. *Pieced by Mother: Symposium Papers*. Lewisburg, Pa.: Oral Traditions Project.

——, ed. 1986. *In the Heart of Pennsylvania: Symposium Papers*. Lewisburg, Pa.: Union County Historical Society.

Lott, Eric. 1993. *Love and Theft: Blackface Minstrelsy and the American Working Class*. New York: Oxford UP.

——. 1992. "Love and Theft: The Racial Unconscious of Blackface Minstrelsy." *Representations* 39 (Summer): 23–50.

Lubar, Steven. "Machine Politics: The Political Construction of Technological Artifacts." Lubar and Kingery 197–214.

Lubar, Steven, and W. David Kingery, eds. 1993. *History from Things: Essays on Material Culture*. Washington, D.C.: Smithsonian Institution P.

Lystra, Karen. 1989. *Searching the Heart: Women, Men and Romantic Love in Nineteenth-Century America*. New York: Oxford UP.

MacLeod, Anne Scott. 1994. *American Childhood: Essays in Children's Literature of the Nineteenth and Twentieth Centuries*. Athens: U of Georgia P.

Maddox, Lucy. 1991. *Removals: Nineteenth-Century American Literature and the Politics of Indian Affairs*. New York: Oxford UP.

Maher, Susan Naramore. 1994. "Laura Ingalls and Caddie Woodlawn: Daughters of a Border Space." *The Lion and the Unicorn* 18 (December): 130–42.

Martin, Theodora Penny. 1987. *The Sound of Our Own Voices: Women's Study Clubs 1860–1910*. Boston: Beacon P.

McAuliffe, Dennis. 1994. *The Deaths of Sibyl Bolton*. New York: Times Books.

McBride, Roger Lea. 1994. *Little Farm in the Ozarks*. New York: HarperCollins.

Melosh, Barbara. 1991. *Engendering Culture: Manhood and Womanhood in New Deal Public Art and Theater*. Washington, D.C.: Smithsonian Institution P.

Metcalf, Eugene W. "Artifacts and Cultural Meaning: The Ritual of Collecting American Folk Art." Pocius 199–207.

Michaels, Walter Benn. 1987. *The Gold Standard and the Logic of Naturalism*. Berkeley: U of California P.

Miller, John E. 1994. *Laura Ingalls Wilder's Little Town: Where History and Literature Meet*. Lawrence: UP of Kansas.

Miller, Nancy K. 1991. *Getting Personal: Feminist Occasions and Other Autobiographical Acts*. New York: Routledge.

Mills, Betty J. 1985. *Calico Chronicle: Texas Women and Their Fashions*. Lubbock: Texas Tech P.

Miner, H. Craig, and William E. Unrau. 1978. *The End of Indian Kansas: A Study of Cultural Revolution, 1854–1871*. Lawrence: Regents P of Kansas.

Mintz, Steven, and Susan Kellogg. 1988. *Domestic Revolutions: A Social History of American Family Life*. New York: Free P.

Moore, Rosa Ann. 1980. "Laura Ingalls Wilder and Rose Wilder Lane: The Chemistry of Collaboration." *Children's Literature in Education* 11: 101–9.

——. 1978. "The Little House Books: Rose-Colored Classics." *Children's Literature* 7: 7–16.

——. 1975. "Laura Ingalls Wilder's Orange Notebooks and the Art of the Little House Books." *Children's Literature* 4: 105–19.

Mortensen, Louise Hovde. 1964. "Idea Inventory." *Elementary English* 41 (April): 428–29.

Motz, Marilyn Ferris, and Pat Browne, eds. 1988. *Making the American Home: Middle-Class Women and Domestic Material Culture 1840–1940*. Bowling Green, Ohio: Bowling Green U Popular P.

Mowder, Louise. 1992. "Domestication of Desire: Gender, Language, and Landscape in the Little House Books." *Children's Literature Association Quarterly* 17 (Spring): 15–19.

My Book of Little House Paper Dolls: The Big Woods Collection. 1995. New York: HarperFestival.

Myres, Sandra L. 1982. *Westering Women and the Frontier Experience*. Albuquerque: U of New Mexico P.

Ortner, Sherry. 1972. "Is Female to Male as Nature Is to Culture?" *Feminist Studies* 1 (Fall): 5–31.

Pascoe, Peggy. 1991. "Western Women at the Cultural Crossroads." *Trails: Toward a New Western History*. Ed. Patricia Nelson Limerick, Clyde A. Milner II, and Charles E. Rankin. Lawrence: UP of Kansas. 40–58.

Penney, David W. 1992. *Art of the American Indian Frontier: The Chandler-Pohrt Collection*. Seattle: U of Washington P.

Phillips, Anne. 1992. "'Home Itself Put into Song': Music as Metaphorical Community." *The Lion and the Unicorn* 16 (December): 145–57.

Pocius, Gerald L. 1991. *Living in a Material World: Canadian and American Approaches to Material Culture*. St. John's, Nfld.: Institute of Social and Economic Research.

Pohrt, Richard A. "A Collector's Life: A Memoir of the Chandler-Pohrt Collection." Penney 299–322.

Pratt, Annis. 1981. *Archetypal Patterns in Women's Fiction*. Bloomington: Indiana UP.

Quantic, Diane Dufva. 1995. *The Nature of the Place*. Lincoln: U of Nebraska P.

Rabuzzi, Kathryn Allen. 1982. *The Sacred and the Feminine: Toward a Theology of Housework*. New York: Seabury.

Radway, Janice A. 1984. *Reading the Romance: Women, Patriarchy and Popular Literature*. Chapel Hill: U of North Carolina P.

Riley, Glenda. 1988. *The Female Frontier: A Comparative View of Women on the Prairie and the Plains*. Lawrence: UP of Kansas.

——. 1984. *Women and Indians on the Frontier, 1825–1915*. Albuquerque: U of New Mexico P.

Rochman, Hazel. 1995. Review of *Walk Two Moons* by Sharon Creech. *New York Times Book Review* 21 May: 24.

Rotundo, E. Anthony. 1993. *American Manhood: Transformations in Masculinity from the Revolution to the Modern Era*. New York: Basic.

Ruddick, Sara. 1989. *Maternal Thinking: Toward a Politics of Peace*. Boston: Beacon P.

Russo, Mary. "Female Grotesques: Carnival and Theory." 1986. *Feminist Studies/Critical Studies*. Ed. Teresa de Lauretis. Bloomington: U of Indiana P. 213–29.

Schlereth, Thomas J. 1991. *Victorian America: Transformation in Everyday Life, 1876–1915*. New York: Harper Collins.

Schlissel, Lillian. 1982. *Women's Diaries of the Westward Journey*. New York: Schocken.

Schlissel, Lillian, Byrd Gibbens, and Elizabeth Hampsten. 1989. *Far from Home: Families of the Western Journey*. New York: Schocken.

Segel, Elizabeth. 1977. "Laura Ingalls Wilder's America: An Unflinching Assessment." *Children's Literature in Education* 8: 63–70.

Shapiro, Laura. 1986. *Perfection Salad: Women and Cooking at the Turn of the Century*. New York: Farrar, Straus and Giroux.

Showalter, Elaine. 1986. "Piecing and Writing." *The Poetics of Gender*. Ed. Nancy K. Miller. New York: Columbia UP. 222–47.

Singley, Carol J., and Susan Elizabeth Sweeney, eds. 1993. *Anxious Power: Reading, Writing, and Ambivalence in Narrative by Women*. Albany: State U of New York P.

"Sister Carrie Has the China Shepherdess." 1990. *Laura Ingalls Wilder Lore* 16 (Fall/Winter): 8.

Smith, Louisa, and George R. Bodmer. 1994, "The Little House of Helen Sewell and Garth Willliams." Children's Literature Association, Springfield, Mo., 4 June.

Spaeth, Janet. 1987. *Laura Ingalls Wilder*. Boston: Twayne.

Spain, Daphne. 1992. *Gendered Spaces*. Chapel Hill: U of North Carolina P.

Strasser, Susan. 1989. *Satisfaction Guaranteed: The Making of the American Mass Market*. New York: Pantheon.

——. 1982. *Never Done: A History of American Housework*. New York: Pantheon.

Summers, K. C. 1988. "Pilgrim on the Prairie: On the Midwest Trail of Laura Ingalls Wilder's Little Houses." *Washington Post* 11 Dec.: E1, 8–11.

Susina, Jan. 1992. "The Voices of the Prairie: The Uses of Music in Laura Ingalls Wilder's Little House on the Prairie." *The Lion and the Unicorn* 16 (December): 158–66.

Toll, Robert C. 1974. *Blacking Up: The Minstrel Show in Nineteenth-Century America*. New York: Oxford UP.

Tompkins, Jane. 1992. *West of Everything: The Inner Life of Westerns*. New York: Oxford UP.

Veblen, Thorstein. 1899. *The Theory of the Leisure Class*. Rpt. New York: Vanguard, 1926.

Walker, Barbara M. 1979. *The Little House Cookbook*. New York: Harper and Row.

Ware, Susan. 1982. *Holding Their Own: American Women in the 1930s*. Boston: Twayne.

Warner, Susan. 1850. *The Wide, Wide World*. Rpt. New York: Feminist P, 1987.

Weslager, C. A. 1969. *The Log Cabin in America: From Pioneer Days to the Present*. New Brunswick, N.J.: Rutgers UP.

Westin, Jeanne. 1976. *Making Do: How Women Survived the '30s*. Chicago: Follett.

Wherry, Peg. 1986. "At Home on the Range: Reactions of Pioneer Women to the Kansas Plains Landscape." *Kansas Quarterly* 18 (Summer): 71–79.

Wilder, Laura Ingalls. 1991. *Little House in the Ozarks*. Ed. Stephen W. Hines. Nashville: Thomas Nelson.

——. 1974. *West from Home: Letters of Laura Ingalls Wilder, San Francisco 1915*. Ed. Roger Lea McBride. New York: Harper.

——. 1971. *The First Four Years*. New York: Harper and Row.

——. 1962. *On the Way Home: The Diary of a Trip from South Dakota to Mansfield, Missouri, in 1894.* With a setting by Rose Wilder Lane. New York: Harper and Row.

——. 1943. *These Happy Golden Years.* Rpt. New York: Harper and Row, 1953.

——. 1941. *Little Town on the Prairie.* Rpt. New York: Harper and Row, 1953.

——. 1940. *The Long Winter.* Rpt. New York: Harper and Row, 1953.

——. 1939. *By the Shores of Silver Lake.* Rpt. New York: Harper and Row, 1953.

——. 1935. *Little House on the Prairie.* Rpt. New York: Harper and Row, 1953.

——. 1934. *Farmer Boy.* Rpt. New York: Harper and Row, 1953.

——. 1932. *Little House in the Big Woods.* Rpt. New York: Harper and Row, 1953.

——. N.d. "A Letter from Laura." Mansfield, Mo.: Laura Ingalls Wilder–Rose Wilder Lane Museum and Home.

Wilder, Laura Ingalls, and Rose Wilder Lane. 1988. *A Little House Sampler.* Ed. William T. Anderson. Lincoln: U of Nebraska P.

Wilkes, Maria D. 1996. *Little House in Brookfield.* New York: HarperTrophy.

Williams, Garth. 1953. "Illustrating the Little House Books." Rpt. *The Horn Book's Laura Ingalls Wilder.* Ed. William Anderson. Mansfield, Mo.: Rocky Ridge Shop, 1987. 27–37.

Wittke, Carl. 1930. *Tambo and Bones: A History of the American Minstrel Stage.* Rpt. Westport, Conn.: Greenwood P, 1968.

Wolf, Virginia. 1984–85. "The Magic Circle of Laura Ingalls Wilder." *Children's Literature Association Quarterly* 9 (Winter): 168–70.

Wright, Gwendolyn. 1983. *Building the Dream: A Social History of Housing in America.* Cambridge: Massachusetts Institute of Technology P.

——. 1980. *Moralism and the Model Home.* Chicago: U of Chicago P.

Wyatt, Jean. 1990. *Reconstructing Desire: The Role of the Unconscious in Women's Reading and Writing.* Chapel Hill: U of North Carolina P.

Yaeger, Patricia. "The Father's Breasts." Yaeger and Kowaleski-Wallace.

Yaeger, Patricia, and Beth Kowaleski-Wallace, eds. 1989. *Refiguring the Father: New Feminist Readings of Patriarchy.* Carbondale: Southern Illinois UP.

Zochert, Donald. 1976. *Laura: The Life of Laura Ingalls Wilder.* New York: Avon. 1977.

Zwinger, Linda. 1991. *Daughters, Fathers, and the Novel: The Sentimental Romance of Heterosexuality.* Madison: U of Wisconsin P.

Research Collections Consulted

Herbert Hoover Presidential Library, West Branch, Iowa. Manuscripts, correspondence, other papers. Designated "Hoover."

University of Missouri, Columbia. Western Historical Collection. Manuscripts and correspondence. Designated "Western."

Laura Ingalls Wilder–Rose Wilder Lane Museum and Home. Mansfield, Missouri. Manuscripts, papers, correspondence, miscellaneous memorabilia. Designated "Mansfield."

Laura Ingalls Wilder Memorial Society, De Smet, South Dakota. Papers, correspondence, miscellaneous memorabilia. Designated "De Smet."

Index

Grateful acknowledgment is made for permission to reprint previously published material, archival material, and material under copyright.

Material from the Wilder/Lane papers housed at the Herbert Hoover Presidential Library, West Branch, Iowa, and at the Western Historical Collection at the University of Missouri is used by permission of the Library, the University of Missouri, and the estate of Roger Lea MacBride.

Short quotations from the Little House books are used with permission of Harper-Collins: *Little House in the Big Woods*, text copyright 1932 by Laura Ingalls Wilder, copyright renewed 1960 by Roger L. MacBride; *Farmer Boy*, text copyright 1933 by Laura Ingalls Wilder, copyright renewed 1961 by Roger L. MacBride; *Little House on the Prairie*, text copyright 1935 by Laura Ingalls Wilder, copyright renewed 1963 by Roger L. MacBride; *On the Banks of Plum Creek*, text copyright 1937 by Laura Ingalls Wilder, copyright renewed 1963 by Roger L. MacBride; *By the Shores of Silver Lake*, text copyright 1939 by Laura Ingalls Wilder, copyright renewed 1967 by Roger L. MacBride; *The Long Winter*, text copyright 1940 by Laura Ingalls Wilder, copyright renewed 1968 by Roger L. MacBride; *Little Town on the Prairie*, text copyright 1941 by Laura Ingalls Wilder, copyright renewed 1969 by Charles F. Lankin, Jr.; *These Happy Golden Years*, text copyright 1943 by Laura Ingalls Wilder, copyright renewed 1971 by Roger L. MacBride.

In different forms, portions of the introduction were published as "The Voices from the Little House," in *Private Voices, Public Lives: Women Speak on the Literary Life*, ed. Nancy Owen Nelson (Denton: University of North Texas Press, 1995); of chapter 1, as "Preempting the Patriarch: The Problem of Pa's Stories in *Little House in the Big Woods*," *Children's Literature Quarterly* 20 (Spring 1995); of chapters 4 and 5, as "*The Long Winter*: An Introduction to Western Womanhood" and as "Writing the Little House: The Architecture of a Series" in *Great Plains Quarterly* 10 (Winter 1990) and 14 (Spring 1994).